THE DAMNED

THE DAMNED

The Canadians at the Battle of Hong Kong
and the POW Experience, 1941–45

Nathan M. Greenfield

HARPERCOLLINS PUBLISHERS LTD

Stephen Spender, "Air Raid across the Bay at Plymouth," *New Collected Poems*, Faber & Faber,
2004, reprinted by the kind permission of the Estate of Stephen Spender.
Rupert Brooke, "The Dead," *Collected Poems*, New York: John Lane, 1916, reprinted from
Bartleby.com, 2000, courtesy of Steven Leeuwen.
Edith Sitwell, "Still Falls the Rain," *Collected Poems*, Duckworth/Overlook, 2006, reprinted
with permission of David Higham Associates, London, UK.
James Dickey, excerpt from "The Performance," *Poems 1957–1967*, copyright James Dickey,
reprinted by permission of Wesleyan University Press.
Everard Owen, "Three Hills," George Herbert Clarke, ed., *A Treasury of War Poetry*, First Series.
Boston: Houghton Mifflin, 1917, reprinted from Bartleby.com, 2002,
courtesy of Steven Leeuwen.
Charles Causley, "Song of the Dying Gunner," *Collected Poems 1951–1997*, MacMillan, 1997,
reprinted by permission of David Higham Associates, London, UK.

HarperCollins books may be purchased for educational, business,
or sales promotional use through our Special Markets Department.

HarperCollins Publishers Ltd
2 Bloor Street East, 20th Floor
Toronto, Ontario, Canada
M4W 1A8

www.harpercollins.ca

Library and Archives Canada Cataloguing in Publication
1. Hong Kong (China)–History–Siege, 1941. 2. Canada–Armed
Forces–History–World War, 1939–1945. 3. World War, 1939–1945–
Prisoners and prisons, Japanese. 4. Prisoners of war–Canada.
5. Prisoners of war–Japan. I. Title.
D767.3.G73 2010   940.54'25125   C2010-903090-7

ISBN 978-1-55468-219-5

Printed and bound in the United States

RRD 9 8 7 6 5 4 3 2 1

To Micheline Dubé, my wife and ideal reader,
and Louise and (late) Pierre O'Neil, and Dedé Marin, who,
thirty years ago, welcomed me to Canada and began teaching
me about the country.

"That I allow," replied the Canadian; "but we must risk that. Liberty is worth paying for; besides the boat is strong, and a few miles with a fair wing to carry us is no great thing."

—Jules Verne, *Twenty Thousand Leagues Under the Sea*
(The Canadian to Ned Land, speaking of
escaping Captain's Nemo's *Nautilus*)

The hand of the LORD was upon me, and carried me out in the spirit of the LORD, and set me down in the midst of the valley which was full of bones,
And caused me to pass by them round about: and, behold, there were very many in the open valley; and, lo, they were very dry.
And he said unto me, Son of man, can these bones live? And I answered, O Lord GOD, thou knowest.
Again he said unto me, Prophesy upon these bones, and say unto them, O ye dry bones, hear the word of the LORD.
Thus saith the Lord GOD unto these bones; Behold, I will cause breath to enter into you, and ye shall live:
And I will lay sinews upon you, and will bring up flesh upon you, and cover you with skin, and put breath in you, and ye shall live.

—Ezekiel 37: 1–6 (King James Version)

Contents

Book II: The POW Years

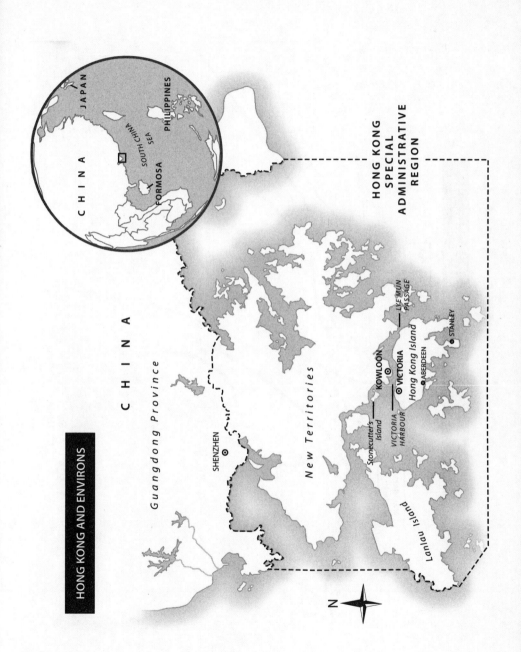

HONG KONG AND ENVIRONS

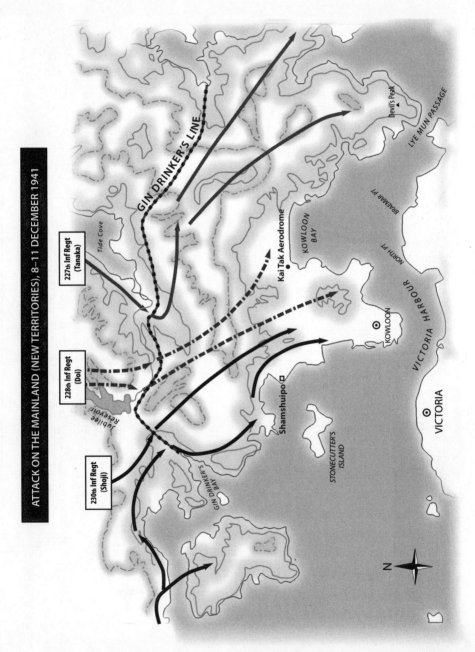

ATTACK ON THE MAINLAND (NEW TERRITORIES), 8–11 DECEMBER 1941

GIN DRINKER'S LINE

227th Inf Regt (Tanaka)

228th Inf Regt (Doi)

230th Inf Regt (Shoji)

Tide Cove

Jubilee Reservoir

GIN DRINKER'S BAY

Kai Tak Aerodrome

KOWLOON BAY

KOWLOON

Shamshuipo

STONECUTTER'S ISLAND

VICTORIA HARBOUR

VICTORIA

Devil's Peak

LYE MUN PASSAGE

BRAEMAR PT

NORTH PT

N

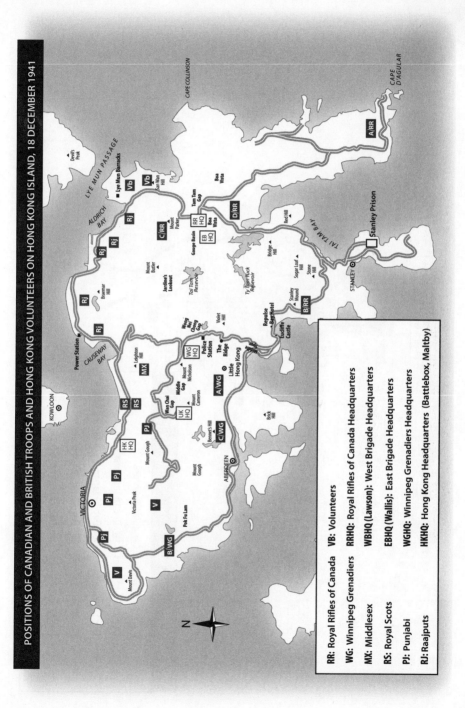

POSITIONS OF CANADIAN AND BRITISH TROOPS AND HONG KONG VOLUNTEERS ON HONG KONG ISLAND, 18 DECEMBER 1941

RR: Royal Rifles of Canada

WG: Winnipeg Grenadiers

MX: Middlesex

RS: Royal Scots

PJ: Punjabi

RJ: Raajputs

VB: Volunteers

RRHQ: Royal Rifles of Canada Headquarters

WBHQ (Lawson): West Brigade Headquarters

EBHQ (Wallis): East Brigade Headquarters

WGHQ: Winnipeg Grenadiers Headquarters

HKHQ: Hong Kong Headquarters (Battlebox, Maltby)

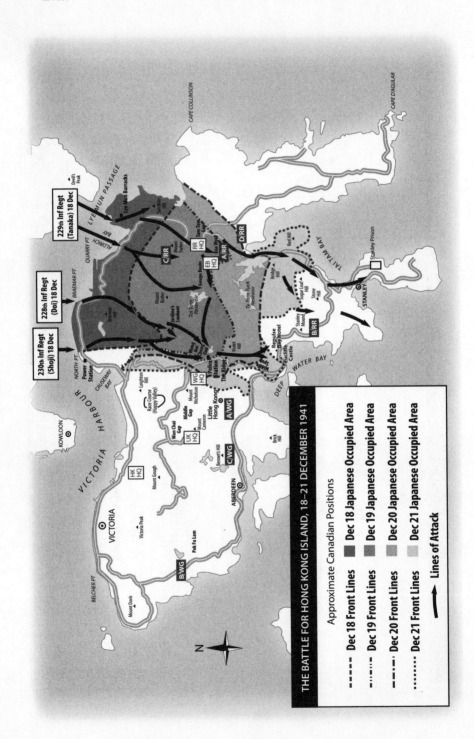

THE BATTLE FOR HONG KONG ISLAND, 18–21 DECEMBER 1941

Approximate Canadian Positions

- - - - - Dec 18 Front Lines   Dec 18 Japanese Occupied Area
- · - · - Dec 19 Front Lines   Dec 19 Japanese Occupied Area
- ·· - ·· Dec 20 Front Lines   Dec 20 Japanese Occupied Area
········ Dec 21 Front Lines   Dec 21 Japanese Occupied Area

⟶ Lines of Attack

229th Inf Regt (Tanaka) 18 Dec

228th Inf Regt (Doi) 18 Dec

230th Inf Regt (Shoji) 18 Dec

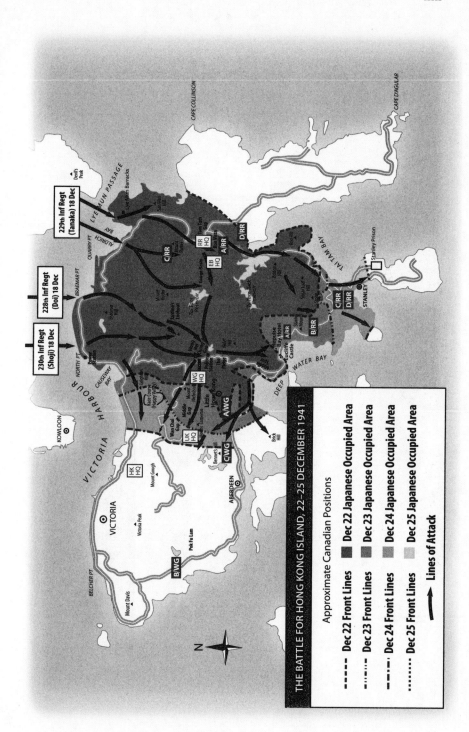

THE BATTLE FOR HONG KONG ISLAND, 22–25 DECEMBER 1941

Approximate Canadian Positions

Dec 22 Front Lines — — — — Dec 22 Japanese Occupied Area

Dec 23 Front Lines — · — · — Dec 23 Japanese Occupied Area

Dec 24 Front Lines — · · — · · Dec 24 Japanese Occupied Area

Dec 25 Front Lines · · · · · · Dec 25 Japanese Occupied Area

→ Lines of Attack

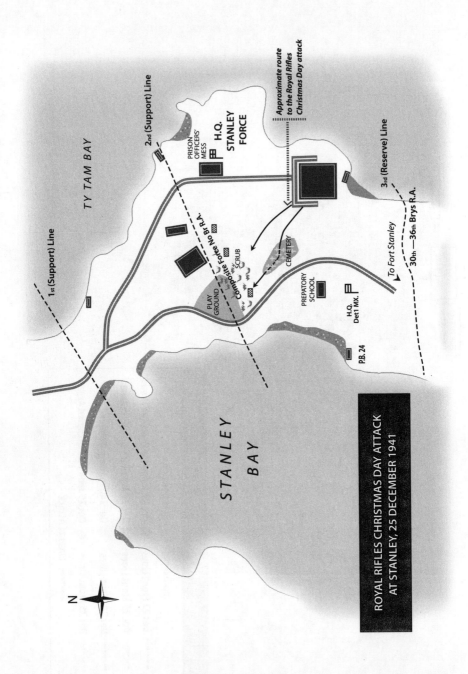

ROYAL RIFLES CHRISTMAS DAY ATTACK
AT STANLEY, 25 DECEMBER 1941

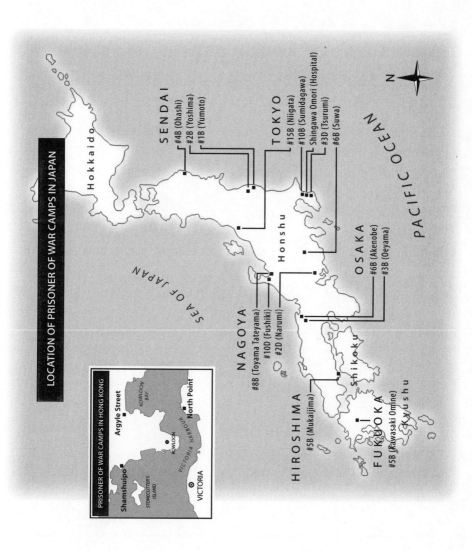

LOCATION OF PRISONER OF WAR CAMPS IN JAPAN

Preface

Under a scorching summer sun, just over twenty uniformed men marched forward. They had done it before. Almost seventy years earlier in Vancouver, they had marched up a gangplank to the SS *Awatea*, and three weeks later and half a world away, down another in Hong Kong. Three more weeks passed and with bayonets in place and bullets in their rifles' chambers, they had advanced in places with familiar-sounding names—Mount Butler, Red Hill, Mount Parker and Notting Hill—and some with decidedly unfamiliar names—Tai Tam Gap, Wong Nei Chong Gap, Wan Chai Gap. In these places and in others, including nameless rises and gullies, they had left brothers, cousins and lifelong friends, for that is what many of the men in the regiments raised chiefly in the small towns of Manitoba and eastern Quebec were to each other. A few days after Christmas 1941, they had marched in formation into North Point Prisoner of War Camp, close to the Japanese troops' first landing point when they invaded Hong Kong Island on 18 December 1941. Ten days earlier, the Imperial Japanese Army had thrown the British garrison, which included 1,974 Canadian troops, off the mainland.

Then, the men had been young (some only sixteen or seventeen), strong and straight.

The distance these men walked to the Memorial Wall that stands just off Sussex Drive in Ottawa wasn't far. Seventy years ago, even with sixty-pound packs on their backs and carrying nine-pound Lee-Enfields, they'd have covered it in seconds. Still, on 15 August 2009, as they fought the bend of age—the youngest had already seen his eighty-fifth birthday—they moved with a precision that recalled the military tattoo they'd learned decades earlier. Those in wheelchairs held their heads as if on parade.

When they reached the Memorial Wall, the western side of which is topped by a representation of the stark, volcanic hills that absorbed so much Canadian, British, Indian and Hong Kong Volunteer blood, their eyes were searching. Each saw his own name chiselled into the Wall, for, uniquely among war memorials, it lists the name of every soldier and the two Nursing Sisters who made up "C" Force.* But these were not the names they touched. Tears welling in their eyes, they felt the names of fallen friends, cousins, brothers, comrades.

The veterans were followed by widows, who cried as they touched their husbands' names. The fingers of sons, daughters, nephews, nieces, grandsons and granddaughters traced the font that etches their families' stories into our history.

---

* Canadian Nursing Sisters held rank—lieutenants—and hence were soldiers in every sense of the word. The Wall also lists Gander, a large Newfoundland dog, who gave his life when the Japanese hand grenade he had picked up exploded in his mouth.

Some 290 men died during the battle: many were bayoneted in cold blood or shot long after they had raised their arms in surrender. Another 267 died in other places Canadians have never heard of: Shamshuipo, Oeyama, Niigata, Narumi, Omine, Tsurumi, Kawasaki 3-D. At these and other Japanese POW camps, the Canadian (and British, Indian, American and Dutch) soldiers were turned into slave labourers. They were systemically starved; often, what food they were given was unfit for human consumption. Hundreds suffered from diseases associated with malnutrition; many died from them. Dysentery alone killed almost a hundred. With the full knowledge—indeed, with the approval—of the camps' commandants, they were beaten and tortured. Four Canadians were executed for doing the soldier's duty and trying to escape.

. . .

The story of "C" Force, as the Canadian military contingent sent to Hong Kong was designated, is little known, and what is known of it is often wrong. They were poorly trained, goes one legend, the foundation of which was laid almost as soon as the guns fell silent by none other than Brigadier Cedric Wallis, the British officer who commanded East Brigade, which included the Royal Rifles of Canada. By the standards of 1944, when Allied armies slugged their way up Italy and invaded Normandy, and American Marines liberated islands like Guam, "C" Force was indeed not well trained. But by the standards of 1941, they were as well trained as any part of the British or Canadian armies.

Another legend holds that they were sent into battle without proper equipment. This one has some truth to it; they lacked both trucks and universal carriers, and they had few mortars and almost no training on them. But both the Rifles and the Winnipeg

Grenadiers had more than their full complement of rifles, ammunition, and Bren and other guns.

Perhaps the most egregious misconception is that, like their fathers and uncles who joined up to fight the Kaiser a quarter-century before, the men who took the King's schilling after the Second World War broke out in September 1939 were dupes in the grip of mindless nationalism. Some octogenarians freely admit that they heard the call of adventure. Others recall the deprivation of the Great Depression and the lure of "three squares a day." Many—and this needs to be emphasized, not only those then enrolled in university or in the media centres of Montreal or Toronto—joined up because they saw Nazi Germany for the threat to morality and democracy that it was. It is one of history's great ironies that the men and women of "C" Force ended up fighting an equally dangerous and pernicious foe in Asia.

None of the thirty men I have interviewed or the thirty or so who have left diaries, memoirs or letters that I have read have said anything that indicates they took up arms because of blood lust, something civilians who have not spent time with veterans sometimes have trouble believing. Like the men I interviewed for *The Battle of the St. Lawrence: The Second World War in Canada,* none of the men I came to know writing this book seems capable of revelling in the fact that he has pulled a trigger with another human fixed in his sights or has used cold steel.

As counted by military statisticians, Hong Kong is the ultimate example of a military disaster: 100 percent of the force was killed, wounded, missing in action or taken prisoner.* By contrast, the casualty rate at Dieppe was near 40 percent. This woeful statistic might serve as an answer to a military version of Trivial Pursuit, but it

---

* This is, of course, true for the rest of the British Army at Hong Kong, as it was for that army at Singapore and the Americans at Corregidor in the Philippines.

obscures much more than it reveals. Behind it lies the fact that the defenders exacted a heavy toll and held out longer than the Japanese had believed they could. Further, the disaster at Hong Kong hides the fact that despite mistakes, more than a few times, the green Canadians held off the better-trained and -armed Japanese troops and at times even caused the vaunted "Knights of Bushido" to retreat. And even more importantly, behind this statistic lies the lived experience of the men of "C" Force, whose war continued even as their battlefield changed from the hills of Hong Kong to POW camps there and in Japan, and to iron foundries, mines and shipyards of Japan, and Kai Tak aerodrome in Hong Kong.

This book is the first to make use of the Japanese official history of the Second World War and Japanese memoirs of the Battle for Hong Kong. Thus, I attempt to tell the story from "both sides of the hill." This does not mean that I have divided morality in half; to do so would verge on blasphemy.[1] Rather, it means that as far as possible, I depict how Canadian (and British, Indian and Hong Kong) and Japanese troops experienced the battle—and how the Canadians suffered and survived their terrible years of imprisonment.

Finally, as will become clear, this book takes seriously Brigadier Wallis's East Brigade War Diary, which remains the official report of East Brigade's performance.[*] Each of the brigadier's comments about the Royal Rifles is examined. Some of what he writes is indeed correct. But taken as a whole, Wallis's war diary is a calumny that deserves to be rebutted.

---

[*] Strictly speaking, neither Wallis's nor the other British or Canadian "war diaries" are true war diaries, which when a unit is in battle are written either during the fighting or as soon as practical afterward and the outcomes of actions. The diaries kept during the Battle of Hong Kong were either destroyed during the battle or lost after the capitulation. The "war diaries" we do have were reconstructed in a POW camp or after the war; some of these last diarists had access to documents buried before the capitulation. None of the war diaries was written with reference to another.

A Note on Style

For the ease of reading, and with apologies to purists, I have made several editorial decisions. With the exception of when I am quoting orders, I have used standard time (8:30 p.m.) instead of military time (2030 hrs). When necessary, I have silently undone abbreviations within orders, for example, spelling out "Bde" as "Brigade."

Traditionally, nicknames are indicated within a name using quotations: Signalman Georges "Blacky" Verreault. But perhaps because I spent a great deal of time interviewing veterans who always referred to their comrades by their nicknames, I too began using them. Accordingly, as do several of the memoirs of the battle, I have used the nicknames as the men's first names: Sergeant Robert "Flash" Clayton is simply Sergeant Flash Clayton. Names are given in the traditional format in the Index.

Unlike most military histories, almost half of this book covers the years after the battle. When talking about their long years of imprisonment, most veterans tended to refer to their comrades by their first names: Sergeant Clayton became Flash. While it was tempting to follow this practice, doing so would probably call too much attention to it. Accordingly, I adopted a half-measure. Except when introducing a new soldier (or reintroducing one who has not been referred to for several chapters) in Book II, I use the men's names without indicating their rank or regiment. My other warrant for this practice is that in the POW camps, their regiment did not matter; they were all Canadian POWs.

To keep from littering the text with notes, I have not cited every war diary, other official document or memoir available online. Instead, I have given enough information in the text for the interested reader to find them either in the items listed in the Bibliography or in the archives where I did my research. I have not cited the pages of the Japanese records I used; the Bibliography provides, however, the publication information necessary to consult these books. Quotations that come from interviews I conducted are signalled by using the present tense, for example, "Dallain recalls." Quotations cited in the past tense, for example, "Laite said," come from published (or online) memoirs, diaries or reports filed after the war.*

None of the sources I relied on—war diaries, official postwar reports, postwar interviews, illegally kept diaries, memoirs, interviews conducted by other historians or those I conducted myself—is entirely reliable. Those who kept personal diaries violated both Canadian and Japanese regulations. Many of the diaries kept in the POW camps were kept on separate pieces of paper squirrelled away. And I hardly need point out that memories of events that happened two, four or sixty years ago can be faulty. In general, my practice has been to include information and provide quotes that can be buttressed by other testimony or sources. Necessarily, my standard of proof is closer to a civil ("probable cause") than a criminal trial ("beyond a reasonable doubt"). In places, I have drawn attention to debates about the evidence.

The Hong Kong veterans fought three battles. The first occurred on a foreign field and the second in POW camps in Hong Kong and Japan. These are what this book is about. Their third—and longest—battle was their five-decade-long battle for restitution. This battle, which ended on 11 December 1998, when the Government of Canada agreed to an "*ex gratia* payment of nearly $24,000 to each living Hong Kong veteran or their surviving spouse for the forced labour under inhumane conditions that the veterans were made to endure while prisoners of the Japanese during the Second World War," is a story of bureaucratic delay and wilful political blindness. It is worth telling in detail, but this book is not the place for this story.

Finally, the Canadians fought as part of the British Army, which

---

* This practice does not apply to the opening interview with Bill MacWhirter.

included the 2nd Battalion/Royal Scots, 1st Battalion/Middlesex Regiment, 2nd Battalion/14th Punjabi Regiment, 5th Battalion/7th Rajput Regiment, 8th and 12th Coast Regiments/Royal Artillery, 1st Hong Kong Regiment/Hong Kong and Singapore Royal Artillery, Royal Engineers, Hong Kong Volunteer Defence Corps (HKVDC), and assorted Royal Naval and other units. In total, Major-General Christopher Maltby commanded some fourteen thousand men: 1,044 died, another 1,068 went missing and 1,332 were wounded defending Britain's small colony; another 2,340 died in POW camps there and in Japan. Each of these deaths and each man who suffered through and survived his captivity is equally to be honoured. To have written about each unit that was in Hong Kong when the war came in as much detail as I have about the Canadians' experience would have meant writing a book of more than a thousand pages, something even my generous editor could not allow. I mean no disrespect to the British and Indian soldiers or the Hong Kong volunteers who fought, died and suffered with the Canadians. Even though your stories are not told in detail here, I trust that you will find what follows to be an accurate portrayal of your war too.

"It Was Canada's Turn to Help"

And I saw when the Lamb opened one of the seals, and I heard,
as it were the noise of thunder, one of the four beasts saying,
Come and see.

And I saw, and behold a white horse: and he that sat on him
had a bow; and a crown was given unto him: and he went forth
conquering, and to conquer.
—Revelations 6:1–2

The two scenes could not have been more different. I was sitting in a warm, well-furnished living room. Beyond the large picture window lay an almost blinding whiteness, the reflection of the early afternoon sun off the huge mounds of snow that had fallen in the harshest Gaspé winter in memory.* On the coffee table before me was a spiral-bound book open to a picture of a badge with three rough-hewn two-inch square wooden pieces. One had a black square, the others numbers: *sanjou shichi.* "Thirty-seven, I had to wear it at all times." A few moments earlier, Bill MacWhirter—who, despite his eighty-three years, was still a tall, powerfully built, gentle man—had shown me a picture from November 1941. He stands in

_____

* This interview with Bill MacWhirter took place on 20 February 2008.

a field, proudly wearing the uniform of the Royal Rifles of Canada, his cap on an angle that—had he been more than seventeen—could be called rakish. And a few minutes before that, he'd chuckled when he pushed on the bridge of his nose, flattening it, an all-too-physical reminder of the efforts a guard named Amana—"Snakes Eyes"—and many others made to break his will and that of almost seventeen hundred other Canadian POWs.

Earlier I had to put down the chocolate chip cookie he insisted I take; it seemed disrespectful even to have it in my hand while he described how, for such a long time, he was *so terribly hungry.* Typed, these words hardly convey his meaning. Neither would *starving* or *ravenous.* The sketches he showed me of Omine, the POW camp he spent years in, include one of gaunt men trudging their way into a mine where they worked at gunpoint. Another depicts shirtless, shoeless men summoning up the strength to wash their clothes at a wooden trough in a hut with paper-thin walls. There is a sketch of two emaciated men fitting into one pair of Red Cross pants, but it too fails to impart the meaning he and the other veterans I interviewed give when they speak of hunger. In their mouths, the "u" opens up and is filled by a mournful tone; a word we use every day becomes the description of a state of being. When MacWhirter spoke of hunger, it becomes almost as solemn as when he told me how his faith kept him going.

Bill was underage when he enlisted, so I assumed he would have signed his attestation papers with his father standing at his shoulder, ready to add his name. Not so. In 1940, urged on by both a sense of adventure and by the harrowing news reports from Europe read by Gabriel Heator on WOR (New York) and picked up on the radio at Woodburn McCrae's general store in the Gaspé hamlet of Hopetown, the then sixteen-year-old high school student joined up. Bill's father was proud of his own service during the First World War. However, instead of signing his son's papers, he knew whom to call to have his underaged but very patriotic son summarily mustered out of the King's service. Bill didn't make the same mistake twice. In August 1941, he waited until his father was away for a day before coming downstairs dressed in his suit to tell his much-surprised mother, "I joined the army last night and I'm leaving." MacWhirter feigned his mother's tone: "Your father will kill you."

As did so many of his comrades, MacWhirter went to war with family—his half-brother, Arley Enright—and friends from just down the road. Like Henry Lyons and Jean-Paul Dallain, both also from the Gaspé, the three Chaboyer brothers from Manitoba and hundreds of others, MacWhirter ran up hills he'd never heard of and crouched on a dozen roads while under fire, knowing that if he could still hear the war he was alive—but straining eyes and ears to tell if his kith and kin were. The importance of these men's lives to MacWhirter could not be missed, for despite the decades that have passed, after describing an engagement, his voice dropped as he recalled the living. He laughed a little when he told me that a bullet split Pierre Delarosbil's helmet. (Delarosbil winked when he told me the same story.) MacWhirter's eyes moistened and his voice broke when he told me of the blood Wilson Major, Ralph McGuire and Leo Murphy poured onto the ridge the Rifles attacked on Christmas Day, mere hours before the surrender.

It is not easy to ask a man on the other side of eighty to continue when he has just asked you to turn off your tape recorder so he can compose himself. But I had three questions left. The first was the most difficult, and here in print seems unduly cold: "What did it feel like to be a slave labourer?" He answered by getting out of his chair and saying, "Come, let me show you something," and led me to a room in his basement where he keeps his wartime memorabilia. After showing me his badge, he handed me a small book, the pages of which are a dark cream colour. The lower right corner of each page carries a red stamp of six Japanese characters.

He'd handed me the diary he'd risked his life to keep. Then he showed me his mess tin and a few other items that he kept during the terrible years at Omine. MacWhirter did not answer my question in words. But by putting his diary in my hands, by showing me his few meagre possessions, including the chopsticks with which he ate what food he was given, he answered my question. He may have been a forced labourer, he may have been beaten, tortured and starved, but he was never a slave, if by that one understands a man without a will.

MacWhirter's wife called down to tell us that she had prepared another pot of tea, so we were back in their living room when I asked my second-last question. Knowing that in the hours before the surrender he'd lost three close friends, I expected to hear him speak of relief or even reprieve when I asked, "What did you think when you surrendered?" MacWhirter took me up short when, his voice cracking, he replied that when he got the order to lay down his arms, what went through his mind was "What would my father think?"

And when I asked him what happened after the surrender, MacWhirter ignored the context of the question: the mechanics of surrender. This gentle old man, sitting in a comfortable easy chair in a Canadian living room now cast in orange by the setting sun, sat up ramrod straight and, for the one and only time in our several hours together, spoke in clipped military cadence: "I never surrendered."

. . .

For the first week after steaming out of Vancouver, the almost two thousand Canadian soldiers aboard SS *Awatea* and her escort HMCS *Prince Robert* heard only rumours. One held that "C" Force was heading for Norway. But most felt that not even the Canadian Army would send an invasion force to northern Europe in late October with shorts and new sun helmets; even fewer believed that, in an effort to confuse spies, the army had the wit to outfit its soldiers in tropical kit on land and exchange it at sea. One rumour pointed to Gibraltar; another, to Crete. Most bet on North Africa, where General Claude Auchin's 8th Army was slugging it out with General Erwin Rommel's Afrika Korps. On 6 November, they learned the truth about the whopper Grenadier Harry Atkinson's father had heard from a friend who worked in a Chinese restaurant: "Those boys are going to Hong Kong."

The thirty-four-day crossing of the Pacific did little to change the Atlantist focus of the men who answered the call in 1939, 1940 and 1941. Nor did the lectures like "Hong Kong, People and Customs," or "Geography of Orient and Hong Kong" do much to explain Canada's long involvement with Japan. While they learned about emperor worship and the military geography of South Asia, they learned nothing about the Canadian missionaries and insurance companies that had been active there since the 1870s. Whatever they picked up in lectures on the Japanese army or on the tensions between Washington and London and Tokyo, they heard nothing of Canada's relationship with and analysis of Japan.

Japan was opened to the outside world only in 1854 when U.S. Commodore Matthew Perry sailed into Tokyo Bay. By 1902, the Japanese Navy was so strong that the British signed a naval alliance with Japan that allowed the Royal Navy to withdraw from its base in Esquimalt, British Columbia; at the same time, the Royal Navy withdrew from Halifax. Three years later, the Japanese Navy destroyed the Russian navy at the Battle of Tsushima; the Canadian National railroad memorialized the architect of the victory, Admiral Togo, by naming a Saskatchewan town after him.* In 1918/19, the Canadian

---

* In 1908, as a Yellow Peril war scare gripped the United States and Canada, Colonel Willoughby Gwatkin, assistant to Minister of the Militia Sam Hughes, warned that Japanese immigrants were organized, possessed arms and were ready, if ordered by Tokyo, to "cut the transcontinental railways."

Siberian Expedition Force, which was part of the international force sent to try to overthrow V.I. Lenin's Bolshevik government, served under Japanese command.

During a tour of Canada in 1919, the British First Sea Lord, Admiral Sir John Jellicoe, warned of Japan's growing strength. In 1922, fears that Japan's navy could raid British Columbia prompted Ottawa to purchase two British destroyers and order two more. Six years later, a Canadian analysis of the Far East concluded that if tensions with Britain escalated into war, Japan was more likely to attack Hong Kong than Canada.

Concern about the rise of Fascism in Europe overshadowed the rise of extreme nationalism in Japan. Four years after Crown Prince Hirohito's fawning visit to King George V in 1921, Emperor Hirohito made the military independent of cabinet and responsible to him alone. In 1929, Hirohito was declared a "living god" and the source of morality for his "divine country," as newspapers declared that Japan should not "confine itself to its own small sphere."[1] Japanese schools taught that the Eight Corners of the World should be brought together under Chrysanthemum Throne—by force if necessary.

In the September 1928 issue of *New Outlook,* the journal of United Church of Canada, Reverend Uriah Laite (who in 1941 would be an honorary captain attached to the Winnipeg Grenadiers) would have read that Japan formed a bulwark against godless Russia and seen editorials supporting Japan's need for *Lebensraum* for its growing population.[2] No major Canadian newspaper reported that, even though the country had been party to the Geneva Convention negotiations, Japan repudiated the part of the convention that governed the treatment of prisoners of war. Japan reasoned that first, the emperor's soldiers were forbidden to allow themselves to become prisoners of war, and second, if they did become prisoners then they had violated the *Bushido* Code and had, essentially, given up their moral right to exist. Whatever disappointment Canadian officials felt about Japan's action did not prevent the opening of a Canadian Legation in Tokyo that same year.

Few things could knock the Great Depression from the front pages in 1931. One that did was Japan's invasion of Manchuria, supposedly to restore order after the bombing of the Japanese-owned railroad near the city of Mukden. Canada's response was schizophrenic. In Geneva, it joined the demand that Japan withdraw; Japan did—but from the League of Nations, not Manchuria. But while Canadian diplomats in Geneva called for trade sanctions against Japan, Canadian trade officers in Yokohama and Kobe worked to increase business between the two countries.

The *Manitoba Free Press* and *Vancouver Province* called for swift action against Japan by the League. With an eye toward Canada's $9 million trade surplus with Japan, the *Montreal Gazette* and Toronto *Globe* supported Japan. *Saturday Night* opined that Japan brought "'order and good government' to a region threatened by Soviet communism and Chinese 'disorder and rapine.'"[3] Returned to office in 1935, Prime Minister W.L. Mackenzie King ended a trade war in which Japan had slapped a 50 percent levy on Canadian wheat, lumber and paper products.

Two years later, following a trumped-up incident at the Marco Polo Bridge near Peking, Japan invaded China proper. On 2 December 1937, the *Globe and Mail* declared, "Japanese Landing Threatens Hong Kong: 50,000 Nippon Reported in Possession of Nearby Island." A few weeks later, during the Rape of Nanking, Japanese soldiers killed more than two hundred and fifty thousand Chinese civilians, seventeen thousand on 16 December alone. On 10 February 1938, Father Francis Deloughery (who in 1941 would be an honorary captain belonging to "C" Force) prayed for the soul of Pope Pius XI, who had died the night before, and thus probably missed the news that Japan had invaded Hainan Island and now commanded the sea lanes between Hong Kong and Singapore.

. . .

The defence of Britain's Asian Empire did not loom large in the Canadian consciousness as Europe lurched toward the Second World War. Nevertheless, Canada's chief soldier, Major-General Harry Crerar, kept one eye warily on South Asia. In the 1934 war games, he played the role of a Japanese officer and concluded that because of the British fleet, Japan could not win a protracted war against Britain. By 1937, however, the Admiralty knew that instead of defending a fifteen-square-mile piece of real estate leased from China, ships from China Station were going to be brought home to counter the German threat in the Atlantic and the Italian threat in the Mediterranean.

In 1938, one of Crerar's oldest friends, Canadian-born Major-General Arthur Grasett, became the General Officer Commanding British Troops in China. Like most British officers, Grasett had a low opinion of Japanese military capabilities and thought Hong Kong could be defended. Even though a 1935 study concluded that the colony's fixed defences were "deplorable," Grasett militated for two additional battalions, which would allow him to push his forward defences off the island and up five miles to the northern end of the New Territories on the mainland, to an east/west defensive line known as the Gin Drinkers' Line (named for the bay on its western-most point).

Exactly why Grasett thought two additional infantry battalions would allow an almost fourteen-thousand-man garrison to adequately man this ten-and-a-half-mile line and the possible seaward approaches to Hong Kong is unknown; in the First World War, a thousand men normally held just over half a mile of trench.* The author of the War Office's refusal of more troops spared Grasett the history lesson, but nonetheless made it clear that "this extra battalion, even if available, should not be allowed to change his mind as to policy, i.e., no undue holding of the mainland."[4]

In August 1940, a British defence review concluded that Hong Kong was not a vital interest and that it could not hold out against a determined Japanese attack. Perhaps thinking that the establishment of the Tripartite Pact, which established the Rome-Berlin-Tokyo Axis, and Vichy France's decision to allow Japan to build aerodromes in northern Vietnam would justifying an increased commitment, in November Grasett asked again for additional troops. Three months later, the newly appointed Commander-in-Chief of the Far East Command, Air Chief Marshal Sir Robert Brooke-Popham, cabled London that, as soon as the situation permitted, he would send one or two battalions from Malaya to Hong Kong.

Prime Minister Winston Churchill was not amused. "This is all wrong. If Japan goes to war with us there is not the slightest chance of holding Hong Kong or relieving it. . . . Japan will think long before declaring war on the British Empire, and whether there are two or six battalions at Hong Kong will make no difference to her choice."[5] Although Canada had not yet been asked for any troops, Canadian and British diplomats must have caught wind of something, for they had already arranged for Argentina to be the "protecting power" for any future POWs Japan might have.

---

* Historians have rightly been critical of Grasett, who seems at times to be almost wilful in his disregard for Japanese military abilities; they had, after all, staged amphibious landings at Canton and elsewhere. In 1939, after Soviet forces destroyed a Japanese army in North Manchuria, there was reason to believe that the Japanese army was weaker than it turned out to be. Indeed, in 1940, Emperor Hirohito himself pointed out to his prime minister that after six years of war, China was no closer to being conquered.

In 1941, as American President Franklin Roosevelt ratcheted up the pressure on Japan by restricting the sale of oil and other strategic materials, Canada imposed an even more extensive ban covering copper, nickel, zinc, lead, antimony and cobalt, as well as iron and steel, which enraged the Japanese ambassador. At the end of June, King's government received a memo from Dr. Hugh L. Keenleyside, who had served at the Canadian Legation in Tokyo, saying that even though Germany had attacked Russia, he doubted Japan would follow suit; rather, the country would abide by the terms of the Japanese-Soviet Neutrality Pact (signed in April 1941) and "direct all her energies to increasing the tempo of the southern advance."[6]

.   .   .

While the British debated what to do about the defence of Hong Kong, the two Canadian battalions that on 16 November 1941 would march behind a bagpipe band from the quay to their barracks at Shamshuipo (on the mainland side of Hong Kong harbour) were doing garrison duty in two different war zones.* Mobilized at the outbreak of the war in 1939, the Winnipeg Grenadiers were part of the 6th Infantry Brigade, 2nd Canadian Division, but not one of the units rushed to England in 1940. After training during the winter of 1939/40 and guarding railheads in Canada, in May 1940 the Grenadiers shipped out for Jamaica, where they guarded a POW camp that held German and Italian nationals from around the Caribbean and captured members of the Kriegsmarine. Corporal Ed Shayler used his knowledge of German to help gather information in the camp about a certain Herr Aramen, "an arrogant Prussian" who had been picked up in Panama and interned, and in capturing one of Germany's sources of informa-

---

* During this march, a British colonist who had apparently read one too many westerns exclaimed, "They're not Indians. They're not Indians."

tion about tanker traffic. On an unauthorized night manoeuvre, one Grenadier used his Tommy gun to cut down a flagpole that was flying a swastika over a POW hut.

Mobilized in July 1940, the Royal Rifles of Canada, which drew mainly from areas east of Quebec City, completed basic training in October 1940. Some 40 percent of the regiment were bilingual francophones like Jean-Paul Dallain and his brother Charles, who grew up in New Carlisle, just down the street from René Lévesque. Like many others, Phil Doddridge, who joined up both because of patriotism and because "nothing much was doing in the small village of New Richmond in 1940," expected that they'd soon be heading off to war. However, instead of shipping out for England, they crossed only the Cabot Strait and began doing garrison duty in Newfoundland. In Gander, they guarded the airfield; at Botwood, the fuel depot.

In late August 1941, the Royal Rifles returned to Canada and began training again at Valcartier. On 10 October, the second of two drafts of Grenadiers returned to Winnipeg.

. . .

MacWhirter, Doddridge, Shayler, the Dallains and their comrades were not the only Canadians coming home in the late summer of 1941. On his way back to England from his tour in China, Grasett stopped in Ottawa, where he met with both Crerar, who was then Chief of the Defence Staff, and Canada's Minister of Defence, John Ralston. A few weeks later, at a meeting at the War Office in London, Grasett once again tried to convince Britain's senior generals to reinforce Hong Kong, suggesting that Canada would be willing to supply the troops.

More than a little controversy surrounds the sequence of events that led to the 19 September 1941 most secret cable from London that (after reviewing the need for troops to bolster the colony's defence) read, "We should therefore be most grateful if the Canadian Government would consider whether one or two Canadian battalions could be provided for this purpose." Writing after the war to C.P. Stacey, Canada's official historian, Crerar said that though he had met with Grasett, "neither to myself alone, nor to the Minister did Grasett . . . raise the question of obtaining these two additional battalions from Canada."[7]

Historians have long dismissed Crerar's claim. While the fact that neither the general nor the minister took notes does not prove that they discussed sending Canadian troops to Hong Kong, this departure from standard operating procedure surely provides what police investigators call "opportunity." More telling is Cable No. 162's summary of Grasett's meeting at the War Office:

1. Canada could probably find the troops.
2. Any troops sent would be practically untrained.
3. The political effect might be undesirable in that it might result in greater attention being given to the Japanese menace to the Canadian Western Seaboard, with the consequent locking up of troops in the Vancouver area.[8]

The first two points suggest that the speaker had the kind of knowledge of Canadian troop allotments that only could have come from the highest levels. Point three is the sort of political analysis that King prized in both his ministers and his senior officials.

After some toing and froing in the War Office, on 10 September Churchill received a memo that outlined the limitations of the four battalions presently in Hong Kong, and said that additional battalions "might be supplied by Canada." The memo continued:

A small reinforcement of one or two battalions would increase the strength of the garrison out of all proportion to the actual numbers involved, and it would provide strong stimulus to the garrison and to the Colony. Further, it would have a great moral effect in the whole of the Far East and it would show Chiang Kai-sheck that we really intend to fight it out at Hong Kong.[9]

This time Churchill agreed.

For a government that was memorialized by the poet F.R. Scott as "Do[ing] nothing by halves/Which can be done by quarters," the speed with which King's government accepted the British request—five days—indicates that it fell on very fertile soil.[10] King may not have been aware of the Grasett-Crerar pas de deux. But he was under pressure from English-speaking politicians who were openly jealous of the battle laurels being won by New Zealanders and Australians in North Africa. Ralston himself felt that "it was Canada's turn to help." That pressure had become at least as strong as the Prime Minister's fear that land battles would lead to massive casualties and trigger the need for conscription, as they had in the First World War, thus touching off another conscription crisis that could sunder the country. After being assured by Crerar that there was "no military risk" (because the troops were going to be doing garrison duty), King's cabinet agreed to the request.

. . .

Historians have made much of Crerar's choice of troops. Deciding against detaching two battalions from the 4th Canadian Division, which was soon to go to England, he skipped over the so-called B-list prepared by Colonel John Lawson, the Director of Military Training who would soon be promoted to Brigadier-General to command the Canadian force sent to Hong Kong. Instead, Crerar chose the Royal Rifles of Canada and the Winnipeg Grenadiers from category C, defined by Lawson as "those units which, due either to recent employment or insufficient training, are not recommended" to be deployed at the present time.[11] Crerar later wrote, "The selection represents both Eastern and Western Canada. In the case of the Royal Rifles, there is also the fact that this battalion, while nominally English speaking, is actually drawn from a region overwhelmingly French-speaking in character and contains an important proportion of Canadians of French descent."[12] Pressure also came from Minister of Defence for Air, Charles Power, whose son, Francis, was a lieutenant in the Quebec regiment.

Garrison duty is not the optimal training ground for battle. However, neither battalion was made up of barroom loafers. While in Newfoundland or Jamaica, and after each returned to Canada, both battalions went through bayonet drills, hours of target practice and foxhole digging, and small-unit manoeuvres. The Royal Rifles had its share of rifles, bayonets and an adequate number of light machine guns and pistols. In April 1941, they began practising with Thompson sub-machine guns. Their greatest lack was live hand grenades and mortars, a problem that also affected the Grenadiers.

Daily schedules recorded in secondary orders tell only part of the story. According to Doddridge, "We were hunters from childhood. I and the other men who joined up from Gaspé and nearby New Brunswick knew how to use a gun long before we enlisted." George MacDonell adds, "By the standards of 1944 no Canadian battalion was well trained in 1941. But 1941 wasn't 1944 and Hong Kong wasn't northern Europe. True, we would not have been able to execute the kind of manoeuvres used there, but Hong Kong is a very hilly place where there is no room for huge formations of thousands of men and armour to move in sequence. We knew very well how to execute small-unit actions by company, platoon and section. And we knew how to march, climb, dig, shoot damned well and use cold steel."

A large percentage of their officers and more than a few men knew war first-hand. The commander of the Royal Rifles, Lieutenant-Colonel William Home, had earned a Military Cross at Mons in 1918.* Major John Price also earned his Military Cross in 1918. Majors Charles Young, Harry Lamb and Thomas MacAuley had earned a Military Cross, a Distinguished Service Order and a Distinguished Service Medal respectively. Lieutenant-Colonel John Sutcliffe, who commanded the Winnipeg Grenadiers, had served in France, Belgium, Mesopotamia, Persia, Russia, Turkey and India. The Grenadiers' second-in-command, Major George Trist, was also a veteran of the Great War. "C" Force's commander, Brigadier-General John Lawson, earned a Military Cross at Passchendaele, where he had served with the British Army.

. . .

Home considered the embarkation on *Awatea* to be a "hopeless muddle." Overcrowding was so bad that some fifty soldiers left the ship without leave. A twenty-minute full and frank exchange of views with their (armed) non-commissioned officers led most of these men to return to the ship. They endured several days of eating mutton (*Awatea* had been chartered from a New Zealand company and had not been fully unloaded before embarking "C" Force), before finding stores of beef and persuading the mess to "cook Canadian."

On board, the troops attended lectures, including one designed to scare the troops away from Chinese prostitutes (99 percent of whom, their officers said, were infected with syphilis). The Canadians also

---

* Home was not an obvious choice to command the Rifles, having earlier been removed from command of a company in the Royal Canadian Regiment "as being unfit to command in time of war" (as General Foulkes put it in a 1948 memo to the Minister of National Defence).

used the endless hours at sea to continue training. In addition to target practice and Bren gun training, many for the first time saw a two-inch mortar. One Canadian recalled not being allowed to touch it because its aiming device was said to be so fragile. When not marvelling at the phosphorescence of fish and the mystery of the stars against the dark night, Signalman William Allister kept his Morse code skills honed by signalling the *Prince Robert* with an Aldis lamp at the rate of four to six words per minute. Others spent hours on submarine watch. Signalman Georges "Blacky" Verreault spent part of the voyage learning the colourful uses soldiers have for the English word *fuck*: "Please, private, kindly pass the fucking butter or for fuck sake, give me that lovely piece of cake."[13]

The trip had its absurd moments. On 2 November, *Awatea* tied up to a wharf in Honolulu. To prevent word of the Canadians' deployment from leaking out, the men were not allowed to leave the ship or to wear their regimental insignia. Thus, they had to content themselves with watching the hula girls who danced so close and yet so far away on the dock, and listening to Grenadier Lieutenant Leonard Corrigan's impromptu saxophone concert. The precaution may have been for naught. Tied up to the next wharf was a Japanese freighter, the master of which may well have signalled Tokyo word of the Canadians' presence in such an unexpected part of the world.

A further stop in Manila was mercifully short. What Manila lacked in dockside diversions, it more than made up for in a heat so intense that by merely touching *Awatea*'s teak deck, one risked a nasty burn. Escorted by a British cruiser, *Awatea* and *Prince Robert* steamed into Hong Kong harbour early on 16 November.

The view was breathtaking. But Hong Kong hardly lived up to its meaning—Fragrant Harbour—it stank like an open sewer.

. . .

Nothing had prepared the 1,974 Canadians for the conditions they would find in Hong Kong.* Built in the 1920s, Shamshuipo was a clean, spacious camp of well-built huts set among manicured greens. The Canadians were, however, rather put off by the absence of Western latrines and by the night-soil trucks that made their rounds every morning. But the beds had mosquito netting, and the messes were good. Men who had scrimped and saved their way through the Great Depression woke to boys carrying hot towels to soften Canadian stubble who washed and ironed for all of 25 cents a day, easily afforded by soldiers earning a daily $1.25. The barber at the Peninsula Hotel was certainly friendly and interested in the Canadians' impressions of Kowloon, Victoria and whatever part of Hong Kong they saw during tours or manning exercises; a little over a month later, that barber turned up in the North Point POW Camp wearing the uniform of a Japanese lieutenant.

The world outside the camp's gates both mesmerized and horrified the Canadians. Chinese refugees fleeing the Japanese invasion swelled the colony's population by almost half, to close to 1.5 million people. Hundreds of thousands of destitute men, women and children lived on the streets. Some of the scenes outside the camp recalled the worst days of the Black Death in medieval Europe. Each morning a truck came by to pick up the bodies of those who had died

---

* In 1941, Canadian battalions counted 807 men, 34 of whom were officers and 650 of whom were privates. When assigned to "C" Force, neither the Rifles nor the Grenadiers were at full strength—and since replacing wounded men would be difficult, it was decided that each would sail from Canada over strength. A total of 206 officers men were added to the Rifles and 387 men to the Grenadiers from manning depots across the country. Depending on how one counts, many of these had received less than sixteen weeks' training. "C" Force also included a Brigade Headquarters (16 officers and 83 ordinary ranks) and assorted medical, communications and ancillary personnel, including George Porteous of the YMCA and Francis O'Neill of the Canadian Auxiliary Service. A total of 1,975 Canadians reached Hong Kong. One was a stowaway who was returned to Canada. One Rifleman had died of hypoglycemia and was buried at sea. The number of Canadian troops in Hong Kong when the Japanese attacked was 1,974.

on the streets during the night. Child beggars with high, weak voices ripped at the hearts of men like Royal Rifles Corporal Bob Barter. "I can still see the little fellahs running to us and saying, ' . . . Give me. No papa, no mama, no money. . . ' God bless them."

Canadian pay and passes stamped "2359 hrs" allowed boys who had grown up in small towns to sample sophisticated nightlife. Some places offered jazz, drink and food. The Sun Sun Café hosted a brawl during which the Grenadiers prevented a squad of Riflemen from advancing up the stairs to reinforce their comrades by pushing a Wurlitzer jukebox down the stairs. Rifleman Phil Doddridge was only one of the many Canadians who, after picking up a "small, round latex device" at the camp dispensary started out for a certain establishment. Before he reached the door beside a burning blue light, Doddridge ran into a lieutenant who brought him up short by asking, "Philip, what would your mother say if she knew you were here?" The young soldier hardly missed a beat, answering, "Sir, I shudder to think of it."

. . .

On 18 November, two days after arriving in Hong Kong, Lawson and his senior commanders toured the colony's defences. They were not impressed with the defensive works, the colony's few planes and old anti-aircraft guns, or with the number of troops in the garrison. "Once a landing is made, we would not have sufficient troops for a long sustained defence," wrote Captain Howard Bush in the brigade war diary. Lawson was so disquieted by the numbers available for the defence of Hong Kong that he supported the 27 November message asking Churchill to request that Canada increase its commitment to Hong Kong from two battalions to an entire brigade. Major Wells Bishop, commander of the Royal Rifles' "C" Company, got on Brigadier Cedric Wallis's bad side when, after Wallis told the

Canadians that the guns pointing across the Lyemun Channel at the mainland were painted wooden logs, he responded, "Well, they sure fooled me, but I bet they don't fool the Japs."[14]

Over the next week, the Canadians practised manning exercises in what they found to be hot, humid weather. What Bush recorded as "reconnaissance of areas," Private Sydney Skelton described on 21 November in his private (and illegal) diary in somewhat more colourful language: "We climbed mountains all day long and we are shown the many posts for which soon we shall be fighting for our own lives. Climbing [in full battle gear weighing sixty pounds and carrying rifles] is no joke and these mountains are plenty hard on greenhorns like me." When they weren't climbing, the Canadians strung barbed wire, dug weapon pits, filled sandbags—and undertook other laborious activities encompassed in war diaries by the phrase "fatigue duty."

. . .

Ten days later (on 31 November) and eighteen hundred miles to the northeast, Emperor Hirohito sat in front of a golden screen listening as his first minister, Tōjō and officers in the military's high command, answered questions put through the President of the Privy Council. After each answer, Hirohito signalled his agreement with but a nod of his head. At the meeting's end, Tōjō promised his emperor that the "nation united will go on to victory."[15] A few hours later, as General Sugiyama explained the war plans to Hirohito, orders went out to the commanders, including Lieutenant-General Takashi Sakai, who commanded the 23rd Army stationed in Canton and from him to the commander of 38th Division, Lieutenant-General Tadayoshi Sano.

A well-established spy network had kept the Japanese army apprised of the colony's defences, and Hong Kong was expected to be a relatively easy nut to crack. Nonetheless, Sano and his field commander, Major-General Takeo Ito, had long been planning his attack and had trained his men in camouflage and infiltration. The men belonging to the 228th, 229th and 230th infantry regiments, trained extensively in night manoeuvres and on territory that resembled the key defensive point on the colony's forward line of defence, the Gin Drinkers' Line.*

Beyond the normal Chief of Staff's duties, which would have included both input into the formation and overseeing the logistical needs of the infantry, artillery and bombers, the role of Sakai's chief of staff, Major-General Tadamichi Kuribayashi, is unknown. But it is likely that his counsel became all the more important once the Japanese learned of the arrival of "C" Force. Indeed, if he did not know Lawson and other senior officers who had been based in Ottawa, he had certainly seen them. For the general, who would become famous for his defence of Iwo Jima in 1945, had lived in Ottawa in 1931 when he served as the military attaché for the Japanese Legation, then housed in the (still standing) Victoria Building directly across the street from Parliament Hill.

Whatever happy memories he had of his time in Ottawa, the general kept them in check. The paper no longer exists, but sometime in the last weeks of November, Kuribayashi, who a decade earlier had written his daughter a postcard describing snow in Ottawa and who kept postcards of Rideau Hall, approved a firing and bombing plan that would devastate the defenders of Hong Kong, including the 1,974 Canadians.

. . .

---

* The 228th was commanded by Colonel Teihichi Doi. The 229th was commanded by Colonel Ryosaburo Tanaka. The 230th was commanded by Colonel Toshishige Shoji.

In the days that followed Hirohito's silent nod, thousands of Sano's men moved south from Fatshan (near Canton) to Shumchun, just north of the line dividing the New Territories and occupied China. A senior executive in the Hong Kong and Shanghai Bank, today's HSBC bank, stymied Maltby's effort to mobilize the two-thousand-man Hong Kong Volunteer Defence Corps; the official feared that since most of the bank's male employees were members of the Volunteers, mobilizing them would mean closing the colony's most important economic engine.

Home may not have known of this or the brouhaha that followed the mining of a beach assigned to the Royal Rifles, but he surely captured the mood of many of Hong Kong's elite when he wrote "We seem to be on some peacetime festival rather than on the brink of war."[16]

. . .

The battle that began early on 8 December 1941 can be divided into two parts. The first occurs on the mountains and hills and in the gullies of Hong Kong. During it, forty thousand veteran Japanese troops defeated almost fourteen thousand Allied troops, of which five thousand became casualties. Some twenty-one hundred died, including 250 Canadians. The battle cost Japan more than two thousand men.

But numbers tell us only so much. Battle is struggle—with the enemy, of course, but also with the elements, the hills and, as day followed day, exhaustion. Battle is seeing your buddies blown apart. And in an army like Canada's, which like Great Britain's was based on a regimental system, often that buddy was either a blood relative or a neighbour from just down a road. Battle—especially a first battle, which is what Hong Kong was for most of the Canadians—is disorder, horror and a welter of confusing orders that barely seemed to connect to the terrible kaleidoscope in which the Royal Rifles and Winnipeg Grenadiers found themselves. Battle is also putting aside a lifetime of believing that killing is forbidden and of trusting that the man closest to you has also set aside this belief.

The second part of the battle, and the second part of this book, occurs in almost twenty POW camps in Hong Kong and Japan, where some seventeen hundred Canadians were interned and where 267 died. A few died from accidents suffered in mines, work sites, shipyards and factories where men raised to believe in freedom and the dignity of man were turned, in direct contravention of the Geneva Convention—which, though it had not signed the part of the convention that deals with POWs, Japan had nevertheless pledged to abide by—into slave labourers. Death, however, came most often for men whose bodies were wasted by disease caused by malnutrition, and, in some cases, by malnutrition alone. The Japanese captors systematically starved their American, British, Australian, Dutch, Chinese and Canadian prisoners.

Equally important is the fortitude with which men, some as young as sixteen and some First World War veterans, all of whom had grown up in a country with a civilian culture, bore the all-but-unbearable. The story of surviving the mines, the shipyards and the forges is not simply one of physical strength. It is, rather, a story of their faith, their love for each other and their refusal to succumb despite having lost on the battlefield.

Book I:

The Battle for Hong Kong

CHAPTER 1

"The Season for Yellowtail Hunting"

The Calm before the Storm
7 December 1941

The cliffs of England stand;
Glimmering and vast, out in the tranquil bay.
—MATTHEW ARNOLD, "DOVER BEACH"

To the thousands who, on 7 December 1941, gave Happy Valley Race Track on Hong Kong Island its highest gate ever, the rising tensions with Japan were just one more distraction. A series of flaps had exercised the colony of Hong Kong since Japan seized Canton in October 1938 and advanced to the northern border of the New Territories. That war scare had died down soon enough. So too had the one in June 1940, when the fighting came so close to Hong Kong that the stench of decaying Japanese and Chinese soldiers' bodies wafted over the border. Observation flights buzzed the colony, which, since the Japanese had seized two islands to its south, was virtually encircled. True, the news from abroad was not hopeful. In response to Japan's move into Indochina in September 1941, the United States, Britain and Canada had tightened their embargoes on Japan. In late November, the United States demanded that in exchange for a resumption of oil shipments, Japan withdraw from both China and Indochina.

In Hong Kong itself, however, things seemed to be going, if not swimmingly, then, at least, in a very British way, ploddingly along. Had not the Japanese border guards agreed to a football match and baseball game? Had not the arrival of the Canadians increased the colony's garrison by some two thousand men and allowed General Maltby to reinstate the 1937 defence plan? What was Japan when measured against the two warships then steaming toward South Asia, HMS *Repulse* and HMS *Prince of Wales* (this last being the very ship that speared the mighty *Bismarck*)?

· · ·

On 3 December, General Maltby had visited the border with Brigadier-General Lawson, whose laconic diary entry, "see Japs," suggests that the Canadian commander found nothing more to say about them than did Maltby, who found them "scruffy, lazy and uninterested."[1] The next day, Maltby dismissed warnings that a Japanese force of up to twenty thousand was set to arrive at Fanling, some five miles north of the border. On 5 December, the Royal Rifles' commanders concerned themselves with what military and educational courses were available, while the men of "D" Company went for a swim at the YMCA's pool.

Twenty-four hours later, the Rifles, the Winnipeg Grenadiers, their British allies and the Japanese were all business. Following Maltby's "warning of impending war," part of the Canadian force moved to its war positions on Hong Kong Island. Shortly after his men were dug in some distance behind Lyemun (on the northeast corner of the island), Royal Rifles Major Wells Bishop banned unauthorized civilian traffic in the area. Later one of his men shot a Chinese man trying to run away from the restricted zone.

Meanwhile, thousands of Japanese troops belonging to the 228th, 229th and 230th regiments—the Doi *Butai,* Tanaka *Butai* and Shoji *Butai*—prepared for battle. Most were in large infantry formations. Some, like the one commanded by First Lieutenant Imai (230th Infantry Regiment), belonged to small infiltration units. In a solemn ceremony under a heavy cloud cover, Imai's men were detached from their company and given a special mission. Imai cut short the backslapping and ordered his men into a truck. Six hours later, they clambered out near the border town of Shenzhen. Tasked with a surprise attack on the British and Indian troops guarding a railroad bridge, their "spirits burned with determination and hope," recalled Soichi Taki. Later, they took shelter from the rain and, as soldiers on the eve of battle have for millennia, spoke of their families, one noting that back home in what they called Nippon, "It's the season for yellowtail hunting" (spearfishing).

Just after midnight, Imai led his men forward. The clouds had moved off and a bright full moon shone. They could hear dogs barking in the distant villages, and the voices of Indian soldiers carried closer on the breeze. Hidden by reeds, Imai waited to slip across the river, sneak up behind the Indian sentry and slit his throat. Taki and the others were then to cross the bridge and attack a guardhouse just beyond it.

. . .

Word of Japanese troop movements intruded into the Sunday morning service at St. John's Cathedral in Victoria, on the northwest corner of Hong Kong Island.* The mystery that seized the minds of the great and the good of Anglican Hong Kong had nothing to do

---

* Because of the International Date Line, the attack on Pearl Harbor occurred on 7 December while Japan's advances against Hong Kong, Burma and the Philippines occurred on 8 December.

with the Eucharist. They wanted to know what was so serious that when a messenger whispered it into Maltby's ear, the general immediately left the service with his officers in tow. Maltby's manning order reached the Canadians at Shamshuipo just in time to cause the cancellation of Anglican Chaplain Honorary Captain James Barnett's church parade. Somehow amid the hustle and bustle of thousands of men grabbing their kits and moving out, Barnett arranged a few moments' peace during which a large number of officers and men attended communion service. For some, it would be their last.

By 4:00 p.m., the Grenadiers were in positions along the southern coast from Repulse Bay to Mount Davis on the northwest coast. An hour later, the Rifles reported that its four companies were in positions more or less in echelon along Island Road, which ran south to Stanley, and on Sheko Road, which ran parallel to Island Road but south to the D'Aguilar Peninsula. The colony's forward defence on the mainland, the Gin Drinkers' Line, was held west to east by the Royal Scots, Punjabis and Rajputs, these last two being Indian regiments. The 3rd Middlesex, a machine gun regiment, manned the pillboxes on the island.

.   .   .

In Hong Kong, the war that began at 7:30 a.m. on 7 December with the bombing of Pearl Harbor—and which was learned of three and a quarter hours later (at 12:45 a.m. on 8 December) when a Tokyo announcer broke into a classical music program—would start as a race between engineers. Within minutes, British Major G.E. Gray's engineers began destroying bridges that crossed the Sham Chun River. An hour or so later, the British and the Japanese seemed to be performing in a surreal Noh theatre play. The Japanese watched as Gray's men destroyed a railroad bridge, though the British knew full well that behind the Japanese picket line, engineers had a replacement bridge ready to rush forward as soon as the British left the stage.

. . .

At 7:30 a.m. on 8 December, Gray received a message from an observation post that "several thousand Japs were pouring over the frontier" on his right flank. Among them was Masakazu Nakamori, whose orders were to "break through the barbed wire entanglements in a hollow" and then attack a pillbox, which, to his disappointment, turned out to be empty.

Chapter 2

"That Was the First Man I Ever Saw Killed"

The Breaking of the Gin Drinker's Line
7:00 a.m., 8 December, to 1:00 a.m., 10 December 1941

. . . for wide was spread that War and various;
   sometimes on firm ground
A standing fight, then soaring on main wing
Tormented all the air
—John Milton, *Paradise Lost*

Kai Tak aerodrome received a warning of an impending air raid at 7:00 a.m., 8 December. No one warned other probable targets such as Shamshuipo. Almost an hour later, as Honorary Captain Francis Deloughery celebrated mass on the parade ground for Catholics who had not yet deployed to their war stations on the island, Japanese infantryman Nakamori looked up and saw the "beautiful sight" of a dozen Ki-36 bombers, each carrying a 500-pound bomb, escorted by nine fighters flying in formation low over Hong Kong.

Only a few hours earlier in Hawaii, an American radar operator had mistaken some unexpected blips on his radar screen for planes due in from San Francisco. When planes neared Shamshuipo, it was the turn of Bill MacWhirter's friend to err when he called out, "Look! Our planes from Singapore."

By the time MacWhirter reached the door of the building he was in so he could see the planes, the formation had broken up as planes peeled off to head for their targets.* Each incoming pilot, with his target clearly in front of him, put his plane into a power dive. The bombers released their payloads a few seconds before they roared over their targets at less than five hundred feet; inertia carried the bombs the rest of the way. The fighters flew even lower, strafing the ground.

"The explosions were terrible. But even worse was the plane that seemed to follow a Chinese man who was running for a fence about 150 yards to my right. He probably thought the trees would hide him," MacWhirter recalls. "To get there, he had to scramble under the fence. There was a little hole, so he had a chance to get under it. The bullets caught up to him when he was halfway through the hole and cut him almost clean in two. That was the first man I ever saw killed."

Moments after the Chinese man died, MacWhirter's sergeant ordered him and other soldiers close by into a nearby barracks and under the iron beds. A few minutes later, the raid was over, and MacWhirter and Rifleman Jackie Coull ventured outside. "We could see the smoking holes where the bombs had fallen and damage done to the Jubilee Building where the officers would have been if they had not been sent to the island. The bombing was timed for the morning parades, so if the boys had been there we would have been blown apart," recalls MacWhirter.

The attack destroyed or badly damaged all but one of the Royal Air Force's few planes, and destroyed all but one civilian plane. The bombs wounded two Canadian signallers who had been loading

---

* The colony's anti-aircraft fire was ineffective and the closest fighters were hundreds of miles away in Malay, which itself was under attack.

45-pound radio sets into a station wagon. Chinese merchants in a nearby market were less fortunate. They and their shoppers were covered in blood and bits of bone and flesh.

. . .

The explosions ruined the start of Lieutenant Imai's Great East Asia War. By the time he slipped across the river, the Indian troops on the other side had "run away to Kowloon." After consoling himself by tearing down the Union Jack and raising the Japanese flag, Imai led his men forward.

. . .

Shortly after the dust cleared at Kai Tak and Shamshuipo, the Canadians on the mainland were on the move—and so were the fifth columnists, either Chinese operatives who worked secretly for Japan or Japanese agents who were ostensibly businessmen. While MacWhirter and the others made their way to their units on the island, the Royal Canadian Ordnance Corps requisitioned cars and trucks. Fifth columnists had, in fact, been active since just after midnight when a small bomb exploded near Waterloo Street in Kowloon. One dumped a tub of soapy water over the batteries that powered a radio in General Maltby's underground Fortress Headquarters (the Battle Box), and snipers were active at various points on the island.

. . .

By late morning, infantryman Nakamori had begun enjoying himself. True, his uniform was heavy with sweat, but his commander had given more than the usual number of rest breaks.* He was struck by the warm welcome the Japanese received from the Chinese villagers.

No doubt Nakamori believed that the villagers who gave the Japanese both coins and cigarettes had been swayed by the leaflets extolling the *Dai-t -a Ky eiken*. Announced in 1940, the Greater East Asia Co-prosperity Sphere was Imperial Japan's answer to Western penetration of Asia. Educated to believe that its role was to civilize Asia, the Japanese public ate up the rhetoric of "Asia for Asians." Anti-colonialists across Asia embraced the Co-prosperity Sphere, until the Japanese occupiers turned millions of Asians into slave labourers. Hundreds of thousands of them died from malnutrition and overwork, and hundreds of thousands of (mainly Korean) women were used as military prostitutes, the so-called Comfort Women.

· · ·

During the early afternoon, bombs again fell on Hong Kong. Since morning, the cost of fish, vegetables and paper had doubled in Kowloon on the mainland. The raid killed many Chinese locals and caused the cancellation of the afternoon picture show at the Oriental Cinema, but not the closure of the building—its stairwells were used as air raid shelters. Several planes attacked three Royal Navy vessels.

· · ·

---

* As the day wore on, these breaks became more important. Nakamori ate persimmons he had found in a house he was billeted in the night before and developed cramps. By nightfall, his diarrhea forced him out of the line of march.

The *politesse* demonstrated between Major G.E. Gray's men at the Sham Chun River and their Japanese counterparts soon frayed. Twice the Japanese fired on sappers affixing explosives to bridge supports. When a group of Japanese soldiers whose *seishin* (strength of will to attack) exceeded their grasp of the sappers' art rushed onto a bridge immediately after Gray's engineers clambered off it, the Royal Engineer calmly pushed down the plunger. Later, he kept a stiff upper lip when the captain of another sappers unit called with word that the Japanese were using peasants as human shields. "Do your job. Halt the enemy advance, blow up the bridge and fall back to the Gin Drinker's Line."[1]

That afternoon, Gray's men destroyed two Japanese platoons. Contrary to what British Intelligence thought, the Japanese were masters of infiltration, flanking manoeuvres and reconnaissance. At times, however, their *seishin* led them to forgo the latter. At 3:00 o'clock, while advancing in close order, their rifles in trail (that is, held in one hand with the arm down), ahead of an artillery train pulled by mules, the Japanese had no idea that a couple of dozen Punjabis and engineers awaited them.

What reminded Gray of "a victory march through Trafalgar Square" came to a bloody end when the Japanese were less than three hundred yards away.[2] A few Japanese men toward the end of the line managed to run back up the trail, the screams of dying men and the nauseating sound of squealing animals behind them. In two minutes, Gray's men killed about a hundred of Hirohito's soldiers. Three hours later, Gray's men ambushed another Japanese force on the narrow causeway that joined Tai Po to Tai Po Market. Lightning struck a third time later in the day when, supported by an armoured car, Gray's men destroyed another detachment coming down the Tai Po Road.

. . .

General Maltby knew that his men were good at night work. In almost pitch darkness, his engineers destroyed several bridges before withdrawing behind the Gin Drinkers' Line. In the early morning of 9 December, Royal Scots commandos, who proudly wore the sobriquet the Jocks, slunk their way through the darkness toward the Japanese position near Telegraph Hill.

British intelligence had assured Maltby that "Japanese night work was poor." That early morning, he wasn't so sure. As Japanese patrols kept pace with the sappers, and put the lie to the cartoon image of bug-eyed men who squinted through coke-bottle glasses, Maltby wrote in his postwar report, "the lesson of today is that the enemy can operate strongly on a moonlit night."

. . .

Air raids punctuated the day. Lieutenant Benjamin Proulx of the Hong Kong Royal Navy Volunteer Reserve watched in horror as bombs "burst among the congested buildings of the Chinese quarter and vomited flame and tile, soil and human flesh in brown cones."[3] Proulx had been born and raised in Ottawa and had worked for Paramount Films in Hong Kong for a generation.

. . .

Shortly before noon, British gunners reported destroying a Japanese observation post on Grassy Hill, just over two miles north of the Gin Drinkers' Line. Japanese records say nothing about an observation post existing there or about artillery disturbing Colonel Teihichi Doi's reconnaissance of the hill, from which he viewed the Shing Mun Redoubt, the key to the Gin Drinkers' Line.

Doi's reconnaissance followed a meeting with Major Oyadomari during which he ordered Doi to break through the Gin Drinkers'

Line near the Shing Mun River.* Doi was bent on "pursuing the retreating enemy" all the way to Hong Kong Island, until Oyadomari reined him in.

The 500-metre climb up Grassy Hill was worth it. Doi could see that the hollow between Grassy and Needle hills was too rugged for his men to use as a jumping-off point. Though disappointed that he did not see any British soldiers, the clothes flapping in the wind told him everything he needed to know about his enemy's readiness.

At a council of war later in the day, Doi's regimental commanders endorsed his attack plan. In the hour before the attack, infantrymen ate from rice balls in their haversacks while their officers toasted victory with sake. Following Shinto tradition, some sent fingernails or locks of hair to preserve their memory in case their bodies vanished in battle.

In his postwar interrogation report, Doi outlined two problems that faced him. He dealt with the first—whether his men, who had not slept for over a day, had just completed a 48-kilometre march and lacked artillery support, could attack over unfamiliar terrain and still triumph—summarily: "I had confidence in the ability of my men." The second concerned Hill 251 at the centre of the Shing Mun Redoubt, the taking of which was a precondition to taking Hill 303, one of Doi's primary objectives. Doi's problem facing Doi had nothing to do with the martial ability of the British defenders. Rather, Hill 251 lay in Colonel Toshishige Shoji's sector. In the clash between protocol and glory, Doi chose the latter: "I was willing to face any reprimand which might come later for making the decision."

. . .

---

* Although of lesser rank, Oyadomari was one of General Kuribayashi's staff officers and, hence, had the authority to transmit orders to his nominal superior.

Despite the fact that the Gin Drinkers' Line was a half-completed, badly situated and rundown defensive line, it had transfixed a series of generals. In 1937, Major General A. Bartholomew had told London that to hold it he would need a division as well as five squadrons of up-to-date aircraft; he had two infantry battalions for the defence of the entire colony and a few outdated planes. Accordingly, Bartholomew and his successor, General Arthur Grasett, planned to use the line only to delay the Japanese while the garrison retreated to Hong Kong Island. The machine gun pillboxes on the north shore of the island provided its primary defence from landward attack (i.e., across Hong Kong Bay). The colony's heavy guns, installed prior to 1937, faced the sea, though many could swing around.

Despite the War Office's wishes, after the arrival of the Canadians, Maltby to reverted Bartholomew's defensive plan, albeit with almost six thousand fewer troops (and no air force). Covering roughly equal portions of the line, Maltby placed half his infantry, the 2nd Royal Scots (somewhat reduced by malaria), the 2/14 Punjabis and the 5/7 Rajputs. On paper, some three thousand men for eleven miles. During a mock night attack, a Royal Scots officer penetrated the line without being detected, hardly surprising the unit's assistant adjutant. "During the hours of darkness," the adjutant recalled, the redoubt was "without any value whatsoever—a large isolated position spread across a hillside, its total armament a few widely separated machine guns laid to fire on fixed lines." Moreover, he added, the guns were fixed on the wrong lines.[4]

. . .

At about 7:00 p.m. on 9 December, as the amateur players at the YMCA in Victoria began performing *The Late Charles Bean,* a play about the Anzac veteran who went on to write Australia's official history of the First World War, a few miles to the northeast, both

Japanese and British troops groped their way through the dark, drizzly night. Second Lieutenant J. Thompson led nine Royal Scots toward the eastern side of Jubilee Reservoir, which, because the British
had only thirty-nine anti-personnel mines available to protect the
Shing Mun Redoubt, lay unprotected. Doi's men, who moved silently
in their split-toed, rubber-soled sneakers, had no trouble avoiding
Thompson's, whose every step was broadcast by their hobnailed
boots crunching on the rocks.

As the performance put on to raise money for the Prisoner of
War fund—for the poor unfortunates held by Germany and Italy—
ended, a sentry just south of one of the pillboxes on the eastern side
of the redoubt saw lights and a party of men approaching. His challenge unanswered, he started shooting. Doi's men scattered, fired
back and threw hand grenades. Overmatched, the sentry broke off
the firefight and rushed back to alert the commander of the closest
pillbox, Corporal M. Robertson.

A few moments later, explosions from hand grenades dropped
down their ventilation shafts rocked Robertson's pillbox and
another a few hundred yards away. Despite the acrid smoke, the
darkness and the deafening roar, the Jocks recovered before the
Japanese attackers could rush into the tunnel.

As soldiers stabbed at each other in the smoky dark of the pillboxes, Doi and his officers came under fire from a machine gun
some distance to the northwest. A few moments later, Hirohito's
soldiers again proved their ability at night work by moving into
position, climbing down rope ladders, swatting a guarding force
out of the way and driving Corporal N. Campbell's crew from its
machine gun.

The men in the observation post commanded by Captain
Potato Jones would have envied Campbell's luck at being caught
in the open. Before the British regular could even attempt to act
on Brigadier Wallis's order to "evict the enemy" from the redoubt,

hand grenades exploded on the other side of the post's steel-door entrance.[5] A burst of machine gun fire drove the attackers off, but only for a moment. One crept close enough to the post for his grenade to blow in an embrasure shield.

The explosions blew out the post's lights and thickened the air with dust and the cutting smell of cordite; they also hid the sound of the Japanese placing a bomb beside the shelter's main steel shutter. That explosion blew the door apart, killed two Indian troops and stunned all but a certain Jock named Thomson, who plugged the gaping hole with a stream of lead from his machine gun.

More grenades and more explosions followed; one knocked Thomson to the floor, which was already littered with shards of glass and stunned, broken men. Another fell near his head. As he reached to sweep it aside, he realized that to do so would send it among the wounded. Instead, he "tipped his steel helmet over his face and waited."[6] The explosion knocked him out, destroying one eye and badly injuring the other. Thomson's observation post held out, as did a pillbox, until early the next day, when, unfortunately, a British shell pulverized it.

Doi considered the artillery bombardment that began just after midnight (or, since the Japanese stayed on Tokyo time, just after 1:00 a.m. on 10 December) to be "conclusive proof" that the redoubt had fallen.

· · ·

Though unprepared for taking prisoners, the Japanese respected the Jocks' defence of the Shing Mun Redoubt and took the surrender correctly, even digging the men out of the ruins of the pillbox hit by the British shell. Doi himself ordered medical treatment for the wounded Captain Jones, whom he mistook for a Canadian and who struck him as "a splendid officer."

The tension of the battle for the redoubt spent, some of Doi's men memorialized their efforts by inscribing on a wall, "Captured by Wakabayashi Unit."

CHAPTER 3

"The Broken Rusted Wire Was Valueless"

Retreat to Hong Kong Island
1:00 a.m., 10 December, to 9:00 a.m., 13 December 1941

All delays are dangerous in war.
—JOHN DRYDEN, *TYRANNIC LOVE*

The attack on the Gin Drinkers' Line had an immediate impact on Private George Hallada and the rest of the Winnipeg Grenadiers' "D" Company. Thirty minutes before Colonel Doi's men scratched Wakabayashi's name into history, General Maltby had contacted Brigadier Lawson, commander of the Island Brigade, ordering the Grenadiers to move immediately to the mainland—and soon non-commissioned officers were rousting men from sleep and their shallow foxholes.

As the Canadians moved toward their positions on Castle Peak Road north of Kowloon, and the Japanese consolidated their hold on the Shing Mun Redoubt, Maltby's Fortress Headquarters descended into what one staff officer remembered as "chaos."[1] The general had thought that the Gin Drinkers' Line would hold out at least a week. True, his men could make a stand at Golden Hill, but without the redoubt, there was nothing to stop the Japanese from advancing all the way to Kowloon and throwing the British off the mainland. Thus, Maltby ordered Brigadier Wallis to counterattack and retake the redoubt.

Wallis would have liked to strike at once using a reserve company of Jocks. However, that company had been moved into position to block a thrust from Smugglers' Ridge and was thus too far away. Captain W. Rose's "C" Company (also of the Jocks) was available, but malaria had much reduced it. Furthermore, to attack, these men would have had to make a difficult climb in the dark up a steep, rocky hillside. Reluctantly, Maltby accepted that Wallis would have to wait until daybreak before making his move.

. . .

Colonel Doi's commander was even less happy with his subordinate. Breaking the British defensive line was one thing, but regimental boundaries were another, and for senior Japanese commanders, the more important. Twice Doi received orders to vacate the redoubt so Colonel Ryosaburo Tanaka's 230th Regiment could attack it. And twice Doi refused. Not until noon did the Japanese brass authorize the facts on the ground.*

. . .

In the hours after the Japanese broke the Gin Drinkers' Line, rumours ran wild. Signalman William Allister heard from panicky despatch riders of "crazy suicidal bastards—racing into the wall of Brens and Lewises, the barrels going steady, getting too hot to

---

* The Japanese were nothing if not consistent. Major Oyadomari was "sharply rebuked" for not keeping Doi on a shorter leash.

handle."[2] On the island, Lieutenant Proulx realized the loss of the Gin Drinkers' Line meant that the collapse of the mainland was inevitable. Still, bolstered by the roar of the nine-inch guns at nearby Fort Stanley, morale in Proulx's station held through most of the day. "We were half deaf but slap happy too. We had weapons to fight with and an enemy to fight against—all a man needs when a scrap is on," Proulx later wrote.[3*]

. . .

By mid-morning, after his men had repulsed two small attacks, Wallis decided the time was ripe for his counterattack. Lieutenant-Colonel S. White, the commander of his chosen instrument, the Royal Scots, disagreed. Perhaps not surprisingly, the Jocks' regimental history passes over White's refusal. A Court of Inquiry (held in Argyle Street POW Camp shortly after the garrison surrendered) found that White refused the order because "most of the Royal Scots had panicked" and streamed back to Kowloon.[4]

Near 10:00 a.m. on 10 December, however, legal niceties mattered less than did Wallis's order to fall back behind what he called his "strong Golden Hill line." That line seemed something very different to the men who struggled up the hill. "Burdened by equipment and ammunition, and weak as some were from malaria, [they] were in a state of exhaustion as they crawled on hands and knees over rocks and scrub to the bare hilltop. . . . There were no mines and the broken rusted wire was valueless."[5] The communiqué issued at 2:30 p.m. surely put the best gloss on things when it said that the line had "stabilized at approximately this morning's position."

---

* Proulx's morale plummeted a short time later when BBC shortwave reported the loss of the HMS *Prince of Wales* and HMS *Repulse*.

A half-hour later, Japanese aircraft went after HMS *Cicala,* which had been shelling Japanese troops trying to remove obstacles on Castle Peak Road. As he had during the attack on his ship a day earlier, the aptly named Captain John Boldero took full advantage of *Cicala*'s three rudders, which allowed her to "turn almost on six-pence" to manoeuvre away from the bombs.[6]

During another attack a little over an hour later, a bomb hit *Cicala*'s stern, the explosion wounding an able seaman and forcing Boldero to order his helmsmen to turn for Aberdeen on the south-ern side of the island.

. . .

Sometime during the morning of 11 December, a rumour reached Canadian Signalman Blacky Verreault that the Scots, supported by the Grenadiers, had recaptured the Gin Drinkers' Line. The rumour was half-right. The Grenadiers were supporting the Jocks, but their mission had nothing to do with reclaiming lost territory. They were covering the Jocks' retreat from Golden Hill.

The British retreat followed a miserably cold and wet night. Even before the Japanese attacked, Captain David Pinkerton's men on Golden Hill were almost at their breaking point. As the sky light-ened, the decision to dig in (if occupying shallow weapons pits can be called digging in) on the exposed slope of Golden Hill meant that even the intrepid men of the Royal Army Service Corps couldn't find a way to bring them breakfast. In its stead, Pinkerton bucked his men up with a tot of rum.

Equally damp and tired Japanese infantrymen spent the night listening to the heavy tramp of British boots. Before moving along a ridgeline, platoon commander Imai cautioned his men (including Taki, who, having recovered from persimmon-induced diarrhea, had rejoined his unit) to keep their faces down so as to prevent a British searchlight from illuminating them. Even with this extra incentive to look downward, though, one of Taki's comrades fell into a deep hole.

A mortar barrage designed to stun the Jocks preceded the attack. But, Taki discovered when he found himself running into a hail of machine gun fire, the barrage had failed. Unsure of where to run, Taki followed a sergeant and some other men, including his lieutenant, Ichikawa, into a gully. Three men trailing them never made it.

As Taki and the others caught their breath, their comrades fell in force on the British defenders a little way down the line. Though the Jocks pushed the Japanese advance back at various points, in less than an hour the numbers began to tell. One after another the defenders fell, one to a sword-wielding officer.

While the southern end of the Scottish line broke apart, Ichikawa, who had also taken shelter in the gully, planned his next move. Though the information was wrong, he heartened Taki and the others by telling them that only six men defended the position they were about to assault. To lighten his load, Taki ditched his mess tin and gas mask just before Ichikawa gave the order to climb out of the gully and rush the British position.

Ichikawa's timing could not have been worse. Moments before the Japanese came rushing into view, Pinkerton's men had pulled the pins on their hand grenades and readied to throw them at a different group of attackers. Just as the men were about to throw their grenades, someone spotted Taki, and the Jocks divided their barrage. Taki saw one of the grenades coming—it looked to him more like a rock thrown in desperation until it exploded, blowing him back down the hill and seriously wounding him. The shower of grenades broke up both attacks.

Realizing that the key to the defence of Golden Hill was its crest, Pinkerton ordered his men to reinforce the British troops he thought were still in position there. As Pinkerton led a bayonet charge that momentarily stabilized his line and later earned him a Military Cross, Taki lay nearby bleeding profusely and struggling to say the word soon to be forever linked with bayonet charges: *Banzai.* The wounded soldier was not, however, cheering on his comrades. Rather, in this instance, *Banzai,* which means "ten thousand years," was an invocation to the emperor said in fear of imminent death. Lance-Corporal Matsuhira soon came to Taki's aid.

Near Pinkerton, Second Lieutenant J.M. Dunlop was not as lucky. A bullet severed a large artery and his blood pooled on the hard ground as he died. Machine gun bullets ripped apart J. Nichol's stomach, leaving him to die an agonizing death. Even the order to withdraw south toward Kowloon did not end the dying. "We tried to take one of the seriously wounded on the knoll with us, but it was rough going down to the road and he died on the way," recalled Ford, whose platoon covered the withdrawal.*

. . .

Had they read it, the Jocks and the Indian troops to their right would have been baffled by Governor General Sir Mark Young's mid-morning communiqué: "It has been a quiet night and there is nothing to report. Some shelling of the Island took place but it had only nuisance value. Damage and casualties are insignificant." Events quickly overtook the governor's words: at noon on 11 December, Maltby ordered the evacuation of the mainland.

---

* Wallis was furious when he found out the Scots were withdrawing. At 10:00 a.m., after the survivors of these companies had joined "A" Company, which itself was barely holding scattered positions south of the Redoubt and with White still unsure of what was happening at the front, Wallis told him that "the good name of the Battalion was at stake" (quoted in Lindsay, *Battle,* 79) and that further withdrawals must stop because they endangered the defensive line hastily thrown together after the collapse of the Gin Drinkers' Line. What many considered the precipitous withdrawal of the Scots led to a barrack room alteration in the regiment's motto from "First of Foot" to "Fleet of Foot."

The decision to abandon the mainland had two important effects on the Canadians. The first involved Captain Allan
Bowman's "D" Company and the signallers still on the mainland.
Just after 7:00 p.m., the last of the Scots passed through Bowman's
line and Private Hallada and the rest of "D" Company marched
south into Kowloon, their heavy machine guns slung over their
shoulders, because the scheduled transport trucks did not arrive.

The Kowloon they had marched through thirty-six hours earlier
was hardly the picture postcard destination it had been a few months
before that. By dusk on the 11th, conditions were much worse. A pall
of smoke and dust caused by Japanese bombs and shells, and by the
burning of oil depots that Maltby ordered destroyed, hung over the
city. Nathan Road, the city's famed shopping street, bore the stain
of the sixty people killed when a shell exploded within minutes of
a communiqué that derided the effectiveness of Japanese shellfire.
Moreover, the stench of putrefying bodies mixed with that of raw
sewage bubbling up onto the streets from shattered sewer mains. At
one point, Allister and his fellow Signalman, Hank Damant, who
took the same streets to the ferry, passed what at first appeared to be
three men sleeping on a bench. But they were not sleeping, Damant
realized; they had been killed by internal injuries caused by the
shockwave of an explosion.

"The city," recalls Hallada, "was filled with screams, the sounding
of breaking glass and panicked Chinese." Rioters looted shops and
godowns (warehouses); armed bands of fifth columnists roamed the
streets. That explains why the Canadians marched through it with
fixed bayonets.

The withdrawal was not without cost. Privates Howard Shatford
and John Gray became detached. The former managed to find some
Indian soldiers—the bulk of the Rajputs had withdrawn at the
same time—and returned to the island with them. The latter was

presumed killed by fifth columnists, becoming, therefore, the first Canadian soldier killed in the Second World War.

The second impact on the Canadians of the decision to abandon the mainland stemmed from Lawson's request that Maltby divide the island's command. The dividing line between Lawson's West Brigade and Wallis's East Brigade ran south from Causeway Bay to Violet Hill to Chung Hon Kok in the south. One of the oddities of choosing this line is that Lawson's headquarters, situated in the Wong Nei Chong Gap, was about a hundred yards from the dividing line between the two brigades. More importantly, since the gap divided the island and was certain to be one of the first Japanese objectives, Lawson was positioned rather further forward than a commanding general's headquarters should be.

The division of the Island Command also divided the Canadians. The Grenadiers remained under Lawson and provided his rear defence. Lawson's forward defence consisted of the Punjabis on the northwest quadrant of the island and the Royal Scots and Middlesex running east to where his command joined Wallis's. The Rajputs provided Wallis's forward defence. The Royal Rifles, holding positions further east and to the south of the Rajputs, came under Wallis.

This arrangement did not sit well with the Canadians, who well remembered the great successes their fathers had had at Vimy and thereafter when they fought together as a corps. Nor were the Rifles impressed with Wallis's first decision, placing his brigade headquarters in Tai Tam Gap. The Canadians believed that the area, which already housed the regiment's headquarters, would now be dangerously overcrowded.

. . .

By dawn on 12 December, the only part of his pre-war plan surviving was the orders for two companies of Rajputs to withdraw south from the eastern extension of the Gin Drinkers' Line to Devil's Peak Peninsula in order to deprive the Japanese of the strategic mountain at its southern tip. The 725-foot-high peak commands the mile-wide Lyemun Channel, which divides the mainland from the northeast corner of Hong Kong Island, and overlooks the eastern half of the island. Maltby believed that, protected by the rugged, narrow peninsula, the Rajputs and Punjabis (who joined them) would be able to hold it indefinitely.

During the day, the defenders broke up two infantry attacks. A third supported by mortars was also beaten back but led to a partial evacuation of the peninsula. Despite the best efforts of the Indian soldiers, the vicissitudes of a night evacuation under fire accomplished what well-trained dive-bomber pilots could not. Machine gun and artillery fire sank sampans carrying some five hundred artillery rounds and, worse, about a hundred mules and ponies were lost either in sampans or in other small boats.

At 4:30 a.m. on 13 December, Maltby ordered the evacuation of the last Rajput company from Devil's Peak. Four hours later, Wallis stepped into a lighter. The famed China Station had contracted to a five-square-mile island.*

---

* Unsure of the Canadians' ability, Maltby placed his most trusted battalions in the forward positions facing the mainland. The Punjabis covered the west side of the island in Victoria. The Royal Scots were bunched around the Navy Yard, just to the west of the midpoint of the island. The 1st Middlesex, a machine gun regiment, held positions around Causeway Bay. The Rajputs, supported by the Royal Rifles' "C" Company, held the eastern side of the island facing the mainland. The rest of the Rifles were spread out over the hills on the eastern side of the island. The Winnipeg Grenadiers were centred in the middle of the island west of the Wong Nei Chong Gap.

CHAPTER 4

"Go Back and Destroy Some More"

The Siege of Hong Kong Island
9:00 a.m., 13 December, to 8:00 p.m., 18 December 1941

"Some of the boys have young beards. Heavy shelling this after-noon. Shrapnel dropping around us. The fragments are quite hot, ugly jagged pieces of metal."
—TOM MARSH, 14 DECEMBER 1941

The siege of Hong Kong Island began with a scene that would not be out of place in a Royal Canadian Air Farce skit. A half-hour after Brigadier Wallis stepped off the mainland on the morning of 13 December, a launch flying a white flag and a banner emblazoned with the words PEACE MISSION approached the seawall in Victoria. As the launch neared, perplexed British soldiers and civilians could see two Western women and a Japanese officer, the officer's hand perched theatrically on his sword.

After strutting up the steps from the dock, the officer introduced himself as Colonel Tokuchi Tada of Japanese Military Information. The ranking British officer present, Major Charles Boxer, barely had time to say "I am Major Boxer of His Majesty's—" before Tada, seeing the camera around American journalist Gwen Dew's neck, turned away from the major and asked if she wanted to take his picture. As the nonplussed major looked on, Tada arranged himself between two of his subordinates, told her when to snap the photo and ensured that she had spelled his name properly before returning to the business at hand. "We have come with an offer of peace from the Japanese Government," he told Boxer, before handing him an envelope.[1]

As Boxer took the letter to Governor Young, Tada released one of his female hostages and allowed the other to give her two dachshunds to a British soldier for safekeeping. Ever the journalist, Dew asked Mr. Othsu, whose picture she had taken with Tada, what the surrender terms might be. "Equitable terms for both sides and safe conduct for all," Othsu said before a nearby British officer brusquely cut in: "Let's leave the terms to the Governor."[2]

Some fifteen minutes later, Boxer returned and told the stunned Tada "No surrender," handing him a letter for General Sakai. Tada replied, "The war shall be resumed if we do not hear from you. Major Boxer, you will order your men to withhold fire until 4 o'clock."[3] More influenced by the precipitous collapse of the British on the mainland than by knowledge of Sir Mark (who, like the Duke of Wellington before him, had learned his trade on the playing fields of Eton), Sakai too was surprised at the governor's response, which ended with the flourish: "British subjects and all who have sought the protection of the British Empire can rest assured that there will never be any surrender to the Japanese."

· · ·

Although Boxer stopped an officer who wanted to shoot Tada's party as it left, the British did not feel themselves bound by Tada's deadline. A few minutes after Tada left his launch back on the mainland in

Kowloon, a British battery opened up on a number of lighters tied up to nearby docks. The Japanese answered the British barrage with an air raid, the first of some twenty-five over the next few days, accompanied by round-the-clock shelling.

Japanese artillerists did not have to guess the coordinates of the big guns, like those on Mount Davis, or of the pillboxes that dotted the island's shore. Fifth columnists had supplied detailed maps. Nor did they have to worry about sighting their guns: Japanese builders had poured concrete emplacements when they built *godowns* in Kowloon.

Before the end of the day, Mount Davis and the Jubilee battery near Victoria had been hit, and a shell that fell near Royal Rifles Captain Martin Banfill's first aid post near Lyemun obliterated the Quebec-born doctor's driver. A day later, shelling killed eleven Indian soldiers.

On 16 December, a dud nine-inch shell burrowed its way into the plotting room of General Maltby's Fortress Headquarters. Snide comments about the efficacy of Japanese artillery manufacturers were stopped cold when the sappers removed the shell and everyone could see stamped on its side: "WOOLWICH ARSENAL 1908." That morning, gunners destroyed three pillboxes and badly damaged a fourth; the pillboxes on the island were built of substandard concrete.

Among the pilots who bombed Hong Kong in six raids between 16 and 18 December, at least one had also bombed the Americans at Clark Air Base in the Philippines. One of his Yoshinki Kubo's flights over Hong Kong was nerve-racking, though not because of anti-aircraft fire, which was negligible. Rather, his engines began losing power after takeoff, causing his plane, weighed down by two 500-pound bombs nestled under its wings, to fall behind his fighter escort. Worse, this loss of power made it difficult for him to attain the proper altitude for releasing the bombs in the short twenty miles from the aerodrome near Kowloon and his target, Aberdeen. After Kubo released his payload, the plane lurched upward, and the pilot's elation rose in tandem with his altitude.

. . .

The misery of the almost 1.5 million Chinese residents mounted daily. After the food distribution system collapsed, Sir Mark established communal kitchens. But to get to them, terror-stricken civilians had to walk by the decaying remains of hundreds of bodies mutilated by shells and bombs. "On one rubbish heap," a British officer "saw a dead monkey and alongside it a dead baby, side by side."[4]

During the first six days of the war, shelling and bombing had killed fifty-five soldiers, wounded scores more, and killed and wounded thousands of Chinese civilians. A bombing raid near Victoria on 15 December caught a Chinese teenaged girl outside. As fire and earth rose around her and the ground shook underneath, the terrified girl ran to Signalman Blacky Verreault, who was firing at the planes with a Tommy or Lewis gun. "Trembling, she cuddled into my arms," he recalled. "I stopped firing to wrap my other arm around her." The next day, on 16 December, a single bomb killed 150 civilians. Of a bombing raid on the Central Market in Kowloon, one memoirist wrote, "The earth opened. Bright lights rolled against us like waves of flame. We tried to drop to the earth but the earth rose up to meet us faster than we could fall. Repercussions after repercussions shook the building. Walls spread outward, shuddered back into place."[5]

The fourteen thousand who were able to cram into air raid shelters traded the terror above ground for the lawlessness of the underworld, where gun-toting gangs robbed at will.* Others took shelter in basements of houses on the Peak on which the well-to-do built country homes to escape the heat. Among those who survived these bombings was a young girl, Adrienne Poy, her brother Neville, and her mother and grandmother. The girl's father, Ng Ying Choi (or William Poy), was a motorcycle despatch driver for the Hong Kong Volunteer Defence Corps. The girl grew up to be Adrienne Clarkson, Canada's 26th Governor General.†

Fifth columnists sowed dissention and defeatism in the general population by raising Japanese flags or distributing Japanese leaflets that asked the Indian troops why they fought for their colonial masters. Others sabotaged cars and trucks, and snipers stalked the roads. On 17 December, a member of the Royal Canadian Ordnance Corps caught a fifth columnist, who was summarily executed the next day.

. . .

Starting with the destruction of the lighters after the "peace mission" on 13 December, Allied forces had some successes. On 14 December, gunners destroyed a concentration of junks at Stonecutter's Island off Kowloon, thus gaining a measure of redemption for a mistake a few days earlier when they had destroyed British lighters carrying munitions. Late on 15 December, a searchlight revealed a large number of Japanese troops attempting to cross the harbour in a junk, small rafts and inflatable boats.

---

* The story of how the gangs were brought under control is worthy of a novel. With Governor Young's approval, F.W. Shaftain, head of Special Branch, British Intelligence, arranged a $20,000 loan from Chang Ji Lin, the head of the Shanghai underworld and influential member of the Triads, to purchase the gangs' loyalty. Following the meeting at the Cecil Hotel at which this deal was made, the *maître d'* discovered that an unusual amount of sterling silverware had gone missing.

† After growing up in Ottawa, Neville Poy, who became a plastic surgeon, married Vivienne Lee, who was born in Hong Kong in 1941; in 1998, Prime Minister Jean Chrétien appointed her to the Senate.

A moment later, Royal Rifles machine gunners opened up; soon the junk blew apart and the rubber boats deflated. Some of the other craft caught fire, their sails becoming sheets of flame that lit the water while Canadian small arms took care of others. Hong Kong Volunteers sunk four other boats before midnight. Just before sun-up the next day, HMS *Thracian* sallied forth and sank two ferries filled with Japanese troops.

On 15 December, there were several reports of Japanese landings on the island. The first, at 8:06 a.m., came from the Royal Rifles, who reported parachutists near the Tai Tam Reservoir. There were indeed parachutes, but no troops—only packages of propaganda leaflets calling on the Canadians and British to surrender. Some twelve hours later, the commander of the Royal Rifles' "C" Company, Major Wells Bishop, misinterpreted the sound of gunfire that destroyed the junk and rubber boats, described above, as indicating that the Japanese had landed and occupied Pak Sha Wan Fort on the northeast corner of the island.

This last incident is important for two reasons. First, it shows quick (if flawed) thinking by the green Canadian commanders. Second, instead of viewing Bishop's error as a rookie mistake, Wallis allowed it to colour his view of the Canadians so much that when a few days later in tandem with the invasion of the island, Japanese operatives occupied Sai Wan Fort, Wallis rejected Bishop's reports out of hand.

. . .

By 16 December, the Royal Rifles had been in the field for nine days and nights and the battalion's war diarist wrote: "Men showing signs of strain. Very little rest or sleep for anyone." Still, as evidenced by Verreault's diary, the unseasoned Canadians were holding up remarkably well. When not mooning over his lost Charlotte, Verreault recorded in a most matter-of-fact way the plaster blown off walls and ceilings, his growing friendship with British troops and his belief that he was "good for 15 Nips by myself."

As smoke from the docks set alight the previous night stained the sky, at 9:30 a.m. on 17 December, Colonel Tada returned to Hong Kong. This second "peace mission" was no more successful than the first. Sir Mark's response was short:

> The Governor and Commander-in-Chief of Hong Kong declines most absolutely to enter into negotiation for the surrender of Hong Kong, and takes this opportunity of notifying Lieut-General Sakai and Vice-Admiral Masaichi Mimi that he is not prepared to receive any further communications from them on this subject.

The Japanese gave Sir Mark four hours to reconsider.

Maltby saw military and/or political meanings behind this second surrender offer. He considered that the Japanese "(a) . . . disliked the prospect of attacking across the water or (b) that the Chinese threat in their rear was taking effect, or (c) that it was an attempt to undermine our morale by thoughts of peace and quiet." Perhaps only the third was true.

. . .

During the short truce, Lieutenant Benjamin Proulx, who had gone to Victoria for supplies, found himself walking past the ruins of some ritzy houses on the Peak. Sitting alone under a large tree, he saw a Maryknoll priest. After saying hello and giving the lieutenant a half salute, the American priest asked Proulx if he could spare a few minutes. "Certainly, Father. What can I do for you?"

The priest, however, had no favour to ask. Rather, he had something to give. For a few moments he and Proulx were almost jocular, with Proulx saying, "I've never been less bored than the past few days" and the priest adding, "This war is not precisely dull." Then, as the growing drone of aircraft engines signalled an end to the truce, the priest became serious. "These are dangerous times," he said, and reached into his pocket. "Why not give me a few moments and prepare yourself?" He pulled out a small container holding communion wafers.

By his own admission, Proulx was not a religious man. Still, he accepted the priest's offer, knelt on the ground and confessed. As the roar of dozens of engines enveloped them, Proulx spoke in Latin, the language of prayer that he and, at the time, every Catholic learned growing up. He shrived "in a voice that was almost a whisper [but] sounded very plain and clear." Before he'd finished, the bombs were falling. "I don't remember them, how near they were or what they sounded like," Proulx later wrote, "because I was receiving Holy Communion."

Proulx did hear the bombs exploding during the next bombing raid, which occurred while he was crossing the field that belonged to the Jockey Club. One bomb blew open the wall of the stables, and moments later the terrified horses rushed out.

> They thunder[ed] through the avenues, swirled around me, stopping, turning sideways, running back, as bombs and shells burst among them with spouts of dark debris and shrapnel. Blood on their slick coats, streaks of blood in their wide staring eyes, heads high in panic, they ran a futile race with death. A horse would suddenly slip and fall; another would balance himself, bewildered and helpless, on three legs. Many lay dead in the littered streets.[6]

As Proulx watched the horses die, General Sakai, who earlier in the day had been given an extension until 10 January to complete the conquest of Hong Kong, issued the order to invade the island, which read, in part:

> Object: The Capture of the British Crown Colony, the Island of Hong Kong
> Intention: On Thursday night, December 18, Japanese Imperial Forces will land upon the Island of Hong Kong at suitable situations between North Point and Lyemun.

Word of Sir Mark's rejection of the second surrender demand quickly made the rounds. By the time Brigadier-General Lawson penned his diary entry for 17 December, it had been distilled to an almost Churchillian phrase: "Jap envoys came over and said all military installations have been destroyed, no sense going on fighting. Gov. told them to go back and destroy some more."

CHAPTER 5

"Japs, Thousands of Japs"

The Royal Rifles' Stand at Sai Wan
8:00 p.m. to midnight, 18 December 1941

Triangles, parallels, parallelograms,
Experiment with hypotheses
On the blackboard sky,
Seeking that X
Where the enemy is met.
Two beams cross
To chalk his cross.
—STEPHEN SPENDER, "AIR RAID ACROSS THE BAY AT PLYMOUTH"

At 7:00 p.m. on 18 December, hidden by a heavily overcast, drizzly night made darker by the oily smoke covering the harbour from fires at the refinery, some three thousand Japanese soldiers put the lie to the British officers' belief that the "Japs would never cross the harbour in the rain. The water's too choppy. They'd get seasick."[1]

Far from fearing *mal de mer*, the soldiers belonging to Japan's 230th, 228th and 229th regiments boarded requisitioned junks, rafts and collapsible boats.* As if to compensate for the roar of their

---

* Order given here is west to east; the 229th was the first to engage with the Canadians.

boats' engines, which they feared would attract unwanted attention, Sakae Ishikawa and the men with him remained silent during the crossing. As tracer shells etched their way through the night, muscle power moved most of Emperor Hirohito's men.

The Japanese did not achieve total surprise. A lookout near Lyemun spotted the boats carrying the 229th Regiment. But even in the face of the daylong bombardment that all but announced an attack on the north side of the island, British and Canadian officers clung to their preconceptions about the Japanese so tightly that as late as 7:30 p.m., Lieutenant-Colonel William Home, commander of the Royal Rifles, dismissed a warning that the Japanese had landed.

. . .

A half-hour later, artillery pummelled pillboxes covering Aldrich Bay, a few hundred yards northwest of the Rifles' position south of Lyemun, and high-explosive shells blasted pillboxes near Wan Chai, further west still.

Some of the Rifles may have seen the flash from explosions of the first few shells fired from the 1st Heavy Artillery Regiment's guns situated near Kowloon that landed less than fifteen hundred feet to the Rifles' northeast. The dull "crump" Hong Kong Volunteer Defence Corps (HKVDC) Sergeant Daniel Bosanquet heard from the gun pit was the last manifestation of the explosion that began a second earlier after a shell moving at about twelve hundred feet per second smashed through the metal grate of the gun position.

As the shell shot from the gun's barrel, a pin in the fuse pushed down, locking the shell's shutter into place. The centrifugal force, an effect of the shell's rotation caused by the gun's rifling, opened the shutter, creating a flash hole. As the shell hit the gate, the striker in the shell's nose depressed with tremendous speed, hitting a small quantity of fulminate of mercury and setting off a small explosion that raced through the flash hole.

Even before the shell's TNT exploded, the metal gates were white-hot shrapnel. Milliseconds after the explosion, so too were the shell's metal casing and the nose cone. The almost 5,000°F roughly spherical shock wave pummelled anything in its path, turning metal and concrete into more shrapnel. The bombardier and the sergeant whose mangled bodies Bosanquet found in the twisted metal of what had been the staircase probably never felt a thing. The blast wave would have knocked them out, and broken their spinal cords or destroyed their brains as it ripped the air from their lungs faster than their bodies could register pain.

. . .

Even as the concrete walls of their pillboxes broke apart, the Rajputs doggedly kept their machine guns ready to fire. When the Japanese flotilla was illuminated by a searchlight and fireballs from the same burning oilworks that produced the smokescreen, the Indian regiment's machine guns turned the crossing, in Colonel Doi's words, into "a spectacular and grim affair." The Rajputs could not destroy the flotilla. But they did slow it down and force pilots to veer away from their assigned routes, which so inter-mixed the units that command and control all but collapsed. After the war, Doi would admit that even those imbued with the *Bushido* Code could flinch in this difficult crossing:

> When exposed to fire on the water, which offers no shelter, it is absolutely useless to turn boats away from the direction of enemy fire, but perhaps it is only normal human psychology to react that way.

More is known about the first minutes after the 230th landed than of the other two regiments. Despite the gunfire he saw during the crossing, when infantryman Sakae Ishikawa landed on the garishly lit shore not far from the burning oil tanks, he thought he and his comrades had caught the defenders napping. A burst of gunfire that cut down five soldiers disabused him of that notion. Quick action by Second Lieutenant Yoshida allowed his platoon to seize the high ground and clear a path for Ishikawa and the others.

A few minutes later, Doi and Colonel Tanaka each made his way across the harbour under heavy fire. As soon as Tanaka landed, he ordered that his regiment's quick firing guns be deployed against the pillboxes still in action.

. . .

The Royal Rifles' Major Wells Bishop did not yet know that the Japanese had landed when he received a report of a suspicious truckload of Chinese heading toward Sai Wan Fort, which commanded the approaches from Lyemun Passage.* Despite having been criticized by his brigadier a few days earlier for reporting incorrectly that Pak Sha Wan Fort had fallen, Bishop acted again to try to protect the fort by ordering Lieutenant Arthur Scott's No. 15 Platoon forward.

As Scott neared the fort, he could just make out armed men standing menacingly near its gates. He ordered his men to fire. While their rate of fire was good, they were hampered by the fact that their targets wore their habitual black—which in the argot of the day was called "coolie black"—on a night "so dark you couldn't

---

* Reports of suspicious movements by groups of Chinese had been noted during the day. An hour before Bishop ordered Scott forward, fifth columnists set three cars alight at Lawson's headquarters in the Wong Nei Chong Gap.

see a Jap at the end of your rifle."[2] When the "Chinese" started firing back, Scott put his faith in cold steel.

The Canadian's charge bore little resemblance to the famed John Wayne charge in the Hollywood epic *Sands of Iwo Jima*. "Unlike the Americans, who run forward and then lean forward on the balls of their feet, and with their bayonets parallel to the ground, Canadians were trained in the British method of bayonet fighting," says Rifleman Bill MacWhirter.

> We sprinted forward but before coming into bayonet range, we went flat-footed with one foot in front of the other so that we were firmly planted. Then we thrust forward from the shoulder instead of the waist. Before thrusting forward, we turned our Lee-Enfields so that the flat side of the bayonet was parallel to the ground. This prevented the serrated edge of the bayonet from getting stuck in the target's ribs.

The Canadians also twisted their bayonets slightly as they pulled them back, so that the wound would open to the air and bleed freely.

Scott got the better of the fight. Still, fearful of being cut off in the dark, he pulled his men a couple of hundred yards back from the gate and deployed them on a north/south line along Island Road before going to report the engagement to Bishop.

．　．　．

Less than a thousand yards away, Akimusa Kishi's men had snuck so close to a British gun emplacement that they were able to kill almost all the sentries before they could sound the alarm. Thus, mere seconds after Bosanquet heard the cry the "Japs are in the gun pits," a hand grenade came through the shelter's partially opened door. The blast blew Bosanquet to the floor but left him unhurt, while wounding others. Knowing that a larger attack would follow, Bosanquet ordered his men to leave the wounded and try to escape.

A British bombardier obeyed the order to leave, but neither he nor several of the men who followed him headed for the hillside to which Bosanquet pointed. Instead, they ran toward the gun pits—and thus the Japanese. Bosanquet pushed others out the door and led them to the roof of the shelter, from which, he knew, they could jump down a hill and, with luck, to safety.

But a few minutes after he pulled himself free of the barbed-wire fence he rolled onto at the bottom of the hill, Bosanquet realized that no one had obeyed his order to follow him and jump. Though safe for the moment, he knew that he could not stay at the bottom of the hill alone. Unarmed and unsure of which direction was which, Bosanquet fought his way through the scrub and the darkness until he found a road.

. . .

Bosanquet was not the only soldier dealing with a hidden fence. Moments after landing on the island, Doi found his way blocked by a chain-link fence, which his sappers could not get through with barbed-wire cutters. A machine gun forced Doi's men to ground and prevented them from flanking the fence. They cleared it only with the help of ladders, an operation that cost a number of his men their lives.

. . .

When Scott reported to Bishop, neither was sure the Japanese had landed. As a precaution, however, Bishop ordered Scott to occupy the Lyemun barracks, and took a Rifleman with him on a reconnaissance of the area around Sai Wan Fort.

They never reached it. While advancing along a hillside, Bishop met a frightened party led by the fort's commander, who told Bishop, "The fort is occupied by the Japanese." The nonplussed Canadian major responded, "What are you doing here?" His tone when he heard that the attackers had chased the British out the fort can be guessed from his words: "Why did you not stay and chase them out?" Bishop could scarcely believe the Royal Artillery corporal's answer: "What with? We have no rifles."

Were it not for the eerie glow from the fires a few miles to the west, the overpowering smell of burning oil, the rattle of machine gun fire and the rumble of exploding shells rolling through the night, Bishop's next question would be funny: "Are you trying to tell me that you are manning a fort without arms and a war is going on?" The hapless corporal answered, "We have Lewis guns but the attack was so unexpected that we had no chance to use them."

By the time Bishop returned to headquarters, it had lost contact with the Rajputs' headquarters near the Shaukiwan Police Station, a mile or so to the northeast. A stream of Indian troops ran past the Canadians yelling, "Japs! Thousands of Japs." Of most immediate concern was the automatic fire from Sai Wan Fort that raked Bishop's positions.

Bishop's low opinion of Wallis was reinforced (and vice versa) in the 8:00 p.m. call in which Bishop told Wallis that the Japanese had occupied Sai Wan Fort. Wallis assured the Canadian that this was impossible, because the Canadians operated the fort.

> Bishop: I am in command of the Canadians in this area, and there have never been Canadians inside the fort. I have not even been permitted to look in the place myself.
> Wallis: I have definite information that there are friendly troops in the fort.

Bishop: They don't act friendly. We are being raked by automatic fire from there this moment. I am ordering an attack to
take the fort at once.

Bishop hung up the phone and ordered Lieutenant Ian Breakey
to retake the fort.

·   ·   ·

By midnight, the Japanese would have advanced the two miles to
Mount Butler and Jardine's Lookout, which put them on the verge of
splitting the island, largely because they used tactics perfected by the
Canadians in what was still called the Great War. Instead of advancing in continuous lines, as the British had during the disastrous first
day of the Battle of the Somme (1 July 1916), a tactic tailor-made for
defenders equipped with machine guns and rapid-fire artillery, the
Japanese followed much the same plan the Canadians used at their
great victories at Vimy Ridge and Passchendaele in 1917 and during
the last hundred days of the war. Small units advanced in rushes or
by infiltration. They flanked most strong points, leaving them to be
mopped up later. Yet as some of Hirohito's men rushed forward, others were engaged in desperate battles.

Infantryman Ishikawa landed near the North Point Power Station.
Weighed down by a forty-pound backpack, a nine-pound Arisaka
model 38 rifle and part of the more than 100-pound machine gun
slung over his shoulder, Ishikawa was pleased that instead of heading into the scrub-covered hills, his squadron leader headed for a
paved road. His relief was short-lived. As he turned onto the wide
road, silhouetted by the light from the nearby fires, Ishikawa came
under machine gun fire and a shower of grenades thrown from the
top of the nearby buildings. Through the maelstrom, Ishikawa heard
his commander call for his men to run to the east side of the road.

Their path took them some distance down the west side of the North Point Power Station, garrisoned by seven Middlesexers and twenty-two members of the HKVDC, the youngest of whom was fifty-five years old, and several pillboxes. The task of Ishikawa's unit was not glamorous, and it placed them in a very dangerous position. To counter the threat of a relief column coming from the city and falling on the Japanese rear, they had to be facing the road. Unfortunately for them, this placed them in the line of fire of a machine gun manned by the 1st Middlesex Regiment, who proudly wore the sobriquet Die Hards, situated in a building some two hundred yards away.*

To silence this gun, Ishikawa's commander ordered one of his gun crews to set up its gun on a rock so that it could fire into the window. British fire soon killed the machine gun crew—leaving the Japanese gun on the rock as mute testimony to the Die Hards' aim.

As Ishikawa and the Die Hards took turns pinning each other down, Doi, after clearing the fence, continued to find the going surprisingly tough.† Out of touch with their platoon and company commanders, Doi's 2nd Battalion made a virtue of necessity and formed small ad hoc units that charged ahead, leaving behind them many strong points, giving the lie to the intelligence report that told Maltby that the "Japanese preferred stereotyped methods and fixed plans."[3]

The Rajputs firing from badly damaged pillboxes destroyed one of Doi's two anti-tank gun companies and cut down many of the runners Doi's commanders sent out to try to re-establish order. The death of Doi's radio operator complicated things. As much as he wanted to strike into the heart of Hong Kong quickly, Doi had no

---

* Coincidentally, in the First World War, the 1st Canadian Division had fought its first battle, Second Ypres (April 1915), alongside the Die Hards.

† Rajputs punished Doi's men; approximately 65 percent of his men became casualties.

choice but to order his men to regroup by a slow process of communicating from one adjoining unit to another.

. . .

Near 11:00 p.m., just as Breakey was about to launch his attack on Sai Wan Fort, a Hong Kong and Singapore Royal Artillery officer, Lieutenant E. Bompas, arrived at Bishop's headquarters saying that Wallis had sent him to lead the attack. Bishop was in telephone contact with his brigadier; hence, it is passing strange that the officer commanding the Canadians had not been informed that another officer was being put in charge of the attack.*

Since Bompas's plan involved two platoons, Bishop ordered Captain Gavey's No. 15R Platoon to join Breakey's. At first glance, Bompas's plan had the virtue of simplicity. Instead of infiltrating around the fort—through Japanese-held territory—and attacking from the northeast, Bompas planned to attack using Cemetery Road, which ran along the east side of the fort. But simplicity can be undone by the facts on the ground.

Bompas may have been, as historian Tony Banham has said, "a highly regarded young officer," but in the minutes before 11:00 p.m., Bishop thought him something of a fool.[4] Instead of leading or positioning himself further back but still close enough to issue orders, Bompas "remained in the roadway, brandishing a revolver and shouting that he would shoot any man who attempted to retire," recorded the regiment's war diarist. Unimpressed, the Canadian major told the lieutenant to stop the theatrics and that, if he was so gung-ho, he should lead the attack from the front.

While Bompas hastened to join his attack, Bishop called Battalion Headquarters to get the searchlight on Mount Collinson (about two

---

* Wallis's war diary says nothing about Bompas being sent to Bishop with Wallis's plans.

miles south of Sai Wan Fort) to illuminate the fort. Bishop's plan could not be gainsaid; the light would make it easier for his men to find the fort and could blind its occupiers. Unfortunately, his request ran into red tape: the searchlight was under another command.

The flaw in Bompas's plan soon became clear: a twenty-foot-high wall that the Canadians could neither scale nor breach, as they lacked mortars and the ability to call down an artillery strike. Light machine gun bullets raked the men. Worse, since the Japanese plan included protecting the fort once they'd taken it, shells started among the Canadians; the shells likely came from the field guns Tanaka's men had recently manhandled ashore.

Bompas had no choice but to cancel his attack and order his men to withdraw. Just as they began to, disaster struck: the light on Mount Collinson switched on, illuminating the Canadians. Before they could dive into the brush for safety, machine gun bullets cut down several of them.

. . .

Bishop too was on the move. A report that the Japanese troops had driven back to the junction of Island and Lyemun roads so alarmed the major that he went to investigate. He had not made it far before he had to avoid a Japanese patrol coming from the same general direction from which his men were retreating. Moments after reaching Scott's position, Bishop noticed movement in the undergrowth; soon men in Japanese uniforms and four in "coolie black" fell to a blast from a Tommy gun.

. . .

As Indian soldiers in the pillboxes died, Tanaka's and Doi's men raced south for the two most important strategic positions on the island. The first, the 1,700-foot-high Mount Parker, dominates the northeastern quadrant of the island. Since Bishop's "C" Company was north of the mountain, if the Japanese took the mountain, Bishop's men would be isolated. The second was Jardine's Lookout. About two miles east of the summit of Mount Parker is Mount Butler; slightly to its southwest is Jardine's Lookout, which overlooks the Wong Nei Chong Gap. This gap was the key to the island's defences because every important road ran through it; it also held General Lawson's headquarters. If the Japanese seized Jardine's Lookout, they would isolate each part of the island and be able to destroy each concentration of troops in detail.

Garrisoning such high points would, therefore, seem to be normal operating procedure. However, as Colonel H.B. Rose (MC) told Canadian interviewers after the war, Maltby did not believe that the Japanese would "attack over the hilltops and mountaintops." Not until 11:00 p.m., some three hours after the Japanese had landed on the island, did Wallis make to occupy Mount Parker. The task fell to the No. 5 Platoon of the Royal Rifles, under the command of Lieutenant G.M. Williams, who when the Japanese attacked were at Boa Vista, about a mile south of the mountain.

While the distances and the gradient the Japanese and the Canadians had to negotiate were roughly equal, about a mile at a 5 percent slope, the Japanese led by Lieutenant Nokajima crossed difficult terrain.* The Japanese won the race. The Canadians were hampered by their heavy marching boots but not, as Wallis asserted, "by their thick winter battle dress which was far too heavy for such operations"; Williams's men were wearing their regular woollen battle kit, chosen to keep them warm during Hong Kong's cold nights.

---

* After the war, a Canadian officer who retraced the Japanese path up the slope of Mount Parker wrote that he "found the climb difficult carrying nothing but binoculars, whereas the Japanese were carrying full equipment" (quoted in Greenhous, 78), as were, of course, the Canadians.

After No. 5 Platoon reached the top of the mountain, a brief battle took place. Williams, his sergeant and most of his men were killed or wounded. Nokajima counted ten casualties.

The distances involved in the race for Jardine's Lookout were greater. Some of Doi's and Shoji's men advanced up the colourfully named Sir Cecil's Ride while others climbed the hills leading up to Mount Butler. The shortest distance from the shore to Jardine's Lookout was directly up the hills. By 11:00 p.m., however, most of the pillboxes had been silenced (more than thirty Rajputs had been killed and scores of others wounded or captured), which opened the way for the bulk of the invasion force to advance on Jardine's Lookout via the Ride. This is the path Doi himself took and on which he found a large part of the 229th Regiment that was pinned down for a time by artillery fire from the British guns north of Stanley.

When he reached the top of the Ride, Doi divided his troops, sending his 1st Battalion to the right and a bit south of the lookout to the police station that stood upon what he referred to as Five-Way-Road Junction on the west side of the Wong Nei Chong Reservoir. Somewhere along this path, one of Doi's soldiers, no doubt nervous about the break in protocol he was about to commit, approached the general and handed him an extremely valuable find: a map showing the coordinates of the British firing positions.

The Winnipeg Grenadiers, who at 10:40 p.m. answered HKVDC Major Stewart's call for help for his garrison at Jardine's Lookout, had an even greater distance to travel than did the Japanese. The closest of Lawson's so-called flying columns, No. 5 Platoon, was at Little Hong Kong and travelled some two thousand yards to a road junction near the north end of Wong Nei Chong Gap. The second, No. 18 Platoon, was four miles away at Telegraph Bay on the far west side of the island.

The third column, No. 17 Platoon, commanded by Lieutenant George Birkett, was three miles to the southwest on the south coast in Aberdeen. The call came soon after the men had bunked down. Earlier in the day they had been more than a little disgruntled when they readied to attack to a small island off Hong Kong that housed a Japanese radio transmitter; that attack was cancelled. Now, in the hour before midnight, the situation was so serious that two trucks were sent to hasten their arrival. It was, Sergeant Tom Marsh recalled, a wild ride:

> Two trucks hurtled down the winding road in pitch darkness. There were now twenty-nine of us. Lieutenant Birkett rode in the front seat of the forward truck. I rode on the front seat of the one following. Ahead of us we could see the red sky and the fires in the City. We careened and bumped over and around obstacles in the road, crashed through roadblocks before being challenged.

At every turn, Marsh expected to see Birkett's truck blown up by a land mine or feel his truck crash into Birkett's as it slowed down to avoid crashing into one of the many obstacles littering the road. The excitement of the drive competed with the knowledge that the Japanese had landed and were advancing into the island.

> The air was bright with sparks and acrid smoke. Guns thundered. Shells shrieked and exploded. The deadly rattle of machine guns and the whine of snipers' bullet added to the bedlam. Steel helmeted figures crouched behind barricades but we saw few civilians. The dense mass of humanity that was Hong Kong lay hidden in their cellars. Many were killed by bomb or bullet and others were burned alive.

· · ·

As Marsh marvelled at his driver's uncanny driving ability, Bompas returned to Bishop's headquarters where, after learning of plans for another attack on the fort, he arranged for the Royal Naval Guns to swing around and lend much-needed support. Heavy shells started falling on the southwest side of the Sai Wan, on the same ground over which Breakey's and Gavey's platoons were to advance. But this second attack never materialized.

The Royal Rifles' war diary and Wallis's war diary give different reasons why the attack did not occur. After praising the artillery barrage, the Rifles' diary says, "Call for reinforcements was refused." Wallis's diary references a message from Bompas: "The [Royal Rifles'] Coy. Comdr failed to stage the counter attack." The difference is important.

Wallis's version of Bishop's decision was incompetence at best and insubordination at worst. Wallis ignores the fact that according to British military law (under which the Canadians served), the commander on the scene has the responsibility of deciding if the facts on the ground fit with the logic of the order. In Appendix H of the war diary, Wallis adds that the Canadians "were inclined to leave their positions and take cover in the various concrete shelters and were loath to return and occupy their weapon pits. Their failure to counter-attack at Saiwan is recorded [elsewhere]. . . . As far as I can judge from the accounts of Captain Bompas, R.A. (dec.) and Officer Commanding Armoured Cars who went to reinforce them, Major Bishop did his best, but the men would not hang on."*

---

* Wallis's words about the Canadians stand in sharp contrast to what he wrote about the Rajputs fighting near Tai Koo docks, some two miles west of Sai Wan. "By 2200 hrs confused fighting was in progress in the streets on the high ground EAST and WEST of TAIKOO H.Q. 'A' BN [the Rajputs] H.Q. were temporarily forced to withdraw to a position SOUTH on the track to SANATORIUM GAP. Later they fought their way back to their old Bn H.Q. but were finally forced to withdraw about 2359 hrs."

Canadian sources make no mention of armoured cars, and the men who were there, like Sergeant Flash Clayton, do not remember their comrades seeking shelter in the concrete shelters or refusing to man the weapons pits. Indeed, Clayton ordered his own platoon to take up exposed positions half facing south and half facing west, an arrangement known as "refusing your flank," designed to allow each side to protect the other's flank. At the same time, Bishop ordered No. 15 Platoon into positions in front of the company's headquarters. No veteran recalls seeing an armoured car.

. . .

While Bishop waited for word of reinforcements, a shell exploded near some of the men who had attempted the first attack as they retreated down Cemetery Road to get back to headquarters. Following the roar of the explosion, calls went up for a stretcher-bearer. The closest was John Russell, who crawled over the bullet-swept road to reach Riflemen Gordon Irvine and Captain Gavey. After clearing each body from the road, Russell and another stretcher-bearer loaded the broken bodies onto a truck for the drive back to the Advanced Dressing Station.

At about the same time, Birkett and Marsh's ride came to an abrupt halt about 150 yards away from a pillbox that guarded the southern approach to Jardine's Lookout. There, within sight of the summit, which despite the darkness of the night they could make out against the even darker sky, thirty-nine Canadians piled out of the trucks. A few moments later, mortar bombs reduced the trucks to burning wrecks. By the light of these fires, the British officer who commanded the pillbox told Birkett that he would give him whatever aid he could, as he guided Birkett's men to a pillbox that they would hold until their advance up Jardine's Lookout, scheduled for just before dawn.

. . .

As midnight approached, the firing on the shore all but ceased. Almost forty Rajputs had died and scores more had fled their blasted pillboxes. Thirty-three Punjabi soldiers had also died, as had a dozen Royal Engineers and twenty-eight members of the HKVDC. The Japanese were attacking every position held by the Royal Rifles' "C" Company and had, in fact, got behind them and both taken Mount Parker and moved onto Mount Butler. Light and smoke from the fires burning in Victoria turned the sky "red as blood," wrote Sidney Skelton in his private (and illegal) diary.

The *Senjinkun*, the pocket-sized Japanese field manual, ordered that the Emperor's soldiers were to "show kindness to those who surrender."[5] However, Hirohito had refused to adopt the Geneva Convention, and Japanese legal scholars argued that prisoners of war had forfeited their moral right to life. This belief grew out of the way the sixteenth-century *Bushido* Code came to be interpreted after the rise of ultra-nationalism in the 1930s.

In medieval Japan, "the Way of the Warrior" was roughly equivalent to Europe's chivalric code, and thus allowed honourable surrender. In the 1930s, however, the code was changed, ostensibly to expunge what officers saw as the disgrace brought upon Japan when some Imperial soldiers surrendered in the Russo/Japanese War of 1905. Like all of Hirohito's soldiers, Tanaka's men had been taught that their highest duty was to serve the Emperor and, if necessary, die for him. In school and again as recruits, they learned that not only was it a disgrace to them and their families if they were captured, but it was also a disgrace for them to retreat.

Canadian and British troops were taught that the aim of battle was to win territory and remove enemy troops from battle. King George's men did not believe that enemy troops forfeited their right to exist. By contrast, Japanese troops were taught: "When you encounter the enemy after landing, think of yourself as an avenger come face to face with his father's murderer. Here is the man whose death will lighten your heart."[6]

Emperor Hirohito's government cast itself as the liberator of Asia, using the rhetoric of the Greater East Asia Co-prosperity Sphere. However, like its Axis partner Germany, it divided the world into a master race and lesser races. The Japanese saw themselves as the masters, the *Yamato* race. The belief that they descended directly from the gods had allowed the Japanese Army to perpetrate the Rape of Nanking. These same beliefs allowed their notorious medical experiments on Chinese POWs and civilians.[*] Late on 8 December 1941, the Imperial Japanese Army committed the first of many atrocities suffered by Hong Kong's defenders.

. . .

In the minutes after 9:00 p.m. when Bosanquet had ordered his men to make a run for it, the twenty-six men left behind had reason to hope they might survive. Despite what they had heard about the Japanese taking no prisoners, word from the mainland was that the Japanese behaved correctly in victory.[†] Thus, when a Japanese officer called out "No harm will come to you; we know you are not regular soldiers," more than two dozen unarmed men surrendered.

The Japanese separated the six officers from their men. Then, as their men watched, Japanese soldiers plunged their almost-sixteen-

---

[*] On the day Hong Kong was invaded, the Japanese held some 350,000 Chinese POWs. At the end of the war, they held 56. Thousands of Chinese POWs (as well as American, Dutch and British POWs, though none from Hong Kong and, hence, no Canadians) were subjected to gruesome medical experiments.

[†] The Japanese did, as noted above, handle POWs correctly. The three days of rape and rapine unleashed on the civilians of Kowloon violated the only part of the Geneva Convention Japan did sign.

inch bayonets into the British officers. After tying the other men's hands behind their backs, the Japanese herded them into a pillbox, where they were kept without food or water until nearly midnight, after which they were taken out one by one and bayoneted.

Tanaka's men had experience in this grizzly business from their days in China. Still, some of the thrusts did not prove immediately fatal. Soon, blood and dead and wounded men covered the ground.

The Japanese contempt for these men did not end with merely bayoneting them. Despite Shinto teachings about fastidious care of the dead and the words printed in the *Senjinkun,* the Japanese soldiers tossed the British dead and dying into a pit and threw rocks at them.*

---

* Two HKVDC men, Martin Ts'o Him Chi and Chan Yam Kwong, survived their wounds and later crawled to safety.

CHAPTER 6

"They Had Already Infiltrated Up to and Past Our Destination"

The Winnipeg Grenadiers' Fight for Jardine's Lookout
Midnight to 6:00 a.m., 19 December 1941

"We were awakened at 3 a.m. and we were told to . . ."
—THE FINAL WORDS OF RIFLEMAN SIDNEY SKELTON'S DIARY

The rumble of exploding shells pulsing through the night could not lessen Signalman Hank Damant's sense of humour. Over the previous few days, he had told his comrades that if ambushed by a "bunch of serious-looking li'l men," he'd jam the despatch into his mouth, chew it quickly and swallow before saying, "Hell-o, little men! Does it look like rain?" As pride alone kept Signalman William Allister from screaming "Stop! Let me live!" into the volcanic night, Damant rose a little from the floor of the communications shelter they were in, handed his fellow Montrealer a cigarette and said with a wan smile, "Time goes so fast when you're havin' fun."[1]

Toward midnight, their commander, Captain George Billings, came into the pillbox and said that the Japanese had advanced so quickly that even though this shelter was two miles inland, it would soon be surrounded, and that four signallers would have to remain to provide communications for General Lawson's headquarters, which was a short distance away.*

Billings asked whose shift came on at midnight. Knowing that whoever stayed would likely die, Allister, who had hated Billings since an untoward incident aboard the SS *Awatea,* quavered: "Ours." During the pause before the officer spoke, Allister offered up a "wordless hopeless prayer." When he heard "The present shift will stay on," Allister—an artist trained at McGill University—masked his guilt with a thankful nod.

A few moments later, Allister and some others followed Billings into the drizzly, dangerous night. After a panicked dash, Allister ran into Signalman George Grant. Together the two "found a path that seemed to wind into the hills—it led nowhere. We tried to retrace our steps. . . . What to do? No orders, no leaders, no equipment, no information. . . ."[2]

. . .

A mile or so away Lieutenant Kenneth Strang's No. 14 Platoon, occupying positions on either side of the road leading to Sai Wan Fort, tried to hold some of the larger Japanese units back. Though they lacked artillery support and the all-important mortars, these Canadians were unusually well equipped; in addition to their regular arms, they had a Vickers machine gun, two Lewis guns and an extra Bren gun, and each officer had a Tommy gun. From makeshift firing pits or hastily established firing lines, men who had grown up hunting in the woods of the Gaspé and New Brunswick fired where they heard rustling or the report of a rifle.

---

* Their comrades in the field, like Bob Acton and Tony Grimston, had had to keep changing positions to prevent the Japanese from using either their long aerials or radio directional finding to get a bead on them and call down an artillery strike.

Though in pain from wounds suffered when an exploding hand grenade blew him so high his body turned round three times, Sergeant Flash Clayton, who had been taken to the shelter that served as Bishop's headquarters, remained very much in the fight. Twice officers sought shelter in the pillbox to unjam their Tommy guns. "Neither Corporal Latimer nor Lieutenant Scott knew I was there," says Clayton, "and I knew from the sound of the Japanese small-arms fire how close they were." Nevertheless, when Lorne Latimer came in to unjam his Tommy gun, Clayton asked how things were going. Latimer didn't miss a beat, saying, "Sarge, I've never had a better time in my life."[*]

Clayton was one of the few Canadians to have taken the four-week arms training course, so fixing the gun made famous by Chicago gangsters was not difficult. Before leaving the shelter, Latimer asked Clayton for the two hand grenades still strapped to his belt; Clayton gave him one. A short time later Lieutenant Harold Scott reprised Latimer's role.

. . .

After the war, British officers like General Maltby and Brigadier Wallis accused the Canadians of being disorganized, a charge, unfortunately, supported by more than a few veterans who complained that their units were marshalled here, then there, and marched up this hill, then that hill. And to be sure, in the fog of war there are incidents like this one. Just after midnight, part of the Rifles' "A" Company was at Windy Gap and another at Point D'Aguilar, each several miles away from the Sai Wan area. Seven hours later, these troops were ordered to move to the Battalion

---

[*] Clayton's voice broke a moment later when he told me, "You know, of course, he died three days later—tied together with three other men and bayoneted."

Headquarters at Tai Tam. Before the truck that collected them had gone a half-mile, new orders arrived sending them back to their original positions at Windy Gap. At 8:30 a.m., still another order arrived: "Move to Bn HQ as soon as possible, as any delay might mean that the Coy would be cut off." While Battalion Headquarters issued these orders, each originated with Wallis's headquarters; similar confusing orders plagued the British and Indian battalions.

. . .

The soldiers in the convoy led by Second Lieutenant M. Carruthers of the Hong Kong Volunteers knew precisely where they were going: down King's Road to the power station (in the middle of the north side of the island) with orders to help the overaged Hughseliers garrison it.* Carruthers's path took him into Sakae Ishikawa's sights. Not long before, Ishikawa had lent a hand when a machine gun in one of the power station's windows chewed up a neighbouring unit trying to advance to the south. After pinpointing the gun's position, he had squeezed his trigger; seconds later, the gun fell silent.

Ishikawa showed his skill again when, instead of aiming for the tires or engines of the armoured cars and trucks, he aimed at much tougher targets. When the armoured car was five hundred yards from the station's gate, he targeted the driver. "The armoured car abruptly turned to the right and crashed," he recalled.[3] Then he fired at the driver of the lead truck, hitting him. When, after that truck crashed, three men ran from the wreck, he cut them down too, before firing on the second truck, causing it to crash as well.

---

* Because of the age of its members, some wags referred to this unit of the HKVDC, named for the founder, A.W. Hughes, as the Methusaliers instead of the Hughseliers.

The driver of the third truck lived for only a few more moments. Of the twenty-four men in these trucks, twelve survived the crashes; only six, including Carruthers, made it to the power station.

.   .   .

Shortly after midnight, Bishop entered the dugout sheltering Clayton. Clayton overheard the major call Lieutenant-Colonel Home and tell him, "The Japs have all the high ground. We have counterattacked and been unsuccessful in dislodging them. I am asking your permission to withdraw, because when daylight comes we will all be killed." Clayton is certain that Bishop received verbal orders to withdraw.

The Rifles' war diary and Wallis's East Brigade War Diary tell two different stories; indeed, one can read Wallis's diary itself as telling two different stories. The Canadians' diary says that the redoubtable Lieutenant Bompas brought them orders to withdraw. Wallis's war diary also places Bompas at the scene, but with a very different mission; he and some other Royal Artillery men and two armoured cars were there to support their positions on the road leading to Lyemun. The Rifles' war diary makes no mention of these men or of the armoured cars.

At all events, by 12:30 a.m. on 19 December, Wallis knew that Bishop's men were falling back, despite the support Wallis claims to have sent them. In Appendix H, Wallis wrote that the Canadians "should have held their positions at all costs as ordered. But they withdrew and once more set an example *which had ruined the defence of C Battalion Sector on the Mainland* of retrograde movement" (emphasis added).* The words "as ordered" suggest

---

* Bishop's withdrawal left the gunners at Sai Wan Hill without protection, so Wallis ordered them to fall back in concert with Bishop's company. When he wrote of the gunner's withdrawal,

that Wallis and Home spoke about the possibility of a withdrawal. The italicized words, however—which contain a slip of the pen ("Mainland" should read "Island")—are damning. The withdrawal of the Canadians "ruined the defence" on the island. Wallis accuses the Canadians of ruining the defence of his brigade when he knew that by then the Japanese had already flanked East Brigade on the west and were atop Mount Parker, which put them in position to isolate Bishop's command.

· · ·

The Canadians were unfamiliar with the terrain and so exhausted that Bishop's men were out on their feet (several even falling down asleep), but still they withdrew skilfully. At times, they found protection in one of the huge water catchments that caught rain running off the island's barren hills and directed it to one of the reservoirs. At other times, they provided their own protection by turning and firing at the Japanese while their comrades slunk forward.

In his book *The Soldiers' Tale,* historian Samuel Hynes argued that one of the defining features of modern soldiers is "stoic courage"; he distinguished it from "heroic courage," which is linked to the dash of the cavalry charge.[4] Stoic courage took shape under the tremendous bombardments of the First World War, when death could come from miles away and in a battle where survival did not depend on one's skill, for example, as a horseman. It is not a virtue

---

the brigadier again criticized the Canadians and blithely ignored the fact that they were about to be enveloped: "Confused fighting followed; information reaching Bde H.Q. being meagre and mainly from 6 positions and it looked as if 'C' Coy [Bishop's Company] had left their GAP positions. 'D' Bn [Royal Rifles] was ordered to ensure that 'C' Coy protected the guns, but it became clear that the Coy had steadily given ground and left the Gunners only time to get clear, removing dial sights and percussion locks."

limited to the trenches or an infantry attack into the face of machine gun or artillery fire, or to men like the Rajputs who remained in their concrete pillboxes as Japanese shells blasted them. In the early hours of 19 December, it fell to Company Quartermaster-Sergeant Colin Standish to lead men imbued with such courage.

Screened by Strang's platoon, Standish's men repeatedly traversed the same dangerous ground between the stores and the trucks, ground raked by bullets and holed by mortars and shells. Working in pairs, one man on each side holding the heavy crates filled with food or ammunition by rope handles, they hoped to hear the next explosion. For as frightening as being shelled in the open is, each man knew that the one he heard was not the one that would destroy him. With each step they took, they hoped their slow-moving forms would not offer themselves to a Japanese rifleman. It is most unlikely at this point that the Canadians carrying the heavy crates still believed that the Japanese were squinty-eyed, nearsighted poor shots, as pre-war cartoons showed.[5]

. . .

Fifteen minutes after Lieutenant Carruthers and his men reached the power station, the Japanese attacked. The battle pit two of the most unequal forces imaginable against each other. The Japanese were well trained and well armed. They were also men in their twenties who had been hardened by combat in China. The Hughseliers had its share of military men: Major J. Paterson, Private Tam Pearce, and Captain Pop Hingston. But they had last fought more than a generation earlier on the fields of France and Belgium, Hingston with the Canadians at Vimy. Two others had cut their military teeth in the Boer War, which had ended nearly forty years earlier.

Aware that he could not let the Japanese see his numbers dwindle, Paterson ordered that even death would not free them from the fight; bodies were to be propped up in the windows to impress the Japanese. Outnumbered twenty to one and using only two Lewis guns, their rifles and, judiciously, their hand grenades, these overaged, nearsighted men (along with a few Middlesexers and Carruthers's men) squinted into the half-light before dawn, many with their hands shaking, and pushed back the oncoming assault troops.

The Hughseliers were respected and cultured men, but after a few hours of battle, they took up the soldiers' age-old tradition of gallows humour. One called out, "This is plain, bloody ridiculous. How the hell do they expect to hold up the whole damned Jap army with a bunch of old fossils like us?" Hingston replied, "What the hell are you grousing about? D'you want to live forever?" When seventy-year-old private Edward Des Voeux said, "We're too damned old for this sort of thing," Hingston (who, like Rifleman Latimer, was in his element) countered, "You speak for yourself."[6]

. . .

For part of the time that Paterson's men stymied the Japanese, and Shoji's men in turn beat back a relief column of Rajputs about five miles to the southeast, Royal Rifles Major Maurice Parker's "D" Company slept in trenches around Obelisk Hill. Sometime after 2:00 a.m. on 19 December, Home ordered Parker to shore up the defence of Battalion Headquarters at Tai Tam. Obelisk Hill is about two miles south of Tai Tam; the seriousness of the situation led Home to send buses to fetch "D" Company. The road was so bad that even with the buses, it still took more than an hour and a half for this force to arrive.

As Parker's men shook the sleep from their eyes and ensured that their water bottles were filled, that they had extra ammunition clips and that their bayonets were sharp, two and a half miles to their left rear, two sub-units belonging to the Winnipeg Grenadiers were also on the move. Under orders from Lawson, Major Albert Gresham led his "A" Company over ground already trod by Lieutenant Birkett; Gresham's orders were to launch a pre-dawn attack on the Japanese on Jardine's Lookout. The second unit belonged to Lieutenant Leonard Corrigan. His goal on the main road was easier to find than most in the darkness of the Wong Nei Chong Gap. When they came under mortar and machine gun fire from Jardine's Lookout, the position must have occasioned more grousing about the brass than about the Japanese. Corrigan had been ordered to establish its firing base at a gasoline filling station.

. . .

At 2:30 a.m., Captain Lynch, a British medical officer who was already working on several wounded British and Indian soldiers, heard a truck roll to a halt in front of his Casualty Clearing Station. It took Lynch little time to pronounce the three Canadians brought to him dead. He ordered Stretcher-Bearer Russell to carry them into a hut to await temporary burial.

Before returning to Bishop's command, Russell wanted one last look at his late commander, so he returned to the hut. Alerted by the beam of Russell's flashlight that someone had entered, Captain Gavey called out, "Go ahead, kill me," giving the young soldier a very queer feeling before he ran back to Lynch to tell him that Gavey was alive. The medic responded to "[get him] the hell out of there." Russell and another stretcher-bearer loaded Gavey, two other wounded Rifles and two other soldiers onto their truck to take them to Queen Mary Hospital four miles away; the trip took more than seven hours.*

---

* One of the Canadians was Corporal Lindsay Mann, who died in a POW Camp in 1942; his

. . .

An hour later, as the sky began to lighten, Gresham's men readied themselves to climb up the southern slope of Jardine's Lookout, and Colonel Doi finally caught up with his own men on the northeast slope. Doi wasted little time issuing new orders. The first told his regimental gunners back at Sai Wan to deploy immediately to support the 2nd Battalion's advance through the lookout. Here the British gunnery map delivered to him earlier came in handy, for it gave the coordinates for the pillboxes and other important points on Jardine's Lookout. The second told his 3rd Battalion to turn west and attack the northern slope of Mount Nicholson, the foot of which meets the foot of Jardine's Lookout in the Wong Nei Chong Gap; their summits are about a mile and a half apart. The third order told his 1st Battalion to turn east and advance "on the five-way road junction west of the Wong Nei Chong Reservoir." At the centre of this Five-Way-Road Junction, at the Wong Nei Chong Gap, stood the police station. Hold Jardine's Lookout, hold Mount Nicholson, hold the police station and—as we will see—Lawson's headquarters is encircled.

. . .

As dawn broke, Signalman Allister's terrifying ordeal continued.[7] Hours earlier, he and Grant had climbed into an abandoned car to get out of the rain. Grant, who "was really more angry and disgusted than afraid," surprised Allister by quickly falling asleep. Perhaps it was the McGill University–trained artist's temperament that kept him from sleeping. "I tried to doze in the back, rifle across my chest,

---

brother, Rifleman Charles Mann, survived the war. The other was Jimmy Royal, who also returned to Canada.

electrically jolted awake at every suspicious sound, a slave to the wildest forebodings."

Forebodings turned to horror when, as the light strengthened, Allister looked down and saw *"dim shapes, bodies, faces of Japanese soldiers, kneeling in firing position all around the car!"* With his heart in his throat, Allister called softly, "George! Ssst! Wake up!" Grant responded as he might have to his young wife waking him on a Monday morning for work: "Mmm? Lemme be." Not quite catching the import of Allister's next words—"Shh! Look! For Chrissake, look out the window. *We're surrounded by Japs!"*—Grant responded with a groggy "Eh?" Only after looking out the window did he realize that near 5:00 on the morning of 19 December 1941 he was, indeed, in Hong Kong in the middle of war: "Holy Jesus!" He'd awakened to a Hobson's choice described by Allister: "Dash, they'll grab us; stay put, they'll soon see us."

Allister thought Grant daft when, after looking out the window again, Grant started to giggle and exclaimed: "Well, fuck me dry. Look!" It took Allister a few moments of looking to realize that the "Japanese soldiers" were, in fact, Chinese and that in among them were a number of soldiers with the letters c-a-n-a-d-a stitched into the two-inch signet on their shoulders.

. . .

As the early morning breeze blew away the smoke from the burning refineries and the Japanese rifle fire abated, the Hughseliers saw mute testimony of their success strewn across the ground. Lest they let down their guard, R.G. Burch said that during the Boer War the Boers would withdraw just far enough to make it seem as if they'd vanished; then they'd attack in force. Des Voeux agreed, adding that he would rather fight and die than spend his last days rotting in a POW camp.

As Des Voeux spoke, the operator of a "knee mortar," having gauged the distance between himself and the power station, turned the knob that adjusted the angle of the gun's tube.* He then dropped a 50-mm shell into the tube, which, together with its stand, measured two feet. A moment later, he pulled the short leather lanyard attached to the trigger. Through a cog and gear series, the trigger compressed a spring that when released drove a firing pin forward against the shell with enough force to hurl it accurately more than a thousand yards. When the shell hit the wall, its impact fuse detonated and two ounces of TNT exploded, blasting a hole in the wall and killing Des Voeux.

But mortars alone do not win battles. They are an important tool in what military planners call "softening up." Mortars, and artillery fire, disrupt defence not chiefly by killing soldiers and destroying defensive positions. Rather, they force defenders to seek shelter from the explosions. Pushing defenders away from the windows of the power station gave the Japanese attackers time to get close enough to the station to shoot the defenders as they returned to their positions or to storm the building itself.

As soon as the barrage ended, the Japanese charged, some throwing hand grenades. One grenade went through a hole in the wall and exploded near Middlesex Private Tommy Tucker's machine gun. The blast ripped out his right eyeball, yet somehow, he kept firing as his unseeing eye hung in front of his cheek. Two Die Hards threw their grenades into the mass of onrushing Japanese soldiers. Paterson's men repulsed them but at great cost; in addition to Des Voeux, three Middlesex soldiers were killed.

---

* The "knee mortar" was not strapped to the leg when either fired or transported. The mistake in the name and in how the Grenade Discharger, Type 89, worked probably came from the fact that when firing, the base was held in place on the ground by the operator's foot; from a distance, it looked as though the tube was attached to the leg.

Fire, lit by an explosion, did what Japanese infantry could not—force the Hughseliers to abandon the power station. Pearce pointed to a derelict double-decker bus and told Paterson, "If it's alright with you, I'd prefer dying there than being roasted alive." His commander answered, "My dear fellow, there's a great deal to what you say."[8]

Among the first to evacuate were Joan Crawford, the daughter of the station's superintendent, Mr. R. Dunlop, and her mother, who had been providing first aid. A machine gun blast scattered the group. Crawford, who was helping a wounded soldier, made first for the bus, but decided against going to it just as several Japanese men came into view. One got close enough to bring his sword down on Mr. Dunlop's neck; his life was saved when the blow hit the strap of his haversack. Mr. Dunlop then followed Crawford and a few others into a tenement. Pearce and the rest took shelter in the bus and awaited the inevitable.

. . .

By dawn, Doi's troops had secured Jardine's Lookout.* As they did, Sergeant Tom Marsh and more than a hundred other Grenadiers struggled up the southwest slope. By the time Marsh crested the hill, the forward units were already under fire, some of which came from behind them. "They had already infiltrated up to and past our destination," Marsh later recalled, "and we could hear the peculiar

---

* As is so often the case in war, the taking of Jardine's Lookout was a near-run thing. As more of Shoji's men advanced silently up Sir Cecil's Ride, they bumped into HKVDC Lance-Corporal Ma's nine-man section, which held them up for a quarter hour. They were bunched up below the lookout not far from a pillbox manned by Lieutenant Field (HKVDC), who opened up on them. According to the regimental historian of the HKVDC, the lead Japanese platoon was almost completely "written off." A bayonet charge from his flank overwhelmed Ma's position. According to historian Tony Banham, archeological evidence "suggests this was the bloodiest single engagement of the 18 day campaign."

cries of the enemy as they sought to make their positions known to each other."

Neither Marsh nor the other men could make out where the Japanese troops were. For, as they had during their attack on Shing Mun Redoubt, they camouflaged themselves by putting twigs and leaves in the seams in their uniforms, and covering their helmets with scrub grass. Marsh saw the men in front of him follow their officers as they ran for cover. Some stumbled over the broken ground and fell. Several men were struck down by machine guns.

Up ahead, the men closest to Birkett reached an artillery observation post and climbed on top of it, placing themselves at an angle beyond the reach of Japanese machine guns. While bullets flew beneath them, two or three machine gun teams quickly set up and began raking the ground to the right and left of the advancing Grenadiers.

Exploding mortars drowned out the zip and zing of the machine gun bullets. As dirt shot skyward, Marsh and the others pushed themselves closer to the ground. They rose again after the dirt blown skyward had fallen back to earth to answer with their rifles, grenades, and Bren and Tommy guns. Because his men had gone to ground where they were when the Japanese started shooting, Birkett's fire was too diffuse. To concentrate it, Birkett tried to gather his men around the observation post, which sheltered the wounded. The lieutenant took it upon himself to supervise the withdrawal of the more-exposed men. "Under heavy fire he then started to climb the slope," recalled Marsh. "He had almost made it when I noticed his leg was dragging. He had been hit, but continued."

A Bren gun crew near Marsh heard Birkett's order and immediately began disassembling its gun. Bugler Kenneth Simpson and Private Lloyd Hallett, in a gully to Marsh's left, however, showed no sign of movement, so the sergeant crawled over the dusty volcanic ground and through scrub grass and small cactus-like plants to a ledge six feet above them. Lying flat on his stomach with his rifle at the ready at his shoulder, Marsh called the order down to them. At the same time as he heard Hallett respond, a "Japanese officer jumped up waving a sword shouting '*Banzai! Banzai!*'"

Hallett may have had a Bren gun capable of emptying its fifty-round magazine in just over eight seconds, but it was pointing in the wrong direction. With a coolness that belied his five hours of battle experience, Marsh aimed his Lee-Enfield and squeezed the trigger. The Japanese officer "spun around and collapsed, lying in full view, his hand still waving."*

Hallett then yelled up to Marsh that Simpson had been shot through the neck. Marsh ordered Hallett back to the pillbox, but Hallett asked what they were going to do with Simpson. Marsh heard Simpson's plea not to be left behind and Hallett's promise not to leave him. Ignoring Hallett's technical act of insubordination, Marsh agreed to help save Simpson.

Marsh passed his rifle down butt-first, after which Hallett ran Simpson's belt through the sling. "We waited for a particularly vicious burst of enemy fire to subside and in the lull that followed Hallett cried 'Ready!' and threw Simpson up. I pulled, or rather jerked, and he fell behind the rock beside me." The Japanese saw the movement but waited a moment too long; by the time they let loose, Simpson was safe behind the rock. When the fusillade ended, Hallett threw his Bren gun up to Marsh and managed to climb up to the ledge. With bullets pinging off the rocks near them, Marsh and Hallett dragged the semi-conscious Simpson halfway to the pillbox. The exhausted men stopped at a patch of open ground.

Marsh called up to the pillbox for help, and soon Corporal

---

* As would Allister later in the battle, Marsh thus became one of the 5 percent or so who actually saw the man they fired at fall (Grossman, 16).

Clarence Darragh darted from rock to rock until he reached a large one on the other side of the open ground. The plan was simple: get Simpson far enough across the open ground so that Darragh could grasp him and pull him out of the line of fire.

Meanwhile, a Japanese machine gunner had the open ground in his sights. He remembered what he'd learned in basic training: wait until you have a multitude of targets. Just as the four of them bunched together, the gunner pumped a "hail of lead" into them, mortally wounding Hallett and riddling Simpson's body. So many bullets shot past Marsh that his pants leg quivered; he felt the burning pain of a bullet cutting into his body and grazing the bone just below one of his knees. To escape the fusillade, he doubled over before flinging himself down the hill and out of the gunner's range of fire. Marsh felt something hit his head as he "tumbled in earnest head over heels down the hill," coming to rest, unconscious, in a gully.

CHAPTER 7

"Dig, You Sons of Bitches"

The Death of Brigadier-General Lawson
6:00 a.m. to 10:00 a.m., 19 December 1941

O For a voice like thunder, and a tongue
To drown the throat of war!—When the senses
Are shaken, and the soul is driven to madness,
Who can stand?
—WILLIAM BLAKE, PROLOGUE, INTENDED FOR A DRAMATIC
PIECE OF *KING EDWARD THE FOURTH*

At dawn on 19 December, Honorary Captain Chaplain Uriah
Laite reached the headquarters of the Winnipeg Grenadiers'
"D" Company in the Wong Nei Chong Gap. The Grenadiers' padre
had not wanted to be there. He believed his place was with Major
Albert Gresham and the men of "A" Company. He'd been with them
since 2:30 a.m. when they had climbed into trucks that took them
from Little Hong Kong to an intersection near the Wong Nei Chong
Gap, and he'd been with them while they sat in the rain as Gresham
figured out how to advance on Mount Butler. He'd be with them
still had not a runner brought orders for him to report to Captain
Allan Bowman's headquarters.

The difficulty of travelling the dark, slippery roads hardly registered with the United Church minister. Neither the rumble of exploding shells nor the sharp crack of rifle fire could drown out the echo of Gresham's last words. The major had asked him to write to Mrs. Gresham, which prompted Laite to say that everything would come out all right. Gresham ignored these all-too-predictable words. Military reports do not describe the tenor of a voice. Laite's didn't have to: "But you will write to her, won't you Padre?"

. . .

About the time Laite reached Bowman's headquarters, Gresham and his men neared the end of their laborious climb (there is much debate about where exactly they were).[1] Gresham ordered two lieutenants to attack with their platoons in open formation. The Canadians' inexperience and the broken ground over which they advanced caused confusion almost immediately. Shortly after Lieutenant William McKillop charged forward, he and the section closest to him became separated from the rest. Company Sergeant Major John Osborn, who had served as an able seaman during the Battle of Jutland in 1916, took charge of the platoon. Watching from some hundred yards behind, Sergeant William Pugsley, holding his men in reserve, saw the bayonet charge that drove the Japanese from what he believed was the southern slope of Mount Butler. He could not see that Osborn had lost his helmet, or the blood dripping from Osborn's bayonet or from the gash on his arm.

While the Canadians were on top of a hill, they were also in a depression, which both increased their chances of being surrounded and allowed the Japanese to fire down at them. Osborn yelled: "Dig, you sons of bitches. Dig like you never dug before. They'll be back for us." Doi's infantry poured mortar bombs, grenades, small arms and machine gun fire onto the men huddled for safety behind rocks and in the few slit trenches they'd scratched into the unforgiving Hong Kong earth. To save ammunition, Osborn's men grabbed Japanese grenades and threw them back at their tormentors. Several times the Japanese came over the lip of the depression waving their swords, and the Canadians drove them back.

.   .   .

On Jardine's Lookout, Corporal Darragh had seen men wounded and shot dead. He'd felt the searing pain of a bullet cutting into his hand. And he was saddened to watch his friend Tom Marsh fall, apparently dead, into a gully. Sometime after 6:00 a.m., however, he looked in disbelief. For now, incredibly, before him stood what appeared to be Marsh, struggling to speak, his uniform dirty, stained with red and ripped, his body akimbo because of a leg wound and his face swathed in bloody bandages.

Some minutes earlier, Marsh had regained consciousness and noticed the blood pouring from his mouth. Though in a haze, he remembered that such bleeding is often caused by stomach wounds; better to put his rifle to his head and shoot himself than suffer the painful death of such wounds. Then he examined his stomach and found it whole. A check of his head revealed that the hole in his face was caused by a bullet that had cut a clean path from under his right cheekbone through his left cheek.

After struggling up the hill, Marsh tumbled into the trench behind the pillbox sheltering Darragh. There he found an even more desperate situation. "All but the seriously wounded were up to along the parapet manning the machine guns or supporting them with rifle fire," Marsh recalled. Inside the box lay the dead and the desperate, the lucky sedated with morphine. Atop it stood

Lieutenant Birkett, determined to save his men, blood from his leg wound soaking through his uniform.

A moment or two after Marsh finished telling Darragh his story, the roar and force of the explosions shaking the shelter became stronger, signalling that the Japanese were now using field artillery. They heard Birkett yell to the few men still able to fire, "Get out of here while you can. I'll hold them off." And then, a Japanese gunner scored a direct hit. The explosion killed Birkett and those with him, and blew Marsh into a connecting tunnel. Somehow, despite his wounds, Marsh had the strength to crawl into the main trench. From there he pulled himself into a smaller trench and once again lost consciousness.

. . .

Lieutenant Alexander Prendergast's No. 7 Platoon arrived near the police station in the Wong Nei Chong Gap as their Winnipeg Grenadier comrades died on Jardine's Lookout. Unsure whether the situation had changed since receiving his orders some three hours earlier, Prendergast deployed his men in a defensive formation and with two men went to General Lawson's headquarters a few minutes away. Lawson told Prendergast that Gresham had already begun his climb and to go support him. Just as the brigadier reached for the map, his telephone rang. No record exists of the call, but Lawson must have learned that even as some Japanese troops fought for Mount Butler and Mount Parker, other units had advanced south of them as still others headed west. The information prompted Lawson to change Prendergast's orders to take his men to near Tai Tam Reservoir and construct a roadblock on Stanley Gap Road to prevent the Japanese from seizing the police station (at what the Japanese called Five-Way-Road Junction).

The meeting with Lawson did not last long. But in those few minutes, the Japanese had occupied a hill opposite East Brigade's headquarters from which they enfiladed the road Prendergast had just taken. Prendergast's party climbed over the hill behind a pill-box and cut around the back of the hill, which shielded them on their way back to the rest of his platoon.

Even before Prendergast reached his men, he heard rifle and machine gun fire coming from their front right, that is, from the police station, which was now occupied by elements of Colonel Doi's 3rd Battalion. Prendergast ordered his men to augment their arms with guns and ammunition from a truck that had fortuitously broken down nearby, and in an effort to prevent the Japanese from infiltrating behind him, moved part of his platoon some way back toward Brigade Headquarters. Then he ordered his men to return fire on the police station.

As soon as they started firing, Prendergast's men faced a heavy barrage from their left flank, from where Prendergast thought "A" Company was. In an attempt to end this "friendly fire," Prendergast sent two officers back to Lawson so that the general could order the firing stopped. The lieutenant soon expected that each explosion or burst of machine gun fire would be the last. About fifteen minutes later the officers returned. They had not been able to get to Lawson's headquarters, for the Japanese now occupied the hill Prendergast had climbed not long earlier. The lieutenant took some solace, however, from the report that his men had killed several Japanese on the hill. And he surmised that the fire came from the Japanese, for they now swarmed over almost the entire area.

. . .

On the morning of Friday, 19 December 1941, Colonel Tanaka's men saw the Red Cross flying above the Salesian Mission, at the time being used as a medical storage depot and Advanced Dressing Station. Captain Martin Banfill of the Royal Canadian Army Medical Corps ran the station, which was staffed by forty personnel, including eight nursing sisters.

Banfill did not know that the Japanese had landed on the island. Home had sent a runner to inform him, but the runner never arrived. The Geneva Convention required medical centres to fly the Red Cross flag and forbade them from posting armed guards. The Convention did not, however, prevent a dressing station from posting sentries, and it was a sentry who interrupted breakfast with word that the Japanese had surrounded the mission.

Banfill ran to the second floor, looked out the window and saw the Japanese troops approaching. He yelled, "Get the women and try to escape!" just moments before attackers kicked in the door and stormed into the dining room. After separating the women from the men, they ordered the men to take off their boots or shoes and tunics. If Banfill and the three Royal Riflemen with him worried that they lacked Red Cross identification cards and armbands, they wasted the thought. The Emperor's soldiers grabbed the cards others quickly produced, threw them to the floor and stomped on them.

Some of Tanaka's men confiscated watches, rings and other valuables. Others bayoneted Rifleman Raymond Oakley, who had been shot through the thigh. An ambulance arrived with two wounded Rajputs. Tanaka's men bayoneted them as well.

Banfill pleaded with Honda, a Japanese officer, who acted as an interpreter.* "I'm sorry. We have instructions from our commander-in-chief. You all must die," he said.[2] A soldier then tied Banfill's arms behind his back and looped the rope around his neck.

---

* Honda Tanaka was likely no relation to Colonel Tanaka. It is, however, likely that he was the same information officer/translator named Honda Tanaka who was later prosecuted for war crimes (see Coda).

The male prisoners were marched a short distance away. When they neared a drainage ditch, some soldiers bayoneted prisoners in the back. "Some of our men had to be bayoneted three times before they would fall," recalled Hong Kong Volunteer Osler Thomas in an affidavit prepared for the War Crimes Trial. "Then their bodies were kicked into the *nullah* [ditch]." The prisoners panicked and Banfill heard the sound of shooting. "I looked up and saw some of my friends falling," he said in his affidavit. Among the dead was Dr. Orloff, a Russian immigrant who had thrown his lot in with the British.

A would-be samurai tried to behead Royal Army Medical Corps Corporal Norman Leath. Luckily for Leath, who had collapsed to the ground as blood poured from his nose and mouth, he looked dead enough, at least for the moment. However, Leath knew that if he lay there, he risked having another soldier bloody his bayonet to ensure he was dead. Safety lay with the dead in the ditch, so he wriggled his way to the edge of the ditch and tumbled in. When a Japanese soldier climbed into the ditch to bayonet or shoot anyone still moving stepped on Leath's hand, he did not move.

Dr. Thomas survived by throwing himself into the ditch and hiding under the bleeding, dead bodies. Ah Tim, who belonged to the St. John's Ambulance unit stationed at the mission, broke away just as he was being shot some distance away from the ditch. Unhurt, he rolled down the hill and played possum.

Forced to lie on the ground, a soldier's foot resting on his face, Banfill waited his turn to die. When the last of the screams died away, he was pulled to his feet and led off. Along the way, Honda asked Banfill if he was a Christian. The doctor replied, "More or less." Honda then asked, "When I shoot you, what do you think will happen? Will you be resurrected or dead forever?" This strange seminar-like disputation continued with Banfill answering, "I don't know. I suppose I'll be dead for a very long time."

Unsure about the theology behind Banfill's answer, Honda

continued, "My mother and sisters are good Christians, but there are certain tenets of Christianity I cannot accept. Yet, I do think Christian morality is a positive force in the world." If Banfill, who had just seen Honda's comrades murder almost forty non-combatants, found his interlocutor's endorsement of "Christian morality" less than convincing, he must have found what happened next surreal.

Honda reached into a pocket and pulled out a map of Canada. He pointed to Quebec and said "Oui," asking if he was correct that it was French. Tanaka's interpreter then told Banfill his given name was Honda. To clarify the correct pronunciation, he continued, "Remember the movie *Wings of the Morning?* With Henry Fonda? Well, my name is the same with an 'H.'"

Once in the camp, Banfill was questioned about the location of minefields. The camp's senior officer soon realized that Banfill knew nothing about them, and ordered him moved to another camp.

The nurses and other female staff at the ADS feared both murder and rape. While it does not appear that any were killed, the Chinese women were gang raped. St. John's Ambulance nurses like Louise Fearon escaped both fates, apparently because at thirty-nine years old the Japanese thought she was "too old to serve the purpose to which the Chinese girls were to be put."[3] After they were released, St. John's Ambulance Captain Tinson placed the younger nurses with a sympathetic Chinese family. Tinson and Fearon found refuge with a Chinese priest and two Chinese nuns.

. . .

While the St. John's Ambulance team awaited their fate, three miles to the east the Hughseliers continued to stymie Colonel Shoji's men, who called up three machine guns to finish the job. Bullets ripped through the thin skin of the double-decker bus, at least two hitting Private Sorby, the power station's technical manager, in the knees. At one point, the men in the bus tried a ruse: they stopped shooting and all movement. Soon, a platoon carefully made its way toward the bus. When it got close, Private Paddy Geoghan jumped into position, cursed and started shooting, killing several of Shoji's soldiers before the machine gunners cut him down.

Their ammunition exhausted, Paterson's men would surrender toward 7:00 p.m. At about the same time, the group with Joan Crawford in the tenement surrendered. As she was herded with the others, Crawford saw one of the wounded men on the ground, shivering in the rain, his face grey from loss of blood. Her Japanese captors stopped her efforts to tend to him or the other wounded. Crawford and her mother were the only prisoners not roped together as they were marched off to a makeshift prison camp.

. . .

Shortly after Gresham received the order to ready his men to climb Mount Butler, Captain C. Clark entered the Royal Rifles' headquarters and found tensions running high. The Japanese had cut through the Rajputs on the coast and the Rifles' positions south of Sai Wan Fort. Several hours had passed since Lieutenant-Colonel Home had sent first Sergeant Hughes's force and then Lieutenant Collinson Blaver's to Mount Parker, and he had had no word from either.* Hoping still to secure the mountain, Home ordered Clark to take Lieutenant Breakey's platoon to Mount Parker to reinforce Hughes and/or Blaver. Clark encountered the same difficulties other Canadians did moving through unfamiliar territory on that dark,

---

* Had Wallis known of Home's action, perhaps he would not have ended the note following the entry for 0600 hrs. that complains of the Rifles' communications thusly: "Their method [of communication] was to send off runners who seldom returned, at any rate for long periods. In the meantime the officer of H.Q. [Home] concerned sat waiting for news."

battle-scarred night. By 5:00 a.m. on 19 December, he had reached Boa Vista, a mile south of Mount Parker, where he hoped a signals unit might have word of where the two other platoons were. It did not. Clark then made the somewhat unusual decision to undertake a reconnaissance alone.

Two hours later, Clark climbed onto a ridge that led to the top of Mount Parker and saw battle flags emblazoned with the Rising Sun fluttering over more than 150 soldiers, some of whom had spent the night manhandling light field artillery up the mountain. One hundred yards from the top of the mountain, he saw Lieutenant Blaver's platoon, which had climbed the mountain at first light. Clark watched as Japanese machine guns, grenades and almost point-blank artillery fire mauled Blaver's men before they withdrew, using a catchwater for cover.

A short while after Clark returned to Boa Vista, Wallis sent for him and asked the captain if he thought he could retake Mount Parker if he were reinforced with another platoon. The experiment had been tried and failed even before the Japanese had dug in. Both Hughes's and Lieutenant Williams's forces had been destroyed. Another attack by two platoons and whatever odds and sods Clark could find near Boa Vista could scarcely achieve anything. Still, Clark answered his brigadier, "I do not think so but will try."

. . .

Near 7:00 a.m., shortly after Prendergast learned that the Japanese had all but surrounded Lawson's headquarters, he noticed enemy troops moving along the southern foot of Mount Nicholson. Canadian Bren gunners added these targets to the police station in front of them. Prendergast's was one of the few Canadian platoons equipped with mortars, and soon it was the enemy's turn to take cover behind rocks.

Prendergast arrived too late to carry out his orders to hold the police station. He thus interpreted his orders (correctly) as being to hold the Japanese at the police station. But time, and the inevitable casualties, now worked against him. He tried and failed to get word to Lawson to expect no relief. At some point, Prendergast would have to declare the situation lost and move to save himself and his command.

The unexpected arrival of a group of Royal Engineers under the command of Lieutenant-Colonel R. Lamb altered Prendergast's plans. More practised in static warfare, on this afternoon Lamb's men were all action. Under a curtain of fire provided by the Canadians, the British stormed to the top of the hill; four fell during the charge. But two made it to the top and tossed grenades onto the enemy below. The Japanese responded in kind, and Lamb and his men rolled down the hill to escape the explosions. As the fusillade ended, the engineers again ran up the hill and rained grenades on the enemy below. After those explosions died away, the Japanese threw another volley up the hill, this time wounding several engineers. Lamb brought his men down the hill, where they established a defensive line that connected to Prendergast's.

By 8:00 a.m., pressure from the advancing Japanese soldiers led Prendergast to abandon his position. He reported to Lieutenant-Colonel Sutcliffe in the Wan Chai Gap an hour later.

. . .

As Lamb's engineers fought as "poor bloody infantry," the crews of six Motor Torpedo Boats were in their element. After casting off from Aberdeen, No. 2 MTB Flotilla sailed around the island's west side. The boats were to attack in pairs.

At 8:45 a.m., two torpedo boats passed the naval dockyard on the east side of Victoria at 30 knots, too fast for the machine gunners at North Point to get a fix on them. Upon seeing boats carrying some fifteen Japanese soldiers each being towed toward the island, Lieutenant R. Ashby ordered his men to ready for an attack. Just as he issued the order, Japanese planes dived toward him spewing machine gun and cannon fire, which missed.

Ashby's five Lewis gunners opened up on the frail transports a mere hundred yards away. Twice during the attack, Ashby dropped depth charges, which failed to explode because of the shallow water. But the disappointment the torpedo artificers felt when two geysers failed to billow out of their boat's wake vanished when they saw that the landing craft had capsized in the boat's wash and that heavily laden Japanese soldiers were drowning.

Ashby's course brought him close to Kowloon and the ships scuttled ten days earlier. Gunners secreted in the ships' hulks added their fire to the mix. Neither speed nor manoeuvring could long protect Ashby's boat in such a maelstrom. A shell ripped through his starboard hull and exploded, killing one man and knocking out Ashby's starboard engine.

His speed cut to twenty-two knots and still under heavy fire, Ashby turned and destroyed a second group of landing craft. Then a shell detonated on his port side, killing his telegraphist and destroying his port engine. His speed cut to twelve knots, Ashby ordered his helmsmen to turn west, pursued by both three planes and the machine gunners on the shore. As their shipmates below deck pumped water and worked to plug holes, those manning the boat's Oerlikon 20-mm anti-aircraft guns fired at the planes. Tracers hit one, and another was last seen flying low over Kowloon.

Japanese gunners severely punished the next pair of attackers. One of the machine gunners was the same Sakae Ishikawa who had all but wiped out Lieutenant Carruthers's relief convoy. To hit a speeding Motor Torpedo Boat (MTB), a gunner had to fire a short distance ahead of it, hoping that the boat would cross the line of fire. Ishikawa fired at a point ten or so metres in front of the boat.

Immediately after firing a short burst, he looked through his binoculars and saw the spray in the air far behind the boat. Aiming twenty metres ahead, he fired and again missed. "On my third try, I was successful in hitting the rear steering wheel and the speedboat lost its bearings. It ran straight across the harbour to Kowloon Bay and hit the quay wall."[4] A shell burst on MTB 11, killing and burning almost ten men, yet the boat managed to get back to Aberdeen.*

. . .

Shortly after Signalmen Allister and Grant joined the detachment of Grenadiers and Chinese troops, the soldier walking beside Allister dropped to his knee, put his rifle to his shoulder and established a respectable rhythm of fire. "Where did you learn to shoot like that?" "Spain," he said. Allister responded, "Hey! Really? Spain? The Mac-Paps? No shit!" A couple of Japanese bullets landing nearby returned him to the business at hand.

After taking shelter behind a bush, Allister saw a target and squeezed the trigger. He missed and spent the next few moments steadying himself, as the recoil of his Lee-Enfield was magnified by the pebbles and sand in the rifle's barrel. He shot again:

> A figure was dead centre in my sights . . . silhouetted against the sky as I pulled the trigger. He dropped. The thought vaguely registered that I had just killed a man. And so *easily*. I only had to line up the sights on the centre of the turtle, tighten my finger–bra-a-am! Down went another.

---

* Aware of the carnage, Commodore Alfred Collinson (Royal Navy) recalled the next two MTBs. For some reason, Lieutenant D.W. Wagstaff's boat did not receive the order and charged ahead. Enemy fire destroyed its engines in front of North Point. If there were any survivors of the boat, the Japanese massacred them, for none was ever seen in the POW camp.

Despite the seriousness of the situation, Allister found the energy and mental space to think about his (lawful) violation of the Sixth Commandment. He thought of *All Quiet on the Western Front*, in which Erich Marie Remarque writes how he vomited the first time he shot a man. In the phantasmagoria of his war, though, the future artist could feel only this: "Nothing."[5]

· · ·

At 8:30 a.m., Canadian despatch rider Lionel Speller approached the massive steel door of Maltby's Fortress Headquarters (the Battle Box) and gave the password. Accompanied by a guard, he walked down a long flight of steps and through several concrete corridors to a room covered in maps that were festooned with pins. A Grenadier captain handed him a sealed envelope and told him to take it to Brigadier-General Lawson at his headquarters in the Wong Nei Chong Gap. Speller replied coldly, "I trust it's important. The snipers are itching to get more riders." The officer likely did not know that a day earlier, Speller had risked his neck ensuring that an asinine officer could feed his canine his favourite chow, but he caught the import of Speller's tone. "Very important. Between you and me, things are pretty hot at the Gap. Lawson has to pull out."[6] To a man as religious as Speller, the order to ride his motorcycle into an area that was so hot that Lawson (in a shelter) had to pull out must have seemed like Daniel going into the lion's den.*

As he kick-started his BSA bike, the air filled with the roar of the engine that would give every sniper along the five-mile windy, narrow dirt road ample warning of a fat target. The first mile

---

* Speller was a regular at the Weekly Remembrance Meetings every Sunday at the Duddle Street Gospel Hall in Vancouver, B.C.

from Maltby's headquarters took Speller through a quiet residential neighbourhood; quiet, that is, except for the sniper who twice narrowly missed Speller's head. Once in the hills, Speller entered a shooting gallery. Every couple of hundred yards he'd hear the crack of a rifle and then the ping of a bullet against a nearby rock. Speller pulled his .38-calibre Smith & Wesson from its holster and shot in the direction of the last bullet fired at him.

Three hours earlier one of the snipers on this road had killed Grenadier despatch rider Elvid Thomas. Now one sniper had Speller in his sights. His rear tire was hit; years of racing on hills paid off as he managed to keep control of the bike and speed around a curve and out of the arc of fire.

After pushing the damaged cycle into a ditch, Speller climbed his way up toward Lawson's headquarters, arriving at the same time as some of the men who had snuck away after Prendergast abandoned his position near the police station. A lieutenant heading for "D" Company's headquarters a hundred yards to the east of Lawson's detailed a few men to escort Speller. They gained a measure of safety when, a couple of hundred feet before the entrance of Lawson's headquarters, they could crouch down behind a thick, three-foot-high concrete wall.

Speller handed the brigadier the envelope and, while sipping a cup of hot chocolate, watched him read the message without any sign of fear. A few minutes later, Staff Sergeant Tom Barton and Sergeant Tony Phillips of the Canadian Corps of Military Staff Clerks tried to convince Lawson that they should all make a run for it. Lawson said, "In a little while. I'm not finished here yet."

At 9:00 a.m., Lawson ordered the men assigned to protect him to evacuate to Victoria. Speller left headquarters, now smoky from Lawson's pipe and the top-secret papers he was burning, with them.

The situation continued to worsen. The Japanese were attacking in a northwesterly direction from the police station, south from

Happy Valley and from the heights to the northeast. The Advanced Dressing Station on Blue Pool Road had fallen. The Japanese ambushed a relief convoy; of seventy British and Chinese sappers in two trucks, only twenty-four survived to reach "D" Company headquarters. When they did, Captain Bowman used some of them in an attack designed to clear snipers enfilading the trench manned by the screen in front of his headquarters. Led by Bowman, Tommy gun in hand, the attack temporarily scattered the Japanese but cost Bowman his life.[4] Still, Speller and many of the Winnipeg Grenadiers managed to make it to safety.

Sergeants Barton and Phillips were not as lucky. After the Japanese had retaken the ground Bowman contested and had again set up snipers and machine guns, the two men made their break. As soon as they emerged from behind the concrete wall in front of Lawson's headquarters, the Japanese opened up, killing Phillips. Barton was badly injured but crawled to safety under cover of night.

.   .   .

Since being woken at sunrise for breakfast, Lieutenant Simons's "D" Company platoon (of the Royal Rifles) dug in near Obelisk Hill had looked at Mount Parker a mile and a half to the northeast, knowing that their "C" Company comrades were fighting there. At 9:30 a.m., they got the order to join the fray.

As both the religious and superstitious among Simons's men ensured that the New Testaments issued to them by the YMCA were, indeed, in the pocket over their hearts, Wallis and Maltby reassessed the situation. The Japanese were on Mount Parker and had surrounded Lawson's headquarters in the Wong Nei Chong Gap, which told Maltby that the Japanese also held Jardine's Lookout, east of Mount Parker. They were closing in on guns at

Gauge Basin, now under the command of Lieutenant Bompas.* The Japanese were about a thousand yards from Wallis's headquarters. A concerted attack would destroy his headquarters and cut off thousands of troops at the Collinson Battery, at Obelisk Hill, on the D'Aguilar Peninsula and, of course, the Canadians still up at Tai Tam. Maltby had little alternative but to accept Wallis's recommendation that he withdraw both his command and his men southwest toward Stanley. At 10:00 a.m., as Simons's men were forming up their march to Mount Parker, a Captain Atkinson arrived with an order cancelling the attack and telling Major Parker to "EVACUATE TO STANLEY IMMEDIATELY."

. . .

With the boom of exploding shells and grenades echoing through his shelter, Lawson called Maltby and told him of his plan to evacuate to the west to a position held by the Winnipeg Grenadiers on Black's Link near Mount Nicholson. He ended the call by saying, "They're all around us. I'm going outside to fight it out," and then destroyed the telephone exchange. Captain Howard Bush did not record what he thought when Lawson ordered him to leave the headquarters. The order to cross the road to the Grenadiers' "D" Company headquarters to arrange for covering fire for Lawson and six other men was the luckiest in the captain's life.

There is a needless controversy over what happened next. As befits an official report, in 1948 General Maltby wrote, "I regret to say [Lawson] was killed together with his Brigade Major."[8] Seven years later, Colonel C.P. Stacey, whose *Six Years of War* serves as part of Canada's official history of the Second World War, wrote in error

---

* Later that day, after engaging the Japanese open sights at 11:00 a.m., small-arms fire nearby would force Bompas to spike his guns and abandon Gauge Basin.

that "no witness survived to tell the story."[9] In his history of the battle published in 1960, Tim Carew likened Lawson to U.S. General Custer at the Battle of the Little Bighorn: "He was still firing his two revolvers up to the very moment he died;" this story is a staple of anniversary newspaper pieces.[10]

Despite the constant stream of machine gun bullets cutting through the air over his ditch near "D" Company's headquarters, Grenadier Sergeant Robert Manchester ignored what drill sergeants at boot camp had tried to drill into his head. Instead of keeping his head down when under machine gun fire, Manchester rose just high enough to look over the lip of his ditch and see Lawson and the other men running from the shelter.

They were not running as Bush had, across the road, but rather along a path next to the shell-scared shelter. The difference is crucial because the path Lawson chose ran along a granite cliff. "They were perfectly outlined against the granite cliffside," recalled Manchester. Whether the gunners tormenting Manchester's ditch "recognized the red bands on their caps as meaning they were officers" is an open question. It's sure, however, that they saw them, for as soon as they were outlined against the rock face, the Japanese shifted targets. "They hit the seven with a terrible barrage of machine gun fire. The brigadier did not have a chance to shoot one gun, let alone two," recalled Manchester.[11]

CHAPTER 8

"The Importance of Fighting It Out"

The Grenadiers Attack North
10:00 a.m. to midnight, 19 December 1941

Honour has come back, as a king, to earth
And paid his subjects with a royal wage
And Nobleness walks in our ways again;
And we have come into our heritage.
—RUPERT BROOKE, "THE DEAD"

Late in the morning of 19 December, two Canadian soldiers walked south on Tai Tam Road toward Stanley. The one carrying a Lee-Enfield, Rifleman Phil Doddridge, still remembers that it had a bullet in its chamber and is sure that the revolver in Major John Price's holster did too. Their destination, Brigadier Wallis's newly established headquarters at Stone Hill, lay more than four miles from where the Japanese had landed a little over twelve hours earlier, and a mile or so south from where the Rifles had established their new defensive line. Yet men belonging to Tanaka's 9th Company had advanced so fast that they had the road in their sights.

As bullets started kicking up dust and pinging off rocks nearby, Doddridge was impressed with his commander's sang-froid, born of his experience in France a generation earlier; Price kept walking straight ahead. Nevertheless, the young soldier felt he'd be safer on the other side of the road. Without first warning Price, Doddridge ran across the road. A Japanese gunner kept pace with him at a distance of one or two steps.

The major was not amused. "Get down, you damn fool. That bullet had your name on it." Doddridge replied with a bit of cheek and in reference to his regimental numbers, "Yeah, but it didn't have E/29986 on it."

. . .

Price and Doddridge may have been under fire, but at least they knew where they were going. At 10:30 a.m., Major Charles Young received orders to take his "A" Company toward Stanley Mound. On the way, a runner arrived with orders for Young to send a platoon to a junction at the southeast end of the Tai Tam Reservoir. While these men were digging in, in order to cover the withdrawal of the Rajputs, Young received a third set of orders, and soon his men were marching back toward Stone Hill to be in position for Wallis's plan to "counterattack the enemy and drive him back into the sea." As the bulk of "A" Company trudged toward Stone Hill, two other groups crept in that same direction: the remnants of Lieutenant Collinson Blaver's platoon and Lieutenant Charles Johnston's platoon, which would arrive at 3:00 p.m.

Elsewhere, things were hardly less confusing. At 10:30 a.m., the Rifles' Headquarters Company received orders "to stay where we were [Tai Tam] till the last," which countermanded orders received a half-hour earlier to evacuate to Stanley. At 11:00 a.m., new orders arrived: "Retire to Stanley." The evacuation of Headquarters Company was complete two hours later. But almost immediately, Captain Frederick Atkinson ordered Lieutenant Francis Ross to take his platoon forward again to cover the retreat of other units. As the last group of trucks moved out of Tai Tam shortly before 5:00 p.m., some two hundred Japanese were spotted near "C" Company's stores. By dusk, the Royal Rifles were in the defensive positions on the southeast quadrant of Hong Kong Island.

Again, Wallis's East Brigade War Diary tells a very different story from the Rifles' war diary. While there was undoubtedly some confusion, Wallis writes, "*The withdrawal proceeded,* but road discipline was bad. All attempts to prevent bunching of men at Tytam [i.e., Tai Tam] and Tytam Fork, cross roads, at the junction of Stanley and Island Rd and at Stone Hill, failed."*

. . .

Word of General Lawson's death spread slowly. Indeed, near noon Colonel Patrick Hennessy, who did not yet know that he had become the ranking Canadian officer, was stopped at a road block at the southern end of the Wong Nei Chong Gap; Sergeant Albert Clark told him that he himself had seen Lawson's body. "Nonsense," Hennessy told his fellow First World War veteran. "I was talking to the brigadier on the phone last night, and I have a luncheon engagement with him," he said, before ordering his driver, Private David Melville, to carry on. But Clark's words had spooked the private, who almost stripped the gears of his '39 Studebaker.

Later that afternoon, Clark was called to a meeting with Captain Roslyn Davies and Hennessy. "Are they back?" Clark asked as he neared the room. His blood ran cold as Davies handed him a glass of dark rum and answered, "Yes, they bloody well walked back. Melville

---

* In fairness, it should be noted that on the same page, Wallis criticizes the officer commanding the 4½-inch guns on Red Hill for misreading an order to be ready "to get out of action" as telling him to "put the bty out of action," which he did by destroying his guns. Likewise, he criticizes a battery commander at Gauge Basin for keeping his guns in position so long that when his position came under fire, he and his men had no choice but to put their guns out of action.

is not with them." Hennessy said, "You were right, Clark. We lost Melville in the Wong Nei Gap." As the first rum Clark had ever drank warmed his body and dulled his senses, Hennessy told him that after their Studebaker came under small-arms fire, Melville tried to turn it around. "Melville opened the door to see where he was backing up and he was hit by a bullet from the other side. He fell out of the car and under the wheel. The wheel," Hennessy continued, "was cramped from starting to turn back and his body stopped it."[1]

. . .

In the late morning, a platoon of Japanese infantrymen belonging to Doi's 5th Company on Jardine's Lookout anxiously moved forward using a water catchment as a trench. They reached their destination, a patch of ground near PB1, before the rain that had begun a short time earlier filled the catchwater with a raging torrent. A few hours earlier, British Private G. Jitts had killed five Japanese soldiers in the water catchment; now the pillbox's commander ordered Jitts and his Tommy gun back into action. He fired first but soon fell mortally wounded. Then an intrepid grenade thrower ran up and managed to toss several grenades through the pillbox's loopholes. The explosions wrecked the box and its machine gun, seriously wounding seven men.

Guessing that any survivors would soon rush out the door, the attackers trained their guns on it. The Japanese intelligence map clearly indicated two enemy positions at the southern end of Jardine's Lookout; however, the Japanese commander was apparently unaware that PB2 supported PB1.* Nevertheless, the relief

---

* After the battle when the Japanese intelligence service surveyed Hong Kong, an officer whose name is lost to history must have smiled when he realized that the service scored a hat trick when it came to identifying the fortified parts of Jardine's Lookout.

party, commanded by Private E. Fisher (HKVDC) never had a chance; as it advanced up the main path that connected the two pillboxes the Japanese opened up, killing Fisher and scattering the others.

What happened next goes some way to undercutting the argument that the Canadians were confused and befuddled. Instead of advancing on the ground Fisher had tried, Second Lieutenant James McCarthy led another small group of Riflemen around the Japanese flank and got behind them. His surprise attack killed them all.

Meanwhile, the wounded survivors of PB1 joined the Canadians and together they set up a defensive formation. Using only rifles and light machine guns, they held off several Japanese attacks. After an hour-long mortar barrage, the Japanese mopped up the last resistance on Jardine's Lookout at 4:00 p.m.

Combined with the loss of mounts Butler and Parker, the loss of Jardine's Lookout was a disaster. The Japanese success had not come cheaply. At the lookout alone, Lieutenant Birkett's men and, even more so, Hong Kong Volunteers equipped with six Vickers machine guns had made the Japanese pay for every step they advanced. Colonel Shoji was upset by the slow pace of his wounded's evacuation; he had suffered nearly eight hundred casualties taking the lookout.[2]

. . .

In the early afternoon, General Maltby ordered the Punjabis, Royal Scots and Winnipeg Grenadiers' Headquarters Company to attack eastward and retake the Wong Nei Chong Gap, the police station and Mount Parker. Maltby's words may have been bold, but as bloodstained puddles formed across the northeast quadrant of the island, problems in command and control and the piecemeal nature of the offensive thrusts doomed the counterattack timed for 3:00 p.m.

The general's favourite regiment, the Punjabis, never received the order to attack north toward the power station. This omission saved men from dying over the same ground that the relief party led by an armoured car had died over a few hours earlier. But Indian troops died that day anyway—on Leighton Hill, about half a mile north of Jardine's Lookout.

At 2:30 p.m., the second prong of Maltby's attack force, the Royal Scots' "D" Company, led by three Bren carriers and two trucks with machine guns, advanced up the main road through the Gap. Step by step, the men behind the Bren carriers and trucks advanced, glancing to their right, then left, rifles at the ready. Each step brought them into a new vector, at the end of which could lie a machine gun or infantryman who had claimed this line of fire as his. Advance, always advance, for advancing is safer than standing still. The air was filled with the iron stench of blood that had poured from the bodies of other Canadian and British soldiers, some with limbs blown away, others twisted into grotesque forms with blackening faces swarmed by thousands of flies. The soldiers shimmied between the wrecks of vehicles filled with the charred remains of their comrades who, a few hours earlier, had tried to relieve Lawson.

The blast of shells exploding nearby drowned out the rumble of distant explosions. One landed directly on the first Bren carrier, destroying it and killing the men inside. Several of the vehicles and most of Captain David Pinkerton's men managed to take cover in vegetation on the side of the road. "After that, if one of us moved a hand, it brought a tornado of lead on top of us from Jardine's Lookout," recalled one officer.[3] Somehow, Pinkerton organized his men and mounted several small advances. One actually came close to their first objective, the police station, but the Japanese broke the attack up with a hail of hand grenades.

. . .

Grenadier Major Ernest Hodkinson understood Maltby's reason for ordering another attack north into the Wong Nei Chong Gap, but he was baffled by Battle Box's view that it was "lightly held." Nothing had been heard from either Lieutenant George Birkett nor Lieutenant Charles French, who had been sent to attack Jardine's Lookout and Mount Butler above it. Nor does it appear that Maltby knew that at 2:00 p.m., each of the three flying column platoons had been engaged and destroyed some distance west of the Grenadiers' headquarters. Even after a rendezvous at 3:30 p.m. with a platoon from "A" Company, Hodkinson would only have about a hundred men, hardly enough for a picket line let alone an attack through a valley, up one rise and onto Mount Parker, where the Japanese were now dug in.

Their bayonets fixed, Hodkinson's men shouldered their packs just before 3:00 p.m. A few minutes later, the Japanese caught them on Black's Link. As machine gun bullets ripped by and mortars blew up, Hodkinson ordered his men into open formation—meaning that instead of advancing in two tightly packed lines, they stepped apart five yards to offer a more diffuse target—but two men soon fell anyway.

A few minutes later (and right on schedule), Hodkinson met up with a platoon from "C" Company commanded by Lieutenant Railton Campbell. When the promised Royal Scotsmen failed to show, Hodkinson decided to move anyway. To cover his left flank, he ordered Lieutenant Leonard Corrigan to take his men a short distance west to Mount Nicholson. By the time Corrigan's men, their climb lengthened by rain-slickened rocks, reached the top of the mountain, only five had not been wounded or killed by machine gunners or field artillery trained on the mountain from points further east. Corrigan led these five men down the mountain to a spot near an abandoned pillbox just west of where Lawson's headquarters had been, where they remained until midnight.

Meanwhile, Hodkinson led his force east on Black's Link. Surprisingly, given the fact that the Japanese artillery was shredding the Canadians nearby, Hodkinson's scouts came back with word that just ahead was a group of some five hundred Japanese soldiers, eating and "apparently unaware they were under observation." Hodkinson ordered his three Bren gunners to move forward as quietly as possible while he put the rest of his men in position to fire their rifles. Then he gave the signal and his gunners opened up on Colonel Shoji's men; many fell while hundreds more broke and ran. Flush with victory, Hodkinson pushed on into Middle Gap.[4]

. . .

Not far from where Hodkinson's men attacked the Japanese, Sergeant Tom Marsh lay where he had fallen unconscious, drawing ragged breaths through his damaged face. When he came to, he found Corporal John Britton lying across him, badly injured but conscious. Marsh tried to get out from under Britton's weight. Britton motioned him to stay still so that the Japanese soldiers, who, Britton could see, were bayoneting wounded soldiers, would not spot them. Britton didn't have to warn Marsh a second time, for moments later he again passed out.

. . .

About the same time as Hodkinson's men opened up on the Shoji's troops, the Japanese atop Mount Butler made another push against Major Gresham's men. In an attempt to usher them to safety, Gresham roared the order to retire toward the southern lip of the mountain. The ground over which the Grenadiers retreated was broken with crevices and gullies. Unable to jump the gully in front of him, Corporal Keith Geddes climbed into it and proceeded some distance before climbing onto a small rise. From the rise, he saw Gresham lead his men into a small depression almost surrounded by Japanese troops, who fired and threw hand grenades at the Canadians beneath them. Realizing that his men were trapped, Gresham made the most difficult decision given to a field commander. Taking a white handkerchief from his pocket, he tied it to a stick and stood up. Geddes watched his commander wave the white flag—and then be cut down by a burst of machine gun fire.

Command fell to Captain Marcus Tarbuth, but it was Sergeant-Major John Osborn who was in position to herd the men closer to the southern lip of the mountain. Their bodies as exhausted as their ammo clips, some of the men began running pell-mell down the side of the mountain toward another small plateau. Some slipped on wet rocks, banged into boulders or tripped over the low trees that seemed to grow out of what men hailing from the Canadian Prairies would call sand, not soil.

"Don't panic," yelled Osborn as he struggled to be heard over the syncopated drumbeat of gunfire and exploding grenades. "Stay together and keep calm." These were seemingly impossible orders to follow for men like Private Stanley Baty. The men at the bottom of the slope were as terrified as Baty, but their faith in Osborn kept them together. In the heat of the battle, reported on by the company's commander, Captain Maurice Parker, in his postwar memoir, the men may even have believed Osborn's next words: "We'll get out of this okay." His encouragement certainly quelled Baty's rising terror; after hearing his sergeant, the private volunteered to cover the retreat down the mountain with a Bren gun he took from an exhausted Grenadier.

There is some confusion about what happened next. According to Private Dennis Murphy, Osborn led the men down a ravine. The sounds of gunfire and grenades died away, replaced by the "heavy breathing of . . . exhausted soldiers and the scraping of their boots on the hard ground." At one point, one of Murphy's comrades looked up toward the summit and called out hopefully, "I think we've lost 'em. There aren't any Japs comin' down the hill." Sergeant Pugsley's report makes no mention of the unit moving down the ravine. Everyone present, however, agrees that at one point the Japanese started throwing grenades and one landed near Osborn and six men, including Pugsley.

As he yelled, "Clear out!" Osborn shoved Pugsley down the hill and flung himself onto the grenade an instant before it exploded. The explosion shredded Osborn's body so completely that six fragments of the grenade hit Private William Bell. According to Pugsley, Osborn's self-sacrifice saved him "and at least six other men" and earned Osborn Canada's first Victoria Cross of the Second World War.*

The shock at having lost their second senior officer in less than thirty minutes did not break what remained of "A" Company. Even when machine gunners cut down the first group that climbed out of a dry slough, discipline held. The fifteen who followed rushed behind boulders and started shooting in the direction of the Japanese gunners. The firefight lasted about ten minutes until, as Pugsley reported, "The Japs rushed our positions and took the remnants of the company prisoner."†

The Japanese did not capture Corporal Geddes, who, with his Bren gun at the ready, hid behind some unusually thick brush. Under the cover of darkness, he climbed down the mountain and made his way west toward Happy Valley Race Track, where he met some Rajputs. He spent the night with them, then headed for his company's last known position.

---

* Osborn died never having learned that his daughter, who had been badly burned the night he boarded the train for Vancouver and who needed more than a score of operations, had lived.

† The hut Pugsley, Bell and others were marched to soon held some two hundred Canadian, British, Indian and Hong Kong Volunteer POWs, many of whom were wounded; conditions there soon resembled the Black Hole of Calcutta.

. . .

For Signalmen Allister and Grant, the afternoon of 19 December was a welter of confusion. It was hard enough for men fighting with their units to understand where they were, but at least they fought under known commanders and, as soon as the battle began, for their buddies. Separated from their units, Allister and Grant took orders wherever they could get them, for example, from a British major, who appeared to have "courage to burn" even as his orders made him seem "mad as a hatter."

> "Men! We're going to hold this position . . . *to the end.*" The *end?* My God—a suicide stand! We a puny dozen men, were to turn back the whole goddam Japanese Army! . . .
> So this was it. Was this where I was to die? There was no other way. . . . I was to die, idiotically, meaninglessly, invisibly, on a distant Chinese hill. . . .
> The Angel of Death was here. . . . [5]

Both men survived.

Later, running after the Chinese soldier in front of him, Allister dove to the ground just ahead of a deadly stream of machine gun bullets passing overhead. And then, when the Japanese gunner paused to prevent his barrel from overheating or to change his ammunition belt, the two rose in tandem and ran again, only to dive for safety a few steps forward. Thousands of bullets—bullets stamped out in factories fuelled by coal mined in places the Canadians would come to know all too well—peppered the ground around Allister's small group. One struck its mark; the soldier running in front of Allister dropped, "blood gushing from his throat."

Riveted by the sight and petrified that he had become the column's leader and hence its first target, Allister froze. Pushed by the shouts of the men behind him—"*Move!*" "*Go!*"—Allister jumped up and ran. It seemed an eternity until a bend in the road took him and the men behind him to a semblance of safety.

. . .

At about 5:00 p.m., a hundred or so yards shy of Five-Way-Road Junction, Hodkinson paused in his advance into the Wong Nei Chong Gap; he was soon joined by a platoon from the Jocks' "A" Company, late, but very much appreciated. Hodkinson's attack plan was simple: a pincer. After synchronizing watches, he sent the bulk of the force, under the command of Lieutenant Railton Campbell, to attack from the west and southwest along Deepwater Bay Road while Hodkinson led five men along a spur southeast of Mount Nicholson.

Before he reached the starting point for the attack, Hodkinson bumped into a Japanese force manning a captured Vickers machine gun. The Grenadiers made short work of them and, some minutes later, destroyed another group at a roadblock. Then, before turning toward the police station, which was already under mortar fire from a two-man mortar unit Hodkinson had detached from his own group, he set out for another point on his map—the headquarters of the Grenadiers' "D" Company. The hulks of the burnt-out cars and trucks that littered the approach to "D" Company's headquarters offered some protection from the fire of the Japanese who held the ground above the headquarters.

Hodkinson was shocked at what he saw in the shelter, starting with Captain Howard Bush's face, torn by splinters from a grenade that had exploded against the shelter's door. The same explosion had badly wounded Captain Robert Philip, whose right eye socket was packed with bloody gauze. Spread out on the concrete floor were men with bandages wound around arms, legs and broken heads.

Hodkinson called Maltby, who reiterated the order that after clearing the police station, Hodkinson was to continue on to take Mount Parker, and told the major he was to do this last "without any artillery support or [further] reinforcements." The daunting task before him did not prevent Hodkinson from assuring Bush that after retaking Mount Parker, he would return and relieve "D" Company.

.   .   .

While Hodkinson was making his way from Bush's shelter toward the police station, Allister found himself attached to a British unit moving along Coombe Road, more or less in the centre of the island, when someone came running down the road yelling that a shell had killed a "whole slew of . . . Signal[men]."

Allister ran up the road and found his friends—Signalmen Tony Grimston, Jack Rose, Horace Gerrard and Roland Damours—pale-faced and gloomy, but alive. "Where's Hank?" Allister asked. They didn't know. "Damant? Normand?" Grimston soberly told Allister how the pair had mistakenly set up their radios in the front part of a house where a shell had killed them and Signalman Charles Sharpe.

Just then, a Middlesex sergeant stepped into the doorway and said he needed help digging graves. Allister rose with his friends. Strangely, Grimston said to Allister, and not to the three men who like him had barely escaped death from that shell, "You'd better not. You—uh—look like hell. Better rest up." Allister insisted. "I'm okay," he said, as he took a swig from the bottle of rum the sergeant passed around.

Allister dug while the sergeant sorted the dead. At one point, he heard the sergeant call, "Anyone here know a Greenberg?" His shovel stopped, Allister turned and replied, "Hank Greenberg? Yeah, me. But he's not here, he's in another sector." Allister noted the curious look on the sergeant's face as he went on, "Well, there's a respirator with that name. Better have a look."

Allister was overwhelmed by the sickening stench of decaying bodies even before he reached the door. The sergeant pointed to the face he wanted identified. "Okay," said Allister, "but it's impossible."

> It was beyond recognition: nose and chin sliced away, leaving flat gaping wounds still wine-collared and glistening. . . . Part of the scalp lay open beside the face, attached by a strand of skin. In it, as in a red saucer, lay what seemed part of the brain floating in blood. . . .

As nausea rose within him, Allister grabbed on to a slender reed of hope: the face was too badly damaged to identify the body. Allister had promised Mrs. Greenberg in Winnipeg that he'd watch out for her boy. "Someone's borrowed . . ." Before he could say "it," Allister saw the "finely knit officer's sweater [Greenberg's] uncle bought him." The words "this mangled *thing*—was him!" screamed through Allister's brain.[6]

. . .

Just before 8:00 p.m., it appeared that Hodkinson's luck would hold. Two armoured cars mounting Vickers machine guns showed up, and he picked up another twenty or so men for his attack on the police station. Mobile artillery would have been more useful; still, with the ability to fire more than five hundred rounds per minute, the armoured cars provided some protection to the infantrymen advancing behind them. Japanese divisional artillery could have destroyed the cars. However, had they done so, the attack might have been called off, which was not what the Japanese wanted. They wanted, rather, to entice the Canadians into what is now called a "kill zone."

The Japanese artillerists disabled both cars by landing shells that exploded under the front axle of each. Their machine guns still operated, though, so the attack continued. The Japanese held their fire until the onrushing British and Canadians were closing in on the police station. Then they opened up, forcing the attackers to dive for safety.

Seeing that his troops had gone to ground but were keeping up a respectable rate of fire, augmented by the machine guns on the crippled armoured cars, Hodkinson led a few men in a flanking manoeuvre. To get to the left flank of the police station, Hodkinson's rain-soaked men, running over slippery rocks, had first to crest a small knoll. The Grenadiers made it about three-quarters of the way up the steep slope, at which point some forty Japanese stepped into the skyline.

Hodkinson had time to order his men to fire but few, if any, could before the Japanese soldiers lobbed a volley of grenades down the hill and dropped back behind the rise. Seconds later, almost eight pounds of TNT exploded, wounding all of Hodkinson's men. One of the two-ounce packages of TNT blew the major into the air and ripped open his left side. He passed out a few moments later, at about 8:30 p.m., when Governor Young walked into the radio station and broadcast these words:

> The time has come to advance against the enemy. The eyes of the empire are upon us. Be strong. Be resolute and do your duty.

. . .

A half-hour before Sir Mark's broadcast, Brigadier Wallis telephoned Lieutenant-Colonel Home at Stone Hill with new orders for the Royal Rifles. At 5:00 a.m. the next day, one company was to attack north from Stanley to recapture the Wong Nei Chong Gap, thus re-establishing communication with West Brigade. Then they were to capture Violet Hill, two and a half miles northwest of Home's headquarters. Another company was to be positioned on the right flank of Stanley Mound, itself about half a mile west of Stone Hill.

The order dismayed Home, who wondered why Wallis had not reached for other troops.

For of all the troops near Stanley, the Canadians were by far the most cut up. Headquarters Company alone had lost twenty men. Since 10:00 p.m. the previous day, "C" Company had been reduced from five officers and 172 ordinary ranks to four officers and 64 men.* Equally important was the state of the remaining men. They had been in the field for eight days; they had not had hot food in five. They had been in battle for thirty hours. The men were so exhausted that during pauses they fell asleep and when they reached Stanley, many simply collapsed on the concrete floor of a gymnasium.

---

* In addition, every one of the thirty-eight men belonging to No. 5 Platoon had been killed, wounded or captured, as were twenty-one belonging to No. 2 Platoon and six belonging to No. 6 Platoon.

CHAPTER 9

"This Heap of Rubble Was Their Cairn"

The Siege of the Repulse Bay Hotel
20 December 1941

Still falls the Rain—
Dark as the world of man, black as our loss—
Blinded as the nineteen hundred and forty nails
Upon the Cross
—EDITH SITWELL, "STILL FALLS THE RAIN"

Before first light on 20 December, the rain that had made the climb up Mount Nicholson a misery for Lieutenant Leonard Corrigan's men slackened to a fine drizzle. The drops that clung to the stubble and dirt on Tom Marsh's face amplified the cold morning air, reviving him. As he became aware that his left arm hung all but limp and again felt the pain from his wounded face, the Grenadier sergeant struggled to see in the half-light. "There was no movement from the pillbox. All was quiet. Only the dead remained. . . . I thought of Lieutenant Birkett and the other gallant lads who lay or were buried there. This heap of rubble was their cairn," Marsh recalled.

Seeing his bayoneted comrades, Marsh knew he had to act quickly. Taking a rifle and a water bottle, he walked unsteadily down the hill and over the next rise, from where he could see a pillbox.

In the strengthening light, he could just make out two figures atop it. Had he been stronger, he might have tried to flank the pillbox and make his way further south. But weak from hunger, shock and loss of blood, he crawled unnoticed under the barbed wire into the trench leading to the pillbox.

When the Grenadier came round a bend in the trench, the Japanese sentry was surprised but had the presence of mind to point his bayonet at Marsh's stomach. Marsh dropped his rifle and lifted his arms over his head.

His captors offered no first aid to the bloody soldier who had fallen into their laps. Only after he started spitting out blood clots and gristle did they offer him anything: an open tin of diced carrots, which, because of his ripped-open mouth, Marsh was unable to consume.

.   .   .

The 5:00 a.m. attack Brigadier Wallis had ordered on the Wong Nei Chong Gap did not get underway on time, but not because as historian Tim Carew wrote,

> the Canadian contingent as a whole had ceased [by late on
> 19 December] to exist as a cohesive force—leaderless, dispirited, demoralized and exhausted, they had scattered to the
> four corners of the island: some sort [sought] solace in sleep
> [,]others in looted liquor.* Others again, were fastened upon

---

* There is only one documented case of a Canadian soldier being drunk. On 22 December, a drunken James Riley was found at the Repulse Bay Hotel after the Royal Rifles withdrew from the hotel prior to its being surrendered to the Japanese. To protect him and the civilians from retaliation, the Rifleman was dressed as a civilian. The Japanese fell for the ruse, which led to him being interned as a civilian and repatriated to Canada in 1942. After the war, Major Charles Young was in a taxi in Toronto in which he vaguely recognized the driver's picture. Before pulling away from the curb, the driver of the taxi leaned out the window and said, "Give my regards to all the boys, Major," thus confirming Young's suspicion and leaving him throwing a string of curses as

avidly by unit commanders and were coerced and cajoled, sometimes at gunpoint, into fighting again.[1]

Rather, arrangements were taking longer to make than Wallis expected. Fearing that if he used the telephones, the Japanese would be tipped off, the brigadier sent a captain to Palm Villa with orders for the Rifles' "A," "B," "D" and Headquarters companies to march west toward Repulse Bay. At Stone Hill, the brigade's headquarters, they were to turn north to attack the Wong Nei Chong Gap and re-establish communication with West Brigade.

No doubt the lieutenants and sergeants resorted to strong language and none-too-subtle nudges with their boots to roust up their tired men. But soon, the hundreds of men who were again called upon to go on the attack shook sleep from their eyes, ate slices of bully beef with their bayonets and bit off pieces of the same sort of hard tack that Admiral Horatio Nelson's men would have eaten before Trafalgar almost a century and a half earlier. To soften what quartermasters insisted on calling biscuit, they took long swigs of water.

Given the failure of the penny-packet attacks of the previous day, Wallis's decision to attack with four companies—almost four hundred men, albeit tired ones—represented a change of strategy. No battle plan, it is said, survives the first contact with the enemy. Wallis's began coming undone even as his officers traced their fingers over their maps to Mount Nicholson, where they were to link up with West Brigade. Unbeknownst to Wallis, the Grenadiers on Mount Nicholson were withdrawing to the west to regroup first at Mount Cameron and, later, at Mount Gough. The attacking force then fell by almost a hundred men after Wallis learned that the Japanese had infiltrated almost to the southern end of the island at Repulse Bay, just over

Riley drove away (quoted in Garneau, 182).

a mile west of Wallis's headquarters at Stone Hill. He tasked Major Young's "A" Company with "brush[ing] aside" the "weak opposition" at the Repulse Bay Hotel. The attacking force fell by another company, thus halving it, when "B" Company (which was now operating under orders to support "A" Company by taking up positions on the Stanley View/Repulse Bay Road) did not meet up with Headquarters Company, commanded by Major Thomas MacAuley.

. . .

Perched high on the bluffs above the bay named for HMS *Repulse*, an iron-clad launched in 1868, the Repulse Bay Hotel was a most unlikely site for a battle.* Little in their experience on the rugged Gaspé coast or the forests around Restigouche, New Brunswick, had prepared Young's men for what they would see: the opulent dining room, tables with full linen service, and manicured flower beds were still there in the middle of a war. Only in Fred Astaire and Ginger Rogers films such as *Top Hat* might they have seen the type of dowager who complained to the hotel's manager that the Chinese families that had taken shelter in the hotel were eating in the dining room. "Can't you keep those creatures in the basement?"[2] In better days, the hotel's guests had included George Bernard Shaw, Noël Coward and British royalty. Now, in addition to Chinese and civilian refugees—including Proulx's family—the hotel held Hong Kong Volunteers like Proulx.

Accounts differ as to who first saw Japanese troops approaching the hotel.† One version holds that, in keeping with the elegant surroundings, Japanese officers in dress uniform, in full view of the stunned breakfasting guests, appeared at the end of the hotel's

---

* HMS *Repulse*, sunk on 10 December, was the eleventh Royal Navy ship to bear this name.

† Official records are not much help. The description here largely follows Proulx's version.

driveway. In his 1943 memoir, *Underground from Hong Kong,* Lieutenant Benjamin Proulx tells how shortly before 6:00 a.m., his ten-year-old son woke him, saying:

> "Hey, Dad! There are a lot of Japs outside on the road in front of the garage."
> "Oh, you're wrong, Sonny. Those are Canadians. We're expecting them in today."
> "No, they're Japs all right. I've been outside and I've seen them."

Proulx jumped out of bed, grabbed his rifle and after seeing thirty Japanese soldiers from the window, ran to the end of the hotel's corridor and snuck out onto the lawn. Hidden by creepers covering a rail, he saw that the Japanese had already captured six men. The bayonet at one soldier's back did not violate the rules of war; the "whipping blows" of a Japanese officer slapping his face, however, did.

Crouching near Proulx were three soldiers, one a Rifleman with a Tommy gun. Proulx inched over to him and asked in a whisper if he could hit the Japanese officer without hitting the others. "He is a dead officer, Sir," replied the Rifleman. Proulx arranged for the other soldiers to fire when he gave the signal.

As Proulx lifted his arm, the soldiers took careful aim and steadied their guns, then looked at him. An instant after he dropped his arm, their eyes shifted back to their guns' sights and their shoulder muscles moved all but imperceptibly as they adjusted for any changes in their targets' positions. The Tommy gun's blast caught the officer just as he had finished another slap, sending him into "a pirouette that ended in a silly lifeless fall." Proulx's plan cost the Japanese five dead, but it did not free the prisoners. In the commotion that followed, other Japanese soldiers pulled them into the hotel's garage.

The Japanese took shelter behind the concrete walls of the car stalls, which neither Tommy nor Lewis guns could blast through. Twice the Japanese raised the Rising Sun in a call for help. Each time a Lewis gunner cut the pole in two.

During a lull in the fighting an hour or so later, Proulx called out, "Come out with your hands up. We will not shoot." Obviously unaware of the complexities of English/French relations in Canada, a Japanese soldier screamed, "Go to hell, you English bastards!" Proulx tried calling out the prisoners' names; their muffled answers confirmed they were alive.

A few minutes later, "Westy" told Proulx he knew where there were some hand grenades.* Assuming that there was a ten-second delay before the explosion, Westy told Proulx to count to five before throwing his grenade. Neither had had grenade training and, like most first-time grenadiers, each threw before finishing their count. This mistake saved their lives, for the grenades exploded after only seven seconds. After throwing a few short, they landed two deep in the garage, and the gunfire from the garage lessened.

A short time later, the soldier with the Lewis gun called Proulx over. Pointing to an open window on the side of the garage, he said, "Nips might try to escape that way."[3] As the gunner crawled into position behind a bush and Proulx lugged forward an ammunition crate, four Japanese soldiers readied to climb up to the window and then jump down from it. The Die Hard won the race. Several short blasts from his Lewis gun ensured that each Japanese soldier was dead before his body hit the ground. The Tommy gunner cut down the lone soldier who ran out the front door.

· · ·

---

* To protect this soldier who was still a POW, Proulx uses a *nom de guerre* here.

Just after 9:00 a.m., Lieutenant Earle Smith called out "Forward march!" and the men of Headquarters Company, some of whom only moments before had been writing letters home or reading from their pocket Bibles, began marching back into battle. Smith's orders traced a line from Stone Hill east toward Repulse Bay and then north toward Violet Hill, a total distance of about two miles, or about thirty minutes' marching under normal circumstances.

Hong Kong, however, was neither the training ground at Valcartier, Quebec, nor that at Botwood, Newfoundland. The way to Repulse Bay included a number of hills, some more than three hundred feet high. Further, to keep out of sight of Japanese gunners, the Canadians kept to the sides of the road, which increased the difficulty of the march as they negotiated wet, slippery rocks.

Japanese field artillerists did not waste ammunition searching for targets. Their maps showed the routes the defenders were likely to take to counterattack. Spotters and gunners worked extremely well together; the first shells did not start falling until the lead part of Smith's platoon was in the most exposed position—the middle of the junction of Island and Chung Am Kok roads.

When the explosions started, some men ran to safety on the far side of the road while others retreated a short distance. As bullets whipped by his head and shells exploded nearby, Rifleman Doddridge recalled Winston Churchill's statement, "Nothing is so exhilarating as to be shot at and missed." Heavy though it was, the Japanese barrage was not constant, and by carefully timing their runs, the rest of the platoon was able to cross the road. As they neared the outskirts of Repulse Bay and the road that would take them north toward Violet Hill, the Rifles came under small-arms fire. The shooting was so heavy that simply ordering his men to return fire was not a useful option. Continuing to advance up was also impossible. Sergeant Shorty Pope, who took command after Smith was wounded, ordered the men to take cover on either side of the road.

Wallis's attack on the Wong Nei Chong Gap had now fallen on the shoulders of "D" Company alone.[*]

. . .

A shell that detonated at No. 8 the Peak (near Victoria), during a heavy bombardment at close to 10:00 a.m. on 20 December, killed Captain Roslyn Davies of the Royal Canadian Army Pay Corps and mortally wounded Colonel Patrick Hennessy. When the shell exploded, Quartermaster-Sergeant Victor Myatt was a few hundred yards away from the house having breakfast at a British Warrant Officers' mess. If he heard the explosion, he paid it scant attention. Much more pressing was the effect of the shell that tore through the roof in the middle of a nearby building, setting off a fire in a storage room containing some three hundred thousand rounds of ammunition.

As the men in the mess and nearby barracks took cover from the bullets shooting out of the fire, Sergeant Charles Clark (Canadian Postal Corps) ran to Myatt. Through Clark's deep breaths, Myatt learned that when Hennessy heard bullets strike the house he and Clark were in, he ordered Clark and two other men to the basement while Hennessy and Davies climbed to the roof to see if the Japanese infantry had attacked. After fifteen minutes without word from either officer, Clark climbed up from the cellar but was forced back by the heavy shellfire. During a lull a few moments later, Clark left the basement to find Davies's body and hear Hennessy's weak voice calling for him. What he saw when he

---

[*] In the entry for 0800, Wallis wrote in the East Brigade War Diary, "The advance of 'D' Bn [Royal Rifles] was slow and over cautious. Men were taking cover every time a distant shot or burst from a L[ight] M[achine] G[un] was heard." It is difficult to square this criticism (and others discussed below) with the statement in Appendix H that "It was clear from the fighting on 20 and 21 Dec. 1941 that provided they had good leaders the men were brave and would follow."

found the popular colonel rivalled anything Clark had seen in the Great War. Hennessy's legs "held only flesh and sinew." To staunch the bleeding, Clark applied tourniquets.

Braving both shelling and the bullets shooting out of the fire, Myatt followed Clark back to the wrecked house. Clark had left Hennessy lying on a board; he returned to a macabre scene. With blood drained from his face and flowing out of his body, Hennessy sat in an almost upright position, the result of his many pleas to Lance-Corporal William Overton, who had come up from the basement, to "Lift my head up. Lift my head up," as if the mere act of sitting would ward off the inevitable.[4]

Myatt assured Hennessy that they would see him through. Meanwhile, Clark crawled his way back to the British barracks where, after a short argument, a captain lent him a car to take Hennessy to the first aid station. By the time Clark convinced Captain Albert Rodriguez (Royal Army Medical Corps) and a few stretcher-bearers to come with him, the driver had vanished. Precious minutes ticked by before he found another, who, because of the shells falling on the main road, had to take the long way around to the house.

To everyone's surprise, Rodriguez loosened the tourniquets, saying that, "unless this was done every fifteen minutes, gangrene would set in due to climatic conditions." The dressings he applied did little to staunch the flow of blood from Hennessy's shredded body. The morphine, though, took effect. Finally, the Canadians carefully lifted Hennessy onto a makeshift stretcher and carried him out of the house. The road was so badly torn up that Myatt almost despaired of making it to the ambulance. They succeeded and then braved shell-pocked roads as they made their way to War Memorial Hospital on the Peak.

· · ·

As Hennessy's life ebbed away, Tom Marsh's captors marched him to the "Black Hole of Hong Kong," the hut that held the remnants of Gresham's command and hundreds of British and Indian soldiers and Hong Kong Volunteers. "Here was gathered all the misery of military defeat. There was no food and, worse, no water. Thirst, doubly prevalent when one is wounded, was an acute torture," Marsh recalled. The two hundred men were so closely packed together in the sixty-by-thirty-foot hut upon which the hot December sun beat that only those who had breathed their last could collapse to the floor. Flies pestered the living and swarmed the dead.

The conditions in the hut and the denial of first aid violated the Geneva Convention. So too did the positioning of a field gun nearby, for that made the area a likely target for counter-battery attack. At some point, Marsh heard shells exploding, which told him that the British were seeking the range of the Japanese gun. Then, a shell slammed into the roof and exploded. Amid the wreckage, smoke and screams of dying men, Marsh threw himself under a table, upon which lay "a dead imperial with half his head blown away."

The blast killed the guard at the door. Bright red blood from the newly wounded and dead splattered bandages that a moment before were stained brown by dried, caked blood. Many escaped death or further injury because they were so closely packed together that their comrades' bodies absorbed both the force of the blast and the thousands of metal shards it generated.

. . .

As the Japanese moved Marsh and other survivors out of the wrecked hut for a harrowing march to North Point, now a POW camp, Major Parker's "D" Company advanced into the Wong Nei Chong Gap. Parker's decision to advance using two catchwaters for protection did not sit well with Wallis, who felt the Canadian major "was cautious and slow and showed a tendency to keep well under cover." Still, the first part of the advance seems to give substance to the first sentence of the communiqué issued at 2:30 p.m.: "Operations have been proceeding satisfactorily to-day."

At midday, it became clear that a Japanese battery likely belonging to Tanaka's Independent Mountain Artillery Company near the Tai Tam Tuk Reservoir would have to be silenced. Sergeant George MacDonell, who reconnoitred the area two weeks earlier, volunteered for the mission. "I was very worried about us being discovered, so I warned my men to be absolutely silent as we crawled through the water catchment. Any noise we made—and we were carrying rifles, mortars and Bren guns and a lot of ammunition in metal cases—must have been masked by the sound of the Japanese artillery," recalls MacDonell.

MacDonell halted his advance when he reached a point nearing the Japanese encampment. "The tension was palpable as I positioned my Bren gunners and as my other men readied their rifles."

With his rifle at the ready, MacDonell peered over the top of the catchment. A moment before signalling his men to rise above the catchment and begin firing, a Japanese staff car drove into view. He recalls, "I waited until the officer stepped out of the car and then fired. In an instant my men were up and firing." The air filled with the sounds of machine gun fire, exploding ammunition, the screams of the dying and wounded, the frightened squealing of mules and the jabber of the Japanese desperately trying to figure out where the fire was coming from.

. . .

Had the men or women at the Repulse Bay Hotel or the men of "A" Company known of it, they would have been astounded to read in the mid-afternoon communiqué that "parties of the enemy have been mopped up in the Repulse Bay area." Indeed, the Rifles had found evidence of at least a platoon of Japanese equipped with machine guns nearby. Proulx had seen enemy soldiers on the ridge north of the hotel. Nor had the siege at the garage ended.

In the middle of the afternoon, Proulx led a small force out of the concrete drainage tunnel that doubled as a shelter for the women, children and old men to a pillbox to replenish the garrison's ammunition supply. Proulx and two other volunteers ran a gauntlet of Japanese machine gun and rifle fire south of the hotel. They thought all was lost when they heard the steady sound of men marching. "Cripes! Nip reinforcements! We have the damnedest luck!" one of the volunteers whispered to Proulx, who ordered his men to ready their grenades.

They kept their "death grip" on them much longer than expected.[5] For instead of men carrying rice balls in their haversacks, Canadian soldiers marched into view and almost into the Japanese line of fire. Proulx risked giving his own position away when he yelled, "Stop. . . . There's a machine gun covering this road just around this curve!" After throwing their grenades down the hill and indicating to Major Young where the Japanese were, Proulx told him about their need of ammunition and the siege at the hotel's garage. Young sent a runner to Wallis and ordered some of his men to deploy along the beach while he and the rest, carrying the much-needed ammunition taken from the pillbox, followed Proulx into the drainage tunnel.

Shortly after hearing from Young, Wallis climbed on the back of a motorcycle and personally delivered the orders to the eighteen-pound battery at Stanley View to begin shelling the garage. The shells killed all but three of the Japanese, who managed to escape. One of the prisoners was also killed.

· · ·

MacDonell and his men had little time to savour their success. Within moments, Tanaka's men on the ridge above them sought revenge. The catchwater worked both to the Canadians' advantage and to their detriment. It gave them a clear path to run down, but it also funnelled them and allowed the Japanese to pursue them from higher ground. From his position at the rear of his men, it took MacDonell a few moments to realize that his plan—exiting the catchment and running to heavily wooded and hence safer area—had run up against a Nambu machine gun spitting out five hundred rounds per minute that pinned down his men in the catchment. A moment later, a machine gunner on the ridge began enfilading the catchwater, threatening to turn it into a mass grave. A blast almost caught MacDonell, who survived by diving to the bottom of the catchment.

MacDonell ordered a corporal to load two Bren guns with magazines with tracers. While he waited for the gun, MacDonell peered over the catchwater and through his binoculars. The machine gunner must not have seen MacDonell, who had time not only to see where the gunner was but for his corporal to hand him a Bren loaded with tracers. It took a second or two to flatten the Bren's bipod so MacDonell could lay it flat on the edge of the catchwater, now serving as a parapet.

"We fired at each other at almost the same time. I could hear his bullets 'chirping' as they passed much less than an inch close to my left ear," recalls MacDonell. To prevent the gun's barrel from overheating, standard operating procedure called for Bren gunners to fire for a few seconds, wait a few seconds and then fire another spray of about ten rounds. MacDonell broke the rule, firing until he had exhausted the thirty-round magazine. "Even though it was daylight, I could see the tracer's arc, and I was sure I was firing into exactly the spot where I'd seen movement earlier."

It took only a moment to knock the empty magazine off the gun and slide in a full one. Then, MacDonell fired in the direction that he thought the second machine gunner was. He ordered his men to be ready to climb out of the catchwater and run the seventy-five yards to where they could take cover in the foliage. Taking deep breaths, the Canadians waited, hearing a pause a few seconds later as MacDonell installed still one more magazine. Only after another few dozen rounds ripped through the Hong Kong air at almost seventeen hundred miles per hour did their sergeant give the order.

"A moment later, I hoisted myself up over the rim of the catchment, jumped down and followed my men. With every step, I expected to hear either the machine gun or a rifle, but I didn't, and made it safely into the foliage," MacDonell says.

Safe for the moment, MacDonell took stock. His men were unhurt. Returning to where they'd started was impossible; so too was moving north toward Violet Hill. Accordingly, MacDonell decided to move his men south toward Stanley, being careful to stay as much as possible hidden in the undergrowth.

. . .

Meanwhile Lieutenants Donald Languedoc and Donald Ross took their mortar section some way forward from the rest of "D" Company to clear Violet Hill of some of the guns punishing Parker's men. There is some confusion about happened next.

The part of the Royal Rifles' war diary that deals with "D" Company's attack, presumably narrated by Major Parker, states: "The mortar Section was routed by enemy and jettisoned Mortar and all bombs (24 H[igh] E[xplosive]) and returned to Palm Villa." The section devoted to Headquarters Company tells a slightly different story. "Due to circumstances no opportunities of using the one mortar with them [on Japanese artillery]. After lugging this Mortar all day decided to dismantle it and did so, scattering it down a steep embankment. Sight destroyed and weapon made completely useless."

Given the brigadier's characterization of Parker's decision to withdraw in the face of overwhelming force on Violet Hill as being "apparently without orders," it is not surprising that Wallis's East Brigade War Diary states: "This Coy had left behind the 3 Mortars sent out to support it not being willing to carry them further." Wallis adds later that "they lost almost all field telephones." No veteran of the battle recalls ever seeing a field telephone in their officer's hands.

. . .

Although most of the men and women in the Repulse Bay Hotel must have known that the British hold on Hong Kong was doomed, the mood in the hotel was not as gloomy as Brigadier Wallis's. His war diary entry for 5:00 p.m. says that all efforts to relieve the hotel had failed, and "there was the danger of the enemy capturing Stanley Mound, cutting the road between Stanley and Repulse Bay and then destroying sub-units in detail." Although the garage had been retaken and twenty-six Japanese had been killed, the enemy still roamed the beach and the hills beyond the hotel. The funeral of Sub-Lieutenant Slay and three Indian soldiers served to pull the men and women together. As the sun set, the shelling ceased.

Darkness was the signal for the women, children and old men, who had huddled throughout the day in the concrete drainage shelter, to climb back up through the greenhouse and re-enter a semblance of the world they had lost. The hotel's "boys" insisted on wearing their uniforms. Water bled from the cold boilers provided enough for cooking and tea. Sister Elizabeth Mosey, a seventy-year-old Scottish registered nurse, ran a makeshift hospital.

The arrival of the Rifles' "A" Company sometime before 7:00 p.m. meant that the garrison could post adequate sentries and allow the men who had been there for several days to get a decent night's sleep. It also meant that men and women who had lived years in the tropics heard very large men "who looked quite able to go out and win the war with a set of brass knuckles" talk about how, with Christmas just a few days away, they were homesick for the kind of snow "that sits all over trees like cotton."[6]

. . .

The hours before the Canadians arrived at Repulse Bay were confusing for both sides. At 4:00 p.m., as part of the defence of the hotel and Stanley, "B" Company was ordered to pass through "A" Company's positions around Repulse Bay to a curve in the road below the Middle Spur, just west of Eucliffe Castle. This castle was located a couple of hundred yards north of the Repulse Bay Hotel. A half-hour later, new orders arrived: proceed to Sugar Loaf, a hill about a mile in almost the exact opposite direction—east. When "B" Company was about half-way to Sugar Loaf Hill, a runner came with orders for the company to "turn about and recontinue its advance on Repulse Bay." Then, these orders too were countermanded and the men, now marching in the rain, turned around and headed back toward Stone Hill.

Things were not much clearer at Colonel Shoji's headquarters. The Japanese had taken Mount Parker and Jardine's Lookout, laid siege to the Repulse Bay Hotel and all but split the island's defences. Yet the messages to and from headquarters were hardly triumphant. Just after midnight, Shoji, who through the late hours of 19 December had been trying to link up with Doi's battalion on his left, heard from Lieutenant Ito that yes, he had found Doi's men, calmly eating their rice and fish balls two thousand yards northeast of Shoji's force. Shoji was not amused and reprimanded Ito for not contacting Doi himself. Shoji's temper was due in part to the fact that his men were short of ammunition and to one of the Japanese Army's surprising weaknesses: the low priority given to evacuating wounded soldiers and treating sick ones.

Word that the first attack on the Repulse Bay Hotel had been beaten off could hardly have improved the Japanese mood. Nor did the two major attacks of the day speak particularly well of the Emperor's forces. The first, a late-afternoon infantry attack on the Ridge from Violet Hill, failed. The second, an attack on the Mound (a ridge near Jardine's Lookout), was somewhat more successful, costing Punjabis and Royal Scots dearly.

Still, by 6:00 p.m., the Japanese were so unsure of the situation that Major Oyadomari could report the alarming rumour that "Shoji's regiment had been annihilated at the Gap." It hadn't been, but that would not be clear for a few hours.

. . .

As MacDonell and his troops, and the men of Headquarters Company, collapsed into sleep in Stanley, their senior commanders were hard at work making plans to try again to establish communication with West Brigade. Though he faulted Major Parker for lacking a certain vigour in his attack, Wallis accepted his judgment that an attack over Violet Hill would fail. Without stating why (perhaps the reason being MacDonell's destruction of the 75-mm gun emplacement on Gauge Basin), Wallis believed that "the enemy was not so strong between Taytam Tuk [i.e., Tai Tam Tuk] and Gauge Basin." Accordingly, he sent Maltby a plan to attack "through Taytum Tuk, thereby relieving pressure on West Brigade and Repulse Bay area, and endeavouring to make contact with West Brigade."

Before midnight, Wallis received Maltby's confirmation of the orders for the attack the next day. Maltby ended his message by saying:

> i. Hold what you have, including R. Bay Hotel and do what you can to get through via Gauge Basin.

ii. Boldness will pay, especially if you get on the enemy's rear.

iii. Use your carriers boldly in recce.

Even several months later when Wallis was reconstructing the brigade's war diary, Maltby's items (ii) and (iii) stung. Wallis was a lifetime soldier, who before coming to Hong Kong had commanded the Rajputs for three and a half years in India. In a note to a sentence in which the brigadier says that despite the Rifles' withdrawals, "never would it be the Brigade Commander's policy to give up trying to fight forward," Wallis laid a careful defence for himself. First, he stated, "This remark was due to the fact that in all Ft. H.Q. phone conversations there seemed to be a hint that it was felt East Bde were doing very little." Then, he pointed his finger clearly at the Canadians: "It was evident that it had not yet been understood how weak in ability the Canadian troops were and how strong was the enemy strength and position."*

---

* These last two points, it should be underlined, are curiously absent from Wallis's more detailed descriptions of what the Canadians and the rest of his command faced on the battlefield.

CHAPTER 10

"Another Bullet Hit Him in Almost the Same Place"

The Royal Rifles Attack Red, Bridge and Notting Hills
21 December 1941

And the enemy's two-handed sword
Did not fall from anyone's hands
At that miraculous sight,
As the head rolled over upon
Its wide-eyed face, and fell
Into the inadequate grave.
—JAMES DICKEY, "THE PERFORMANCE"

The second entry for 21 December in the Royal Rifles' war diary reads: "0001 hours to 0600 hours—All quiet during the hours of darkness on all fronts." This hardly describes the night experienced by thousands of men across the east side of Hong Kong Island. True, there had been little fighting. Seeking shelter from the heavy rain and cold wind, men on both sides of the line huddled under hastily constructed lean-tos in the wreckage of pillboxes or in shallow trenches.

Meanwhile, hundreds of Japanese soldiers moved toward the Repulse Bay Hotel and other points south and west. Teamsters spent the night coaxing wet and chilled mules, their hooves struggling for purchase on slick rocks, to pull field artillery into position to shell the hotel, Stanley, Aberdeen and scores of other positions.

. . .

Before and just after dawn, King George's officers and men took part in two meetings that could not have been more different. At the first, Brigadier Wallis explained to officers of the Royal Rifles and two companies of the Hong Kong Volunteers at Stone Hill his plan for the attack that General Maltby had authorized the night before. Having already fought over the ground that led north to the Tai Tam Reservoir and Gauge Basin, it's unlikely that the Canadians thought much of the plan. Perhaps the only bright spot was that Wallis tasked the Hong Kong Volunteers' No. 1 Company with spearheading the attack because its commander knew the terrain.

Later, Wallis tore a strip off the Canadian officers for costing him victory the day before. Ignoring the fact that forty-five-pound radio sets were too heavy to carry up steep inclines and through the catchwaters, Wallis chastised the Canadians for "slowness in Battalion intercommunication" and for relying on runners who often did not return. The responsibility for their failure, the Canadians must have itched to say, surely lay more with Japanese bullets than with lack of Canadian vigour.

Given Wallis's decades of service in the British Army in India, it is difficult to make sense of the brigadier's argument. Indeed, it is almost as if, instead of conceptualizing the tropical battlefield before him, he reverted to the fields of France and Belgium where he had fought as a subaltern. Though few senior commanders had led from the front during the First World War, they could generally see the battlefield for themselves because, more often than not, it was actually a field. Hong Kong's open spaces often formed the steep sides of hills. The ground was covered with small, slippery rocks or volcanic earth that formed a sort of dry slurry or with low scrub that caught pants and hid tangles of roots that could trip men in heavy boots. One Canadian remembers seeing monkeys swinging through the trees in one of the few heavily forested places. Surely, the brigadier did not think that the Canadian officers were so thick that they did not realize that they risked being pinned to the ground if they used the roads. When they could, they used catchwaters, but often the steep hillsides or the vegetation meant that the only path between two points was a road.*

Wallis was right about one thing: because the Japanese held the high ground, they could pin the Canadians down. He glossed over the fact that General Maltby had not believed that the Japanese would seize the high ground and thus had failed to issue orders to garrison Mount Parker and Mount Butler. Officers who commanded men who had barely seen two- and three-inch mortars before arriving in Hong Kong, and who were not issued live shells until the battle had begun, must have been dumbstruck by Wallis's criticism of their handling of mortars to "dislodge the opposition."

No Canadian knew that when he had written his entry for 11:00 a.m. on 20 December, the day before, Wallis made the exact opposite criticism of Major Parker's advance. And while the battalion's war diary suggests that its officers had some trouble organizing and feeding the men once they had returned from the aborted attack on Violet Hill, Wallis went much further when he wrote: "They kept on withdrawing to the road to feed, leaving far too this [?] detachments to hold the high ground. Once down Island Road, men did

---

* At a question and answer session held prior to the dedication of the Memorial Wall on 15 August 2009, veterans reacted with a justifiable mixture of stunned disbelief and indignation when I read to them the sentence that ends this entry: "The men would wander off and pick up anything they fancied."

not hurry to return to their positions, in some cases slipping off to the Bn cooking area near Stanley Police stn."

Though Wallis was tone deaf, as it were, he was not entirely unwilling to listen. After both HKVDC and Canadian officers pointed out that as they travelled north on Island Road toward Tai Tam Tuk, their left flank would be open to attack as they passed Notting and Bridge hills, the brigadier agreed to detach a small force to occupy them.

. . .

The second meeting was more solemn. In the centre of the main yard of St. Stephen's College in Stanley, beneath a leaden sky and with a stiff, cold wind blowing, stood Chaplain James Barnett, holding a book and carrying a small bag. Around him stood a large number of patients, some leaning on crutches, others with white bloodied gauze wrapped around their heads, faces, arms or legs. Some stood defiantly; others could barely see. Many had a most unsoldierly amount of stubble on their cheeks.

Neither the Reverend nor most of the men really needed the book. Perhaps the smattering of Protestants and Catholics among the Anglicans could have benefited from some of the directions in it, but even without it, they had little trouble following the padre. Even the few French speakers would quickly have recognized what Barnett was reading after he opened his copy of *The Book of Common Prayer*: "Our Father, who art in heaven, Hallowed be Thy Name, Thy Kingdom come, Thy will be done, in earth as it is in heaven. . . ." Images of dead men, of buddies who had died next to and in some cases for the men standing there, must have cascaded through the minds of the men before Barnett as they joined in. ". . . And I look for the Resurrection of the dead, And the life of the world to come."

. . .

As Barnett placed the Host on the tongues of the men around him, less than two miles away, more than a score of Winnipeg Grenadiers were in need of extreme unction, for the attack in which they'd die had already begun. Major Harry Hook divided his "B" Company force, sending Corporal Ed Shayler's section over the north slope of Mount Nicholson with orders to cross its crest and break into the Wong Nei Chong Gap via the mountain's southern slope. Hook stayed with the bulk of his men, whom he planned to take up the same stretch of Black's Link from which he had retreated the previous night when a machine gunner and antipersonnel mines blocked his path.

The purpose of anti-personnel mines is only partially to blow up hapless soldiers who step on them. A more important function of mines is to channel an enemy's advance into your field of fire or cause the enemy to hesitate rather than advance quickly. A sergeant spotted the channel and correctly guessed that a machine gun lay beyond the bend in the road. His grenade attack might have succeeded had the machine gunner not pulled his trigger in time.

Hook ordered his mortar section forward. Fifteen explosions and several Bren gun blasts later, three of Hideo Maseo's men lay dead. The destruction of the machine gun emplacement did not mean that the way was clear, something that became apparent when two men in the lead section were shot as they started down the road. The fire came from an enemy position south of the road. Taking advantage of the strengthening light, Hook ordered one section to try to get beyond the fire by climbing up the side of Mount Nicholson and another to use a nearby valley to do the same thing.

The light also showed No. 11 Platoon heavily engaged on the slopes of Mount Nicholson. Corporal Ed Shayler was in the middle of this fight. "The fire started just as we reached the top of the mountain. We could look to our side and see Happy Valley. They had machine guns there and they started firing on us and we hit the dirt. But we didn't have many places to hide or find shelter. The bullets ripped through the air and kicked up a hell of a lot of dirt. Pretty soon we started losing men," he recalls.

Lance-Corporal Charles Edgley and Private Keith Lawrie used their Bren gun to provide covering fire for the men trying to get to the southern slope of the mountain. Shayler watched as his friend Lawrie fired and then fell back, thrown by the force of a bullet that cut through his brain. Edgley took Lawrie's place, getting off a few rounds before being hit in the leg.

"I saw Edgley go down and I crawled over to bandage his leg," recalls Shayler. "He was sitting up watching me. I had just ripped off his pants leg when his body jumped up; another bullet hit him in almost the same place. The pain in his stomach told me that this one had gone much further. Bullets were flying around, so I had to stay low to the ground. He groaned that he wanted water." One of the privates reached for his water bottle. The corporal stopped him. Knowing that any water Edgley drank would flow out of his torn stomach and thus make his death even more agonizing, Shayler said, "Giving him that is not an act of kindness."

With the Japanese climbing up the mountain and the fire from Happy Valley, Shayler knew they could not remain long where they were. He also knew that they could not evacuate the 250-pound lance-corporal. "Even though doing so increased his pain, we pulled Edgley some distance to a tree that gave him some shade," says Shayler. "We then escaped by climbing down the perpendicular side of the mountain to the road below."

· · ·

The battle near Hook went no better. Hook recalled the men he'd sent forward. In quick succession, a sniper wounded him and artillery began pounding the area.

Taken together with the failed advance the night before, Hook's attempt to break into the Wong Nei Chong Gap was an expensive failure. Every officer of Hook's company, the company sergeant major, both platoon sergeants, both lance-sergeants, two corporals and a lieutenant in charge of an attached mortar section was killed or wounded. Ninety-eight men went into battle; twenty-nine became casualties.

. . .

Daybreak had ended the quiet at the Repulse Bay Hotel. Shortly after gunfire woke him, Proulx joined two Canadian Bren gunners at a small window. The two recruits from a town east of Montreal were French Canadian, which allowed Proulx to practise his rusty mother tongue. A spray of tracer bullets from one of the Riflemen's guns lit the underbrush under several Japanese soldiers. When one of them rose to beat at the flames, the Canadians fired, and he fell dead into the burning brush.

The three *Canadiens* did not have long to savour this small victory. While they concentrated on the soldiers on the ridge, Japanese artillerists checked their maps, rotated cranks that brought their guns to bear on the target indicated by a rectangle and, after a countdown that end with *san, ni, ichi,* pulled levers. Seconds later, several eighteen-pound shells smashed through the thin wall of the Repulse Bay Hotel's ornate dining room, detonating against the far wall. Proulx reached the dining room as the guests beat a hasty retreat to the culvert that now doubled as a bomb shelter.

Proulx had seen men fall, victims of his decision to squeeze the trigger at just that one moment. He had seen fellow soldiers come into the hotel with ghastly injuries. He had seen Sub-Lieutenant Slay fall at his feet. As he looked out the window after coming back upstairs, he could still see the charring body of a Japanese soldier. The terrible equation of battle now dictated that a Middlesex private who ran down the steps and jumped into a parked car would be next. The private's inability to turn the car around quickly sealed his fate. A hidden Hotchkiss gunner opened up, and the car slowed suddenly before nosing into a hedge. Proulx heard "the screams of the trapped soldier as the lead found and riddled him."

Some deaths affect soldiers more than others. Perhaps because the "gun kept up its idiot chatter long after the screams were stilled," this death drove Proulx into a frenzy. Each time he heard it, "it seemed to rattle and jeer at me from an entirely new location." Proulx scanned the hillside, on which he saw Major Young's recce patrol. Proulx noted that the Canadian battle dress stood out against the ground and the sun shone off their helmets.[7]

Finally, Proulx saw a movement in some shrubbery about five hundred yards away. "I picked up a Tommy gun and went to work on the spot with a long, savage burst and I think I felt incapable of missing. . . . There was a sudden convulsive movement."[8] The Hotchkiss gun fell silent.

. . .

Led by a platoon of Hong Kong Volunteers, temporarily under the command of Royal Rifles Major Thomas MacAuley, Wallis's attack moved off on schedule at 9:15 a.m. It is a measure of how far south the Japanese had infiltrated that within fifteen minutes—perhaps one or two thousand yards—the attack faulted when the lead platoon came under fire from Red Hill on its right and Notting Hill on its left. MacAuley sent back a message to Captain Walter Royal to take his HKVDC men and part of "C" Company, which was in the reserve, pass through the Rifles, clear Notting Hill and provide covering fire for the men attacking Red Hill.

Neither Royal nor any of his men had ever been on Notting Hill. Still, having been shoved out of position after position, these men were eager for a fight in which they were the aggressors. Over the last few days of battle, they had learned a thing or two. Regulations be damned: they threw away the yellow fatigues that made them stand out and discarded their bulky respirators, which, because they were strapped to their stomachs, meant that even when they went to ground they still presented a rather too high target.* Rifleman Ken Cambon and the others crawled up the hill as Japanese bullets whizzed past them a few inches away.

A few mortars or an artillery barrage would have been useful, Cambon thought, as he inched forward on his belly, his face so deep in the dirt that he later joked that he had eaten his way up the hill. More than once the scrub vegetation on the hill had to choose sides: serve as a shelter behind which the Rifles and Volunteers could hide or catch fire from the Japanese tracer bullets. As they neared the top of the first summit (like many hills in Hong Kong, Red Hill has two summits), the machine gun fire became so heavy that Cambon almost despaired. Fate in the form of another catchwater intervened, and Cambon's section was able to take a position behind it for a few moments.

They may have been out of the line of fire, but they were not safe. A grenade landed near Cambon, who kicked it a mere six feet away. Terrified of the coming explosion, he pushed his face into the soft ground. One minute passed. Another passed and a nausea born of terror rose in his chest. Then the spell broke, and Cambon realized it "was a dud."[3]

---

* The ditching of authorized kit deeply upset Wallis, who incorrectly places this incident on 20 December.

. . .

Several hundred yards to Cambon's rear, the attack on Red Hill quickly turned into a disaster. Moments after it began, Japanese gunners killed several men and wounded HKVDC Captain A. Penn, his second in command, a sergeant and a number of other men.

Forty-five minutes after the advance began, and thirty minutes after it was stymied in the col between Red and Notting hills, MacAuley called for reinforcements from "D" Company, which held the position of main guard of the attack, for his left flank (Notting Hill).* As if to provide fodder for Wallis's complaints about the Rifles' communications, no one bothered to inform the commander of "B" Company that the Volunteers' "D" Company would soon be moving through their lines.

"Liaison is crucial on any battlefield, and more so when the enemy engages in infiltration tactics, so that an attack can come from any direction," says historian Bill Rawling. "By not sending an officer to warn that Canadian troops would be coming through their lines, MacAuley risked a fratricidal battle, with all its possible consequences to cohesion and morale." Fortunately, this clash did not occur, but only because "D" Company was soon engaged in fighting for its life on these hills.

. . .

MacAuley waited for reinforcements, and Lieutenant William Fry led No. 12 Platoon in a frontal assault on Red Hill. Lieutenant

---

* The attack's structure was:

Advanced Guard:	No. 1 Coy HKVDC
Vanguard:	B Coy RR (less two platoons)
Main Guard:	D Coy RR
Main Body:	Battalion HQ Coy, C Coy RR, and No. 2 Coy HKVDC

Bompas led another on a flanking attack on the hill. Sergeant Shorty Pope motioned for Cambon to get out from behind the concrete wall and start moving up Notting Hill again. After clambering to the summit, his face still all but in the dirt, Cambon looked up and saw seventy-five Japanese soldiers, likely commanded by First Lieutenant Hiroshidi Yamada, about fifty yards away, shooting at a number of stragglers on the road.

The moment had a surprising theatricality about it. The Japanese soldiers were smaller than Cambon expected, and at the back of their caps hung a flap that recalled the French Legionnaires he'd seen on posters of the film *Beau Geste*. Cambon was also struck by Yamada, who, in place of the excellent camouflage worn by his troops, wore a white shirt and encouraged his men by waving his sword about.

Pope knew he did not have much time. Silently he arranged his two Bren gunners and his ten riflemen. A sheen of sweat lay between the barrels of their Lee-Enfields and their left hands, which grasped the guns by the wooden handhold twenty-one inches from the trigger guard. Breathing hard both from the exertion and the tension, each rifleman tried to steady himself so he could look calmly through his gun's sight and pick out a target, always recalling what was drilled into them in basic training: aim for the body. Like the vast majority of soldiers who fired their weapons in battle, they missed. "Our first burst took them completely by surprise and they scattered for shelter as our bullets raised clouds of dust. We kept firing as the [thirty-three] survivors fled down the other side of the hill."[4] Notting Hill was in Canadian hands by around noon.

. . .

Different parts of "D" Company attacked Bridge Hill from slightly different directions. Corporal Bob Barter's platoon climbed up in a skirmish formation. Barter's commander, Lieutenant Breakey, chose this organization, which places each man six feet apart from the one to his right, because it would make it more difficult for Japanese gunners to find their marks.

Shortly after MacWhirter's No. 18R Platoon crested the hill, the Japanese ran toward a white cottage some distance down the side of the hill. Though he did not know how to pull the pin and throw a hand grenade, MacWhirter gathered up several grenades and followed Lance-Sergeant Lance Ross. At the edge of the hill, the young Rifleman handed the grenades to Ross, who threw them at the retreating Japanese. At one point, MacWhirter and Rifleman Raynald Murphy noticed a little way down the hill a fallen Japanese soldier "screeching and yelling in agony."

As explosions rocked the hillside, Murphy moved toward the fallen enemy soldier. When Murphy reached him, he knelt to examine him. In an instant, the injured man rolled over and pulled his sword. "He killed Raynald with one stroke of his sword," recalls MacWhirter.[5]

As Henry Lyons neared the top of Bridge Hill, rifle and machine gun fire forced his platoon to go to ground. Behind Bren gunfire and some well-placed grenades, the Canadians advanced, albeit slowly, making use of what scrub cover there was and a few depressions that were just deep enough to ensure that Japanese bullets fired low over the ground were just too high.

At one point, Rifleman Leverette Trites and a few other men took shelter in a hole partially surrounded by shrubbery. The Japanese were behind a nearby bluff. Thinking that he might be able to get a shot off when the Japanese appeared on the bluff, Trites peered over the lip of the pothole. "He got his head up a little way, and they put a bullet through his neck. He was dead before his body fell back into the hole," recalls Lyons.

Although "D" Company had control of Bridge Hill sometime before noon, the agony of battle continued. For some, like Corporal Little Jo Fitzpatrick, the end came quickly when a shell turned him into pink mist.[6] Others, like seventeen-year-old John Duguay, a bandsman/stretcher-bearer, tried to ignore the bullets and explosions and focused their attention on caring for shattered bodies.

Unlike the infantrymen who hugged the dirt, Duguay worked on bended knee. Of one wounded soldier, who would not have long to live, Duguay recalls, "He was alive, but a grenade shredded his leg. I ripped open the dark green waxed paper that protected the bandage and began winding it around his leg. His blood was flowing pretty freely and before I'd managed to wind it around his leg and over the stump, my hands were covered in blood."

As the battle petered out, the men who conquered the hill, and who had had mighty little sleep in days, fought to stay awake and tried to ignore their hunger. "But," says Lyons, "worse was the fact that we could not get water. Nothing means half as much to you as water."*

. . .

Through the last part of the battle for Bridge Hill, Wallis paced nervously outside his headquarters at Stone Hill. As Lieutenant Frank Power led a charge that earned him a Military Cross, Wallis, the author of the attack, looked north to the hills, "worried over the terrible slowness and lack of training of the 'D' Bn." When he saw the Canadians on the crest of the hill, his worries lessened. Still, at 1:00 p.m., calling Maltby to tell him that the Rifles had secured the three

---

* A few hundred yards to the east, Cambon realized that filling his water bottle with rum was not as good an idea as it had seemed at the time, for after his buddies had each had a slug, the bottle was empty.

hills, his words damned with faint praise: "They were really doing their best that day at any rate and [are] fighting gamely."

.   .   .

The clearing of Red, Bridge, and Notting hills opened the way for the Royal Rifles to try to reach the "Y" crossroad just south of Tai Tam Tuk Reservoir. Their orders were to take the left spur that leads to the Wong Nei Chong Gap. The lead units had not advanced far before a machine gun at the crossroads stopped them again. Several well-placed mortar shell stunned the Japanese gunners, who were routed by a rain of hand grenades, fire from a Bren gunner aboard a universal carrier and volleys fired by thirty Dominion soldiers.

The enemy were still nearby, however, for as the Canadians approached the crossroads, they could hear Japanese being spoken from the direction of the nearby pumping station. Hoping that these troops had neither mortars nor secreted machine guns, MacAuley's troops turned left at the crossroads, moving ever closer to the Wong Nei Chong Gap.

.   .   .

As the Rifles moved forward through the afternoon, the mood in Chaplain Laite's and Captain Bush's shelters in the Wong Nei Chong Gap worsened. Since no relief had arrived, the men surmised that Hook's attack had failed. They also knew nothing of Sutcliffe's order to garrison Mount Cameron, but a look at the map would have suggested that with the Wong Nei Chong Gap lost, Mount Cameron was the next place to try to establish a defensive line. Had they known that at 2:30 p.m. two companies of Japanese soldiers had occupied Mount Nicholson, they might have despaired. The presence of such a large body of enemy troops at the top of the gap indicated not only that no relief could be expected from that quarter but also that a new wave would soon break on them.

Conditions also continued to worsen. Mortar blasts rocked them and machine gun fire kept up a sickening drumbeat. Lieutenant Alexander Blackwood, the officer to whom Bush had turned over command of the Grenadiers' "D" Company's headquarters, had been wounded.* Shot by shot, his stock of ammunition dwindled. Each bite of food and drink of water or juice from a tin of fruit brought them closer to exhausting these supplies. The moans of the wounded, the sight of dried blood and oozing wounds, the stink of unwashed bodies and the smell of decaying flesh made all the more putrid by the unseasonable heat of this last Sunday of Advent filled the air.

.   .   .

Late in the afternoon, coders in the Battle Box were busy with three important signals. The first message, from Generalissimo Chiang Kai-shek, arrived at 4:00 p.m., just about the time MacAuley's advanced guard was stopped by three light tanks blocking the road near the dam at the southern end of Tai Tam Tuk Reservoir.† The message flatly contradicted Admiral Chan's claim made two days earlier that sixty thousand Chinese troops were ready to fall on the Japanese rear. Given that the Japanese had managed to seize close to half the island and shatter his defence plans in just over two days, Maltby's heart must have sunk when he read that

---

* During the night of 18/19 December, Blackwood earned a Military Cross for risking his life to retrieve (along with Private William Morris) Lieutenant-Colonel R.D. Walker, OBE, MC, of the Hong Kong Volunteer Defence Corps, who had been shot in both legs a short distance from the shelter. Blackwood died in the early hours of 21 December when a Grenadier sentry shot him while he was trying to slip away from a Japanese patrol.

† Chiang Kai-shek commanded the Chinese armies allied to Britain and the United States.

Chiang now said his men could not begin operations before 1 January, more than a week away. More promising were the words that "it was hoped" that twenty bombers would operate at once against Japanese aerodromes. However, Chiang, who was a master at leading British and American leaders by their noses, never did order either a land or air attack on the Japanese besieging Hong Kong.

At 5:00 p.m., Governor Young signalled the Admiralty with a summary of the baleful military situation. As the decoders in London read that the Japanese held key positions in the hills, a force commanded by a staff officer named Norizakia reoccupied Red Hill and began firing at MacAuley's rear. This action forced the major to order his men to fall back toward Stone Hill, thus surrendering all the ground Cambon, Lyons and MacWhirter had fought for and men like Trites had died for in the morning heat. Sir Mark told the War Office that the island's defence force was "rapidly approaching the point at which [the] only resistance open to us will be to hold for a short time in small pockets" and this, the governor underscored, would leave the "bulk of the fixed population [of more than 1.5 million Chinese] to be overrun." Conscious of the untold suffering this would cause, Sir Mark told London that he considered it his duty to do something that no British governor had done since Lord Cornwallis surrendered the American colonies after the defeat at Yorktown almost two centuries earlier. "If His Majesty's Government feels able to give assent please cable single word ability repetition ability."

. . .

The Battle for Hong Kong merits barely a mention in Winston Churchill's history of the Second World War. Perhaps charity for what Sir Mark suffered while in prison prevented Churchill from pointing out the difference between the spirit of the governor's signal and the one the prime minister sent at about the same time:

> The eyes of the world are upon you. We expect you to resist to the end. The honour of the empire is in your hands. Ends. In spite of the conditions you and General Officer Commanding [Maltby] are facing, the difficulties of which are clearly understood, His Majesty's Government's desire is that you should fight it out as in the Prime Minister's message.

Had he considered the battle for Hong Kong in detail, Churchill would have found his spirit of resistance in both British Major Robert Templer, who took command of the Repulse Bay Hotel after Major Young was ordered to take his men forward, and the British, Indian and Canadian soldiers in the field.

The diminutive Templer arrived at the Repulse Bay Hotel with orders to attack north from the hotel toward the Wong Nei Chong Gap. Amazingly, given the Grenadiers' failures to break into the Gap from the east, his orders ended with the command to capture Jardine's Lookout. Whatever innate abilities Templer may have had, the one concrete difference between his attack and the earlier ones undertaken by the Canadians was his access to trucks, which, he hoped, would get them quickly to their jumping-off point.

Between the time when Templer arrived and when part of the Rifles' "A" Company clambered onto the trucks, a Japanese machine gunner sighted his gun on the hotel's entrance. As soon as Templer's lead armoured car left the hotel, a well-aimed burst of fire ripped through the radiator and two of the car's tires. Subsequent bursts knocked out another carrier and an ammunition truck. Templer likely said something more earthy than "A good start!" when he climbed into the back of the first truck carrying the Rifles, which, along with the other trucks, then sped safely past the gunner. As

1. Rifleman Bill MacWhirter in September 1941, at age seventeen.

2. Lance Corporal Charles Dallain and Rifleman Jean-Paul Dallain in October 1941, at age nineteen.

3. Company Sergeant Major John Osborn (Winnipeg Grenadiers). Osborn earned Canada's first Victoria Cross of the Second World War on the afternoon of 19 December when, after leading his men in a retreat from Mount Butler, he threw himself on a grenade and saved the lives of several officers.

4. Lieutenant Colonel Home, commander of the Royal Rifles of Canada. Home clashed bitterly with Brigadier Cedric Wallis, the British officer who commanded East Brigade. In the brigade's war diary, Wallis writes that he would have liked to have had Home and his senior officers shot.

5. British Major General Arthur E. Grasset. In September 1941, the Canadian-born Grasset, who had just finished a three-year posting as General Officer Commanding China, convinced the British government to ask Canada to send two battalions to strengthen the Hong Kong garrison.

6. Major C. Lyndon, Brigadier J. Lawson (Commander of "C" Force), Colonel Patrick Hennessey and Captain Howard Bush aboard HMTS *Awatea* en route to Hong Kong. Only Lyndon and Bush would survive the Battle for Hong Kong.

7. Royal Rifles debarking HMTS *Awatea* in Hong Kong.

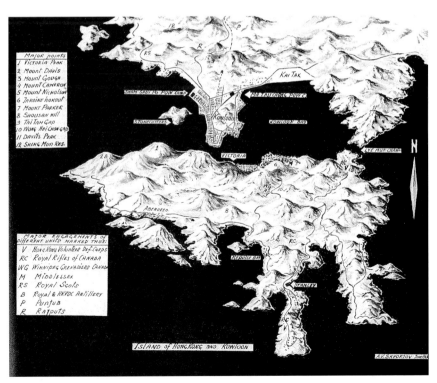

8. Topographical map of Hong Kong.

9. Lyemun Passage. Colonel Tanaka's 229th battalion crossed Hong Kong Bay at this narrow point.

Bde H.Q. Shelters

Brig Lawson's
body found here

Mount Nicholson

Police Station

Kitchen Shelters
used as hospital

Ammunition Storage

Company Shelters
held by "D"coy Wpg Gren

10. Wong Nei Chung Gap. The absence of trees on these hills meant that the Canadians were easy targets for Japanese machine guns and artillery.

11. Ty Tam Tuk Reservoir.

12. A house in Victoria after being hit by a bomb.

13. Eucliffe Castle. Leslie Canivet and several other Canadian Army Ordnance Corpsmen escaped from this building after the Japanese attacked it near dawn on 23 December 1941.

14. Colonel Tanaka overlooking Aldrich Bay.

15. Silesian Mission where Captain Banfill's medical station was located. On the morning of 19 December 1941, numerous war crimes occurred here.

16. St. Stephen's College. Royal Rifles Private Sydney Skelton and Chaplain James Barnett were among those who survived the Japanese attack on the makeshift hospital on 15 December 1941. Colonel Tanaka's men gang raped and murdered the Chinese and British nurses they found here.

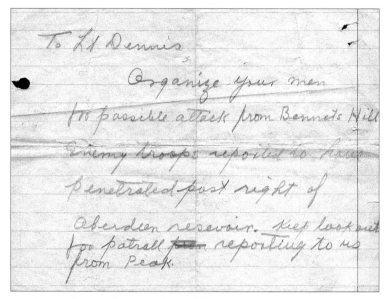

17. Message from Major Kenneth Baird (Winnipeg Grenadiers) to Lieutenant Elmer Dennison, ordering him to prepare for an attack from Bennet's Hill.

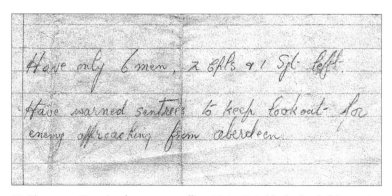

18. Lieutenant Dennison's response, telling Major Baird he had only "6 men, 2 captains and 1 sergeant left."

they drove by burned-out trucks and the bloated bodies of Royal Navy ratings killed in a failed attack the day before, an eerie silence fell over the Canadians.

Templer's force arrived safely at the police station a mile and a half up the Repulse Bay Road from the hotel, and not far from the Ridge where Major Young had sent two platoons earlier in the day. He was able to reach that far into Japanese-held territory, however, not because of his trucks' speed but because the Japanese let him; a postwar report written for the United States' Department of Defence suggests they held off in order to draw Templer's force into an ambush.

However much Templer wanted to continue, the odds were against him. First, it was getting dark, and while it is true that the infantry had trained for night attacks, the troops at his disposal did not know the terrain over which they were to attack. Second and more importantly, Templer had no idea of the number of troops holding the Wong Nei Chong Gap. Had he known that there were only two battalions in it, he might have trusted to the element of surprise. But just as he was about to decide, he received word that two of his Bren guns were jammed. Without the fire from these two guns, any attack would be suicidal. He ordered his men to withdraw to Altamira, a house opposite the Ridge on Deep Water Bay, while he returned to the Repulse Bay Hotel, where he called Maltby to tell him the attack had been aborted.

· · ·

In the minutes leading up to his 11:00 p.m. meeting with Wallis, Home—who, in addition to being the ranking officer of the Royal Rifles, had been since the deaths of Brigadier-General Lawson and Colonel Patrick Hennessy the commander of "C" Force—contemplated what the Rifles had endured in the fifty hours since the

Japanese invaded. On 19 December, after the Japanese cut through the Rajputs, the Rifles had been shoved back from Sai Wan to Tai Tam and they'd bled on Mount Parker. On the 20th, they attacked the Wong Nei Chong Gap. After fewer than six hours' sleep, on this day, 21 December, they had attacked Red, Notting and Bridge hills. "A" Company, which had been at the Repulse Bay Hotel, was divided: two platoons had taken shelter in a house on the Ridge, part was at Altamira and part was still at the hotel.

No doubt still smarting from the dressing down Wallis had given the Canadians before dawn, Home knew that his brigadier would likely refuse his request to speak to either Sir Mark or Maltby about how Wallis used (and, in Home's and Sutcliffe's view, misused) the Canadians. Legally, Home did not require Wallis's permission. Unlike his fellow lieutenant-colonels, he served not as a British officer but as a Canadian officer under the Visiting Forces Act (Canada). Wallis may not have liked it—indeed, he might not even have known about it—but the Act put Home in a unique position. Wallis was the unit's field commander, but as the senior Canadian officer, Home alone was directly responsible to Ottawa for the well-being of Canadian troops. Home was unaware that Wallis had already concluded that Home "had not the drive and determination to fight a losing battle" and that Wallis considered him something of a coward for remaining "under cover" while his men advanced.[*]

Home may not have required Wallis's permission, but he respected the chain of command. Exactly what each said went unrecorded, though the general tenor can be determined from the mere fact that Home asked for Wallis's permission and from the resumé in Wallis's war diary, which ends with these words: "I wondered at

---

[*] Taken with Wallis's criticism of Home waiting at his headquarters to hear how his men were doing, one must ask how Wallis expected Home to be in each part of an advance. On 20 December, three different companies were engaged in three different places.

the time whether it [the meeting] was all a bad dream. Could a Canadian officer and one who looked a gentleman, have made what seemed to me to be a dishonourable request?"

According to Wallis, Home wanted to tell Sir Mark that "his Bn was dead beat and he felt further resistance would only result in the wasting of valuable Canadian lives." Wallis took great offence at "talk of 'Canadian lives' being wasted—as if they were of higher value than those of other members of H.M. forces." Although Wallis does not say so, clearly the reason Home asked for permission to speak to the governor was because he did not believe that Wallis fully appreciated what the Rifles had been through and the sacrifices they had made. Wallis tried to dissuade Home, even saying "it would be disloyal to speak direct[ly] to His Excellency and not first inform his G.O.C. [General Officer Commanding] Major General Maltby."

Given that they were officers in the middle of a battle and that their trade was making quick decisions, Wallis's reported response is curious, to say the least. He told Home that he "had always found it best to rest and have a sleep before acting on a big problem not of any urgency." It is also hard to understand how this response could have satisfied Home, for the whole point of his complaint was that Wallis did not understand the urgency of the situation confronting the Rifles. Equally strange is Wallis's statement that "Home was sent to rest. It was clear that he was physically and mentally exhausted." The meeting ended with Home withdrawing his request.[*]

. . .

---

[*] A half-hour after the meeting with Home ended, Wallis ordered the Rifles on the Ridge to withdraw to Overbays, where they joined a group belonging to the Royal Canadian Ordnance Corps that had taken shelter there.

It took the Admiralty seven hours to respond to Sir Mark's message. The word "ability" did not occur in the message once, let alone twice. Churchill's message to fight on stood. The hard-nosed officers at the Admiralty, however, were less concerned with rhetorical flights of fancy and fighting on than with denying what they could to the Japanese. They ordered Maltby to turn his guns on the remaining oil installations and destroy them.

CHAPTER 11

"My Sergeant Was Wounded and Bleeding"

The Battle for Stanley Mound
22 December 1941

There is a hill in Flanders,
Heaped with a thousand slain,
Where the shells fly night and noontide
And the ghosts that died in vain,—
A little hill, a hard hill
To the souls that died in pain.
—EVERARD OWEN, "THREE HILLS"

For a few moments after his eyes fluttered open at dawn on 22 December, Rifleman Ken Cambon remained somewhat disoriented. As he groped to consciousness, he heard only an ominous quiet in the house where he and his buddy Joe had taken shelter the night before. Clean sheets caressed his body, which lay on a proper bed.

The two Riflemen broke the quiet as they pulled on their damp clothes, grabbed their rifles and ran downstairs. Their worry about catching hell for leaving their platoon turned to dismay when they could not find the old Chinese woman who had given them some whisky and orange soda, a few crackers and a can of condensed milk before showing them to the clean beds. Dismay turned to terror when, running toward the gate in the yard, a light tank rounded a bend in the road. They dove into a catchwater just as the gunner atop the tank opened up.

Running down a catchwater in Hong Kong may have been "a hell of a place to die," but, Cambon noted to his surprise, he felt little of the fear he had experienced on Red Hill the day before. He knew that soon the tank would be close enough to fire over the lip of the catchwater, and fully expected to be hit any second. Then he heard the ripping sound of a Vickers gun, which stopped the Japanese tank dead.

The Middlesex machine gunner, who had been covering the retreat of Cambon's platoon, was blunt: "Where the fuck have you stupid fuckers been?"[1] Joe mollified him by giving him the half a bottle of Scotch he grabbed before leaving the house.

. . .

Daylight also brought an end to Bush's old headquarters, now commanded by Captain Robert Philip. At dawn, a two-inch shell blew in the doors and steel window of the shelter, driving shrapnel into Grenadier John Gunn's back, buttocks and testicles; he would die in agony from septic shock. An hour later, two small parties made a break for it; both managed to get through but suffered casualties. At 7:00 a.m., his ammunition gone, Philip dragged his twice-wounded body up the steps to wave the white flag as Laite threw the men's guns and bayonets out the window. He wanted to be able to truthfully answer no when the Japanese asked if there were any arms in the shelter, which held thirty-seven severely wounded men.

Laite planned to stay with the wounded men. The Japanese had other plans, though; after searching him, they took him to an inter-

preter. The emperor-worshipping officer was less than impressed
with Laite's official or religious status, which the padre tried to
establish by showing him his field dressings and Bible. Nor was he
impressed with the niceties of the Geneva Convention; he ripped
the list of wounded from Laite's hand. The officer was impressed,
however, when Laite gave the wounded men water before he drank
some himself.

Fearing the Japanese would massacre the wounded, Laite urged
them, "Boys, if you *can* walk, for God's sake walk." Men swathed
in dirty bandages who for days had subsisted on a little bit of juice
and a few pieces of tinned apricot and whose only joy had been
their morning cigarettes, forced themselves, despite their injuries
and sheer exhaustion, to rise. Two Canadians and four other men
were too badly wounded to leave the shelter.

As the wounded struggled to leave the shelter, an armed guard
took Laite along the paths that led to the other shelters and made
him call out to the men to surrender. A few hundred yards from
Lawson's headquarters, Laite saw his brigadier's body, stiff with
rigor mortis and beginning to decompose. Laite's first request to
remove Lawson's identification tags was denied. In any event, as
much as Colonel Toshishige Shoji may have damned Lawson and
his men for stymying his advance into the Wong Nei Chong Gap,
Shoji apparently saw him as a worthy adversary.* Not only did Shoji
come in person to see Lawson's body, he ordered his temporary
burial "on the battle ground on which he had died so heroically."

While the victorious Japanese infantrymen amused themselves
by writing on a wall "This particular place had been captured by
the Okada Platoon," Laite returned to the shelter to care for the men
who had been unable to leave it. He gave each a little milk and some

---

* The delay caused by the Canadians prompted a 9:00 p.m. call in which Shoji was rebuked for
not keeping up with Doi's advance.

biscuits that he had found in one of the other shelters. The privates detailed to guard them shared little of Shoji's battlefield *politesse:* "They spent most of their time in what seemed to be an attempt to terrify us as well as in searching kits . . . and taking watches, rings, etc. from us," Laite recalled.

· · ·

The authors of the 8:00 a.m. communiqué that began, "It has been a relatively quiet night and our positions have been maintained," apparently did not know that the last Grenadier post in the Wong Nei Chong Gap had fallen. Thirty minutes later, Major George Trist worked his way to Mount Cameron with a Grenadier detachment and a platoon of Royal Engineers. The ravine he moved through was under such heavy fire that he had to pull his revolver to scotch an incipient mutiny by his Chinese carrying party. His efforts to place his men on a ridge near the mountain were hampered by shelling that caused a number of casualties.

At 10:00 a.m., the detachment belonging to the Royal Canadian Ordnance Corps were on the Ridge. They had been ordered to fall back at nightfall; now they successfully beat off a Japanese attack, causing heavy casualties. Around the same time, the Japanese moved on to the forward slope (southern side) of Stanley Mound and Red Hill, from where they looked down on the Canadian positions at Stone Hill and the defences of Stanley itself. At 10:30, Maltby placed Brigadier Wallis in command of Stanley Garrison with orders "to hold."

· · ·

At midday, Japanese infantrymen attacked the Rifles on Notting and Sugar Loaf hills. In short order, they evicted the Canadians and silenced three machine guns manned by the Die Hards, one at Palm Villa and two at Sugar Loaf. By taking these hills, the Japanese not only seized ground the Canadians had bled for the day before, they also broke open the defensive line Wallis had been ordered to hold just a few hours earlier.

Amid the tumult of shellfire and men running down the hill, the Canadians rallied to seal the rent in the line. Captain Walter Royal and Corporal Lorne Latimer sewed the first stitches when, after advancing through heavy fire, they got the machine gun at Palm Villa working again. Latimer did not, however, have long to relish the sound of .303 rounds firing back at the Japanese; he was killed almost as soon as Royal began firing.

A second group, including Lance-Sergeant Murray Good-enough, who at sixteen years old was probably the youngest Canadian in Hong Kong,* and Corporal Aksel Sannes raced up Sugar Loaf together while Lance-Sergeant Melvin Roberts ran up himself through a blistering barrage. Goodenough and Roberts made it to the gun but at great cost: Sannes was dead and Good-enough had been hit twice. The gun was functional, though, and they soon had it firing at the Japanese.

The thousands of rounds these two guns pumped out bought Major Bishop's men what they needed: time to regroup. Lieutenant Kenneth Strang, Company Sergeant-Major Clifford Kerrigan and Sergeant Shorty Pope organized three parties that, under the cover of the machine gun fire, took back the hills. The cost, however, was high, with four non-commissioned officers dead and seven others wounded. Wallis makes no mention of either of these actions in his 10:30 a.m. diary entry; it records, however, that he spoke to Maltby and told him that Home continued to "hold the same opinion as last night," and "he hoped however to keep 'D' Bn

---

* Goodenough was certainly the youngest NCO.

[Royal Rifles] going somehow but it was impossible to make them operate offensively."

. . .

Two thousand yards to the northeast of Sugar Loaf, Laite was again led away from the shelter that housed those too wounded to walk. Laite was taken to the Japanese regiment's new field headquarters and given two biscuits, a slice of bully beef and water. He was, however, denied permission to join the men now herded by the roadside. A few minutes later, when a Japanese non-commissioned officer came up to him and put a revolver to his side, the chaplain, whose heart had not flinched during the hours of terrible shellfire endured over the last four days, felt that his end had come. The NCO did not, however, shoot Laite. Nor did the soldiers who soon marched behind him plunge their bayonets into the back of the padre, who stumbled as he walked with his hands over his head.

Having survived the shells that burst on the high bank that ran beside the road they were on, Laite began to think, with the passage of time, that he might indeed live. His heart sank when they came upon a small group of Japanese soldiers, one of whom yelled out, "British bugger, kill him now." After a short halt, during which the NCO berated the soldier who had called for Laite's execution, Laite's captors again hurried him along the road. They soon came upon another group of soldiers who levelled their rifles at him. "Again my NCO spoke and there was a second reprieve." The NCO then led Laite to the top of a knoll, where, to Laite's surprise, he released him. Ever the gentleman, Laite gave him a smile, stuck out his hand for a handshake and thanked him. "He understood this gesture. His handshake was firm and he smiled as if to say 'the best of luck.'"

By the time Laite walked to safety, the wounded men left behind in the shelter had, in all probability, already been bayoneted.

. . .

Officer cadets are wont to talk of strategy and tactics, with the former taking pride of place. Veteran officers speak of logistics, logistics and logistics. The most important is water, which explains why the Japanese cut off the flow from Tai Tam Reservoir. The second most important is ammunition, which explains Maltby's order to Wallis to hold out as long as "ammunition and water were available."

The third logistic is food, which explains why, when possible, the Canadians ate before going into battle and why they carried iron rations in their backpacks. It also explains why, late in the morning of 22 December, Corporal John Burton of the Royal Canadian Army Signals Corps and two other men were ordered to Aberdeen after an advanced party of Japanese soldiers abandoned it to salvage ten thousand pounds of beef. The destruction that the Japanese had wrought on the picturesque seaside town shocked Burton. "The very small town was a scene of chaos and devastation. Many motor cars, riddled with bullets, had been smashed into the sides of buildings and in most cases had been burned down to the chassis. . . . There was an abundance of blood on the streets."

Soldiers under the command of a British officer had gathered the dead from one section of town together. When Burton and the other Canadians left, the bodies—charred or shot—lay in a clearing waiting for burial as shells fell among them.

. . .

Throughout the day, pressure built on the Repulse Bay Hotel. In the early afternoon, heavy fire forced a platoon on a ridge a few hundred yards north of it to fall back. Even more alarmingly, Japanese echoed into the end of the drainage culvert in which the hotel's guests sheltered during the day.

By mid-afternoon, the committee running the hotel called Maltby to say that the hotel could no longer be used as refuge for civilians and a fort. Maltby wanted it to remain part of the forward defence of Stanley. Aware of the Japanese atrocities in Kowloon, he proposed moving the civilians. The committee, led by Jan Marsman, was not impressed with the idea of a nighttime withdrawal. "How are the women and their babies and young children going to get from the sands of the beach to barges?"[2] Maltby reluctantly agreed that after dark the Canadian and British soldiers would pull out, and that at daybreak the hotel would surrender.

. . .

As Laite made his way to Happy Valley and from there, disguised under a long Chinese robe, to the Royal Navy Hospital at Wan Chai, large parts of Wallis's defensive line broke apart under the repeated hammer blows of the Shoji *Butai*. At 3:00 p.m., while under heavy artillery and mortar fire, HKVDC Captain D. Strellet's attempt to surrender his position on the Ridge failed when his white flag was shot out of his hand. Lieutenant-Colonel R. Macpherson's surrender attempt cost him his life. An hour later, the Japanese swarmed over Violet Hill.

The blows also fell on the Rifles at Stanley Mound. "B" Company had been dug in on the mound since the day before. Despite heavy mortar and machine gun fire, they were reinforced by, among others, Rifleman Jean-Paul Dallain, who after becoming detached from his company on 20 December had been with Major Parker's "D" Company. "We were taking supplies and rations up to the Canadians on Stanley Mound when I saw, coming down the hill, Sergeant Conway, my sergeant, who was wounded and bleeding. I asked him where the boys were and he told me. Nobody really knew where I was, so I didn't have to go up the hill. But I figured, 'If I'm going to die, I might as well die with people I know,'" recalls Dallain. His resoluteness stood him in good stead, for once he got to the top of the hill, Dallain spent hours hugging the ground as Japanese shells and mortars burst around him and men he had grown up knowing: Privates Smitty Smith, Lorne Newall and Phil Gallie.

Shooting from shallow foxholes scratched in the hard earth or from behind a few rocks, the Canadians drove the attackers back. Toward dusk, Smith told Dallain that he was going to get the cigarettes he had left in his kit a short distance away. "Right after he lay down next to me on the upper slope of the hill," recalls Dallain, "Smitty got up on his haunches to have a better look ahead. A second later he fell just dead as they come."

Immediately after Smith fell, the Japanese opened up a ferocious mortar and machine gun barrage that pinned the Canadians down while the attacking force moved close to the hill. Their coordination was excellent; explosions of shells and mortars gave way to those of hand grenades thrown by the Japanese vanguard.

Despite these smaller explosions, Dallain remembers the men around him rising, shouldering their rifles, peering through their sights and squeezing their triggers. Then, with a well-practised motion, each pulled his right forefinger out from the trigger guard as he lifted his right arm so that it was level with his right shoulder. A short movement backward allowed him to grasp the Lee-Enfield's bolt, which was about eight inches from his nose. To eject the spent casing, each man pushed the bolt a quarter turn to the left and then pulled it back. The push forward forced a new bullet into the gun's chamber; it was locked into place by pulling the bolt down to the right. Each man then slid his arm forward, stopping only when his finger again lay on the trigger. In about thirty seconds of firing, he would have exhausted the ten bullets in his clip.

Dallain did not join his comrades in firing, but he wasn't frozen by fear. Rather, he was concerned about what would come next:

a close-order bayonet fight. "I had decided during bayonet practice," recalls the five-foot-four, 117-pound Dallain, "that I was not
going to go anywhere fighting with a bayonet because whoever I
fought was bound to be as heavy as I was. So, I made sure to keep
my rounds until I was able to get the first Japanese who came within
bayonet range."

As their ammunition began to run low and the Japanese moved
closer, some of the Rifles started throwing hand grenades. The
assault momentarily shuddered but soon recovered as the Canadian
supply of grenades was exhausted. "They kept coming. Lieutenant
[James] Ross was killed and they kept pushing us further back,"
recalls Dallain. Sergeant Emile Bernard, who had been severely
injured, earned a Military Medal for "directing his platoon in con-
spicuously fearless and efficient manner . . . under heavy fire."[3]

The weight of the Japanese assault was too much, and the word
came to withdraw; the command had to be yelled across open
spaces from one clump of men to another. Where the distance was
too great, runners risked their lives carrying the order. Dallain and
his comrades ran when they could, but they were not routed. When
they had a chance, they turned and fired, trying to provide some
cover for their comrades. "We knew it was damn prudent to get the
hell out of there and down the hill as the dark settled in." Dallain's
section ended up in a pillbox some distance beyond the southern
slope of the hill; only then did Dallain find that the wetness in his
pants was caused by a bullet that had punctured his water bottle.[*]

.   .   .

---

* In his entry for 1400 hrs, Wallis summed up this fight churlishly: "About this time P.B. 27
opened fire on enemy advancing from Red Hill and Bridge Hill direction with some effect. Unfortunately, men of 'D' Bn [Royal Rifles] who were unused to overhead fire or fire past their
flanks, began running off the Eastern portion of Stone Hill and the enemy were able to make
further small advances."

At 6:15 p.m., Wallis ordered his signaller to connect him to Maltby so he could discuss his plan to counterattack at first light. It was not a difficult job. The only telephone line still functioning connected Wallis to Fortress Headquarters. To be fair, trying to push the Japanese back was Wallis's only option. What is surprising, however, is that he again planned to use the Royal Rifles, even though, as Cambon and others discovered when they withdrew there, there remained at Stanley a host of British soldiers available.

Cambon had seen the writing on the wall. In the last few hours, the Japanese had isolated the Repulse Bay Hotel and pushed Wallis's defensive line so far south that it now ran just a few hundred yards north of his headquarters. North of the Wong Nei Chong Gap, which the Japanese held, the Japanese had begun pushing west toward Victoria and its teeming streets. At 4:00 p.m., mortar fire forced the Middlesex Regiment to withdraw its headquarters from Leighton Hill. This action opened another route into the Wan Chai Gap, where the Grenadiers were concentrated. Throughout the day, Major Trist's positions near Mount Cameron was heavily shelled, mortared and dive-bombed.

Cambon knew he had the courage to fight on. However, he also knew that doing so was worthless.* Fate had cheated him, but not of military glory. As Cambon contemplated a premature death

---

* In neither Ottawa nor London did the prime ministers agree. Prime Minister Mackenzie King's telegram read: "All Canada has been following hour by hour the progress of events at Hong Kong. Our thoughts are of each and every one of you in your brave resistance of the forces that are seeing to destroy the world's freedom. Your bravery is an inspiration to us all. Our Country's name and its honour have never been more splendidly upheld."

After declaring that "there must be no thought of surrender," Churchill's telegram ended by saying: "The enemy should be compelled to expend the utmost life and equipment. There must be vigorous fighting in the inner defences, and, if need be, from house to house. Every day that you are able to maintain your resistance you help the Allied cause all over the world, and by a prolonged resistance you and your men can win the lasting honour which we are sure will be your due."

from a Japanese bayonet or years rotting in a POW camp, he didn't regret the great books he had not read or the symphonies he had not heard. Rather, the eighteen-year-old "thought of how few girls I had laid."[4]

.   .   .

Squaring the Japanese account of their attack on Trist's positions (held by a mixture of Grenadiers and Royal Engineers fighting as infantry) with the Canadian and British records is not easy. Both report fierce fighting. According to Colonel Doi, every officer of No. 4 Company, which attacked Trist's right, was killed or wounded. As well, Doi reported that during the attack on Mount Cameron, "the enemy bombarded us from our rear, just as they had in our attack on Mount Nicholson, and they harassed our forward elements to a considerable extent." Doi was wrong about where the guns shelling his men were located; the 9.2-inch guns were some six miles to his right front at Stanley. The harassing fire to which he refers came from Middlesex machine gunners at Little Hong Kong, who fired twenty thousand rounds.

Both Doi's and Trist's accounts begin with runners bringing the commanders information about the location of the enemy. Doi's story tells of one of those odd moments in war. After cresting the eastern slope of Mount Cameron, an Imperial Japanese soldier stepped away from his comrades into the clearing, undid his pants and with the sound of his urine splashing on the ground heard someone speaking English on the other side of the shrubbery.

Trist's runner brought word that at 8:00 p.m., a listening post heard "a sound like some digging on the lower forward slope of [Mount] Cameron," prompting Trist to send a machine gun crew forward. A few minutes later, the report Trist heard was not a spoken one but the sound of a Japanese machine gun firing into his right flank. Then came word of movement on that same flank. It is a measure of the seriousness of the situation that Trist dipped into his small supply of flares. But if the harsh light burning in the sky helped any soldiers, they weren't Trist's: the Japanese machine guns tore into them.

A half-hour later, the staccato sound of the machine gun on Trist's right was joined by another heavier gun, and the explosions of the mortars and artillery shells that showered his position with thousands of shrapnel balls and red-hot metal splinters. Somehow, through all of this, Trist heard the sickening sound of machine bullets hitting his own headquarters, from—of all directions—the south.

As his men took shelter where they could, Trist ventured out into the hailstorm. He had not gone far when he heard the panting of a runner heading toward him. Between gasps, the Grenadier said that the Japanese had broken through their forward position. Trist ran back to his headquarters, where he ordered Sergeant Cecil Whalen forward with a section of his No. 7 Platoon.

No record exists of Whalen's advance. His men must have fought ferociously, for Doi reports that the "enemy counter attacked with a strength of about 400" when, in reality, Whalen attacked with a dozen men. A few moments later, word came that the Japanese had overrun the Royal Engineers' position on Trist's right and that they were now using a captured light machine gun and two-inch mortar as they worked their way along the rear of the right flank in an attempt to encircle the Grenadiers.

Trist, the war diarist for the Winnipeg Grenadiers, later wrote, "Runners were sent to the right platoons instructing them to withdraw [west to the Wan Chai Gap], evacuate casualties, destroy all guns and equipment they could not take out, and leaving a covering party who were to withdraw as soon as the Company was clear of their forward positions." The same Lieutenant Prendergast who forty hours earlier had tried and failed to reach Jardine's Lookout now commanded the last covering party. The lieutenant was so severely wounded that he had to be carried to safety, first to the headquarters in Wan Chai Gap and, after the decision was made to abandon it, to Mount Gough a mile further west.

. . .

After dark, the soldiers at the Repulse Bay Hotel prepared to evacuate. To prevent panic, the civilians were not told that by morning a white flag would be flying over the hotel. Only after the civilians had gone to sleep did the soldiers destroy anything that could be of military value and, hoping to prevent a drunken rampage, hundreds of bottles of booze.

Because he knew the terrain, Lieutenant Proulx volunteered to lead the first batch of 250 soldiers out of the drainage culvert and toward Stanley. Even though he had his men take off their boots to lessen the noise as they walked through the tunnel, their backpacks and guns clanked against it, causing loud echoes that Proulx feared would spill out onto the beach and alert the Japanese. Nor was the tunnel free of hazards in the dark, such as small piles of bricks over which men would trip, making more noise as they tumbled down.

At one point Proulx tripped over some bricks and stopped himself from falling on his face by quickly extending his right arm. Despite the need for haste, he did not immediately get up. Surrounded by darkness, threatening echoes and the breathing of men, he felt a small piece of metal under his hand that demanded attention. "My fingers traced it and I recognized the shape. It was a crucifix," Proulx remembered. The discovery made the blackness that enveloped them not quite so dark.

As soon as Proulx rose, he turned to the soldier behind him, a French Canadian, and "pressed the grimy little crucifix into his hand. *'Touche ça!'*" he whispered. A kind of shiver ran through the tunnel as the "crucifix was passed back from man to man." The men had been ordered to be silent, but they could not be. Their whispered prayers could be heard even over the clang of their equipment. When he stepped from the tunnel and found that the Japanese were not waiting for them, Proulx could not help but think their prayers had been answered.

Proulx's joy, however, was short-lived. Instead of 250 men behind him, he counted fewer than thirty. "Where are the others?" he asked the last man in the line. The soldier could only answer, "No one was behind me." After secreting the men in the mouth of the tunnel, Proulx made his way back to the hotel. He discovered when he appeared unexpectedly (and given the reason for the soldiers' departure, most unwelcomely) at the reception desk that because of the noise the men with Proulx made moving through the tunnel, Templer had decided to take his detachment out a different way. A few moments later, Proulx heard a Japanese soldier yelling just outside the hotel; looking out the window he saw three officers with swords dangling from their belts. Since his presence in the hotel would have vitiated the white flag and almost certainly cost him his life, he quickly ran back to the greenhouse and climbed down into the culvert: "Three thousand years seemed to go leisurely by before I joined my men at the end of the tunnel," he later wrote.[5]

· · ·

As Proulx ran back down the tunnel, Marsman called out to the bayonet-wielding soldiers who no longer slunk in the shadows or behind the trees: "Come in . . . Come in. No sold-iers here! No sold-iers here! [. . . .] Come in. . . Don't shoot . . . All civilians. . . . No sold-iers here." He watched as the door to the west wing of the hotel opened very slowly to about three inches; behind the door were two

Japanese soldiers, one standing and one crouching, bayonets at the ready. "Up hands!" one yelled.[6]

Elsewhere in the hotel, the Japanese bayoneted the No. 1 Boy who had brought Proulx his breakfast. Others rushed into Sister Mosey's makeshift hospital with the intent of bayoneting the wounded. Before they could get to the beds, which contained both wounded men and an Indian officer who had snuck into the hotel just ahead of the Japanese and was hidden among the wounded, Mosey stepped in front of the lead Japanese soldier and said in her most imperious tone, "You will have to kill me first before you kill them."[7]

The soldiers hesitated briefly before moving on to other prey.

CHAPTER 12

"They Walked among Them and Bayoneted a Few"

Murder at Overbays House and Eucliffe Castle
23 December 1941

Oh mother my mouth is full of stars
As cartridges in the tray
My blood is a twin-branched scarlet tree
And it runs all runs away
—CHARLES CAUSLEY, "SONG OF THE DYING GUNNER"

The dark of night protected Grenadier Major John Baille's "C" Company. Come daylight, the Japanese then moving onto Mount Cameron would be able to pour fire on his position a short distance northeast of Aberdeen. Baille's force was too small to guarantee his left flank for long. And the loss of this position would lead inexorably to the loss first of Baille's headquarters at Pok Fu Lam (two miles further west) and the vital Wan Chai Gap–Aberdeen Village Road, all but isolating the naval and other forces in Aberdeen.

But Baille's brigade commander, Colonel H.B. Rose, who at 10:00 p.m. on 20 December had replaced the late Brigadier Lawson as commander of West Brigade, realized that Baille's thirty-five men could do nothing to prevent either of these events. Nor did Rose believe that Baille had enough time before dawn to evacuate north to Mount Gough. Instead, he ordered Baille to join the navy detachment in Aberdeen. Baille agreed but in what turned out to be a prescient request, not just the unrolling of battlefield red tape, requested a written copy of the order. Circumstances precluded a written order being delivered, however. Baille then called his commander, Lieutenant-Colonel John Sutcliffe, but could not reach him.

Carrying what ammunition and food supplies they could, Baille's men withdrew. The condition of the roads stretched the two-and-a-half-mile journey out to about four hours. Baille's men did not know it, but had their commander not stood up to General Maltby—who, surprisingly, had answered the phone when Baille had called Fortress Headquarters seeking more information—they would have soon been marching back to their positions. Maltby "expressed regret" at Baille's withdrawal, which is the Grenadiers war diarist's way of saying that the general bawled out the Canadian major. After telling Baille "that no British Officer had issued any orders to [Baille] to leave his position," Maltby had ordered him to reoccupy the position at once.

Baille's next act goes some way toward dispelling the view, voiced here by Blacky Verreault but felt by many, that they could no longer rely on their officers, whom they considered "idiots."[1] Baille, a Canadian major, told the senior British commander in the theatre that he would not comply with the order because his "men were exhausted and had been without any relief for the whole period of the war." Major-General Maltby relented.

· · ·

As night merged slowly into day, the Japanese moved to deal with Overbays House and Eucliffe Castle, each of which sheltered an assortment of Allied troops. As soon as he thought it would be visible, the British sergeant at Overbays raised a white flag. He needn't have bothered.

One of the first "Knights of Bushido" to reach the house behind a fusillade of hand grenades tore down the flag. Another burst into the house spraying machine gun bullets, killing, among others, British Quartermaster-Sergeant Singleton, who commanded the house. The British interpreter who had arranged for the surrender a few hours earlier was killed by being pinned to the door with bayonets.

Whether or not the Japanese suspected that, in addition to the wounded men they had been told about, the house also sheltered able-bodied soldiers, including Royal Canadian Ordnance Corpsmen, they were not taking any chances.* After climbing the stairs, the attackers kicked in the door, sprayed machine gun fire, wounding and killing several men, and trusted to their hand grenades to finish the job. Corpsman Leslie Canivet and others threw the slow-timed hand grenades out of the window as fast as they could. One exploded before it could be thrown, blasting a piece of shrapnel into Canivet's jaw. Amid the confusion, dust and screams of pain, at least two of Canivet's comrades retrieved their rifles and, shooting from the window, killed three Japanese soldiers.

A few moments later, the Japanese poured kerosene on the ground floor and set the house alight. Canivet was able to help some other wounded men out the window before jumping to safety himself. The comrades they were unable to help began choking and burning to death, as Canivet and a few other men ran down the Repulse Bay Road and immediately came under heavy machine gun fire.

---

* The Royal Canadian Ordnance Corpsmen who had taken shelter in the house after a failed attack on the Ridge had not received the order to leave the house and make their way back to Stanley.

The only path open to them was to jump down the cliff into the sea and try to swim across Repulse Bay. From the southern end of the peninsula, they could try to make their way to Stanley. According to Canivet,

> Eight of us started out to swim; four of us reached the other side.... When we first started to swim the Japs fired on us with rifles and machine guns, but nobody was hit. When I reached the shore, I was almost completely exhausted, through loss of blood from my jaw and excitement, to say nothing of the hard job of swimming roughly two miles.

It is unknown how the Japanese attacked Eucliffe Castle, a replica of a Scottish castle with a dining room that could seat two hundred and where some fifty other British and Canadians had taken shelter.* What happened after they did, however, was made clear at Colonel Tanaka's war crimes trial. As soon as the Japanese took the mansion, and quite possibly with Tanaka present, they beat the British and Canadian soldiers. After beating British Company Sergeant-Major Hamlen, the Japanese led him with his hands tied behind his back onto a grassy bank behind Eucliffe Castle. "There were pools of blood on top of the bank with dozens of dead bodies at the bottom of the bank near the sea," testified Hamlen. As the Japanese set up Tanaka's headquarters in Eucliffe, some of his men took aim and fired at Hamlen and members of the Royal Rifles.

---

* Some time before dawn, Major Young's hundred-man force that left the Repulse Bay Hotel to attack the Ridge the previous day received orders to withdraw to the hotel. When Young saw that the Japanese had occupied it, he took his men a few hundred yards north toward Eucliffe Castle, which was already under attack. At 6:00 a.m., Young ordered his lieutenants to take their men and try to infiltrate back to Stone Hill. While most of their men made it safely, two lieutenants were killed near Stanley Mound. Others, including Collinson Blaver, swam their way to safety across Repulse Bay. Young and thirty-four other men hid out in the hulk of HMS *Thracian* until after the Christmas Day surrender.

Hamlen must have been shot first, for the other bodies "rolled down and over" him. Hamlen survived because he turned just before one of Tanaka's men pulled the trigger, so "the bullet passed through my neck above the left shoulder and came out my right cheek"; he played dead the rest of the day.

. . .

At 6:30 a.m., a half-hour after Lieutenant Proulx's exhausted, bleeding group clawed their way through the last barbed-wire entanglements around Stanley, the guns on Stanley Peninsula opened up a barrage on Stanley Mound. This barrage was the "softening up" part, as military planners call it, of an attack that was to be carried out by the Royal Rifles' "B" Company. Wallis had ordered the attack in an attempt to push the Japanese back from his forward defensive line.

The roar of the shells woke Jean-Paul Dallain. Though the shell-fire signalled another attack that he would soon be part of, Dallain had a more immediate concern: "As soon as I woke up, I realized that I was alone, apparently having missed hearing the order to move out." He reached for his boots where he had placed them just before collapsing into sleep. "Even before I saw the first boot, I knew they weren't mine," recalls Dallain. "One of the guys in our section had the worst athlete's foot; within a minute of taking a shower his feet could be smelled across the room. We all knew that a quarter of his feet were white and that he got into the regiment in the first place by walking in the dust before his medical. The son of a bitch had taken my boots. We were the same size, though, and I was able to pull his on and run to join my platoon."

. . .

As Dallain and the rest of "B" Company readied to attack Stanley Mound, the civilians at the Repulse Bay Hotel awoke to a white flag over the building and began learning the realities of being prisoners of the Japanese. The first lesson violated the Geneva Convention but was as old as war itself: Imperial Japanese soldiers pulled rings off fingers, necklaces off necks and watches off wrists.* They then marched the 150 civilians, including children as young as four and five, toward Eucliffe Castle. On the way, they saw Canadian and British soldiers bleeding to death from bayonet wounds and several incidents of torture. "The Japanese have a simple, ingenious, effortless and economical device for torturing their captives," Jan Marsman told the world in 1942:

> The arms of these . . . officers and soldiers were tied tightly together behind their backs, just above the elbows. A rope then was tied to the link binding the arms, strung up over the left shoulder, drawn through their parted lips, and pulled down under the right shoulder, where the other end also was tied to the arm link. The bonds were taut. The moment fatigue forced the victim to slump from the rigid, unnatural position in which the bonds held him, the rope cut into his lips savagely. At the expenditure of two pieces of rope, the Japanese forced their captives to torture themselves.
>
> All of the captives we saw were held together by a long rope drawn through their bound arms, from one end of the line to the other, tied to poles at each end. The soldiers were glassy-eyed, their tongues lolled and their chins dripped with blood.

At Eucliffe Castle, Tanaka hectored the prisoners: "Why that

---

* Although Japan did not sign the part of the Convention that dealt with POWs, it did sign the part that dealt with non-combatants.

man and that man no fight? The young men. Why they no soldiers? . . . What you mean civilians? . . . Japanese lady stay home."
recalled Marsman. Just before ordering them back to the Repulse
Bay Hotel, Tanaka barked out another order. A few moments later,
several soldiers joined those guarding a group of bound prisoners.
A moment later the Japanese brought their guns to their shoulders
and shot the Canadians and British soldiers. "Then they walked
among them and bayoneted a few in their death struggles." On the
way back to the hotel, a "coolie" recognized his "English master"
and, with his arms over his head, ran toward him.[2] Japanese soldiers bayoneted him twice before his body hit the hard ground.

. . .

Toward 7:00 a.m., machine guns manned by the Middlesex Regiment
joined the fusillade falling on Stanley Mound and Stone Hill a few
hundred yards to its east. It did not take long for the Japanese to get
a read on where some of this fire came from, and soon shells fell
on PB27 in Stanley, and on cottages and bungalows nearby. By the
standards of later battles like Iwo Jima, the weight of artillery fire
hardly amounted to a rounding error. Still, by the standards of the
Rifles' attacks on Red and Bridge hills, when there had been no artillery or machine gun support, the covering fire heartened Dallain,
even as the thought of the explosions tore at his heart.

"The guns were blasting the hell out of the Japanese at the top of
the hill," recalls Dallain. As the sound of the shells shrieking overhead merged with the deep rumble of the explosions shaking the
ground, Dallain could not keep himself from thinking, "We needed
the covering fire, but as I walked up the hill with my rifle held across
my arms, as much as I saw the ground in front of me, in my mind's
eye, I saw the shells blowing apart the boys, like Smitty, that we had
left on top of the mound."

The covering fire made all the difference to the attack. "At one point as we made our way up the hill, off to our left, we could see a whole platoon of Japanese soldiers taking cover from the bombardment. They didn't see us; probably, they thought, nobody would be stupid enough to try to climb the hill while the shells were still falling. Anyway, we saw them clearly and somehow lined up and we began firing at them. Some fell, some broke and ran down and then up toward the next hill. They were sitting ducks on the horizon."

By 7:30 a.m., the Canadians had retaken Stanley Mound. They held it for almost three hours. During this period, the Japanese on the northern side of the island pushed the Rajputs back from their position on the north side of Leighton Hill, thereby exposing the right flank of the Die Hards on the hill, and occupied St. Albert's Convent Hospital.*

. . .

Word that the Japanese were pushing the Rifles back down Stanley Mound led Lieutenant-Colonel Home to meet again with Brigadier Wallis. No record exists of Home's reaction to the 4:00 a.m. order that, after only a few hours' sleep, "B" Company undertake another attack. Given their meeting the previous day, though, Home must not have been pleased. Much is known about their 10:00 a.m. meeting.

While it appears that Home apparently did not again ask to speak to either Sir Mark or General Maltby, the Canadians' commander told Wallis that the battalion must be withdrawn for rest. Home laid out the numbers: his battalion had been cut by almost two-

---

* At St. Albert's, the Japanese tied up the doctors and civilian nurses. At one point the commander and chief matron were "dragged outside and a machine gun trained on them." They and the other prisoners were untied after the Japanese learned that one of their comrades "had been decently cared for" before he died (Roland, 27).

thirds, to 350 effectives; eighteen officers were dead, wounded or missing. Home then went further, advising Wallis that East Brigade, which had already been driven back four miles, should pull back still further to a line across the Stanley Peninsula. Wallis reluctantly agreed, and a few minutes later informed Maltby that by 6:00 p.m., his headquarters would be in Stanley and the line across the peninsula would be manned by the Royal Rifles.

The first part of Wallis's summary of this meeting is accurate. "O.C. 'D' Bn [Royal Rifles] insisted his unit must fall back as the men were exhausted and he felt they would fight better on the flatter ground around Stanley village." The second part, though, begins with the suggestion of mutiny and ends by coming close to making a charge of cowardice. "It was evident that whether permission was to be given or not, the position was being steadily lost. This was partly due to small withdrawals by sub-units of 'D' Bn and partly to enemy infiltration." Both charges are unjust, but within days Wallis would make them even more strongly.

. . .

Throughout the day, Japanese gunners and dive-bombers kept up a constant tattoo. High explosives pounded Leighton Hill, the centre of West Brigade's line running from the Lee Theatre at Causeway Bay over the hill itself, down Canal Road at the north end of Happy Valley Race Track. A shell killed two men at St. Stephen's College Hospital in Stanley. At one point during the morning, Chaplain Barnett and some other men took shelter in the cemetery, where explosions blasted earth, tombstones and skeletal remains out of the ground.

At North Point, a mortar operator targeted a building in which some Grenadiers manned a machine gun. Just before the Japanese soldier dropped his mortar bomb into his tube, Lance-Corporal

Ross McGavin and Lance-Sergeant William Laidlaw lessened the tension generated from the endless explosions and their dwindling food supply with some good-natured banter about what food would be like in prison camp:

> Laidlaw: Instead of hardtack, it'll be hardtack with boiled rice.
> McGavin: On the contrary. I have it on good authority that the Peninsula Hotel caters all Japanese POW camps. Seven-course meals. And that's only for breakfast.

A moment later, a mortar bomb passed through an open window and between Laidlaw's open legs before its explosion knocked him out, wounded McGavin, and killed two others.

Canadian Signalmen Gerry Gerrard, Tony Grimston and John Fairley survived a shell that hit their signals shelter in the Wan Chai Gap. Gerrard would have been in the room that was shelled had he not mistakenly entered the room next door just before the shell hit. Even at that distance, the force of the explosion blew him into still a third room, from which, as soon as he could, he ran toward the screams coming from the room he should have been in.

The screams told Gerrard that his friends were still alive, but he could hardly see them because of the brick and mortar dust that soon filled his eyes, mouth and nose. Still, he could make out a dozen or so men who were badly wounded. "I took one to the other room and patched him up as best I could," Gerrard recalls, "and went for another one. Then I heard my name called out and it was Signalman Fairley . . . I picked him up and took him into the back room. He was wounded five times. By this time an ambulance arrived and we had to pass the men through a small window, as we were still under shellfire."[*]

---

* Fairley would die of his injuries on 29 December.

A bomb dropped from a K-29 bomber hit a truck that had just left Pok Fu Lam under the command of the Royal Canadian Ordnance Corps, killing seven Chinese workers. At 4:45 p.m., shell-fire destroyed the wireless station, which left the Royal Navy's radios the only link to the outside world.

. . .

At 3:00 p.m., as a scratch force assembled by Maltby tried to push the Japanese back near the Happy Valley Race Track, some two and a half miles to the northeast, Captain Edward Walker, Major Baille's second-in-command, reported to Baille at Pok Fu Lam with orders to move "C" Company to positions some two miles east near Aberdeen Reservoir. Because these orders came from Baille's immediate superior, Lieutenant-Colonel Sutcliffe, Baille followed them. After distributing a dozen or so stragglers among his platoons, Baille ordered his tired and dirty men to move out and back to where they had withdrawn from earlier. Accompanied by two men, Baille went on ahead to recce. Safety dictated that Baille's party eschew the road and use hill trails, which lengthened the trip from one to three hours. By 8:30 p.m., the majority of Baille's men were in position.

Although Baille may not have questioned his orders, he was uneasy about his position. This unease could have only increased when Lieutenant John Park informed Baille that he had been unable to connect with Major Hook, who was supposed to be on Baille's left. After learning of this failure, Baille walked to the Aberdeen Reservoir Company Headquarters to try to reach Sutcliffe, but found that the phone line was broken. On his way back to his position, Baille met up with Grenadier Captain Njall Bardal and some eighty men. Bardal's orders were vague: "take up positions in the vicinity of Aberdeen." Bardal asked for Baille's help in deciding where.

Baille suggested that Bardal reoccupy Baille's old position, thereby securing Baille's flank. Since Lieutenant William Nugent was familiar with the Bennett's Hill position, to the east but essentially in front of Baille's Aberdeen position, he should take some men and occupy it. Bardal and Nugent agreed and before midnight were in position.

. . .

As Baille's men moved into position, Hong Kong Volunteers Company Sergeant-Major Stewart "Trudy" Begg and some Canadians who had taken refuge in a cave when they fled the Ridge decided that under cover of darkness they would make a break for it. Like Canivet, they escaped across water. Though several of the Canadians protested that they could not swim, even they agreed with their comrade who said, "I'd rather drown than get carved up by those monkeys."

Just before they rose to leave the cave, a horrifying sight stumbled into view: Company Sergeant-Major Hamlen, his face and neck covered by dried and oozing blood and caked with dirt. Despite suffering from shock, Hamlen, who had crawled away from where he'd been hiding under the bodies of dead Canadians hours earlier, joined Begg's impromptu swim team.

Perhaps alerted by the splashing Begg's men made as they swam for safety, machine gunners aided by the phosphorescence of the water were soon firing from the top of the cliff. Begg and Hamlen, who against all odds would survive at least twelve hours in the water, heard the sickening sound of machine gun bullets splash into the water amid the screams of men whose blood, for a short time, stained red the gentle waters off Hong Kong Island.

. . .

During the night, tempers again flared between Home and Wallis. At a meeting that also included Wallis's Brigade Major, Lieutenant-Colonel Wilcox, Home again demanded to speak to Maltby to tell him that "in his opinion continued resistance could only endanger further Canadian lives." Wallis countered with several arguments:

(i) We were a formidable fighting force holding a strong though badly overlooked position. A position it would be costly for the enemy to attack.

(ii) We had ammunition, food and water enough (in spite of the damage which was and could be repaired). That no other troops dreamt of surrender.

Since neither of these points swayed Home, it is hard to imagine that Wallis believed that the first part of his third argument would sway the recalcitrant Canadian commander.

(iii) Anyhow we were paid to fight and now was our chance.

The second part of this argument appeared stronger:

We were containing a strong enemy force, thereby relieving pressure on our sorely pressed comrades elsewhere on the Island.

But it too failed to move Home, who knew that Sutcliffe agreed with him.

Whether or not British soldiers thrilled to Churchill's order that "there must be no thought of surrender" is an open question. However, Home answered to Ottawa. And while there is no doubt that Home would have followed a direct order from Ottawa to stand and fight, no one who knew anything about how Canadians felt about their prime minister (Prime Minister King had been booed by Canadian troops he reviewed just a few months earlier in England) would expect Home to change his mind when Wallis said "that he felt sure the Prime Minister of Canada also expected us to fight on."* Wallis added that "to surrender in such circumstances would be an action on the part of a Unit Cmdr which the B[rigade] C[ommander] had never heard of in British history. Such an action the b.c. said he considered dishonourable."

This time Home did not budge, and Wallis called Maltby, who refused to speak to the ranking Canadian. Maltby wanted to know if the Rifles would fight. Wallis assured Maltby that he "would go on trying to make 'D' Bn do the right thing" and then again played for time: "Lt. Col Home who was in a state of physical and mental exhaustion was told to go and get some rest."

The section of Wallis's Appendix H that deals with these events expands on his critique of the Rifles. Wilcox's complaint to Wallis that the Canadians came into the officers' mess established at the Prison Club at Stanley Fort and "took the place over, rather than going to their new positions" is likely true. The Canadian gloss on this clichéd colonial insolence was, not surprisingly, a taunt at British preoccupation with rank.

Much more important is Wallis's claim that Wilcox reported that "when he had to issue orders to an officer of the R.R.C., the order and its suitability or otherwise (as they saw it) would be discussed in a sort of 'soviet' by any present at the time. If the Canadians thought the action ordered a good thing it would be obeyed. If those present did not care for it, in all probability it would not be carried out."

Technically, a "soviet" is a workers' council; the first national soviet occurred during the Russian Revolution of 1905. Almost certainly,

---

* The troops who booed King did so largely because they had been left standing in the rain waiting for him. Later, they cheered him. But the point is that *they were willing to boo him.*

Wallis did not mean to make the risible suggestion that men like Doddridge, Dallain, Lyons and Eric Maloney were "fellow travellers," that is, dupes of the Soviet Union. Rather, he likely had in mind the "soviets" that formed in the Russian Army during 1917 (prior to the Bolshevik Revolution) when the czar's soldiers simply refused to fight on. Combined with the statement that the Canadians carried out only those orders of which they approved, Wallis suggests that Wilcox faced something more than a bunch of irascible Canadians. Wallis sketches something little short of a mutiny.

It is one thing to complain that the boorish colonials ruined the tenor of an officers' mess. It is quite another to suggest that they were in violation of both the Mutiny Act of 1879 and the Articles of War. If Wallis truly believed this in 1947 when he transcribed the East Brigade War Diary and submitted it as his official record of his brigade's battle at Hong Kong, one wonders why he did not call for charges against these Canadians.* Even today, Wallis's claims remain a stain on these Canadians who travelled halfway around the world to answer Britain's call for help.

. . .

At midnight, the commander of the Grenadiers learned that Mount Cameron had been taken and the West Brigade's headquarters were falling back a mile to Mount Gough.

---

* As is noted below, charges were brought against several Canadian and British troops for their actions in the POW camps.

CHAPTER 13

"Each Reluctant to Relinquish the Sword"

The Japanese Close In
24 December 1941

*"The smell of death was heavy as fog and
as piercing as acid. It crawled into our nostrils,
it seemed to paint our clothes with a cloying brush"*
—GWEN DEW, *PRISONER OF THE JAPS*

While Wallis and Home sparred, the Royal Rifles in the field were beginning to buckle. At 3:00 a.m. on 24 December, Lieutenant Peter MacDougall found Captain Everette Denison suffering from such "extreme exhaustion" that the lieutenant took the extraordinary step of directing his superior officer to the battalion's headquarters under the guidance of a sergeant. MacDougall then reported to Major Price that neither of the two platoons was in its assigned position and that he should consider Stanley's first line of defence as being lightly held.

Two hours later, the Japanese launched a small attack in the centre of the line held by sixty-six men commanded by Captain Frederick Royal. The Canadians became aware of the attack when a Japanese soldier answered a sentry's challenge with the word "Canadian" in heavily accented English while lunging forward with his bayonet-tipped rifle. The bayonet slightly wounded the sentry, but, courtesy of a blast from a Bren gun in the hands of another sentry, the Japanese soldier never straightened up. The gunner's second burst wounded several more Japanese soldiers.

Though stymied, this attack demonstrated the weakness of Royal's position. Acting on his own authority, soon after daybreak he moved his men back to a position that, though somewhat better, was also "too thin to hold for any length of time if attacked."[89]

. . .

Reprising the sorts of battles that had raged during the First World War when German or Allied sappers broke into each other's tunnels beneath the Western Front, Royal Marines fought the Japanese soldiers who entered tunnels adjacent to Stubb's Road on the eastern side of Victoria. The Japanese guards at the Repulse Bay Hotel, meanwhile, herded their civilian prisoners out of the hotel for a march to North Point to be interned. From poking exhausted men and women with bayonets, to denying them food and water, few of the Japanese would have realized how ironic their actions were on this hot Christmas Eve Day. Suitcases quickly became burdens that bent backs and all but broke spirits. The detritus of war, burned trucks and cars and bloating, blackening bodies of Canadians, British, Indian and Chinese troops, lined this *via dolorosa*. To avoid British shellfire, Dew recalled, the exhausted and terrified civilians flattened themselves against cliffs, as, of course, did the Japanese soldiers.

They passed Japanese on horseback and supply and artillery units using mules. High heels broke off and fashionable shoes burst. Blisters formed and broke, squeezing bodily fluid into socks that wore thin. Two infants became feverish. More than once, the civilian captives watched in horror as the Japanese used Chinese stragglers caught along the way for judo and sword practice.

.   .   .

At 9:30 a.m., the field telephone rang in a trench manned by Grenadiers near the southern slope of Mount Cameron. Lieutenant Leonard Corrigan's orders were simple: take six men and do a reconnaissance to determine the strength of the Japanese forces nearby. Seventy-five yards after climbing out of their trench, Corrigan thought he heard movement in the deep grass to his left. He motioned for his men to get down and stay quiet. After sending a runner to warn the rest of his men, Corrigan moved his force forward.

They had not gone more than a few steps when Corrigan heard the swish of men marching through grass. Signalling again to his men, he peered through the tall grass and, a little to his left and less than forty feet away, could just make out a dozen soldiers heading for the trench that held the rest of his men. As the lead Japanese soldier came even with him, Corrigan dropped to his knee, fired and missed.

Since his rifle was in trail, the lead soldier had time enough only to raise his rifle, grasp it with his left arm and charge, trusting his safety to his bayonet. Corrigan pulled the pin on a grenade, held it for a few seconds before tossing it "under hand into the midst of the advancing Japs, where, fortunately for us, due to the closeness of the range, it exploded waist high immediately behind the enemy."

One soldier who had not been riddled with shrapnel rushed Corrigan; as he lifted his rifle, Corrigan realized to his horror that before leaving the trench he had forgotten to attach his bayonet. For the want of a two-second twist and turn, Corrigan found himself all but defenceless. He turned his rifle around, grasped it by the barrel and used it as a club. Corrigan's first swing knocked the rifle out of the onrushing soldier's hands. Dropping his own rifle, Corrigan picked up the Japanese bayonet-tipped gun and ran the soldier through.

Unlike those forged in Canada, Japanese bayonets had neither the grooves nor the bevel that facilitated withdrawing them from another man's chest. (The grooves allow blood to flow around the bayonet, providing a lubricant; the bevel pries open the ribs and its taper allows easier withdrawal of the weapon.) As he struggled to pull the bayonet out of the soldier's chest, Corrigan caught the flash of a sword raised to strike him. Letting go of the rifle, he jumped toward his attacker, managing to grasp the blade with his right hand while circling the attacker's neck with his left arm, which forced the man's head down against Corrigan's chest. "Locked together in this fashion we struggled for a few seconds, each reluctant to relinquish grasp of the sword." Corrigan used his weight to bend the Japanese soldier's arm and prevent his feet from gaining the purchase needed for judo. Trying to knock the soldier out with an uppercut, Corrigan hit the man's steel helmet and sprained his own thumb.

Then, in a shrill voice, his Japanese opponent called out something that sounded like "Kill! Kill!" Fearing that the soldier's comrades would rush to his aid, Corrigan remembered his pistol—it had fallen out of his holster but was still attached to its lanyard. When he grasped the sword, Corrigan suffered a cut that must have severed a muscle, for while he could get his finger onto the trigger, he could not pull it. The flapping skin then acted as barb, all but preventing him from pulling his finger out of the trigger guard. The pain notwithstanding, Corrigan finally pulled his finger free, inserted another, put the gun to the base of the Japanese soldier's neck and "ended the weary struggle," wrote Corrigan in a 1946 report that at the time he requested not be made public.

As his opponent's body slipped to the ground, Corrigan saw the sword a foot or two away from him, quickly bent for it and then readied to face "the Jap who, I felt certain, was coming to the aid" of his comrade. Breathing hard and feeling the pain of the sprain and the cut from the sword, Corrigan soon realized that he was alone.

The struggle had so exhausted him that it took a few minutes before he could climb the hill and return to his men.

. . .

Three miles away from the nameless gully in which Corrigan fought for his life, the feud between Lieutenant-Colonel Home and Brigadier Wallis was boiling over. This time Home was accompanied by Major John Price. According to the Royal Rifles' war diary, Home demanded the withdrawal of the Rifles holding Wallis's advance line, *"otherwise [Home] would not be responsible for what would happen"* (emphasis in the original). Home reminded Wallis that his men had borne the brunt of the fighting since the invasion and that they had had almost no rest and little food.

His next statement, that "it was the considered opinion of the Battalion as a whole that the fighting should cease," almost got him summarily court-martialled and shot. Wallis angrily responded, "The Canadians must either fight or march out under a white flag to (say) Repulse Bay." What Wallis did not say (but wrote in his war diary) was: "The Brigade Commander . . . considered arresting or shooting Lt. Col. Home and placing Maj. Price (2nd in Command) in command. He had refrained from doing so as he had come to the conclusion that many officers would require shooting—that it was in fact a bloodless mutiny."* Home refused to surrender the Rifles alone.

---

* This incident uncannily echoes one that occurred during the Second Battle of Ypres, coincidentally Canada's first First World War battle. Late in the afternoon of 24 April 1915, Brigadier-General Arthur Currie left his brigade's position at Gravenstafel Ridge to search for reinforcements. After failing to find any, he happened on Major-General Thomas D'Oyly Snow's dugout; unbeknownst to Currie, Snow had been given command of all reinforcements in the area a few hours earlier. Snow flew into a rage when Currie explained his need for reinforcements, and again when Currie took a few moments to write a message for his commander, General Edwin Alderson. Snow later told Sir James Edmonds, the author of the British official history of the war, that had Currie been "an English officer, I would have put him under arrest and he would have been shot" (quoted in Greenfield, 269).

In a 1948 letter to Canada's official historian, Price said nothing about Home demanding to speak to Maltby. Rather, he wrote, "I cannot believe that ... Home asked Brig. Wallis to see the Governor. This does not make sense as we were cut off from the other sector and there was no practical way of carrying this out."[2] Having decided that it was "imperative to clear the battlefield of disaffected troops liable to jeopardize the defence," Wallis called Maltby and, while remaining silent about the "bloodless mutiny," informed him that he was "temporarily withdraw[ing] the Canadians to Stanley Fort on the southern tip of the Peninsula so that they could rest and reorganise."

The withdrawal of the Rifles did not occur quickly. As late at 3:00 p.m., Wallis's and Home's staff dickered over the details of how and when the Middlesexers and Volunteers would replace the Rifles. A front-line soldier's view of the fighting is something like twenty yards on either side of him. But desperately glad as they were to be relieved, Riflemen like Dallain felt their anger rise when they saw the Royal Artillery playing soccer. Lance-Sergeant Lance Ross summed up the feelings of the men who collapsed into sleep after they trudged into Stanley: "Almost played out. Can't stand it much longer."

At noon, events shifted Wallis's attention from his fantasy of shooting Dominion officers. A Japanese flag had been hoisted a few hundred yards from St. Stephen's College Hospital, which then held more than four hundred patients. And equally importantly, all communication lines between Stanley and West Brigade and Fortress Headquarters had gone dead. Meanwhile, a platoon-sized group of Middlesexers left their positions on Leighton Hill, but not because of orders to relieve the Rifles. Rather, after resisting serious attacks, they finally gave way at 4:45 p.m.

. . .

Late that morning, Lieutenant Proulx had had another chance to prove his mettle when the commander at Aberdeen asked for volunteers to carry a package containing codes and maps captured from the Japanese to Maltby's Fortress Headquarters. Proulx and a man he called "Arthur" volunteered to take the attaché case through roads that were being shelled and on which it was thought the Japanese had already set up roadblocks.*

The ride began with a dash through the naval base's open gates in a small Vauxhall car. To avoid being hit by gunners, Arthur sped through the gate in second gear, building up enough speed that when he swung the steering wheel to the right, the car pitched onto its two right wheels, thus making it a more difficult target. As the car came back down onto four wheels, they heard the sound of bricks being blown off a building by a shell that had just missed them. The attacking gunner overcompensated; his next shell exploded thirty yards in front of the speeding car.

To get a soldier ahead of them off the road, Proulx pushed the front windshield down and, with the wind whipping past him at seventy miles per hour, fired one shot, causing the soldier to dive into the brush beside the road. Forced to slow down by the hulks of burned trucks near Queen Mary Hospital, Proulx could not help but fill with emotion when he saw the bodies of Chinese men, women and children who had been killed by the shelling. "Half the world around us seemed dead or dying."

A tree that had been blasted was blocking the road that led to the Battle Box, forcing Proulx and Arthur to run the rest of the way. About a hundred yards from the entrance, a Canadian sentry appeared and asked for the password. Proulx responded, "Smiling," the consonants "s" and "1" being absent from Japanese. Once inside,

---

* Banham suggests that "Arthur" was the Vancouver-born Francis Woodley "Mike" Kendall, head of the Special Operations Executive.

he handed over the attaché case and was given lunch, which he described as "more edible than glory." The culinary failings of the British Army were not, however, his greatest disappointment.

What really took Proulx aback was the officer who asked, "How many Japs do you think may have landed on the Island? And have you any idea where they are located?" Proulx's stunned reply, "Dear God, don't you know?" elicited the honest, if less than comforting response, "We're a bit in the dark down here. I thought you might help us out." Proulx's wartime published prose is more restrained than some, but he captures the attitude many had when he wrote, "If the men at the top were not in possession of the detailed information . . . , how were they to regulate the fighting? The situation might have seemed almost comic opera had it not involved the freedom of our Colony and our very lives."[3]

The first part of the trip back to Aberdeen was uneventful. The Japanese, however, were waiting for the party on the approach to the naval base. The first shell missed the speeding car by a wide margin. A second hit the wall directly above them. Had the shell not been a dud, the resulting blast would likely have sent the car spinning out of control, that is, if the concrete torn from the wall did not crush the car first. "A second later, with tires screaming, we swung through the gate and ripped off the rear fender."

Annoyed at having twice let the little car through their gauntlet, the Japanese gunners contented themselves with raining shells into the compound. Proulx and Arthur moved fast, emptying the car of some tinned goods and champagne that they had stopped to pick up at the remains of Arthur's office before leaving Victoria. As they ran from the car, a shell hit it and the car burst into flames. Safe for the moment, Proulx suddenly remembered that he had forgotten two cans of Quebec-brewed Frontenac Beer, the beer favoured by Canadians in Hong Kong, in the car. He and Arthur "mourned" the loss.

. . .

Although the commanding general had decided, against Colonel Doi's wishes, to wait a day before launching any further major attacks, the Japanese kept up the pressure. At 2:45 p.m., the defenders of Brick Hill (on the west side of Repulse Bay) came under attack from Tanaka's men to the northeast. Fifteen minutes later and two miles away, a group of engineers commanded by Lieutenant-Colonel Tsuneo Iwabuchi, fighting as infantry, attacked Leighton Hill from the north, east and south. The Die Hards held on for two hours before giving way. Late in the afternoon, Wallis sent thirty-three HKVDC officers and men to his third line of defence, the St. Stephen's College line.

. . .

Throughout the afternoon the march of terrified and exhausted civilians from the Repulse Bay Hotel continued. At one point, they passed a group of Japanese photographers drinking water. The photographers took pictures of the civilian prisoners, paying particular attention to the women. Thinking that perhaps the photographers would be less cruel than the soldiers, Jan Marsman begged for water. "No, no English water here," replied a lieutenant, whose smile sent a chill down Marsman's spine.

At dusk, the Japanese commander summoned Marsman, Major C.M. Manners and Mr. Shields before him. He reminded them that three times already the Imperial Japanese Army had asked Governor Young to "surrender at his headquarters." Now, the emperor's army was demanding that they take the message to the governor that "he must come through the lines to us and surrender must be unconditional."[4] As a Philippine citizen, Marsman demurred. Manners and Shields passed through the Japanese lines intent on telling the governor that on their march from Repulse Bay they had seen at least five thousand troops and thousands of horses and mules, many pulling field artillery, and that any further resistance was futile.

. . .

In the gathering dusk, the defenders of Morrison Hill, which became the anchor of West Brigade's defensive line after the fall of Leighton Hill, came under heavy fire. Among them were a couple of Winnipeg Grenadiers, including signaller Frank Christensen, who found himself as part of a three-man machine gun crew secreted in a market. Theirs was one of the first positions hit.

The explosion destroyed the gun and wounded two men, one of them severely. Christensen's report that the "less wounded fellow and I carried him back about three blocks to where an English officer and a driver of a three-quarter ton truck were" hardly captures the moment. Under constant shellfire, Christensen and the other man held between them a wounded comrade. One of Christensen's blood-smeared arms wound round the man's waist, trying to support as much weight as possible; the other held his rifle. Christensen and the man helping him breathed heavily, the wounded man's breath coming in ragged, shallow intakes. Half bent over, they made a ghastly version of a three-legged-race team, the middle leg being the dead weight of a terribly wounded man. As explosions roared around them, they hunched closer to the ground while struggling to keep the wounded man from sliding onto the pockmarked street covered in broken glass. Adrenaline-fuelled strength allowed Christensen to pick up the wounded soldier and place him in the truck.

Shortly after Christensen returned to the line, a burst of fire caught him in the arm. The force of the bullets spun him around, and he flopped into the gutter. Neither the searing pain in his arm nor the disorientation from being spun around was enough to stop him from thinking of what he needed to do: push himself below the lip of the gutter. He couldn't do so completely because of the gas mask strapped to his belly. Three bullets soon ripped into his backpack and two through the leather of his right boot. As his boot filled with blood and with little chance of surviving a third blast, Christensen "played possum," and the gunner soon moved on.

. . .

For a moment or two just before 9:00 p.m., the shelling of HKVDC Major Forsyth's position on Wallis's first line gave way to the sound of engines as three light tanks rolled into view, and behind them masses of Japanese infantry. One or more of the two-pound guns secreted in this line made short work of the tanks. They could do little, however, against the infantry.

The few Volunteers who escaped brought harrowing tales of hand-to-hand combat, of men dying with bayonets in their stomachs. Forsyth stayed with his men until the last possible moment, which earned him a recommendation for a Victoria Cross; he was badly wounded when he ran for his life. As the survivors who made it back to Stanley coughed out their story, the Japanese overran the gun that had destroyed their tanks and another gun at the Stanley Police Station a few hundred yards to its left.

Japanese machine gunners quickly moved into Forsyth's old position and joined their field artillery comrades in pummelling Stanley itself. The machine guns were now close enough to hit St. Stephen's College, then serving as a makeshift hospital. Just as Padre Barnett and three other captains lay down in the medical inspection room "to try to get some sleep," a Japanese machine gunner swivelled his gun just a little. Instead of his bullets pinging off the wall, they now hit the windows, showering the room with thousands of shards mixed with a stream of bullets that drove the four captains out of the room.

. . .

The attack that fell on Baille's men and on Bennett's Hill late on Christmas Eve interrupted Grenadier George Peterson and his comrades' Christmas dinner. As close-order fighting raged in and around their well-dug-in-position, Privates John James and Harry Orvis, a couple of hundred yards away, readied their three-inch mortar. It is unclear whether they managed to get off a shell before Orvis was killed. There is no question that a Japanese shell exploded near them, driving shrapnel into James's foot and eye. The men in Peterson's group were luckier; when their position became untenable, they retreated over an open area near the Aberdeen Reservoir. The plan was to draw the Japanese behind the retreating Canadians. They knew it had worked when they could hear the sound of three hidden Vickers machine guns opening up.

Earlier that morning, when they had been unloading mortars from a wrecked truck, Orvis and James found three Indian soldiers, one with a terrible wound above his elbow. James had used his own first aid kit to help staunch the bleeding and then, using an overcoat, made a makeshift stretcher on which they carried him to a roadblock and put him in the care of a sergeant. Now, James was alone, badly injured and without his first aid kit some three miles from Aberdeen. Earlier, "one of the men dropped to his knees and kissed my hand for getting them safely down the hill and to help." Now James, mourning Orvis and thinking of the many Christmas pageants showing angels and wise men on the road to Bethlehem, crawled all night with his "foot flapping" toward the little village on the bay.

· · ·

At 10:00 p.m., Maltby and his officers had little doubt as to where the Japanese were. Their three-inch mortar bombs were exploding on the Battle Box itself.

A half-hour later, the same troops who had broken through Wallis's first line attacked the second line, further wounding Major Forsyth and killing another officer. Forsyth was carried under fire further back to the schoolhouse. "The whole narrow isthmus was rocketing fire like a burning munitions dump. Nearby, on our left, a house was surrounded, Bren guns blazing from each quarter and automatics returning fire at point blank range. All over the place were similar close exchanges," recalled Hong Kong Volunteer gunner James Bertram.[5]

· · ·

For a few moments before midnight, as the firing lessened, some might have thought that their war too might have tales of a Christmas Truce. It wasn't to be.

As they had before, the Japanese gunners let up only to allow their infantry to charge forward. Price and the Canadians were now not at the front, but the lull followed by the ripping sounds of machine guns told them all they had to know. With their experience of Japanese tactics, the low explosions that soon followed would have told them that the Japanese had been stopped and were now resorting to their favoured weapon: the knee mortar.

Shortly after midnight, one of those mortars landed on Sergeant Leslie Millington's machine gun, killing Millington and setting off the ammunition boxes. The explosion and the thousands of bullets that fired out from it killed almost every HKVDC man on the left side of the line. Those on the right saved their lives by staying low to the ground. Sharpshooters, however, seized the opportunity and picked off several Japanese infantrymen under the garish light of the exploding ammunition.

CHAPTER 14

"Anyone Who Can Get Out the Door Will Be Spared"

The Christmas Day Attack
25 December 1941

And one day some Greek soldier will stick me
With cold bronze and draw the life from my limbs,
And the dogs that I fed at my table,
My watchdogs, will drag me outside and eat
My flesh raw, crouched in my doorway, lapping
My blood.
—VIRGIL, *THE ILIAD*

Chaplains Uriah Laite, Francis Deloughery and James Barnett had never spent a Christmas Eve like the one they did in 1941. None of the three had experienced the Great War. For decades, first as children and then as men of the cloth, the holy night had been a pageant of the three wise men from the East bearing gifts. On this night, soldiers who believed their Emperor to be a living god and that every step they took toward victory increased his glory stormed forward.

In the early hours of Christmas Day at the Bowen Road Hospital, Deloughery heard gunfire from a Japanese attack on Bennett's Hill not far away. General Maltby's Battle Box was more than a mile northeast of Bennett's Hill, and Mount Gough stood about the same distance directly to the east. Still, the loss of the hill combined with the overwhelming force the Japanese could bring to bear meant that the fall of Maltby's headquarters was simply a matter of time.

Chaplain Barnett at St. Stephen's College Hospital in Stanley was much closer to the fighting. At 1:00 a.m., Colonel Tanaka's men broke through on the east side of Stanley and proceeded south toward the prison before turning west toward the college's playing field.

. . .

The Japanese were less concerned about the hospital and the few units left around it than they were about the thousands of bullets a Lewis gun was firing into waves of Japanese attackers and about high-explosive shells fired "open sights." One of these shells destroyed a party of Japanese soldiers who had advanced some distance up Prison Road. And still the Japanese kept moving forward.

After receiving word that the Japanese were threatening his second line and just a few hundred yards from his last defensive line, Wallis called again on the Royal Rifles. At 2:30 a.m. the brigadier ordered Home to rouse his men and occupy the high ground immediately north of Stanley Fort. Just south of the third defensive line, this ground afforded an unobstructed view north to St. Stephen's and thus of the new Japanese positions.

Home resisted the order, pointing out that his exhausted men had had only four or five hours' rest. Wallis replied that "nobody else had had *any* rest at all," which is not exactly true, since large numbers of the Middlesex Regiment had not been in the field for days. Wallis then appealed to Home's pride: the Canadians "could not sit inactive and watch 1 Mx, the Royal Artillery and the

H.K.V.D.C. fight a battle as infantry for which they were not trained when much of 'D' Bn [Royal Rifles], probably the largest unit intact on the Island, were available."* Despite the seriousness of the situation, Home continued to object but relented when Wallis "insisted." This description comes from Wallis's East Brigade War Diary, so it remains unclear what he said to change Home's mind. By 4:00 a.m., Bishop's "C" Company was in position on the high ground immediately north of the fort and the Officers' Club that housed Wallis's headquarters.[†]

. . .

As dawn broke, Barnett prepared to celebrate the morning of Christ's nativity. Japanese soldiers, for whom 25 December was *Taish Tenno Sai,* the commemoration of the death in 1926 of Emperor Taish , Hirohito's father, stormed into the hospital. The hospital's commander, Hong Kong Volunteer Lieutenant-Colonel G. Black, rushed forward to tell the Japanese that the building under the flapping Red Cross flag was, indeed, a hospital.[‡] Black was shot and bayoneted.

---

* Wallis's argument here is curious to say the least. First, by early Christmas Day morning, the Rifles and the 1st Middlesex had suffered a similar number of men killed: eighty-five Rifles and seventy-three Die Hards. Added to this number, however, must be the hundreds of wounded Rifles that cut its numbers by more than one-half. True, neither the Middlesex nor Royal Artillery were infantry, but both were professional army regiments that had had basic training. Military history is replete with examples in which cooks, signallers and other ancillary personnel were handed rifles and sent into the trenches or used in an attack.

† Wallis's East Brigade War Diary incorrectly states that Home gave this task to Major Parker's "D" Company.

‡ The Tokyo War Crimes Trials made clear that there can be no accepting of the Japanese claim that the atrocities that took place in St. Stephen's Hospital were a military necessity. Nevertheless, it is worth noting that at least as they approached the hospital, the Japanese had reason to doubt the veracity of the Red Cross flag. According to Sergeant H. Peacegood (RAMC), on Christmas Eve machine guns were placed on the hospital veranda. These guns fired almost continuously during the night. Sergeant J. Anderson (RAMC) told the war crimes investigators that machine gun emplacements on the grounds of the hospital were sandbagged with mattresses and hospital

Hirohito's men then turned their fury on the hospital's patients. Helpless, Barnett watched as the Japanese bayoneted some twenty wounded soldiers as they lay on their cots. Somehow, Rifleman Sydney Skelton, who had just been prepped for surgery on wounds suffered two days earlier, understood that the shouts of *"Banzai"* and the cloudy images of Japanese soldiers stabbing men elsewhere in the room were not products of the anaesthetic coursing through his veins. A moment before a Japanese soldier saw him, Skelton threw himself to the floor, the blinding pain from his wounds piercing his half-conscious state and keeping him awake enough to roll under the cot.

As Skelton hovered near unconsciousness, a Japanese soldier bent down, reached under the cot and pulled the limp, bandaged body into the open, but he did not plunge his bayonet into the prostrate Canadian. The anaesthetic, which caused Skelton's head to loll to one side, made him seem dead—even as his attacker kicked him in the face. One soldier who had not found anyone to bayonet vented his frustration on an empty bed, failing to notice that beneath it British Sergeant-Major Stewart Begg and his wife, Emma, an auxiliary nurse, huddled for safety.

A few moments later, Skelton heard someone yell that anyone who could get out the door would be spared. Wrapped only in a thin sheet, Skelton dragged himself forward as the Japanese searched each soldier and nurse. Before Skelton reached the door of the dark storeroom into which the Japanese were herding the prisoners, he saw a Japanese soldier motion a Hong Kong Volunteer out of the line, point to the sheathed knife that hung from his belt and plunge a bayonet into the Volunteer's stomach. For a moment,

---

linen. According to Barnett, both of these violations of the Geneva Convention worried Black, who asked the padre to go out to the veranda and ask the men manning the machine guns "to be as quiet as possible, so that they would … not attract [the] attention of the enemy to the hospital."

Skelton thought he too was going to die, for, after confiscating his wristwatch, a soldier lifted his sword over the Canadian's shoulder. But the soldier swung the sword so that instead of decapitating the Canadian it only slapped him on the face.[*]

. . .

Shortly after dawn, the Japanese outside the hospital broke through Millington's position, killing him as the two sides of their wave swamped the sections to his right and left. Somehow in the half-light, Second Lieutenant H. Jones rallied his section and counterattacked; Jones and half his men were soon dead. HKVDC Second Lieutenant H. Muir led his men into a thick-walled bungalow. Four miles to the northwest, notwithstanding a truce arranged near Happy Valley so that the Repulse Bay refugees could safely continue their march toward North Point, the Japanese continued to shell and dive-bomb the roads.

. . .

Toward late morning, a Japanese soldier opened the door to the room that held Barnett, Skelton and the others. An interpreter ordered them from the room. As they exited, the nurses were separated out. Barnett watched in horror as one of the nurses, dressed in regulation uniform with a Red Cross brassard on her arm, was "hit on the head with a steel helmet, slapped in the face, and kicked by a soldier." Much worse was to come.

The Chinese nurses were taken to a room into which the Japanese had thrown the bodies of the men they had bayoneted.

---

[*] Barnett wasn't surprised that his steel helmet, respirator and cash were confiscated; the taking of his prayer book hurt more.

On top of the bodies, they piled the bloodied and torn mattresses. None of the Chinese nurses survived to tell their tale. The seven British nurses were also gang raped. The bodies of three of them, including Emma Begg's, were mutilated. Nursing Sisters A. Gordon and Elizabeth Fidoe were repeatedly raped, returned to the room holding the other female staff, and then taken out to be raped again.* Despite the Japanese soldiers' fears of contracting venereal disease, which could merit a capital sentence, the rapes—often gang rapes—continued all day.

. . .

At 8:00 a.m., as Christmas Day mass began at St. John's Cathedral in Victoria, the Japanese launched another attack on Bennett's Hill. An hour later, they drove the last company of Royal Scots off Mount Cameron. At about the same time, Manners and Shields, who crossed the lines in front of Maltby's headquarters under a white flag, met with the general, giving rise to an impromptu local truce that lasted on this part of the island until the final surrender, which Maltby signed in Kowloon a few hours later.

Repeatedly, the Japanese attacked Muir's small detachment sheltered in a bungalow at the north side of Stanley. The Japanese brought up a flame-thrower. Muir and most of his men burned to death. The Japanese advance had not cut off Bishop's "A" Company at the fort on the.eastern side of the approach to Stanley, but it was impossible to get them food and drink.

. . .

---

* Canadian Nursing Sisters Kay Christie and May Waters were at the Bowen Road Military Hospital when it was captured; there were no atrocities at this hospital.

Shortly before 10:00 a.m., Maltby's headquarters informed Wallis of the three-hour truce. For reasons that remain unclear, despite this truce, the commander of East Brigade ordered Home to organize an attack to retake the bungalows above Stanley. Once again, the brigadier and the ranking Canadian in Hong Kong locked horns.

Wallis tried to assuage Home by promising that the attack would be supported by artillery. Home, who had heard this promise before (and rightly predicted that it would again go unfulfilled), "protested against such an attack in daylight as likely being unproductive of any result but additional Canadian casualties." (It is unclear whether Home was aware of the truce at Maltby's headquarters.) Wallis, however, was "adamant," and Home again bowed to his commander and ordered Major Parker to ready his "D" Company to move to Stanley Prison, the jumping-off place for the attack.

The officers charged with leading the attack, including Sergeant George MacDonell and Lieutenants Frank Power and Angus MacMillan, of Nos. 18, 17 and 16 platoons respectively, did not, of course, know about Home's objections.* According to MacDonell, they considered the plan "madness." His men, including such tough nuts as Lance-Sergeant Lance Ross, were stunned when they heard that they were to attack across open ground without machine gun or artillery support.

Over the previous few days, the men of these platoons had had precious few hours of sleep. Over the last two days, two of MacDonell's corporals had been killed, and he had had to reorganize his sections. Since his men knew how fast the Japanese advance had been, MacDonell "said something to his men to the effect that attacking the village was no worse than sitting here waiting for the inevitable last attack."[1] Despite what Wallis had confided to his

---

* This is the order of the platoons as they attacked; MacDonell's platoon was on the left of the Canadian line and thus attacked the right front of Stanley Village.

diary, the Canadian mettle was demonstrated, MacDonell recalls, by the fact that "not a single man asked to be excused from this idiotic attack."

. . .

As Parker's men cleaned their rifles, filled their sacks with ammunition, counted their grenades and then, as amazing as it sounds to a civilian, "lay down again to sleep until it was time to form up for the attack," atrocities continued within the walls of St. Stephen's College Hospital.[2] Barnett and some ninety other men were crammed in a room so small that they could not all sit down at once. At one point, a soldier entered the room with a bucket. It contained neither water nor food, but rather .303 bullets, which the solider grabbed by the handful and threw in the prisoners' faces.

Barnett tried to keep spirits up by retelling the story of Jesus' birth and leading the men in prayer. In that small, dark, hot, increasingly fetid room, they could hear the screams of Royal Riflemen Elzie Henderson and John McKay, who had been led out of the room and were being tortured to death. "We all thought it was the end," recalled Barnett.

. . .

Before attacking, Major Parker's men ate Christmas dinner: Henry Lyons shared his can of bully beef, a package of Indian hard tack and about half a bottle of water with his brother, Lance-Corporal Jack Lyons, and good friend Reggie Haley.[*]

---

[*] Wallis, in his East Brigade War Diary, characterizes this normal procedure thusly: "The men were going with a bad grace—grumbling and some remarking 'well I'm going to have my B . . . [blasted?] breakfast first anyhow.'"

The attack began sometime after 12:30 p.m. Despite Wallis's promise, there was no artillery barrage, so as soon as the Rifles began running across the field, the Japanese saw them and began firing mortars. Rifleman Phil Doddridge, who, along with Parker, ran down the road to the observation point on the west wall of Stanley Prison, found that instead of measuring the odds of whether the next shell had his name on it, he thought of his family back in the Gaspé and how they would be worried about his safety. The roar of exploding mortar bombs and rattle of machine guns hardly registered against the words of one of Doddridge's mother's favourite gospel songs:

> *Will the circle be unbroken*
> *By and by, Lord, by and by*
> *There's a better home a-waiting*
> *In the sky, Lord, in the sky.*

Henry Lyons strengthened his resolve with silent prayers and thoughts of his young wife, Isabelle. As Lyons and the other men of No. 17 Platoon ran forward on the left, MacDonell's men dodged their way from rock to rock heading for his first objective, the cemetery. Japanese soldiers hiding behind gravestones had an open field of fire over the last several dozen yards MacDonell's men would have to cross to reach the cemetery. Just before those last dangerous yards lay a small patch of dead ground. Gathering his men there, the sergeant with a week's battle experience ordered his men to fix their bayonets and spread out in a skirmish line some forty yards across. Then, on his signal, they rose as one, "emitted fearful war whoops" and charged into the graveyard.[3]

Their screams bought a few precious seconds, during which MacDonell and his other Bren gunners, shooting from the hip, laid down a curtain of fire that allowed his men to get into the graveyard. In the "confused and bloody melee of hand-to-hand fighting with bayonets" that followed, the Canadians broke the Japanese and forced them to run for safety in a row of thick white-walled bungalows about fifty yards to the north. After giving his men a few moments to catch their breath, MacDonell ordered them to attack the bungalows.

Some distance to MacDonell's right, No. 17 Platoon attacked another set of bungalows. Lance Ross told Doddridge that "Big Ed Bujold stood . . . pulling the pins out of grenades and hurling them like baseballs through the windows of the bungalows."

Leo Nellis was the first Rifleman to die in this attack. "As we approached the house," recalls Private Henry Lyons, "a Jap rushed toward him. He got his bayonet up and shoved it into him." Nellis's bayonet must have been an angle, as he couldn't pull it from his dying Japanese opponent. "Bullets were flying around and he had to act fast, so Leo then put his foot on the Japanese and tried to push him off. But then, his bayonet broke off. He never moved far though; a moment later he fell dead."

Private Lyons and the others raced into the bungalow after the retreating Japanese. Lyons ran from the back door first and although bullets whipped around him, did not go to ground. Instead, knowing that in just a few seconds his brother Jack and his good friends would themselves run from the door, he continued to a small rise, fell to his knee and began squeezing off round after round to give them some covering fire. "They got out and ran toward the right. Then I saw Jack drop," Lyons recounts.

Henry Lyons didn't have time to worry about his older brother, for an instant later, he was facing the charge of a Japanese soldier himself. Surprised by the onrushing soldier, Lyons wasn't able to get a shot off and the Japanese soldier had the instant he needed to thrust his bayonet forward. However, instead of the blade plunging into Lyons' body, the blow glanced off his webbing. "You bastard," thought Lyons. "You've hit me. Now, get ready to die." But, before Lyons could thrust his bayonet forward, his brother Jack shoved his bayonet into the Japanese soldier.

The three Canadians then ran toward a bluff. Corporal Jack Lyons and Haley went around it in one direction and Henry Lyons in the other. On the other side, they could see hundreds of Japanese reinforcements rushing forward. Corporal Jack motioned Private Henry toward the graveyard secured by MacDonell's men. "I obeyed the order and turned toward a fence that I jumped over before taking cover. I never saw my brother again," recalls Henry Lyons.

. . .

As Parker's three platoons fought their way forward, casualties began streaming past the major and Doddridge. A bullet broke Sergeant-Major Frank Edben's jaw and ripped out eight teeth. Another smashed Ursel Kaine's ankle. Morris Delaney staggered back, and Doddridge could see that he'd apparently been hit by a glancing blow just over the left ear. But Delaney was fatally wounded. Doddridge saw machine gun fire tear another Rifleman apart.

. . .

When MacDonell learned that Lieutenant Power had been wounded, he took effective command of his No. 17 Platoon, gathering both platoons behind some hedges to redistribute ammunition and hand grenades.* On the other side of the hedge ran Fort Road. "To

---

* Before the attack, No. 17 Platoon had been reinforced with elements of No. 18R Platoon, including men like Bill MacWhirter, who just days earlier had marvelled at Lance Ross's sang-froid. In this battle, young MacWhirter and his brother fought like the grizzled veterans they had, in fact, become. In an action not far from the cemetery, he, his half-brother Arley Enright, their old friend Leo Murphy and some forty other Riflemen used their superior weight and reach to break another Japanese force.

my shock and surprise," MacDonell recalls, "when I looked up we saw a squad of Japanese soldiers trotting briskly toward the graveyard, their rifles at the trail, obviously heading to reinforce what they thought were their comrades in the graveyard." The sword-bearing Japanese officer saw MacDonell's men an instant too late.

"Our guns were loaded," MacDonell told me in a normal conversational voice. Though his opinion of the orders to attack has never changed, MacDonell, who rose in the 1980s to be Ontario's Deputy Minister of Trade and Technology, remains proud of his men and his wartime performance. I was, therefore, surprised when, after telling me the guns were loaded, he said in a soft, almost melancholy voice, "I gave the order to fire." After a short pause, his voice dropped almost to a whisper and he added, "We cut down half of them in a few seconds.'"

The other half ran into a nearby driveway that sloped down to an underground garage. MacDonell's men were not far behind. "We just walked down the road and hosed them with our automatic weapons. We killed every single one of them."

A troop of Japanese soldiers had been destroyed, but MacDonell was anything but sanguine about his position. He'd taken many casualties; one section leader was dead and another wounded. His men were low on ammunition, and even more importantly under the hot sun, their water was gone. Things got worse a few minutes later when the Japanese unleashed a furious artillery and mortar barrage, and a runner arrived from Major Parker with word that the Japanese had penetrated between the Canadians' line and the prison.

"We have to get out of here," MacDonell told Lance-Sergeant Lance Ross, the ranking non-commissioned officer of No. 17 Platoon. "Why don't you and I stay with your Bren and my Lewis gun and send the men back? We'll walk up and down the line firing so the Japs don't realize we're evacuating the line." The order given, those who were able to began retreating toward the prison. The order did not admit of his men helping the wounded who could not walk; there wasn't time.

MacDonell and Ross kept up the fire, but when they started taking fire from the direction of the prison, which was the only way out, they realized that they had waited too long. To clear the way, the two men stood close together and blasted away at where they thought the shooting from their rear was coming from. Then they started running. Their fire bought enough time to reach a drainage ditch. It protected them, but it was so shallow that as they crawled downward they could feel bullets hitting the trench inches above their heads.

The two men saw a car at the end of the trench, ran for it and were soon under heavy machine gun fire. They listened for the pattern of the fire so that they could judge when machine gunners had to reload. They ran toward safety just as a lull began. When they reached the prison, Major Parker was waiting outside.

"Is this all? All that's coming out? How many are left?" he asked.

"Not many. We are the last," answered MacDonell.

. . .

There is no way to square Wallis's account of "D" Company's attack with the Canadian record or with the memories of the men who were there. Nor does Wallis's version have much in common with what Royal Air Force Cadet Pilot Forrow recalled: "We saw the last glorious charge of the Canadians, up through the graveyard and into the windows of the bungalows at the top. We saw the Japanese escaping through the back of the houses and then return with grenades, which they lobbed among the Canadians in occupation. Very few of the Canadians survived that gallant charge."[4]

Wallis is correct that the attack "advanced N.W. and North across the open fire-swept ground and up through the Cemetery." Later he writes that "the counter-attack . . . failed through not obeying orders and attacking by the most exposed route and out of control," apparently forgetting that the only route from the prison where the Canadians had been told to firm up for the attack and the Japanese in the cemetery and village was across the field running north from the prison. Perhaps Wallis's most egregious claim is that the "men were in bunches almost shoulder to shoulder as if they found greater courage by this method," which flatly contradicts MacDonell's memory of the attack, as it does Lyons' and MacWhirter's.*

According to Wallis, "after some 15 minutes the disorganized Coy withdrew in a broken manner and suffered more casualties in once more crossing the open ground near the Prison." In contrast, the Rifles' war diarist wrote, "after about 3/4 hour the attack had come to a halt, the Coy suffering as foreseen terrible casualties amounting to 26 killed and 75 wounded and without having dislodged the enemy from their positions in the bungalows." Both war diaries agree that by evening, Parker's battered men were close to Stanley Fort, about a mile south of the prison. They disagree as to when and why they so withdrew. "Instead of hanging on, or occupying fire positions S.W. of the Prison, Maj. Parker withdrew all ranks right back to Stanley Fort," wrote Wallis, which means that Parker's battered men would have been out of the mix somewhere around 1:00 p.m. According to the Rifles' war diary, they did not collect their wounded and withdraw until near 5:00 p.m.

Both the proverbial fog of war and the fact that both war diaries were reconstructed after the fact could explain these time differences. Neither of these explanations account, however, for the calumny that comes after Wallis writes that Parker withdrew his men

---

* In his 21 December attack, it will be recalled, Corporal Bob Barter had also ordered his Riflemen to advance in open formation.

back to Stanley Fort. "It was more than ever apparent that 'D' Bn [Royal Rifles] were of little or no fighting value, being badly led and commanded by a C.O. with little fighting spirit [and] think mostly of his own safety and comfort."* Even though Wallis did not have access to the Canadians when he wrote the first draft of his report, he did when he transcribed it after the war. At that point, he would have known (or if he did not, he should have) that Parker's command was in no shape to hold "fire positions" anywhere. The attack had exacted a casualty rate of 84 percent.

In the 1960s when Wallis was living in Vancouver, MacDonell had occasion to ask him why he ordered the attack when it was clear the battle was lost. Wallis answered simply, "It was a mistake."

. . .

Through the early afternoon, the Japanese continued their advance to the west, though not without cost. Some died at the hands of the Middlesex and Rajput machine gunners secreted in the Wan Chai market. Nevertheless, Winnipeg Grenadier commander Sutcliffe moved his headquarters from Wan Chai Gap to defended positions southwest on Mount Gough. Soon, however, the Japanese were attacking the Grenadiers on Bennett's Hill, a short distance south of Sutcliffe's new headquarters.

The Grenadiers held off the attack until mid-afternoon, when they threw down their guns and raised their arms in surrender. Emperor Hirohito's men accepted this universal signal from, among others, Private James Fowler—and spent the next twenty minutes

---

* It is worth contrasting Wallis's language about the Canadians' failed attack and an equally unsuccessful attack undertaken by the Middlesex regiment a few hours earlier. "At about 0830 hrs a 1 Mx fighting patrol was sent to drive the enemy from the houses S.W. of St. Stephen's. After some initial success, heavy fire from the windows forced this patrol back to a position overlooking the Cemetery."

"thrusting their bayonets through the many wounded men lying on the ground."[5]

. . .

At 3:15 p.m., General Maltby sifted through the reports—of the loss of communication with Wallis's East Brigade, of the Japanese relentlessly pushing back West Brigade's line, of the deteriorating situation in Victoria—and reached the "inevitable conclusion . . . that further fighting meant the useless slaughter of the remainder of the garrison, risked severe retaliation on the large civilian population, and could not affect the final outcome." After speaking with Governor Young, Maltby ordered all British, Indian, Hong Kong Volunteer and Canadian commanders to cease fighting and formally capitulate to the nearest Japanese officer.

Neither the Japanese in the field nor the commanders of West and East Brigades were inclined to believe the first word each had of the surrender. Colonel H.B. Rose refused to believe it until he had confirmation by telephone. The Japanese thought the white flag raised over Mount Gough was a ruse; they continued sporadic firing in the west until close to 5:00 p.m.[*]

The surrender ended the horrors at St. Stephen's Hospital. Suddenly, the door to the room in which Barnett and the others had been held was opened by a smiling Japanese officer. After telling them of the surrender, he said "we were now friends and let some of us move to a larger room." The victors gave the vanquished some water.

---

[*] At 5:00 p.m., the Winnipeg Grenadiers destroyed their ammunition stocks and marched to the Mount Austin barracks where in a room later locked they stacked their arms and then bedded down for the night to await the arrival of the Japanese.

. . .

Word of the surrender, which had been signed around 5:00 p.m., did not reach Wallis until near midnight. The delay was costly for the Royal Rifles. Still operating on his last orders—"To hold to the last"—at 4:00 p.m., as the Japanese artillery pounded Stanley Fort and the surrounding area, Wallis once again ordered the Rifles into the field. At 4:30 p.m., "A" Company started moving into position "in full view of the enemy." The Japanese artillerists did not waste the opportunity; soon six Canadians were dead and another twelve wounded.

At first, Wallis too refused to believe the order. Home, who considered Wallis mentally unbalanced, never knew of his commander's Strangelovian fantasy recorded in his war diary of "blowing up the Fort by detonating the magazine should the enemy penetrate into the whole Fort area. Survivors would be permitted time by [sic] harboured with wounded in cover . . . near Bluff Point."* Shortly after midnight on 26 December, Wallis issued the order for East Brigade, made up of units belonging to the Middlesex, Hong Kong Volunteers, Royal Artillery and Rajputs and the entirety of the Royal Rifles of Canada, to surrender forthwith.

Surrender was not, of course, culturally beyond the pale for the British and Canadians; hundreds of thousands had been POWs during the First World War. Still, soldiers come to fight. Moreover, while sixteen days of battle had exploded almost all of the preconceptions of the Japanese as fighters—and, indeed, given birth in Canadian (and American) media to an equally unrealistic image of the Japanese superman—surrendering to them stunned the Canadians. Winnipeg Grenadier Private Tom Forsyth recalled the

---

* These words go a long way to confirming George MacDonell's belief that Wallis was "confused and erratic."

words "What, surrender now . . . after so many good men we've lost" breaking through his comrades' sobs. Surrendering, even after been shoved out of position after position, could not help but stick in the craw of the Canadians who had travelled halfway around the world and, in two weeks of terrible battle, learned the dark arts of war. Capturing the thoughts of many, Signalman Blacky Verreault wrote, "We gave up to these imitations of men. What a disgrace."

Book II:
The POW Years

CHAPTER 15

"The Stench of Ordure Ran among the Cobbles"

The First Days as POWs
26 December 1941 to April 1942

Thou shalt not be afraid for the terror by night;
nor for the arrow that flieth by day;
Nor for the pestilence that walketh in darkness;
nor for the destruction that wasteth at noonday.
A thousand shall fall at thy side, and ten thousand at thy right
hand; but it shall not come nigh thee.
—PSALM 91

The usually adroit government of W.L. Mackenzie King had done little to prepare Canadians for what Colonel George Drew, Conservative leader of the Opposition in Ontario, called the Canadian Gethsemane, a reference to the garden in which the Romans arrested Jesus. Indeed, on 22 December Minister of Defence John Ralston assured the nation that the British and Canadians were not only resisting the Japanese but that one Canadian battalion was attacking the Japanese rear. The next day the *Globe and Mail* went a step further, declaring "Jap Invaders Hurled Back by Defenders of Hong Kong."

Word that the Canadian contingent had suffered 100 percent casualties did not cause the political earthquake that might have been expected. Announced in the *Globe and Mail* in a banner headline—"Hong Kong Resistance Ends"—on 26 December, the defeat was page 4 news the following day.[99] The next issue of the paper, Monday, 29 December, carried a forty-eight-word article on page 3 reporting that Ottawa had requested Swiss help in obtaining a casualty list.* The scant coverage has nothing to do with wartime censorship or the phlegmatic temper of the times; rather, the rush of world events overtook the military disaster.

On Friday, 26 December, King's government announced that Winston Churchill would be coming to Ottawa the following Tuesday to address the House of Commons. Together with battlefield news from Europe, the *Globe and Mail*'s headline on 27 December was:

> Churchill to Speak in Ottawa Tuesday;
> Smash New German Lines in Russia;
> Hitler Prepares for Drive in Near East

The disaster at Hong Kong was in the news again in late January 1942. Drew published an open letter criticizing King for sending an undermanned, undertrained and underequipped force to Hong Kong, and Defence Minister Ralston admitted in the House that the Canadian mechanized transport had been mistakenly sent to Manila (just in time to be seized by the Japanese). Pressure from Drew and the press forced King's hand and he appointed Sir Lyman Duff, the Chief Justice of the Supreme Court, to head a one-man royal commission into "C" Force's formation and mission. In June there were some fireworks when Luff, predictably, largely exoner-

---

* On 26 December, the government released the names of the men who composed "C" Force, but not a causality list.

ated King's government. But even though newspapers and newsreels showed the pictures from Pearl Harbor; the bombing of Darwin; Australia; the fall of the Philippines; naval battles and the years of island-by-island advance on Japan, for Canadians, the Pacific War was America's war. Canadians focused their attention on their sons fighting on the North Atlantic, on the St. Lawrence River, in North Africa and Italy, over occupied Europe and Nazi Germany, and after storming Juno Beach, in France, Belgium and Holland. The Europe-first policy decided on by Roosevelt and Churchill governed Canada's war effort and the lives of almost a million Canadian servicemen and -women. The titanic struggle against the Nazis left only the families of the almost two thousand men who had sailed from Vancouver in October 1941 standing vigil.[*]

. . .

First World War veterans' were familiar with the systematic way that the British, Canadian and German captors recorded the names, ranks, serial numbers and health conditions of their prisoners. That made the Japanese disregard of these Geneva-mandated procedures and their control of the thousands of prisoners they took on 25 December all the more shocking. Lieutenant-General Sakai's men neither took names nor posted strong guards around Stanley and Mount Austin barracks. Save for kicking the Grenadiers out of the barracks on the 26th and the Peak Mansions the next day, for the first few days after the surrender, the Japanese left the Canadians to their own devices. The Japanese attitude was not, however, rooted in a touching sense that King George's troops played by the Marquess of Queensberry's rules.

---

[*] Raised in January 1942, the 1st Reconstituted Grenadiers provided coastal defence for British Columbia and participated in the combined U.S.-Canadian attack on the Japanese in the Aleutians in 1943.

Rather, after the surrender, Sakai gave thousands of his soldiers three days' leave, turning the Wan Chai district over to rape and rapine. One family that escaped this horrible fate was Adrienne Poy's.* When the Japanese soldiers came looking for women, her grandmother hid her mother and aunt under some coats and blankets while Adrienne and her brother pretended to be playing with their grandmother. On 27 December, some two thousand men marched behind General Sakai on his white horse through the streets of Victoria—suitably bedecked with Japanese flags—while sixty planes roared overhead.

However, the most important reason that the Japanese left the defeated soldiers alone is that they simply had no plans to cope with more than ten thousand Canadian, British and Indian POWs, as they themselves had been enjoined against being taken prisoner. Ensign Kazuo Sakamaki, who had commanded one of the midget submarines that attacked Pearl Harbor on 7 December and was captured a few hours after the attack, begged his captors, "Kill me [in] an honorable way."[2] At Tarawa in November 1943, of 2,571 Imperial Japanese soldiers, eight would be taken prisoner. Wounded Japanese soldiers famously waited until Marines came to their assistance before detonating hidden grenades.

. . .

For the first few days after the capitulation, the Canadians lived off their own stores. Rumours abounded: Chiang Kai-shek's army had fallen on the Japanese rear; the American fleet was steam-

---

* Fearing that the Japanese would kill his despatch rider, Lance-Corporal William Poy (Adrienne Clarkson's father), because he was Chinese, Poy's HKVDC commander ordered him to exchange his uniform for civilian clothes and to try to blend into the civilian population. The Poy family was among those evacuated from Hong Kong in mid-1942. Poy later debriefed the Canadian government.

ing to the rescue or had been destroyed at Pearl Harbor. None, of course, was true.

On Boxing Day, Rifleman Alfred Babin and four other men helped Chaplain Barnett with the grisly task of collecting the men killed on Christmas Day. Without regard to creed, in front of each body, including those of Riflemen John MacKay and Elzie Henderson, who had had their "eyes, ears and tongues cut out," Barnett read the Anglican burial service. He read it before the pile of mutilated nurses that included nurse Emma Begg; when Sergeant-Major Begg saw his wife's body, he suffered an immediate mental collapse. The Japanese refused permission to bury the dead; instead, more than one hundred and sixty bodies were placed on a pyre made out of mattresses.

Babin could never forget the smell the burning pyre or "how the bodies curled into a foetal position, or how the backs arched as the fire caused them to shrink and blacken—how the flames flared as the body fat melted—how the bodies emitted an unearthly whuhh as the air in the lungs expanded and forced its way out of the mouth."

At one point, a wounded soldier asked for communion. "I used a cup and saucer for the Chalice and Patten," Barnett wrote in his report, "and water and hard tack for the Elements." Moments later, the soldier died.

. . .

Beyond the Japanese sentry line lay still more fallen Canadians, who weighed on George MacDonell. Major Parker doubted that the Japanese would allow MacDonell to bury the men who had died in the bungalows and around the cemetery, but after MacDonell insisted, Parker agreed to let him try to tend to them.

As MacDonell's small party approached the Japanese line, he raised his arms to show he was unarmed. When the soldier challenged him, MacDonell made it understood that he wanted to speak to an officer. He recalls, "The officer spoke passable English and I told him we wanted to bury our men, and he ordered that we be allowed to enter the Japanese position."

The search for their dead took the Canadians down the road on which they had caught the Japanese the day before. The scene shocked MacDonell: "In the street where we had shot down the troops, the bodies were removed, but the gutters were filled with blackened dried blood."

. . .

According to Lance Ross, 29 December was extremely solemn. The daylight was stained by "terrible sights," perhaps the most baleful of which were seen by a burial party at Eucliffe Castle. Of the more than fifty bodies British Lieutenant W. Markey saw there, at least fifteen had "had their hands tied behind their backs with thin cord and had obviously been captured alive and destroyed later," he later told the War Crimes Tribunal. British Lieutenant Charles Johnston told the same tribunal, "All the ones I saw with their heads chopped off had wound[s] in the back of the neck." Among the mutilated were the remains of three Canadians.

. . .

The next day, spirits rose as men given up for lost reappeared. After three days of hiding in the hulk of HMS *Thracian* and then on Lamma Island, Major Charles Young paid a boatman to take him and his men to where they could surrender. No one would have bet a nickel on Leslie Canivet being alive.

After escaping from Overbays House on 22 December, Canivet and several other men had tried to make their way to Stanley. En route they met a Rifleman who "had had his privates almost completely shot away" and whose legs had been reduced to pulp. Canivet, weakened by a shrapnel wound to his jaw, passed out shortly thereafter. When he came to, Canivet spent the better part of another two days trying to get to Stanley, but he and several other men were captured and marched toward Repulse Bay. Before reaching the bay, the Japanese captors lined the men up in front of a ditch and started shooting. The volley boomed in Canivet's ears and turned a sergeant's prayerful words into his "death rattle."

Hit several times, Canivet fell and played dead. Some time later, the wounded soldier Canivet had seen earlier treated Canivet's wounds. Canivet then lost consciousness. When he awoke, he was weak from loss of blood, lack of food and water, and completely alone.

Summoning up the last reserves of his strength, Canivet climbed a hill from which he could see Stanley. Along the road, he encountered some Chinese travellers, who, upon seeing him, screamed and ran away. Lazarus rising from the dead might have seemed less frightening to the medical staff at an advanced dressing station Canivet found, for by the time he arrived, "maggots were falling quite freely from the hole" a bullet had made in his jaw.*

. . .

On 30 December, a time ended that, in comparison with what was to come, Canadians would look back on with nostalgia. The Royal Rifles at Stanley were ordered to North Point and the Grenadiers

---

* Though they suspected that there had been a surrender, Stretcher-Bearer John Duguay and several other Canadians he was tending in the field did not receive the order. They hid out, surviving on bully beef they found in blasted pillboxes and on water taken from the Tai Tam Tuk Reservoir. Pushed by the worsening infections in two of the men's legs, on 1 January, Duguay disposed of their guns and grenades and surrendered to a Japanese patrol, which gave them neither food nor water but did arrange for a truck to take them to North Point.

were transported back to Shamshuipo on the mainland. Bob Barter remembers with pride that the Canadians marched into North Point in formation. The Grenadiers stayed at Shamshuipo until 23 January 1942, when they would join the Rifles at North Point. (At the same time, the British at North Point would be sent to Shamshuipo.) While some of the specifics differ, it hardly mattered in which camp the Canadians spent their first three weeks of captivity.

Both camps had sustained significant damage during the battle; neither met even minimal standards of hygiene. At Shamshuipo a few buckets constituted the "latrine." Diarrhea set in within a few days as a consequence of the dirty, poor-quality rice and unsanitary cooking conditions; the latrine was soon overburdened and men were forced to "crap all over the place," recorded Harry White in his secret diary. At North Point, the "latrine" consisted of a plank that extended over the seawall—beneath which bodies of dead Chinese floated on the ebb and flow of the tides. Men weakened from wounds and/or dysentery tied themselves to the plank to keep from falling into the foul water.

Neither camp had adequate shelter, their roofs and walls having been ripped open by shells; neither had electricity (though the Signalmen at North Point soon rewired the huts there). The Grenadiers slept on bare concrete, something they would recall fondly when, after moving to North Point, their mattresses (canvas bags filled with crushed coconut) crawled with bedbugs whose bites deprived them of sleep and made them look as if they had measles. At North Point, flies—attracted by the garbage dump blasted open during the battle and the decaying Chinese corpses and dead animals that littered one end of the camp—were so numerous that the food the prisoners were served could hardly be seen beneath the seething black mass of flies. In February, in an attempt to staunch an outbreak of dysentery partially caused by fly-borne feces, the camp's commandant ordered inmates to catch a quota of flies each day.*

Neither camp had a hospital, though for a time the worst medical cases were taken to the one at Bowen Road. Worse, neither camp had adequate facilities to cook what amounted to a tea cup of rice per man per meal, and fish heads, rancid whale meat or chrysanthemum tops. The Geneva Convention stipulated that POWs must be fed the same rations as the host army. For most of the time of their imprisonment, the Canadians did not receive such rations. Even when they did, they were still drastically underfed because the average Canadian soldier was significantly taller and heavier than the average Japanese soldier. The Canadian calorie requirements were at least 2,500 per day and more than 3,500 for those doing heavy labour. In these early days of their captivity, rarely did the calorie intake rise above 1,300; some days it totalled only 900. Similarly, the Canadians were consuming significantly less than the two ounces of protein required by grown men.

At North Point, the Japanese guards provided a couple of cooking kettles and mouldy rice. For the first few weeks of January, they allowed foraging parties to retrieve supplies left behind in dumps. Equally important were the field cookers, tools and building materials used to patch up the barracks and build an oven in which to bake bread. At Shamshuipo, meagre Japanese rations were also supplemented with British and Canadian supplies—bought from Chinese looters who had taken them from the camp.

On 3 January, White wrote, "Am getting sick of rice already, it seems to bloat you up and then in a short time you are as hungry as ever again." That same day, the Japanese drove four pigs

---

* The order was not unique. In *Prison Doctor*, his memoir of Haruku, a POW camp in the Spice Islands, Richard Philips reports that he was not allowed to build the camp's latrine so it emptied into the sea because the sea belonged to the Divine Emperor—and that the fly problem was handled by having each POW capture a hundred flies per day.

into the camp holding more than two thousand men. Across the bay at North Point, Ross wrote, "Whale meat isn't very good and rice isn't very nutritious either." Three days later, when Grenadier Nelson Galbraith wrote that he was "getting thinner every day," inflation had driven the price of two small loaves of bread outside Shamshuipo to two Hong Kong dollars. The arrival of a different group of guards at the beginning of the second week of January put an end to the over-the-fence trade. Without that trade, the men's weight loss accelerated. Between Christmas Day and 15 January, some had lost twenty pounds—almost a pound a day.

. . .

While cultivating rice requires significantly more labour than does cultivating wheat, in its natural form (that is, brown rice), rice compares well with whole wheat and enriched flour. However, when they were not giving the Canadians mouldy rice, the Japanese gave them white polished rice from the captured British stores. White rice is significantly less nutritious than brown rice or enriched flour. It is especially lacking in B vitamins and trace elements like phosphorus, and totally lacking in zinc. Within a few months, the lack of these vitamins (avitaminosis) would lead to beriberi, pellagra, temporary blindness and a painful condition called "electric feet."*

. . .

By 18 January, however, a diet built on rice was not just gnawing at the Canadians' stomachs, it was having a devastating impact on their

---

* Caused by a lack of thiamine (vitamin B1), "electric feet" or peripheral neuritis, dry beriberi, begins with numbness in the toes, extending to twitching feet (sometimes called "happy feet") before turning into shooting pains from the arch to the tip of the toes, which for reasons that are not understood are worse at night.

sleep (already badly disrupted by the plague of bedbugs) and their morale. Young men who prided themselves on their physical condition were beginning to lose muscle; moreover, as though they had aged prematurely, they had to urinate four or more times a night.

. . .

The Japanese authorities were relatively benign during these early days. Under the watchful eyes of only two guards, Major Bishop and some twenty men went to Lyemun to retrieve the unit's band instruments, which, they discovered, had been pilfered. Foraging parties brought back books. Jean-Paul Dallain took advantage of the lax camp rules in early January to read both *Gone with the Wind* and a collection of Rudyard Kipling stories while sitting with his feet in the sun to dry them out, a successful effort to treat the athlete's foot he contracted from the boots that had been switched for his during the battle.

The casual brutality of the Japanese was, however, never far from view. On 12 January, in full view of the Grenadiers, a Chinese boy was tied to a lamppost and two other Chinese civilians were publicly stripped to humiliate them. A week later, Verreault saw a guard shoot down a twelve-year-old girl who had tried to sell something across the fence. "The bastard threw her on his shoulder and dropped her brutally down the street where an old woman in tears picked her up," he wrote. Guards used a Chinese man who had forgotten to walk on the other side of the street from the camp's fence for judo and bayonet practice before throwing his body off the end of the dock.

. . .

The transfer of the Grenadiers to North Point on 23 January did not unite all Canadians behind one fence. Many injured men and others sick with dysentery remained at the Bowen Road Military Hospital.* Kept in operation until April 1945, partly as a show for the Red Cross and partly because the Japanese had no plan of their own to provide medical care to POWs, the hospital was staffed by British and Canadians, operating under Japanese regulations that determined the type and number of patients the hospital could accept. Here too the Japanese failed to supply adequate rations.

When William Allister fell ill and was taken to the hospital in January 1942, he found the hospital on quarter rations, and dysentery patients like himself were on a quarter of that. For breakfast one morning, he and seven other men were given a dozen corn flakes each and a 1½-inch cube of cheese to be divided among them. Enraged, they confronted an officer, "Can you tell us how the fuck eight grown men are expected live on this?"

Allister's anger at the Japanese (and at British medical orderlies suspected of pilfering rations) was matched by the bile that rose in him when he spoke to Captain George Billings, who was also a patient at the hospital. Allister did not begrudge his commander a private room with a fireplace; he was, after all, an officer. What Allister couldn't understand was how, after hearing his complaint about the lack of food, Billings could go on baking flat biscuits (made from water and flour) in front of his subordinate and not offer him even one of what the secular Allister thought of as "home-made matzo," the Biblical bread of affliction hastily made by the Israelites fleeing Pharaoh.[3]

Scant food and nights and days of running to pass watery stool had weakened Allister's and the other men's bodies, but it did not

---

* Though they were military personnel, each holding the rank of lieutenant, Canadian Nursing Sisters Kay Christie and May Waters were allowed to remain at the Bowen Road Military Hospital to nurse the sick until August 1942. Thereafter, they were interned with civilians like Gwen Dew at a camp in Stanley. Christie and Waters were repatriated in late 1943; the Japanese did not release the British nurses.

break their spirit. They told a British officer to "go to Hell" when he told them they were going to be put in work parties to help rebuild the hospital. The next day, the fat British colonel who gave them a dressing down ignored the "Fuckin' bullshitter" whispered audibly after he threatened to send them to North Point. The colonel tried again: "The Jap has left us to our own, not crowded us into rat-infested huts like sardines, surrounded by vicious guards and barbed wire. Of course, if you feel well enough for that, it can easily be arranged. Either you stay and follow orders or get out. . . . Now. How many of you choose to leave? Raise your hands."

The only things to go up faster than the colonel's blood pressure were Allister's and the other men's hands. Stunned, but able to get even, the colonel ordered, "Pack your damn kits! You'll be on the march in the morning."[4] Allister arrived at North Point on 19 January, the day Verreault wrote that he was no longer strong enough to wear his boots and that he wouldn't have the strength to twist Charlotte's little finger. "I still have enough energy to write as I lay on my bunk with only my hand having to make the effort. . . . it helps to forget this hell I'm in."

. . .

When Allister returned to North Point, where as many as two hundred men lived in 125-by-18-foot huts and slept in bunks ranged five high, the camp included a dysentery hospital. Ignoring the etiology of disease, the Japanese blamed the dysentery outbreak on their captives' weak spirit, which supposedly allowed them to get shamefully sick. The number of sick men, however, forced the commandant to allow the creation of a hospital in a nearby *godown*. It reminded Tom Marsh of the medieval dungeon on Lake Geneva immortalized by Lord Byron in the poem "The Prisoner of Chillon." Lieutenant-Commander R.B. Goodwin recalled that in the makeshift hospital,

[the] floor was of cobblestones, ventilation and light were provided by two very small windows and a small door, and the interior was always in deep gloom. Two four-gallon conveniences provided. Four or five patients were always clustered about each of these inadequate receptacles, needing to use them at the same time and the place reeked with the stench of ordure which ran among the cobbles and fouled the blankets of those lying on the ground.[5]

Without medicines, the only treatment the medical corpsman could offer was cleaning of the desperately ill men. To be washed, a man was first carried outside and stripped; his stinking clothes were then put in boiling water. The corpsman "scrubbed the crusted shit and corruption from head to toe—ears, armpits, feet, hair, under the testicles where the shit was glued in layers—scrubbed and scraped with rags and fingers, nearly drawing blood, till all the skin shone pink and fresh and glowing."[6] And then the corpsman would do it again to another man.

. . .

Veterans of German POW camps have rightly criticized *Hogan's Heroes* for making light of their ordeal. Still, the campy 1960s situation comedy underlined at least one important fact about life in a POW camp. Contrary to what civilians (who are apt to confuse the POW experience with that of an incarcerated criminal) might expect, young men who continue to conduct themselves as soldiers—and the Canadians in Hong Kong did—quickly adapt as life becomes regularized under the command of known officers.*

---

* The orders for 23 March included a number of promotions of Signalmen. Corporal Donald Penny became an acting sergeant; Blacky Verreault and Lionel Speller became acting lance-corporals.

"After the pell-mell of battle and the anxious days of waiting after the surrender," says MacDonell, "it was almost a relief to once again live the structured life of a soldier. Soldiers woke to reveille, took part in morning muster, had breakfast, took part in sick parade, evening muster and then went to sleep at the last post—and that is what we did.* We were hungry, terribly hungry, and at the mercy of a savage and arbitrary enemy, but we not only believed in our cause, we believed in each other. We were nothing like criminal prisoners. We had done nothing dishonourable. Quite the opposite. We had held up honourably under a terrible onslaught and had damaged the enemy."

With the exception of regular beatings, the POWs had remarkably little contact with their Japanese guards. Orders could, of course, be issued directly to a POW, but most of the time orders were issued to the Canadian officers who relayed them to their men. The POWs also ran the messes.

. . .

Observant Catholic veterans are as dismissive of those who did not regularly attend to take communion but scrambled forward for it before battle as Protestant veterans are wary of the old axiom that there are no atheists in foxholes. Nevertheless, there is no question

---

* In these early days of their captivity, a typical daily routine was

0630	Reveille
0715	Breakfast
0800	Muster Parade
0805–0825	Physical Training
0900	Sick Parade
1200	Dinner
1700	Supper
1800	Muster Parade
2130	Lights Out

that for many POWs the celebration of the Eucharist was important. These age-old rituals, the singing of hymns like "Unto the Hills," "Faith of Our Fathers" and "Abide with Me" and the repetition of prayers learned as children were the only actions the POWs could undertake that they knew were performed in the same way by their families half a world away.

Laite, the United Church padre, and Barnett, who was Anglican, shared services, giving communion to each other's adherents, and even conducted some services in the style of the (Baptist-like) Plymouth Brethren. In April, the Japanese stopped allowing Father O'Brien, SJ, Chaplain of the French Hospital at Causeway Bay, to supply Father Francis Deloughery with altar breads and sacramental wine. Using a flat iron as a press, a cook began supplying Deloughery with communion wafers.

Equally important were the padres' more private moments with the sick, those struggling to find or keep their faith and those nearing death. On Ash Wednesday (13 February), Laite wrote that the previous night he had had "a pleasant chat with a small group who, without question, spoke of their faith in the Church, and how belief in, and the acceptance of the principles of Jesus only could save our civilization." Deloughery kept the most detailed records; over the course of 1942, he celebrated 360 masses, administered 11,817 Holy Communions, made 250 hospital visits, prepared 125 men for death and buried 17 soldiers. The padres helped the men cope with the loss of brothers, cousins and lifelong friends, often by reciting with them the poet Laurence Binyon's words that today end the Remembrance Day service:

> They shall grow not old, as we that are left grow old:
> Age shall not weary them, nor the years condemn.
> At the going down of the sun and in the morning
> We will remember them.

. . .

Two other manifestations of POW camp life helped gird morale. The first consisted of organized diversions such as ball games (for those still strong enough to play), lectures (including one with the gripping title "How Canada Is Governed") and reading. By June, a lending library with four hundred books operated. For some, reading was an important diversion and, in the case of francophones like Verreault—who proudly recorded on 1 March that he had read three 300-page English books—a means to demonstrate achievement. For others, reading was akin to therapy. When Lance-Corporal James Mitchell, who had sunken into despair after the surrender, reached for a book, Allister wrote that he had "beaten back the ogre of darkness."[7]

For Allister, reading connected him to the Republic of Letters beyond the camp fence. It allowed him to make sense of the world he lived in—a world of awful uncertainty and arbitrary power in which survival meant following not just the rules handed to you, but also anticipating unstated rules that must be followed to avoid being beaten. Reading proved to him, as it proved to members of the German Resistance, that *"Die Gedanken sind frei"* ("Thoughts are free").

For many, as their hunger increased—something that can be tracked from poignant diary entries like "Allowed to pour tea on rice"—baseball, lectures and reading lost their allure.[8] Hunger, sometimes kept at bay by men recalling favourite meals or describing those they'd cook, sometimes by singing (Allister's hut had a piano) or listening to records or, most commonly, by cigarettes, was never far away; some men took up smoking to assuage their hunger. How else could it be when on those days that their hearts rose when they heard they were to be given eggs, more often than not they found them to be green and rotten, and when every day their uniforms became looser? In early March, hunger and, more to the point, the belief that those charged with ladling the rice into the men's tins were shortchanging them, became so palpable that Royal Rifles Captain Edmund Hurd feared mutiny. He quelled the rising anger by convening a Court of Inquiry and appointing Company Quartermaster-Sergeant Colin Standish, who was trusted by the men, to oversee the rations.

.   .   .

Also important in maintaining morale was what some Canadians called their "chum" but which is, perhaps, better captured by the Australian term "mateship."[9] In some cases, especially in regard to work details, mateship could extend to four men, a number that allowed one man to be sick and the others to cover his work quota. This number allowed them to "pool their food so that he would have a bit extra, try to scrounge him a duck egg, take turn[s] visiting him, wash his clothes [and look] after his belongings in the sleeping hut."[10] Most of the time, however, mateship involved two men.

In regiments like the Rifles, which contained many sets of brothers, cousins and pre-existing friendships, many of the mates were obvious. Jean-Paul Dallain belonged to a larger group that included his brother Charlie, and Charlie's pre-war friend, Andrew Flanagan. Because Allister published his memoir and Verreault's son published Blacky's, much is known about this quintessentially Canadian odd couple, whose mateship spanned the country's two solitudes.

Verreault is present in Allister's resumé of the battle. Allister does not surface in Verreault's diary until 11 March. "Ally," Verreault wrote, is a "very different type. . . . He's Jewish but not of strong convictions." Though something of a lady's man, Verreault proudly recorded the many times he took communion (and, later in Japan, when he could not take it, how long it had been). Thus, it is somewhat surprising to find him adding that Allister "has his own ideas on religion and I respect his sincerity. He's deeply intelligent and witty."

Allister's views on the Catholic Church and its role in Quebec were quite at odds with the extremely conservative Catholic views Verreault learned in church and at school. On 10 June 1942 Verreault wrote: "Strange! I used to despise Jews and now my best friend is a Jew. It's regrettable to see the injustice shown to this race in the way we were raised especially us French-Canadians, in despising and even hating Jews. I'm closer to Allister than to Bruno [a fellow French Canadian] and I'm looking forward to meeting his family as I am sure I will like them."

Ironically, it is the intellectual Montrealer Allister who writes in more emotional terms about his mate.* The night Allister returned to North Point, he shared a "miserable little wick" with Blacky and Tony Grimston. "Blacky lay pressed against me, locked away in his own bitter world. . . . Unlike me . . . he had revelled in battle, stood ready to be tested by any challenge of courage and strength. . . . He'd been sold off into slavery, humbled, locked away in this god damn leper colony."[11] The nights were cold and they huddled together for warmth—as so many others would over the next few years.

．　．　．

Back in Canada, the political manoeuvring that began with Drew's attack on King's government and the report of the Duff Commission is interesting for those who study what is now called "crisis communications." But what mattered to the Canadian government and Phil Doddridge's mother, Ed Shayler's wife and some thousand other Canadian families was whether their sons, husbands and fathers

---

* I do not mean to imply that there was a sexual relationship between them. By March, malnutrition had extinguished most libidos.

were alive and if they were well. On 12 January 1942, the Adjutant General wrote these families saying how much he regretted having no information to give them and assuring them that the government was making every effort to get information about their loved ones. The letter ends:

> You may rest assured that on receipt of any particulars respecting the welfare of your son/husband you will be advised immediately by telegram, as it is fully realized that suspense may cause even greater distress than a full knowledge of the facts, whatever they may be.

The government knew almost nothing, and what it did know, it didn't want publicized. Almost a month after the capitulation, neither Britain nor the Red Cross had received any information from Japan, though an intercepted radio message indicated that the POWs had been interned at Kowloon (referring to Shamshuipo). On 29 January, Hirohito's government issued the following statement:

> The Imperial Government has not yet ratified the Convention relative to the treatment of prisoners of war on 27th July 1929. It is, therefore, not bound by the said Convention. However, it will apply *mutatis mutandis** for the provisions of the said Convention to English, Canadian, Australian and New Zealand prisoners in its hands.[12]

---

* *Mutatis mutandis* means "changes where necessary" and is usually used to indicate that changes to a text that have been made, for example, changing the title of an officer of an organization from "Chairman" to "Chair," should be assumed to have been made in all documents so pertaining. Given the number and extent of the violations of the Convention already perpetrated by the Japanese, this phrase here is almost a ghastly joke.

By the beginning of February, the Canadian government knew that dysentery had broken out and that some POWs had been shot. On 9 February, the British informed the Japanese that failure to allow either Argentina, who had been made the "protecting powere," or the Red Cross to verify the status of the British Empire's POWs would be taken as proof that they were being mistreated. Tokyo ignored the message.

On 13 February, Defence Minister Ralston, then visiting London, cabled Ottawa that a broadcast originating in Berlin indicated that the Canadian POWs were in good shape, but he cautioned against putting too much faith in the report. Equally importantly, given the roiled political waters in Ottawa, he noted that it was only a matter of time until the North American press picked up this report and published it. Two days later, papers across Canada carried, mostly on inside pages, an Associated Press story that five thousand men at Kowloon were being badly mistreated and that dysentery raged through the camps. On 16 February, Tommy Douglas (of the Co-operative Commonwealth Federation, the forerunner of the NDP) asked what the government knew about the report. King answered that the British were trying to verify the information and then pointed out the government's difficult position as it tried to balance the need to censor rumours with the public's desire to have information at the earliest possible moment.

Three days later, Ottawa learned that the "conditions [in the camps were] undoubtedly deplorable and Japanese completely callous. Doctors [were] unable to treat many cases of dysentery owing to absence of medical stores. No proper arrangements for cooking, feeding or sanitation." The cable also said that after the battle "there were many authenticated cases of brutality, including murder of prisoners and nurses and rape of nurses." On 24 February, Vincent Massey, Canada's High Commissioner to the United Kingdom, cabled a report that detailed several atrocities and spoke of "studied barbarism undoubtedly employed with the object of breaking morale." Canada's Chief Press Censor told the wire services to spike the story.

He needn't have bothered. Earlier in the day, Sir Percy Harris rose in the British House of Commons and asked several pointed questions about the reports coming from Hong Kong. Churchill's government waited to answer until 10 March when Sir Anthony Eden, Secretary of State for Foreign Affairs, confirmed that atrocities had occurred and were still occurring, and that Japan had refused to allow either the Red Cross or Argentina access to the prisoners. "The Japanese claim that their forces are animated by a lofty code of chivalry, *Bushido,* is a nauseating hypocrisy."*

The Canadian press handled stories about the mistreatment of Canadians carefully. In a 31 March story, O.D. Gallagher reported that after the battle at the Repulse Bay Hotel a banker saw fifteen Canadians roped together, with knots shoved in their mouths, kneeling by the side of a road, and later heard shots; it appeared on page 11 of the *Globe and Mail.* The story prompted a government official to write to Under Secretary of State for External Affairs Norman Robertson complaining that the article was "the height of ghoulishness."

Letters by worried relatives and concerned citizens received attention at the highest levels of the government. In April, the head of the Medical Aid to Russia Fund, Colonel H. Mackie, wrote Robertson suggesting that the prime minister appeal to Russia's leader Joseph Stalin to intervene on the Canadians' behalf. Russia, Mackie argued, owed Canada both a financial and moral debt "for saving 100,000 Russian children during the famine twenty years ago," a reference to

---

* Forewarned on 9 March that Eden's speech would contain "facts that will come as a great shock to the public," Robertson telegraphed the Commissioner of the Royal Canadian Mounted Police asking him to take "precautionary measures . . . to prevent the indignation, which must follow on the publication of the reports from Hong Kong, venting itself on persons of Japanese origin in Canada." There were no incidents.

the famine Stalin had engineered in the Ukraine during his drive to collectivize agriculture. Robertson thanked Mackie, but there is no record of the Canadian government requesting Stalin's help.

The men half a world away, of course, had no idea what their families knew about their battle, defeat and imprisonment. Coincidentally, at just about the point when stories of their mistreatment at the hands of the Japanese appeared in the papers, several men recorded in their diaries not just what their internment was doing to them but also what it must have been doing to their families. In the privacy of their thoughts, they tried to imagine their wives, sons and daughters, a task made all the more difficult for some like Leonard Corrigan; he had lost his pictures of his family in a shallow trench.

. . .

The approach of Easter (5 April) carried significant meaning to the men in the camps. Even to the less-than-devout, Jesus' death and resurrection was an all-too-obvious metaphor for their plight. The coming of Easter also threw into sharp relief the difference between the outcome of their battle and their fathers' great 1917 victory on Easter Monday at Vimy. Whether they chose to acknowledge the importance of Holy Week or because an important Japanese holiday fell on the same day as did Good Friday, the Japanese paid the officers for the first time, each officer receiving the same pay as his equivalent rank in the Japanese army.*

Like so many men, even as he joined the other padres in leading the Easter celebration, Laite's thoughts were of his wife, Sally, his two children and the rest of his family. The money the Japanese paid on Good Friday allowed Laite's mess to buy an extra tin of

---

* There being no honorary officers in the Japanese army, chaplains Deloughery, Laite and Barnett were not paid; the officers in their mess pooled their pay and distributed a portion to each padre.

milk for rice, porridge and tea. While he enjoyed the largesse, he regretted that it was not shared by the men sick in hospital or by the hundreds of ordinary ranks.

The terrible scourge of dysentery had sickened hundreds and killed two Grenadiers, Privates Earl Till and Orville Rodd, in January. Septicemia killed Rifleman Gordon Kellaway in March. Malnutrition had led scores into near-madness from pain and others toward progressive blindness. On Easter Monday, malnutrition—manifested as anemia, dysentery and beriberi—took its first life: the commander of the Winnipeg Grenadiers, Lieutenant-Colonel John Sutcliffe.

Word of Sutcliffe's death at the Bowen Road Hospital shocked Barnett and the other prisoners. It also seems to have affected the Japanese commandant. The same officer who had refused to respond to repeated entreaties for more food and had resisted the establishment of a hospital to the last minute, trucked thirty-two officers and men to the hospital for the funeral. Conducted by the three Canadian chaplains and a British padre, Colonel Reverend Strong, Sutcliffe's funeral was the largest for any of the five hundred men who died during the battle or in the prison camps. Strong read the 90th Psalm, the second verse of which is

> Before the mountains were brought forth,
> or ever thou hadst formed the earth and the world,
> even from everlasting to everlasting, thou *art* God.

When they heard these words, many men must have asked themselves the same sort of question that the Jews at Auschwitz asked when they put God on trial: Did God not see the suffering in the camps?*

---

* Though this story may be apocryphal, it was used by Elie Wiesel as the basis for his 1979 play *The Trial of God*.

CHAPTER 16

"All Canadians Will Be Slaves as You Are Now!"

The Kamloops Kid
May to December 1942

"There are worse evils than war."
—OWEN WISTER, *THE VIRGINIAN*

Late on the night of 12 May 1942, Lance Ross began his diary by writing that it had rained very hard that day. The final nine words of Ross's entry—"Great sea battle reported going on in Indian Ocean"—were probably gleaned from a gossipy guard or from a newspaper carelessly left in the open; although there was a clandestine radio in camp, only the senior officers knew of it. Like all governments do in wartime, Tokyo controlled what could be published. Big battles, however, produced large numbers of casualties that could not be completely hidden, especially as tins filled with the ashes of cremated soldiers began arriving on doorsteps across Japan. Accordingly, while the Japanese used newspapers to shore up the home front (trumpeting the sinking of the aircraft carrier USS *Enterprise* at least three times), they also reported on the general course of the war. The particulars Ross had heard were wrong, but their essence was right; during the Battle of the Coral Sea fought 4–8 May, the United States had halted the Japanese advance on Australia.*

.   .   .

The Japanese did not provide the Canadian government with a list of casualties until October, but scores of families wrote Ottawa seeking information before then. Thinking that Ottawa might know something from soldiers who had escaped Hong Kong, Mrs. E.R. Thomas wrote asking about the status of her husband, Signalman Ernest, and eleven other men. In June, Mrs. Mina Doucet, cousin to Rifleman Edgar, wrote to Norman Robertson saying how difficult it was not knowing if Edgar was alive or dead and that the government's response to the published reports of atrocities has been "a poor salve for [the families'] wounded hearts." After telling Robertson that she would rather know that Edgar had died a martyr for his country than that he suffered at the hands of "Orientals," she ended her letter by "ask[ing] God to bless you And help you in all your great problems." Robertson did not know that Edgar had been killed on 23 December during the attack on Bridge Hill; he did reply that "every effort has been made since the fall of the garrison to obtain every scrap of information" and that the government had sent aid to the POWs through third parties. He ended the letter by writing, "Mr. King wishes me to thank you on his behalf for the expression of appreciation of the difficult task with which he is faced in these trying times and for your kind words of encouragement."

In the absence of definitive word, most families held out hope. On 1 May, Winnipeg Grenadier Major Kenneth Baird's father-in-law voiced his hope in a letter to his son-in-law: "After weeks and

---

* The battle was fought off the east coast of Australia, not in the Indian Ocean.

months of terrible anxiety, the worst we have ever experienced, it seems we can write and just hope that it reaches you some time, so you will know that day by day we have waited for real news of just where you are and how things are going." Thousands of letters were written. Hundreds of times over four years, the family of Winnipeg Grenadier Corporal Tiny Martyn addressed letters to:

Cpl. F.D.F. Martyn
Winnipeg Grenadiers
H 6053
Taken Prisoner of War at Hong Kong,
Force "C"
General Post Office
Ottawa, Ontario
Canada

The letters were filled with news of family, friends and sports; any discussion of politics or the war being, of course, forbidden. Martyn's father worked hard. Lil and the kids were quarantined because Evelyn had a mild case of scarlet fever. Ed Freeman's wife had died. On 7 March, Martyn's father wrote, "it looks like Detroit Red Wings and Boston for first and second with Chicago, Toronto and Montreal and the New York Rangers bringing up the last spot."*

Mother's Day was an especially hard day for the men. But this 10 May was a wonderful day for Mrs. Molly Baird, Major Kenneth's wife. She wrote something that more than a thousand other Canadian families hoped desperately to write:

---

* Sports was a constant theme. In October 1943, Martyn's cousin Fred dashed off a short note: "Greetings from Winnipeg. Mother and Dad are fine. Dad has been promoted at his work. The Yanks won the World Series."

My dearest Ken,

I feel like a different person today, I can tell you—just 100 years younger. Yesterday I received a wire telling me you were safe. I can't tell you what I felt when I read it. I just sat down and wept for sheer joy. It has been so dreadful not to know all these months. . . . Harvelyn [their daughter] is so excited. This is Mother's Day, and Harvelyn spent her two weeks' allowance and bought me four lovely tulips. Wasn't it sweet of her, because she has to do it on her own, without her dad's help. Then to get my wire—wasn't that a wonderful present from you?

In the middle of the letter, Harvelyn wrote one line: "Dear Daddy; we are so happy to know you are well. XOXO Harvelyn."

Such letters are today a treasure trove of information about the everyday lives of Canadians and, especially, of those whose hearts and prayers were focused on the men of "C" Force even as the country's attention was on the North Atlantic, Sicily, Italy; and the skies above Germany and France. Even the fact that, in most cases, both the writer and the intended readers have now passed on does nothing to ease the ache behind the words "we have not heard from you."

. . .

As important as letters were, the piece of paper that most concerned the Canadians in late May was the No-Escape Pledge that Colonel Isao Tokunaga demanded all prisoners sign. Triggered by the escape of four British POWs from Shamshuipo and of Benjamin Proulx and several others from the Argyle Street POW Camp in January, the pledge violated the Geneva Convention. So did both the threat to cut rations to force men to sign it and the savage beating administered to Royal Rifles Lance-Corporal Jack Porter, a First World War veteran, who outright refused to sign it. British military law (under which the Canadians served) required that, if possible, soldiers try to escape; the Geneva Convention recognized this duty.

Tokunaga, whose girth riled the hungry Canadians almost as much as his sadistic nature, asserted otherwise. Allied POWs were under the control of the Imperial Japanese Army, and it ordered them not to try to escape. By this logic, violating the order was mutiny and thus warranted the death penalty. Tokunaga flew into a rage when the Canadians refused, but he was no fool. After a harangue, he produced a copy signed by General Maltby. Seeing it, the Canadian officers told their men to sign the pledge. In a nice piece of legal legerdemain, the officers explained the requirement to sign, the consequences of not signing and the total irrelevance of an oath sworn under duress. Harry White would never have any trouble remembering the day he signed; 24 May 1942 was his thirty-fifth birthday.

Six days later, Japanese War Minister Tōjō issued the following instructions concerning POWs to the commandant of a camp in Japan. The second sentence reads as if Japan intended to follow the Geneva Convention: "Prisoners of war must be placed under strict discipline as far as it does not contravene the law of humanity." The next sentence, however, is chilling: "It is necessary to take care not to be obsessed with the mistaken idea of humanitarianism or swayed by personal feelings towards those prisoners of war which may grow in the long time of their imprisonment." The order continues: "The present situation does not permit anyone to lay idle doing nothing but eating freely. With that in view, in dealing with prisoners of war, too, I hope you will see that they may be usefully employed."[1] These words authorized turning the POWs into slave labourers.

. . .

On 3 June, Tom Forsyth and some others were taken to a studio to record propaganda messages to be broadcast on shortwave. To ensure that the messages achieved the desired ends, an English-speaking Japanese officer stood ready to halt the recording. The Canadians could not, of course, mention the recent 20 percent cut in rations or relate that the day before their first letters home had been returned with orders to shorten them to no more than two hundred words and not to ask for anything. Forsyth's message was not broadcast until late 1944; it was picked up in the United States and South Africa and relayed to his family.

To ensure that each recording carried the central piece of information the prisoners wanted transmitted—who was alive—they found ways of naming as many men as possible. Nor was it impossible to get information past the censors. In a recording he did later in the war, Allister said, "We are being well treated here and the food is great. Please tell this to all my friends in the army and navy and, above all *tell it to the marines*."[2] The Japanese heard what they wanted to; any North American would have known that the last five words meant *bullshit*. Donald Penny ensured that his upbeat letter of 10 June, which spoke of idling away days at concerts and softball and volleyball games, was understood to mean much the opposite by referring to his wonderful tan (Penny disliked heat) and by asking if his parents had chosen a place in North Vancouver to which he could retire; Penny's family knew of his intense dislike of North Vancouver. At least two Canadians wrote home saying how much they looked forward to a holiday at Stony Mountain and Oakalla, prisons in Manitoba and British Columbia respectively.

. . .

Toward the end of the first week of June, the Japanese requested a Canadian work party to go to Kai Tak aerodrome on the mainland where the runway was being extended.* Though weakened from lack of food, as many as a hundred men volunteered, mostly, according to the Rifles' regimental historian, "to have a diversion from the idleness" of North Point.[3] It is a measure of how powerful the experience of being a POW was that, according to White, the men found being outside the camp a "most peculiar . . . sort of unprotected and deserted and strange" feeling.

The Canadians' job was to remove an ancient burial hill—using nothing but muscle, shovels and traditional baskets hung from a pole balanced across their increasingly bony shoulders. The pay, between 10 and 25 sen, was negligible, but the hot, sweet bean stew was very real. Within days the extra pay and food vanished, and the beatings began. Even as dysentery sickened hundreds, the Japanese demanded four hundred workers a day. An outbreak of diphtheria that killed nine men in September alone did not end the march of men to work beginning at 4:30 a.m. and ending sixteen hours later.

The worst moments were not the sweating and strain under the broiling sun or drenching rain. Rather, they followed the docking of the ferry at Kowloon, when belligerent guards forced the POWs out of the sleep into which they had fallen while crossing the bay. Wordlessly, recalled Allister, they dragged "their emaciated frames down the road in a straggling group, faces fixed with permanent grimaces of fatigue and misery. Some limped, some . . . on stretchers to fill the bureaucratic quota."[4]

Few mastered the jogging gait necessary to haul the "coolie baskets" efficiently, which upset one guard so much he handed Ken Cambon his rifle to hold while the guard demonstrated the proper technique. The guards were less understanding about the inept way the Canadians mixed the cement to be used for the runway; the

---

* British POWs had been used there as slave labourers since early February; landslides had already killed several men.

workers were beaten for it. The Riflemen would have been executed had the guards realized that, in order to weaken the runway, they were intentionally mixing too much sand into the concrete.

. . .

The Japanese gave the Canadians a day off on 1 July for Dominion Day, allowing them to play baseball or volleyball and at night put on a minstrel show. The joy was tempered, however, by the fact that twenty-eight men were sick with dysentery, electric feet and in recent days beriberi, and the rumour (spread, no doubt, to demonstrate the reach of the Imperial Japanese Navy) that the Japanese had attacked Canada by shelling Vancouver.* The next day, the camp's commandant called the senior officers to a meeting at which he told them that negotiations were taking place to arrange a prisoner exchange; since civilians such as Adrienne Poy's [Clarkson's] family and Gwen Dew had sailed for West Africa a few days earlier, the commandant's words seemed tantalizingly true.†

On 3 July, the Canadians had even more reason to hope that their conditions would improve when two Swiss representatives visited the camp. The visitors' minders kept them from speaking to Major John Price, the senior officer in the camp, until they entered the hospital and saw the blood- and mucus-soaked pieces of toilet paper and "cakes of excrement and pools of urine" that lay everywhere through which rats ran.[5]

---

* The rumour that Canada had been attacked was true. I-26, commanded by Minoura Yokota, surfaced off Vancouver Island near 10:00 p.m. on 20 June. His gunners' first few rounds fell short of the Estevan Lighthouse, prompting the authors of *No Higher Purpose*, the official history of Canada's naval operations in the Second World War, to quip "Yokota thus found himself in the embarrassing position of being unable to hit the broadside of a continent" (p. 355).

† The Poy family's escape started with a horrific moment: a knock on the door in the middle of the night by the Kempeitai, Japan's equivalent of the Gestapo. William Poy was told his family was to be evacuated the next day.

Shocked, one of the Red Cross representatives momentarily ignored the presence of the guards and asked Price, "Do you have trouble getting drugs and medicines?" Price quickly answered, "We hardly get any at all." The Red Cross representatives saw that the Japanese cared as little for their own military law, which required a year's worth of medicine be available, as they did for the Geneva Convention.[6]

. . .

The appearance of the wet form of beriberi, which by the end of the year would kill four men and sicken dozens, increased the quotient of suffering significantly. Caused by a combination of a lack of vitamin B1 and a high-carbohydrate diet, beriberi results from the body's inability to excrete liquids, leading to generalized swelling as fluids accumulate in tissues. Pressure on his brain caused one Rifleman to forget his son's name. Most of the afflicted, however, swelled into what more than one veteran referred to as a blob. Arms and legs would resemble hunks of dough, retaining the dents of fingers poked into them. Testicles would swell so large the men could not walk, a condition dubbed "Hong Kong balls."

"I was puffed up like a balloon," recalled Frank Christensen. "My bottom lip was touching my chin and my top was touching my nose. My eyes were swollen so bad that I couldn't see out of them. . . . After about a week of this, I gradually deflated."

. . .

Late on the evening of 16 July, Laite recorded two rumours and news from the BBC heard on the clandestine radio.[*] The rumours that a

---

[*] On 11 June, the camp commandant issued an order banning the keeping of a diary. Strangely

prisoner exchange was in the offing and a division of Canadians had landed in Egypt to reinforce the British, then fighting for their lives at El Alamein (neither of which were true), lifted his spirits. The BBC report that Red Cross visitors to North Point said "that we 1,600 soldiers here are being properly cared for" did not. The chaplain had no way of knowing that in private, in their secret report, the Swiss said something quite different and that within hours, Lieutenant Benjamin Proulx, having escaped from Hong Kong on 28 January and crossed China, would sit down in Ottawa and give the Canadian government its first official report of the fate of "C" Force.

Proulx told how Brigadier-General Lawson died, about the siege at the Repulse Bay Hotel and of what he believed to be the unjust removal of Major Charles Young from command of the garrison there. Proulx told of the masterly camouflage used by the Japanese and how the Canadians had been betrayed by the sun glinting off their helmets and buckles. He reported on the rapes and murders at St. Stephen's Hospital and how the Japanese had allowed "violation, murder and looting for days in the native sections of Hong Kong." And he revealed the terrible conditions in the POW camps.

Proulx's defence of the Canadians had nothing to do with a new-found sense of patriotism now that he was safely in Canada. Indeed, he does not cite a single Canadian source. He does not appear to be aware that Brigadier Wallis was preparing the report that was so critical of the Canadians. However, at Shamshuipo he had heard Royal Navy Admiral Alfred Collinson say that Hong Kong fell because "the Canadians wouldn't fight." Neither Collinson's staff nor Colonel Ride agreed; they blamed the Royal Scots and to a lesser extent (and completely unjustly) the Rajputs.

---

enough, some months later, the Canadians were ordered to write essays in which they described the battle. In August 1943, to protect his diary, Grenadier White kept it buried for a week or so. MacWhirter hid his in a gap in the wall of his hut.

Commander J. Douglas of the Royal Navy Reserve told Proulx that when the Royal Scots detachment near him realized they could not hold against the Japanese, they got drunk. "But somebody's going to be made the goat," he told Proulx, and he was "afraid they're going to make a goat out of the Canadian regiments. . . . None of those people who say that the Canadians ran can tell you where they did run. There was no evidence of any specific kind against the Canadians."

After hearing the details of his escape, officers who debriefed him could hardly have been surprised that Proulx doubted if there would be many more escapes from Hong Kong. Few Westerners and no Canadian would have known that the sewer that ran through the camp also ran near a mountain on which they could hide in the first hours after Proulx's escape. Nor would they have known the Hong Kong terrain well enough to move through it at night, how to bargain with the Chinese (in front of whom dangled a HK$300 reward for every Westerner turned in) or how to contact the guerrillas on the mainland who spirited Proulx and his fellow escapees out of China. No one in Ottawa would have argued against Proulx's conclusion that "insufficient food has weakened the men, and they would be unable to embark on the hazardous journey of 500 miles to Chungking," Generalissimo Chiang Kai-shek's capital.

. . .

Proulx was wrong. Within days of his debriefing, Grenadier Sergeant John Payne began planning his own escape. Saying that all they had to look forward to was "years of slavery and then death," Payne tried to convince fellow sergeant Tom Marsh to join him. But Marsh, believing escape impossible, demurred. Three other Grenadiers—Lance-Corporal George Berzenski and Privates John Adams and Percy Ellis—joined Payne.

Just before midnight on 19 August, Payne led his small band from the hospital's orderly room and by Lance-Sergeant William Hall's bed. A few minutes later, the orderly who was rubbing Hall's feet to ease the pain of electric feet said softly, "Well, they've finally got away."[7]

Neither Hall nor the orderly knew what Payne had confided in a letter to his mother he had given to another Grenadier. In it, the twenty-three-year-old from Winnipeg shows a sense of humour— "I'm ruddy sick of Japanese hospitality"—and underscores the role faith played in his decision to try to escape:

> You share, I know, my own views of fatalism, so for that rea-
> son I know you won't condemn my judgement. So just in
> case I shouldn't make it you must remember that according
> to our beliefs I have departed for a much nicer place (I hope)
> although it will grieve me to exchange the guitar for a harp
> even though there is a higher percentage of gold in the latter.

Payne ended the letter with an impish P.S.: "Best Regards to Di & Yvonne. Tell them to join the Air Force next war."

The guards noticed the Canadians were missing just after they had been sent to bed. Colonel Tokunaga struck with a vengeance, ordering the prisoners to parade in the pouring rain. He gave no exemption for the sick, who were carried onto the parade ground on stretchers. Weak from dysentery, Grenadier Lieutenant Richard Maze took longer getting onto parade than pleased Namura, Tokunaga's interpreter. Heedless of Maze's condition, Namura slapped and then began punching his face.

Tokunaga kept the Canadians shivering in the rain until 5:30 a.m. Once back in their huts, the prisoners dried off as best they could and crawled into bed. Reveille sounded as usual an hour later;

the sick and those who trudged to work at Kai Tak were the lucky ones. Thinking that he knew something about his brother's plans, Tokunaga himself beat Private Nicholas Berzenski.

The Japanese recaptured the four Grenadiers after their boat capsized as they tried to cross to the mainland. The Kempeitai military police beat them with baseball bats and tied them up with barbed wire before killing them. Fearing "loss of face," Information Officer Honda Tanaka sent a false report to Tokyo saying that the Canadians had been shot while trying to escape.* Unable to find the graves the Canadians may have been forced to dig for themselves, Major George Puddicombe, who prosecuted Tanaka for war crimes, came to think of the patch of land he explored as "that terrible Golgotha." He erected a small marker listing the Grenadiers' names and saying, "They have died doing their duty."

. . .

Mail started arriving in Hong Kong at the end of August, a month after Grenadier Harry White had such a vivid dream of his wife, Maxine, that he "could almost touch her."† The route to and from Japan guaranteed that the frequency of mail exchanged would never come near the six or seven weeks it took letters to travel from Canada to Germany. Letters to Japan went first to England, then

---

* It is likely that this information officer is the same Honda Tanaka who acted as a translator during the battle and who had released Padre Uriah Laite.

† Letters mailed before the capitulation were not delivered. Among those returned to their sender is one written on 11 December 1942 by Gladys Corrigan, Lieutenant Leonard Corrigan's wife in which, after telling her husband how she had read his first (and last) airmail letter three times after going to bed, told her husband honestly, "You don't really have to worry about me. Please have faith in me. When I married you, I took my vows seriously and I intend to keep them. I don't intend to have moments of weakness. And if such did come up, I'm assured my love for you is deep enough to put my personal feelings aside and wait until such times as we are together again. And may it be soon" (quoted in Corrigan, 53).

Tehran, where they were transhipped to the Soviet Union; the letters then crossed Russia to a port near Vladivostok and were put on a ship to Tokyo, where they were censored and then shipped to Hong Kong. Delivery was arbitrary. Some men received many letters. None of the scores of letters Phil Doddridge's mother wrote reached him.

There are two reasons that armies deliver mail to men even when they are in battle. Words from home take a soldier, at least for a short time, out of the stress of battle. Mail delivery also demonstrates the efficiency of the organization upon which his life depends. This second reason cannot apply to POWs, but if anything, the first applies even more so. According to historian Gavan Daws, for POWs, letters were a balm "for the mind and soul."[8]

Of his first receipt of mail, Allister later wrote, "Contact! . . . This paper had actually been in my home in Montreal! It had been touched, handled, folded by loving compassionate hands. . . . Touching it was touching them, an invisible embrace, a reunion, a banishing of all the grime and horror and ugliness."[9] He "sucked up the life-affirming images of real and civilized people doing the make-believe things I dreamed of. . . . I read it again and again, over and over, to retain the secret tenuous thread that still bound me to a dimming reality." The importance of images of the quotidian world—where people worked, families gathered and loved ones died (albeit in a bed surrounded by family)—can be glimpsed from the fact that men who did not receive mail surreptitiously read other men's mail. "True generosity was sharing mail."[10]

Letters home were almost as important, for they allowed the caged men to reach out to the normal world. Often the Japanese dumped these letters on a rubbish heap. Those that were sent to Canada had to travel the reverse of the circuitous route the letters from Canada travelled. The letters had to be printed and written in English, which meant that francophones like Verreault wrote to his family in a language they only partly understood. Their letters were rigorously censored; they could not say much more than the postcards the Japanese supplied:

> Dear _____,
> I am interned at _____. My health is—excellent; good; fair; poor. I am————injured; sick in hospital; under treatment; not under treatment. I am—improving; not improving; better; well. Please see that _____ *(depending upon the card, there would be room for a ten-, twenty-five- or fifty-word personal message)*.

Not one of the dozens of letters Doddridge wrote his mother reached her.

. . .

In August 1942 when the Japanese allowed the prisoners to make the huts at North Point a little less forbidding, Verreault became the driving force behind Allister's painting business, stealing the canvas and the materials to make brushes and paint. Within a week, Verreault crowed to his diary, "My Jewish friend continues painting and has eight canvases complete, masterpieces!!!"[11] Allister disagreed but relished the cigarettes or yen (from Japanese guards) , which the prisoners "happily converted to 'extras'" in the camp's underground economy.

Through the latter part of 1942, Verreault, who proudly boasted of protecting "my little Jew" and who swung like Tarzan from the rafters of the bunkhouse, was weakening, the victim of slow starvation. He avoided the diphtheria epidemic that sickened hundreds and killed scores, but in October suffered incredible pain from electric feet. Like all patients, Verreault tried rubbing his feet and plunging them into ice-cold water. Some days the pain radiated as high as his knees. When the Canadians were transferred to Shamshuipo in late September, a ward housed the many patients who screamed with pain through the night.

Allister fetched and carried for Verreault, who refused to go to the Agony Ward, but he could not relieve his pain. The cause of the disease, malnutrition, wasted Verreault's muscles and, together with the searing pain, weakened his mind. "I watched," recalled Allister, "as he gradually acquired the blank, dull, faraway look of the Agony Ward inmates, a non-caring, introverted look that made me afraid." One day, while Allister was telling how before being wasted by electric feet, Blacky could do seventy-five push-ups with each arm and leg on a chair, his chum's mind snapped and Verreault lashed out at Allister, who parried punches while retreating beyond the view of the other men before grappling Verreault safely to the ground.

When, a few minutes later, they returned to the rations line, the exhausted Verreault leaning on Allister, another soldier said to Allister, "He was hurting you—I thought he was your pal." Allister nodded sadly and answered, "He is."[12]

. . .

The diphtheria outbreak that began early September killed many. In October alone, more than 283 Canadians were admitted to a special diphtheria ward. The deaths began slowly: one each on five days in September, one on 1 October. The tempo soon increased. Two men died each day on 7, 10, 11 and 15 October. Even more than the misery of dysentery, the diphtheria outbreak cast a pall over the men that is easily traced in diaries like Verreault's:

Monday 5 October: Two dead this a.m. A Grenadier and a Royal Rifles. Two little women back home will shed tears.

One of my buddies just left for the hospital with diphtheria. He told me with a smile "So long Blacky. I've had it but I have no one to miss me." I wanted to cry.

Friday 9 October: Diphtheria is spreading. We average two deaths a day for the Canadians alone. . . . The only place of comfort is the chapel where I go as frequently as my legs will allow. . . . In the evening the Padre blesses the Host.

Friday 16 October: Another death during the night. Every day we hear the "Last Post" bidding goodbye to these unsung heroes.

Ville-Émard, my 6268, how I fear I won't see you again!

On 10 October, Lance Ross came down with diphtheria and was placed in the ward. Like the other two hundred men, including Charles Dallain (whose throat, his brother Jean-Paul saw to his horror, "was lined with white bubbles, just like the tips of wooden matches"), Ross lay suffering on the building's cold, hard cement floor, which ran wet with excrement. The original of Ross's diary shows how weak he was the next day when he managed to scratch out the words "Can hardly write today . . . so sick my tonsils as big as eggs . . . can hardly breathe."

Caused by the *Corynebacterium diptheriae* bacterium, diphtheria manifests itself as a membrane that forms across the throat. While the membrane can cause asphyxiation, death usually results from toxins released by the bacteria that degrade the central nervous system. Almost eradicated today by inoculation and antibiotics, in 1942 diphtheria could be treated with an antitoxin. As he did with dysentery, Captain Shunkichi Saito, a graduate of the Kyoto Prefectural Medical School, ignored the cause of the disease. Instead of supplying the serum that would have ended the epidemic, he

berated and slapped (at least once using a rubber hose) the doctors
and orderlies caring for the sick men.

Cambon, an orderly at Bowen Road Military Hospital at the
height of the diphtheria epidemic (who had not been inoculated
for the disease), watched helplessly as men wheezed toward death
and the bacteria burned its way through their bodies, bursting out
in secondary infections that ulcerated their noses, faces, penises and
scrotums.

As the deaths mounted and his preferred method of spurring
medical progress failed, Saito reluctantly handed over ten thousand
units of antitoxin; according to Captain John Reid, who was a medical doctor, one hundred and fifty thousand units were required.
Reid knew the medicine would save lives, and found, to his surprise, that even in severe cases, he could save a life with less than a
thousand units. Still, Reid did not have enough to save everyone. Ed
Shayler remembers the test Captain Martin Banfill applied. "I was
choking and Dr. Banfill came through and said, 'Stand up if you
can.' I did and he gave me a shot in the ass and said, 'This might not
work because we are limited in the amount we can use.'" In a postwar interview Reid recalled the horror doctors felt as they chose
whom to give what antitoxin they could: "We would say this one is
too late, this one will, this one won't; just playing God . . . signing
life and death warrants."

. . .

In addition to dysentery, diphtheria, and wet and dry beriberi, doctors like Reid found themselves coping with pellagra and blindness caused by lack of B vitamins. About the time Charles Dallain
contracted diphtheria, his brother Jean-Paul began losing his sight.
Though sick call was held every morning, reporting sick risked a
beating, so Jean-Paul Dallain held off as long as he could. Finally,

he could wait no longer and reported for sick call. "I was in pretty bad shape. I weighed seventy-two pounds and could hardly see anything. Instead of getting a beating, a Jap medic ordered me to military hospital at Bowen Road."

Because of a lack of riboflavin, Jean-Paul Dallain's eyes ulcerated, a condition that struck scores of men, some several times. Each morning Andrew Flanagan washed Dallain's eyes, which were "stuck solid with puss." To shade them from the unbearable pain of daylight, Dallain wore a cloth over his eyes. His friend Shorty Lapalme's eyes were in even worse shape; Lapalme had gone totally blind. When they had to use the outhouse—between ten and twenty times a day—the two men went together. Dallain, painfully peering through the cloth, led the way while Lapalme supported his fellow soldier who was unable to walk by himself. Even a small egg that Flanagan brought Dallain when he could provided the protein that tied him over until the arrival of the first Red Cross parcel, which surely saved Dallain's life. When he squatted over the latrine hole, all Dallain passed was a "mucus-like substance. . . . I don't recall having a single solid stool."

Despite Saito seizing much of the hospital's surgical equipment and the fact that such simple things as tongue depressors had to be reused, Bowen Road Hospital provided surgical care—using razor blades and jackknives, a jury-rigged operating table that even had a tiltometer to allow the use of spinal anaesthetics. On 26 July Lance Ross was operated on for appendicitis. Dr. J. Crawford tested for the loss of sensation (caused by malnutrition) with a tuning fork manufactured by the ordnance corps. Crawford, Reid and other POW doctors traded on the black market for medicines. Crawford took advantage of the fact that Japanese guards came to him because they were so frightened of going to their own doctors to treat venereal disease, the contracting of which was a serious crime. "For such treatment, the Jap had to supply his own medicine, purchased on our advice. Depending upon whether our own troops were particularly plagued by malaria or beriberi at the time, it was surprising how much quinine or thiamine was necessary to treat syphilis in a Japanese soldier, in addition, of course, to a small amount of intravenous arsenical. . . . Perhaps we were not strictly following the ethical teaching of our profession, but the Japs were pleased and the College of Physicians and Surgeons was not watching us."[13] Crawford also stored in plain sight medical records detailing the Japanese mistreatment of the POWs, although the Japanese wanted these records destroyed.

. . .

By the time the diphtheria epidemic had run its course in mid-December, it had killed almost a hundred Canadians, more than one in five of those who contracted the curable disease. At no point did the Japanese lessen the demand for slave labour for Kai Tak. Day after day, malnourished, sick and increasingly hope-starved men, many now wearing the Japanese sarong and wooden sandals (their regulation fatigues having worn through and their boots rotted away), worked seven days a week rain or shine taking down a mountain with bamboo picks and shovels. Rising before dawn and returning long after sunset, they went months without seeing their camp in daylight.

The Japanese language remained largely a mystery, as Henry Lyons discovered one day when a Japanese guard yelled at him to fetch what he thought was an oil drum. The guard wanted a *kanji*, a plank. The mistake occasioned a terrible beating. They all, however, learned their number; Bill MacWhirter can still quickly recite his: *sanjou shichi* (thirty-seven).

. . .

Through the last months of 1942, the camp's jungle telegraph worked reasonably well, if not entirely accurately. On 7 October, Laite recorded that the U.S. Navy had sunk a convoy of transports, a heavy cruiser, two light cruisers and several destroyers, none of which was true. What the United States *had* done was hold Henderson Airfield on Guadalcanal despite fierce counterattacks.[*] Word of the November invasion of North Africa, Operation Torch, made the rounds in early December.

Some information announced itself. In late October, Americans bombed the last remaining oil tank in Hong Kong. Every diary and memoir records how, despite the risk of being bombed themselves by mistake, the men were heartened by the sight of Allied air power and the roar of the attacks.[14]

Lyons was outside the day the American bombers hit the oil tank. "I was with my friend Dick Irvine when they came over," he recalls. "They were in formation—the prettiest thing. 'Look, look,' I said as the bombs started coming out of them clear as your fingers. When they started exploding, blessed Jesus, we were ten miles away and we felt the concussion that just drove us back. We looked at each other and smiled as the flames shot upward. A Jap guard saw us and came over and slapped our faces."

• • •

Their captors' attitude toward religious observance varied over time and, to some degree, depended on religion.[†] Through 1942, United Church Chaplain Laite had little trouble holding services

---

[*] On 11 October at the Battle of Cape Esperance, the U.S. Navy did sink a cruiser and several destroyers. The discrepancy in dates suggests that Laite might have written entries later than the day indicated and interpolated information that became known later.

[†] Even though the identity discs worn by Canadian soldiers indicated their religion, Signalman William Allister asked Captain Billings that he not inform the Japanese that Allister was Jewish.

and ministering to the men. In a joint service with the Anglican Barnett, Laite preached to two hundred men on John 19:41, "In the place where He was crucified there was a garden." After the move to Shamshuipo in September, every Sunday Laite held two Communion services in the morning and preaching services at 12:30 p.m. and in the evening. On 11 November, coincidentally Remembrance Day, the Japanese took Laite from the prison camp to officiate at the funeral of a downed American airman.

The Japanese put more restrictions on Roman Catholic Chaplain Francis Deloughery. As noted earlier, they had cut off his supply of altar breads in April. Between May and September, he conducted six funerals and made numerous visits to the Bowen Road Hospital. However, as the diphtheria epidemic took hold, Deloughery was not allowed to go to the hospital to minister to the suffering or to administer extreme unction.

Although Deloughery was treated humanely, the Roman collar did not shield Father E.J. Green from Tokunaga's anger after the British padre wrote asking that a portion of the funds Pope Pius XII had donated to the relief of POWs in Hong Kong go toward purchasing medicines. Tokunaga had Green beaten with sheathed swords. As scores of men around him died of diphtheria, Tokunaga spent the money on sports equipment and band instruments, which were used as props in propaganda pictures.

The conversion of Grenadier Art Ballingall increased Deloughery's flock by one. The ceremony, recalls John Duguay, who stood as godfather, was simple, "just a few men and a priest but it meant a lot to us. It was a sign that life continued despite what we were going through."

.   .   .

In late September, the Canadians moved back into their pre-war barracks at Shamshuipo. Though the British had repaired the electric wiring in the huts, the move hardly improved the Canadians' living conditions. Gaping holes in the walls and roofs let in the cold wind and rain. Sanitation remained rudimentary and the remains of decomposing Chinese corpses still floated close to the seawall.

In the hospital ward, Rifleman Harold Englehart lay ill with dysentery. Through his own fever he heard even sicker, delirious men "get up at night and go to the window and order all kinds of food. . . . In a day or two they would be dead." Englehart would live, but for several minutes one day, the orderlies thought that he, like the Grenadier next to him, had died—and they came with strips of cloth to tie his legs together before rigor mortis set in.

.   .   .

For a short time after the Canadians' arrival back in Shamshuipo, a camp canteen allowed the men to purchase some poorly made chocolate, which at least offered much-needed calories and fat, and bean curd. In general, however, the move to Shamshuipo coincided with a decline in nutrition. The Japanese provided oil drums to cook in but gave the prisoners green wood, which produced only enough heat to turn the rice into a gelatinous goop. Swept off warehouse floors, the rice "had to be soaked to get the matchsticks, paper, and other rubbish to float to the top of the water."[15] Bags of rice stamped 220 pounds held only 150. The half-pound of vegetables allocated to each man per day was made up of weeds and garden flowers. Fish was provided that was often unfit for human consumption. By October, four months had passed since Laite had last eaten meat.

The move to Shamshuipo also had the perverse effect of increasing the time the Canadians spent on back-breaking labour at Kai Tak because they no longer had to take the ferry. By late October, however, conditions had improved somewhat. Verreault placed his bunk in the rafters of his hut, and the painting business he and Allister ran was flourishing. On 24 October, sitting before a photograph of his family and still wondering if they had learned that his name was not on the casualty list, Laite wrote, as if in a letter to his wife, about the pomelo he'd eaten at dinner the night before. "To underscore its importance, believe it or not, this is the first fruit—apart from a wooden apple brought in months ago— we have tasted since our surrender." Laite had had a good day. In addition to eating a piece of fruit and finding a door, as he wrote Grenadier Sidney Sheffer was bricking up a hole in the wall at the top of which would be placed one of Laite's prized possessions, a piece of glass to make a window for the door to his hut.

. . .

Relations with the guards were never easy. "We were in the grip of a powerful and completely arbitrary enemy," recalls MacDonell. "At no time did the norms of military justice obtain. We had to be constantly on the watch to make sure that we followed rules: both written and unwritten." Lyons remembers a large Japanese guard who, one day while Lyons and some other men were carrying heavy concrete blocks, repeatedly lit a cigarette, ostentatiously took a few puffs and then threw it on the ground. Lyons and the men fairly salivated at the smouldering smokes, but knew they were forbidden from picking them up.

"He threw one down just in front of me and I kept on walking. Then he grunted like a pig and pointed to the cigarette." Lyons bent down, picked it up and handed it to the guard, who refused it. Knowing the rules, Lyons threw the still-burning cigarette on the ground and returned to carrying the blocks. "You never knew what they were going to do. So imagine my surprise when I came past him a few minutes later and he took a package of cigarettes out of his ammo pouch and handed it to me."

Nicknamed the Kamloops Kid because of where he was born and Slap Happy because of his sadistic nature, Kanao Inouye was a Canadian of Japanese heritage. His father, Tou, had earned a Military Medal while serving in the army of his adopted country, Canada, in the First World War. After Inouye graduated from Vancouver Technical High School in 1936, he followed the path of many first-generation Japanese-Canadian males and travelled to Japan for university. He attended Waseda University in Tokyo for two years before transferring to an agricultural college in 1940. Under Japanese law, a son of a Japanese father was a Japanese citizen; thus in 1942, he was called up and, because of his fluency in English, was quickly posted as an interpreter for the Kempeitai and sent to prison camps in Hong Kong.

Inouye took full advantage of the fact that he spoke unaccented English. Signalman Gerry Gerrard recalled Inouye sneaking up to groups of Canadians and criticizing the Japanese in strong terms. If anyone agreed before realizing that it was Inouye, "he would quickly put the boots to them."

Shortly after arriving at Shamshuipo, Inouye gave Lyons "a son of a whore of a beating." Inouye had ordered him to pick up a plank. However, Lyons, who had lost sixty pounds, played coy and pretended that he could not lift it without help. Inouye caught on and called over two guards, who held Lyons while Inouye punched away at him. After he'd satiated himself, Inouye told the guards to go. Displaying more guts, perhaps, than judgment, Lyons then said, "They've never made a Jap in Tokyo who could knock me off my feet." Inouye lifted his rifle by the barrel, swung it like a club and hit Lyons squarely on his collarbone, breaking it.

After catching Gaston Oliver trading for food with a sentry, Inouye ordered that the Grenadier be made to stand in front of the guard room for two days and nights holding a bucket of water in front of him at arm's length. "Every time I moved the guards struck me with their belts," Oliver recalled in an affidavit. Art Ballingall was beaten for not saluting a general who was visiting the hospital in which he worked—even though at the time Ballingall was carrying a basin of water up to his ward. Inouye began the beating with his fists and then used the side of his sword. "He hit me with the sword across my mouth and broke my teeth," said Ballingall in his affidavit, in which he did not mention that he had been beaten so badly he spent two months in the hospital.[16]

"The Japanese flag will soon be flying over Ottawa. All Canadians will be slaves as you are now! Your mothers will be killed. Your wives and sisters will be raped by our soldiers and anyone resisting will be shot," Inouye told his former countrymen. He tied Grenadier Jim Murray, one of the several Native Canadians in the regiment, to a pole and beat him with his fists, before taping Murray's mouth closed and sticking burning cigarettes up his nose. When Murray passed out, Inouye had him doused with water. The torture continued for two days. Inouye beat and tortured dozens of men who, like him, had grown up listening to Foster Hewitt call the game on *Hockey Night in Canada*.

Inouye took especial delight in beating the Canadian officers in front of their men, a violation of the laws and usages of war. He beat them if at roll call he found a unit had an extra man in hospital (beyond the number the Japanese allowed on sick call). And he did it twice on 21 December, coincidentally the day two Red Cross officials visited the camp and, just before they were to leave, were directed to the Jubilee building, into which, in Allister's words, God himself "didn't venture."[17] Later, when two men were not present in the Grenadiers' roll call, Inouye did not accept Captain John Norris's explanation that they were in hospital and slapped him in the face. Norris recalled in his postwar affidavit:

> Then he closed his hand and hit me on the face with the inside portion of his clenched fist many times. After about 15 or 20

blows, he put his foot behind my leg and pushed me over. Then he kicked, I believe at my head but the blows landed on my shoulder probably four or five times.

He said "Stand up and take it like a man." I stood up. He continued to strike me in the face. After some time my knees caved in and I fell down.

After Norris collapsed, Inouye turned to Major Atkinson, yelled at him and then kicked him in the knee. The beating almost cost Norris an eye; at the war crimes trial, it would help cost Inouye his life.

.   .   .

Even as Inouye terrorized the Canadians and November's death toll mounted to twenty-nine, toward the end of the month Shayler, Lyons and their thirteen hundred comrades had reason to celebrate. On 29 November, they received their first—and for some their only—Red Cross parcels.

The importance of the fifteen-pound boxes can be measured in two ways. Each was a tangible link to the world beyond the fence. Indeed, the parcels were filled with tastes and scents from the outside world—canned stew, bacon, condensed milk. For the few fleeting moments during which the contents were tasted and their smells savoured, the dirty, beaten-down prisoner of war didn't just figuratively drink in the forms created by words written at home, their senses made the world beyond the fence part of them. "Surprise! A gift from heaven! . . . I just ate a chocolate bar and cried doing it," wrote Verreault the night the parcels arrived.

The second measure uses the dry terms of nutrition. How many milligrams of zinc, iron, calcium or manganese? What is the calorie content of oleomargarine, cheese, chocolate or canned beef? How much protein is in a slice of bully beef?

When Dallain received his package, he was so weak he could not open it, but it did not take long for the food inside it to set him on the road to recovery. The day after the parcels arrived, Lance Ross wrote, "Sitting eating my food from the Red Cross. It will save a lot of lives." Somewhat fortified, the next day he struck a more mournful tone: "This Red Cross stuff will only make us want more."

.   .   .

The terrible pace of deaths slowed in December when the men mourned their comrades who had fallen a year earlier. They wrote to their families. Somewhere between Canada and Hong Kong were letters like this one written by Bernard Castonguay's mother on 5 November, a few days after receiving the telegram saying "Fusilier Bernard Castonguay E306659 prisonier de guerre dans un camp a Hong Kong":

> My Dear Son:
> We have received a telegram from Ottawa saying that you are a prisoner and it is the first news that we have had in a year, imagine how worried we are, my poor child. What can I tell you in this letter to console you. Pray a lot and we pray for you, so that you don't lose your courage. I hope your health is good. Here everyone is well. . . . It's fall here, it's starting to be cold and for you it may be the opposite. If I could, I'd send you seeds to make a garden so that you would not be bored. I would have lots to write. Maybe I've said too much. We've already sent many letters in a package. . . . We hug you and kiss you.
> Your Father and Mother who pray for you.

Though the particulars would differ, Major Baird's letter of 18 December speaks for his comrades.

Five more shopping days to Christmas. How I wish I could be with you, Sweetheart, to help do the many things that have to be done—going down with Harvelyn to do her shopping, secrets galore, and all kinds of hiding places that would be taboo for all of us. . . . We are planning our Christmas meals here also. We are hoping to have, as an extra special treat for breakfast, porridge, fried eggs, toast and coffee. I have saved my can of bacon . . . to have a real binge. We are trying to get enough ducks for our Christmas dinner.

As does Baird's Christmas Eve letter:

I have been fighting off a bout of blues for the past two weeks and today they descended in full force, but then I soon found it to be a bad way to spend a day. I cheered myself up by thinking that I really am darn lucky. I am alive, my health is OK. . . . Three Christmases are too many to miss by at least three.[18]

On Christmas the Japanese distributed to each man an envelope with Christmas trees printed on it containing ¥10, a Christmas gift from the Government of Canada.

Each chaplain conducted several Christmas Day services. Laite read four and, as hoped, had both a special breakfast that included fried eggs and a dinner with meat and plum pudding with cinnamon sauce. Allister was able to spend Christmas dinner with some Russians who were interned on the part of Shamshuipo that held members of the Hong Kong Volunteer Defence Corps. These internees were able to smuggle a selection of food into the camp, and Allister found it hard to believe he was drinking sake and eating flavourful dishes instead of "flavourless rice, tasting of sacking and filled with white worms and mouse turds."[19]

Verreault's last entry for 1942 came a day later and captures the pain at the end of Christmas:

> Christmas! Christmas! All over with. We attended midnight mass and were emotionally tortured by memories. I had organized a small choir that performed beautifully. I sang "O Holy Night" and cried like a girl. The excitement and emotion were too much for what strength I had left after mass. . . . Ah! I don't have the will to write. I'm half blind. I'm all dried up on all counts. I'm fed up . . . I'm . . . I'd like to die.

On the last full night of 1942, Laite wrote about his visit to a Sergeant C. More, who was in the hospital, a snapshot of his wife and children hanging on the wall above him and his fiddle bow beside him on his bed. "He had, apparently, been trying to play and found that his hands were so cramped with pain that he could not do it. I tried to cheer him a bit but his comment was 'What will my wife say? What will my wife say?'"

CHAPTER 17

"We Stood on Loose, Shaky, Unfastened Planks"

The First Canadian Hell Ships
1943

"Victory belongs to the most persevering."
—NAPOLEON

During the second week of January 1943, Mrs. Greenberg of Winnipeg received a telegram telling her that her son, Hank, whom William Allister had promised to watch out for, had died in Hong Kong. Similar telegrams arrived at homes across the country, including those of Signalmen Robert Damant and John Fairley. A few days later, these families received two letters of condolence. One was signed by Canada's Minister of Defence, John Ralston, the other by King George VI. The King and Queen Mary offered their sympathy and their prayers "that your country's gratitude for a life so nobly given in its service may bring you some measure of consolation."

On 13 January, the same day the *Winnipeg Free Press* carried Greenberg's obituary, one hundred envelopes postmarked in Ottawa arrived at Shamshuipo. Some remained unopened, mute testimony to the fact that they had been written before Ottawa received a casualty list.

.   .   .

Less than a week later, after being vaccinated for diphtheria and tested for cholera and amoebic dysentery (the exam for this last involving a glass rod inserted into the rectum), 1,320 POWs—including 668 Canadians—left Shamshuipo. A few hours later, guards herded them aboard *Tatsuta Maru*,* which had long since left behind the luxury that Charlie Chaplin and Albert Einstein enjoyed when the almost-600-foot ship plied the Yokohama–San Francisco run.

The crossing to Japan, the first of five (and at seven days the fastest) that Canadians would take to labour as slaves in factories, mines and shipyards, rivalled the infamous "middle passage," the final leg of the triangle trade that brought African slaves to America. The almost four hundred Riflemen in Hold No. 1 were crammed so close together that they could not all lie down at once; another hold held hundreds of Grenadiers and other POWs. Back in Shamshuipo, the rumour made the rounds that the men who left the camp had been given beer and hot food; the men aboard *Tatsuta Maru* were given nothing more than small rice balls and water. The air soon grew fetid, partially from the stink of hundreds of men sweating in airless holds at temperatures over 100°F, and partially from the stench of shit that flowed out of those stricken with dysentery and from the buckets that served the office of a latrine.

The voyages were terrifying. The Canadians, who were not issued life vests, knew that *Lisbon Maru*, carrying British POWs,

---

* Also known as *Tatuta Maru*.

had been torpedoed by an American submarine the previous October, and that the Japanese had machine gunned the prisoners in the water.[1] "We are like rats in a trap," wrote Lance Ross on 19 January. "Should we be torpedoed not one would be saved." As if in disbelief, the entries for the next two days begin with the words "Still afloat." Almost a year later, another Hell Ship, the SS *Soong Cheong*, laden with ninety-nine Canadians and other POWs and a load of iron ore, hit a fierce December gale that buckled the ship's plates. *Soong Cheong* made Formosa safely, but just; after the last barge filled with disembarking POWs left, the ship turned turtle.

When the Canadians aboard *Tatsuta Maru* reached Japan— gaunt from hunger and stinking from sweat and excrement— their condition shocked the famously clean Japanese. They caught something of a break when the officer commanding the Emperor's Guard recognized the Canadians' commander, Captain John Reid, from their days at a Canadian university. "What an odd place to meet. I'm to escort you. Is there anything you need?" the officer asked. "The men are cold and hungry. They need food and clothing," answered Reid.

A short while later, a truck arrived with thick greatcoats. Another brought "wondrously fluffy buns, oval, half a foot long, of pure white flour covered with a thick sweetened crust." Soon "gurgles and giggles and animated talk" replaced the sullen silence of men a short step from the limit of endurance.[2] The following August when Ken Cambon's draft arrived, the Japanese would be ready with sanitation teams equipped with spray guns filled with phenol to clean the grimy men.

. . .

By January 1943, Tōjō's government knew that Japan could not win the war. Her navy had been neutered at Midway six months earlier. The Imperial Japanese Army was losing its grip on Guadalcanal, a harbinger of things to come. Still, Hirohito ruled an empire several times larger than Hitler's.

The riches of Asia, rice from China, iron ore from Korea and oil from the Dutch East Indies poured into Japan. Save for the Doolittle Raid on Tokyo in April 1942, which caused much consternation but little damage, the Home Islands stood inviolate behind both a still-formidable navy and a ring of conquests arcing from the Aleutians in the north Pacific to the Mariana Islands in the south central Pacific to the Indian border. Most importantly for the Canadians who would arrive in Japan in January and August, the country's rolling stock was on time and food—pork, vegetables and strong tea—was plentiful enough to be given to them. On the way to Tsurumi (near Yokohama), Allister snuck a peak out of the blind-covered window. The landscape seemed like a *National Geographic* photo come to life and the people seemed to him as if they'd stepped off the set of Gilbert and Sullivan's *Mikado*.

. . .

The Japanese divided this first draft of prisoners between two camps: Omine and Tsurumi.* For men used to squalor and damaged buildings, Omine, a new camp, was something of an improvement. It lacked furniture, however, which meant that Bill MacWhirter and 162 other Canadians had to sleep on mattresses on the floor. Fleas soon infested their mattresses. Not until mid-August were the men able to raise them off the floor using the wood from the crates that

---

* Omine, near Nagasaki, should not be confused with another camp by the same name near Tokyo.

held Red Cross parcels. Each parcel, in violation of the Red Cross rules, was divided among four men.

Constructed from bamboo and thin plywood, the huts at Tsurumi were arranged around a central corridor with ten narrow aisles running off it. The men slept on tatami mats on raised, seven-foot-long sleeping platforms, each of which held fourteen men. The individual sleeping areas were divided by a raised slat every thirty-seven and a half inches. Neither the wood fibre blankets nor the thin walls offered much protection against the cold winter wind.

At each camp, the Canadians were welcomed by speeches like this one delivered via an interpreter by Lieutenant Yoshida, Commandant of Niigata POW Camp: "You are prisoners of the Imperial Nipponese Army. The war will last a hundred years and you will be here forever. This is the punishment for disobedience." The last sentence was accompanied by theatrical slashing through the air with his sword.[3] Even though the Japanese general who delivered the speech at the Kawasaki camp added that soon Hirohito's army would invade Canada, the Dominion's soldiers had trouble taking it seriously. When several hours later the Canadians were heard laughing hysterically, the camp commandant summoned Reid to explain their odd behaviour. Reid didn't make mention of the French Canadian who perfectly mimicked the general's demeanour while apologizing "for the bad food and accommodations." When the Japanese asked if his men were insane, he had answered, "No, we were Canadians, and we were going to resist to the very end, whatever that end might be!"[4]

. . .

To resist, to remain soldiers at war, which is how the Canadians never stopped thinking of themselves, meant not giving in to malnutrition, sadistic guards, despair and ironically, given Japan's reputation for lotus flowers and kimonos, an old Canadian foe: winter. With only thin work clothes, thin running shoes and thin cotton socks, on 31 January at 5:00 a.m. they were mustered on parade to salute the Rising Sun, the symbol of Imperial Japan. In the snow, the saluting was the hardest part of the freezing morning ritual.

The Kamloops Kid may have been left behind in Hong Kong, but each camp had its equivalent. Just days after the Canadians arrived at Omine, a foreman zeroed in on the Metis Marcel Chaboyer, one of three brothers who had enlisted in the Winnipeg Grenadiers. Exactly what Chaboyer did is unclear. One version has it that he punched the guard who was beating him. In any event, Chaboyer was dragged away, and his fellow Canadians never saw him again.*

Sometime later, Sergeant Kabachi caught MacWhirter skirting the rule that each POW's tag had to be placed on the peg indicating where he was. Sick with dysentery, MacWhirter had run to the latrine without stopping to move his tag. Kabachi noticed the infraction and with other guards confronted the six-foot-six Rifleman, who now weighed only ninety-five pounds. The guards unsheathed their bayonets and stood behind MacWhirter while Kabachi pummelled him. "He blackened my eyes and knocked out several teeth. Each time he drove me backwards, I pushed against the bayonets and had to step forward and take the next punch."

The beating destroyed the cartilage in MacWhirter's nose and damaged his trigeminal nerve, leaving him with a lifetime of facial neuralgia. The bayonet pricks are still visible; black marks were left by the coal dust that sceped into the cut skin as he loaded coal in the mine at Omine.

---

* Chaboyer was sentenced to two years' hard labour, which for an unknown reason was extended. Japanese records indicate that he died a month before the war ended. His ashes were returned to his widow; in 1973, the Manitoba government named Lake 63 K/16 as Chaboyer Lake.

In July at Tsurumi, a certain Amana, "Snake Eyes," stopped Blacky Verreault for having his hands in his pockets. Unable to hear the guard's order over the noise of the metal shop, Verreault failed to remove his hands. A few moments later, Amana and another guard made an example of the Quebecer.

First, they had him hold a bucket filled with water in his out-stretched arms. When Verreault's arms tired and he dropped it, Amana filled it again. After an hour, he changed tactics and ordered Verreault to keep a push-up position—with outstretched arms and on the tips of his toes. Then, as he and another guard laughed, Amana placed a shovelful of glowing coals under the straining man. As Verreault's strength ebbed and the heat became intolerable, he arched his back, only to have a rifle butt smashed into his lower spine to force him back into the position Amana had ordered him to hold.

Torture continued back at Shamshuipo as well. On 14 September, White recorded that the POWs "had to spend 9½ hours on the square in the boiling sun" while the guards searched for a clandestine radio.

. . .

As their comrades in Hong Kong continued to take down the hill at Kai Tak and Harry White contracted dysentery and then malaria and wasted to 109 pounds, equally ghostly forms moiled for coal in Omine. They worked in shifts and were paid the equivalent of a cent a day; the pace of work was set not by the demands of the rock formation but by Japanese fists. In early May, an American POW named James Murray, so weakened from malnutrition that he could hardly walk, worked too slowly and a guard beat him. The next day, a guard saw him apparently lying down, ran over and kicked him. When the prisoner did not move, the guard realized Murray had died. On 4 May, Ross wrote poignantly, "We buried Murray today. He was so light one man could carry him. A light rain is falling; they say 'happy is the corpse that the rain falls on.'"

Most days, advances could be measured in shovelfuls and hoe tailings, but advance the Canadians did, filling as many as twenty-five railcars full of six tons of coal to fuel the furnaces of the Japanese war machine. When they blasted away rock, advances could be measured by the amount of coal crushed by sledgehammers and by how many supports men like Bob Barter could install before the roof caved in.

Their troglodyte existence fifteen hundred feet below the surface was dangerous. Working in the darkness turned at best a foggy grey by battery-powered lanterns or weak electric lights, injuries and deadly accidents punctuated their days. Clad only in sarongs and canvas running shoes, they lived with skinned and cut knees, painfully blistered hands and soon with a condition that resembled trench foot. A cable break on 18 March hurt three men. On 22 October, Ross barely escaped a cave-in that killed Rifleman James Main: "The agonizing cries he gave would make one shiver.... His back and spine are broken and both his legs in many places, his hips also." The following day, a cave-in injured another five men and killed a guard.

. . .

As terrible as the mine at Omine was, at least through the winter months, it held one great advantage over the Nippon Kokan Shipyards at Yokohama, where shivering men with numbed hands scraped rust, drove in rivets with sledgehammers and painted ships battle grey—it was warm. Fed a half-ration of rice, a few beans and thin soup at 6:00 a.m., Grenadier Frank Christensen and four other men spent twelve hours a day pulling a two-wheeled cart filled with oxygen tanks to the yard's various welding areas. By mid-morning, William Allister would shake with hunger.

Slave labour in Japan didn't just mean sweat, strain and ever-present hunger; it meant following the complicated forms of Japanese etiquette, including, for Allister and the painting crew he was assigned to, bowing at Kando-san the paint master, or *ichiban*, who then, to the Canadians' surprise, bowed to them and asked who they were:

> "Canada *heitai* [soldiers]," we said.
> "*Kanada, heitai-ka?*"
> "Yup."
> "*S-ka.*"
> This called for another round of bows and salutes. He asked
> for our leader;
> Tommy [Marsh] stepped forward.
> "*Watakushi gunso* [I am the sergeant]," he said bowing.
> "*S-ka.*" Another bow.

The theatrical etiquette was a daily occurrence, but so did the demand that the increasingly weakened Allister and the rest of the crew climb up four flights of rickety bamboo ladders carrying a heavy can of paint and a brush. "At the top, with nothing to hold on to, we stood on loose shaky unfastened planks.... We were expected to keep our balance [buffeted by cold winter winds] while leaning forward painting the sides of the ship."[5] As the winter winds and lack of food made the paint gang feel colder day by day, these men envied those who worked in the pipe-bending shop. But no one envied those who spent each day swinging heavy sledgehammers down onto the plates that formed ships' hulls.

. . .

In the months before Jean-Paul Dallain, Tom Forsyth and 374 other men boarded *Manryu Maru* in August 1943, they heard of the Russian victory at Stalingrad in early February and of the Allied invasion of Sicily in July. The men continued to labour at Kai Tak. They received their first Canadian-packed Red Cross parcels, which meant familiar chocolate, Carnation condensed milk and, most importantly, Sweet Caporal cigarettes, which commanded a higher price on the camp's black market than did British cigarettes. In honour of Hirohito's birthday at the end of April, the men received another parcel. They also got to enjoy the communal bath opened in April. They laughed and cheered at Sonny Castro, a Portuguese national who fought with the Hong Kong Volunteer Defence Corps, who convincingly played Carmen Miranda and other women in minstrel shows.*

In addition, they suffered the communal punishment of being confined to barracks that the Kamloops Kid—in another contravention of the Geneva Convention—meted out on 9 April after a guard discovered a clandestine radio. A day later, two Canadians were beaten unconscious for talking to a sentry. That same month, their officers were moved from Shamshuipo to the Argyle Street camp.

Dallain and the others did not know it, of course, but the Lenten and Easter celebrations would be their last organized religious observances until the end of the war. Despite exhaustion caused by overwork and malnutrition, and the fact that association of the

---

* The POWs' wholehearted acceptance of Castro's performances, one Canadian confiding to his diary he "is a 'wow' of a girl," raises the question of their sexuality. No Canadian diarist or memoirist admits to homosexual urges, though it is worth noting that elsewhere straight men recorded homosexual urges that did not centre so much around sex as "the urge for companionship of one of my fellow men and the desire to be of service and to share all things with him" (quoted in Roland, 116). While malnutrition severely reduced most libidos, two Canadians recorded masturbating at least once. Assignations with Chinese women at Kai Tak led one British officer to marvel at the Canadians: "I don't know how you do it on this food, Sir."

beginning of Lent, Shrove Tuesday, with pancakes and maple syrup made the constant gnawing hunger starker still, a full slate of events were held in the lead-up to Easter. On five successive Wednesdays, men attended lectures on God in the Universe, Education, History, Mission and Field, and the Post War World. During the next-to-last week of Lent, the camp must have seemed almost Biblical as some fifty blind, legless and armless Canadians (who had been in Queen Mary Hospital) rejoined their comrades. The heightened religious feeling led the two Durrant brothers (Christopher and Frank), Tom Forsyth, Kenneth Hogarth and four other men to seek out Chaplain Laite's spiritual advice.

According to Father Jerry Pocock, a now eighty-six-year-old priest who served as an able seaman in the Canadian Navy during the Second World War, despite the doctrinal differences between the chaplains, it is likely that many of the hymns sung at Protestant services were also sung at the Catholic ones. Laite mentions several, including "When I Survey the Wondrous Cross" and "Throned upon the Awful Tree," the horror of the latter hymn's echo of the second to last words of Jesus being all too real:

> You, the Father's only Son,
> You, His own anointed One,
> You are asking "can it be"
> "Why have You forsaken Me?"

Whether in English or Latin, the stately tones of the Lord's Prayer—"Our Father, who art in heaven/*Pater noster, qui es in caelis.* . . . Give us this day our daily bread. . . . But deliver us from evil"— allowed the men to reach beyond the camp's gates to their past, their families and, for the devout, beyond time itself. In 1943, Good Friday fell on St. George's Day, which celebrates the patron saint of England and of King George VI. Both services would have offered prayers to St. George for England and for the King of both Britain and Canada. More than a few of those present would have noted the juxtaposition of the agony of Calvary and a half-remembered speech from Shakespeare's *Henry V:*

> Once more unto the breach, dear friends, once more;
> Or close up the wall with our English dead. . . .
> The game's afoot:
> Follow your spirit, and upon this charge
> Cry "God for Harry, England, and Saint George!"*

Between Lent and the departure for Japan of the second draft of Canadians, the POWs buried more than one man a week, including Grenadier David Johnston, who had fought at Vimy Ridge. And they cheered, albeit silently, on 29 July when the Americans again bombed Hong Kong. Every soldier understood the importance of hitting the naval yard, but perhaps more importantly, the presence—even for a few minutes—of a dozen American bombers overhead told them that they had not been forgotten. After the beginning of June, never far from their minds was the (prescient) rumour White recorded: "When the going gets tough for the little yellow bastards, they will turn on us in earnest and probably do away with a lot of us."

. . .

Starting in late March, when almost three hundred letters arrived in two days, mail began arriving at Shamshuipo fairly regularly.

---

* Less than a month later, Deloughery was ordered to pack his kit, forbidden to speak to anyone and mustered into a lorry that delivered him to the Argyle Street camp where he ministered to some forty men. Thereafter, he again received a regular supply of sacramental wine, altar breads and candles.

George Grant's wife, who had been married for all of two weeks before Grant shipped out, wrote that a man who "looks so much like my darling husband" now lives nearby that she feared meeting him on the street and weakening.[6] The soldier who read that his wife pledged not to drink water until her man came home must have smiled.

Neither Cambon nor Dallain received any mail, though not because their families had not written. The emptiness they felt—and until he received the first letter from his wife on 20 June Captain Lionel Hurd felt too—can perhaps best be glimpsed by the fullness of Hurd's diary entry that follows the receipt of his wife's letter: he copied it word for word.

Hospitalized men who were too weak to write said to Laite, Burnett or Deloughery, "Padre, here's my wife's name and address, you do the rest."

. . .

Conditions on *Manryu Maru,* the Hell Ship that brought Jean-Paul Dallain and Cambon to Japan in August, were so bad that during the fifteen-day trip Rifleman Dallain developed a case of "Hong Kong balls." Slick with oil from coal, Dallain and the more than 350 Canadians could lie down only in shifts. They were allowed out of the hold every evening to use a head built over the side of the ship. The Japanese threw overboard what they did not loot from the Red Cross parcels loaded onto the ship. Food consisted of burnt rice and a watery soup twice a day.

When these Canadians arrived in Japan in late August, one hundred, including John Duguay, were sent to Onekama north of Kyoto; the rest were sent to Niigata. Divided into three parts (*Shintesto,* the foundry; *Marutson,* the dockyard, *Rinko,* the coal yard), Niigata 5B could have been the setting for *The Bridge over the River Kwai.* At the first sick call, only 10 percent of the men were fit for work; most had diarrhea and were still dehydrated from the long voyage to Japan. The officer who received this report ordered the Canadians to march by him. Guards slugged those who walked slowly or showed signs of falling away because of weakness; any movement to avoid the blow was taken as proof of being fit for labour.

At *Marutson*, Tom Forsyth and seventy-five others laboured twelve hours a day, hoisting 200-pound sacks filled with rice and grain or charcoal onto their backs and carrying them fifty yards into warehouses. The day of 31 October was especially miserable, with two hailstorms and constant rain. "Socks completely worn out. Boots in bad shape, chafed and blistered feet, causing festering sores. Hands numb with cold at work today. . . . No mitts, very hungry," wrote Forsyth, who noted a few days later that many then felt "the fellows who died in battle at Hong Kong were the lucky ones."

In *Shintesto*, Dallain and seventy-five others laboured in a Dantesque world, where the white-hot heat of the furnace caused them to sweat so much that some passed out due to lack of salt. When their uniforms dried out, they were stiff from sweat. Dallain recalls:

> I worked on a great big furnace by the main door of the building. Using a pulley and winch system, we would load a huge steel ingot into the furnace and then brick up the door—the heat coming out was so great that our faces felt red hot. The furnace would then be heated even further, until the ingot was white hot and the bricks were almost transparent.
>
> When the time came to pull the ingot out, we had to knock down the bricks. Then the heat that came out was almost unbearable. Sometimes our silk mitts caught fire. We would then lower a chain and pick up the ingot and move it to a steam press. We were fashioning huge gears and other parts

of ships' crankshaft. We'd stamp once and make one side and then the stamped piece of steel would be too cool to stamp again and we would have to put it back into the furnace and begin the whole process again.

Working at the coal yard almost killed Cambon and pushed another 125 to the edge. After a derrick unloaded a thousand pounds of coal into cars on a trestle thirty feet above ground, they had to push each car along the trestle until it was over the storage area or into a railway coal carrier into which they then dumped the coal. Other men carried coal loaded into baskets hung from a pole balanced across their bony backs. Here the *hanchos* were less understanding than the one in Hong Kong had been; they responded to errors or slow jogs by using their sticks. Soon, Cambon's weight was down to ninety pounds.

Cambon probably saved his life when he lied that he had some medical training and Corporal Takeo Takahashi took him to be his medical orderly. Takahashi's preferred treatment for pneumonia, camphor injections, was useless. So too were the powders he gave for dysentery, the burns caused by moxibustion (a Japanese folk remedy) and the needles two acupuncturists used to combat dysentery and diseases caused by malnutrition. Major Bill Stewart (Royal Army Medical Corps) tried to save lives by setting up a rotation that allowed the sickest to be excused from work. "It was extraordinary that a simple rest from work for three or four days should have been the means of preventing a man's death. Such was the delicacy of the dividing line between life and death," he wrote in his postwar report.[*]

---

[*] After the war, Captain Reid recalled his modus operandi was "to take back as many men as possible to Canada whether well or ill. . . . I would rather return with five hundred men in various stages of beriberi which perhaps in the future could be cured than to return with three hundred men in good health and leave two hundred behind."

The Japanese were having none of it. After the sick list rose from 150 to 240 a month, Tokyo sent an investigator with orders to ensure the highest number of workers. Henceforth, Stewart could withhold no more than twenty, and soon men began losing ground. The regimen at Niigata all but destroyed some three hundred Americans who, after being captured in the Philippines, had been held (and well fed) on a prison farm. "They were in top shape," recalls Dallain. "They were dancing and yelling. The Japanese hated them and took people like me off the hardest work on the furnace. But in about a month, the lack of food, hard labour and terrible living conditions had reduced those fine boys to our level."

. . .

While the Japanese did not perform the sort of heinous medical experiments on their Canadian prisoners that they did on Chinese POWs in Unit 731 in Harbin, China, Japanese doctors and medical students at Sagaminahara, a Tokyo hospital, performed torturous procedures on a few Canadians.* Rifleman Joseph Lawrence was made to stand with one foot in ice water and the other in hot water. The following day, a medical student pumped his stomach, and he was denied food for twenty-four hours, after which he was encouraged to gorge himself on rice. Six medical students then watched him throw up. Lawrence testified that he and other patients were given injections of unknown substances and that the medical students then recorded the results. A doctor injected Grenadier David Turk's spine with what he said was vitamin B, but the next day Turk became ill with dysentery, leading Turk to surmise that he had been experimented on.

---

* In December 1941, Japan held some three hundred and fifty thousand Chinese POWs. When the Second World War ended, Japan held 56 Chinese POWs, a survival rate of 0.0001 percent. Some two hundred thousand died at Camp X (Unit 731), where the Japanese military carried out gruesome human medical experiments.

Lawrence saw orderlies beat a Royal Scots POW who was suffering from dysentery, and who had run afoul of the rule forbidding men from leaving the room during roll call. The torture was more than physical. On several occasions, the medical students would come into the ward and ask "if anybody wanted to have his legs amputated."[7] A chronic lack of clean gauze and bandages led to many cases of gangrene, some of which led to otherwise unnecessary amputations.

.   .   .

The jungle telegraph did not, of course, connect the Canadians to each other or operate equally well at each camp. Nevertheless, through the second half of 1943, at least one group knew that in August Churchill had met with Roosevelt at Quebec and that the Russians had pushed the Germans out of Korkov; in September that the British 8th Army had invaded Italy and that German troops had occupied Rome; in October that the Americans had defeated the Japanese in the Solomon Islands; and in December that the Gilbert Islands had fallen. None knew that among the British forces that invaded Sicily were twenty-six thousand Canadians or that twenty-six hundred—six hundred more than the entirety of "C" Force—had become casualties on that island alone.

As much as the Canadians thrilled to the news from Europe and, especially, news of the American advances in the Pacific, their hearts would have beaten even more strongly had they known that thousands of their fellow countrymen were fighting and killing Japanese soldiers on the western end of the Japanese Empire. Over the course of the war more than seven thousand Canadians fought or flew into battle in Southeast Asia. During the POWs' first year of imprisonment, fifteen Canadian pilots accounted for sixteen kills. In March and April, Canadians flew supply missions for the famed Chindit invasion of Burma, while Roy "Mac" McKenzie—undoubtedly the only employee of the T. Eaton Company Limited ever to command Gurkhas in battle—led his men in a thrilling escape from the Japanese through the forbidding rainforests of eastern Burma.

. . .

As 1943 drew on, the families of the men of "C" Force could not help but feel that they and their men had been forgotten. True, they received financial support from the government. But aside from the regional papers in Quebec and Manitoba, there was limited reference to the first Canadian soldiers to go into battle in the war. On 12 January a press release had reported that Red Cross officials who visited Shamshuipo a month earlier found that the Canadians' condition had improved, though they were still underfed. The press release did not report the dreadful conditions that Red Cross officials found in the hospital. Hansard records only a few perfunctory questions in the House of Commons about the fate of "C" Force.

Seeking more information than the Canadian government gave them, Signalman Don Beaton's family asked the Vatican if the Apostolic Delegation in Tokyo could find out anything.

At least one Canadian contacted Sir Anthony Eden. Mrs. Jean Callahan of Arnprior, Ontario, began her letter by asking if he recalled that "five years ago a sixteen year old boy wrote to you . . . ask[ing] as a favour, [if] you would help him get over to England to join the R.A.F" before going on to say that "that boy is missing at Hong Kong with his older brother." She feared that her sons were on the "boat that had been sunk by the Japanese."* She continued, "And if the news is the worst that can come to me, I still want to know." Callahan ended her letter "And may God keep you, and our

---

* The *Lisbon Maru* was, as noted above, torpedoed by an American submarine.

King and Empire safe is my earnest prayer and send us victory and peace."*

By the time Mrs. Callahan wrote to Eden, the war had, quite literally, passed MacWhirter and Forsyth's battle by. The bombing raid on Hamburg on the night of 24/25 June 1943 saw 791 aircraft hold aloft some three thousand men, more than one and a half times the number of Canadians sent to Hong Kong. In the 22 December raid on Berlin, 5,300 men took to the skies. The Battle of Ortona in December cost more than 2,250 Canadians casualties, of whom more than 1,300 died. On the Eastern Front, Stalin fielded armies numbering in the millions. Ten million Americans were under arms. The Canadian army, navy and air force totalled almost one million, and tens of thousands more served in the merchant marine.

"In school there was a large map on the wall with many coloured pins in it that moved as the troops advanced," recalls Harvelyn McInnis, Winnipeg Grenadier Major Kenneth Baird's daughter. "This map covered Europe. There was no map of Hong Kong or any mention of Hong Kong. To me this meant that we were a forgotten group."

The absence of public statements did not indicate inaction. As it had through 1942 (and would until the end of the war), King's government worked through the International Red Cross to better the Canadians' condition, chiefly by sending money and Red Cross parcels and facilitating the exchange of mail.

Especially after they learned of the drafts to Japan, scores of relatives wrote the government asking for information about their loved ones. On 30 August, Under Secretary of State Norman Robertson answered one such letter from J.H. McArthur, Esq, of Campbellford,

---

* Eden's response read in part: "The Foreign Secretary will gladly make whatever enquiries are possible with regard to their present whereabouts, and if any information should prove to be available he will let you know at once."

Ontario; after checking the list supplied by the Japanese, the secretary found "that there is no record of his having been moved from Hong Kong." Robertson was quite forthcoming about the Red Cross inspections of Shamshuipo: "I am glad to be able to say that these Delegates are allowed to visit the camp occasionally, although it would seem that they are not permitted to make a very thorough inspection."

On 6 December, the Adjutant General's office wrote to the families of the POWs in the Far East telling them that 979 letters had arrived but that very few of them were from Hong Kong because the Japanese were still censoring them. For a country that had been at war for more than four years, and had seen tens of thousands of casualties already, Ottawa's response is surprising gentle:

> I hope that if you have not received a letter, you will not take this as an indication that there may be something the matter with your dear one. . . . Lists of casualties now come forward regularly and as you have not been notified in this regard, you have every reason to believe that he is safe, even though he has not been given an opportunity to write to you.[8]

According to McInnis, "Getting a letter meant suddenly that we had closeness. Even though it was a year old, it signified that he was alive or, at least, that he had been. And we could still hope."

. . .

When possible, the POWs turned the logic of slave labour on its head. Most often, this was done by the slave's oldest gambit: going slow. *Sur m shon* conserved scarce energy and reduced the POWs' contribution to the Japanese war economy. In some cases, a guard or an *ichiban* who held a jaundiced view of the war abetted the

POWs. Tom Marsh's *ichiban* taught him to make soap that he then smuggled out of the camp and sold; the proceeds were used to bribe other guards.

Perhaps the most adept poker player among the Canadians was the artist Allister. Kando-san enjoyed Allister's portrayal of the silent Marx brother, Harpo, so much that he joined him in aping "Hawpo-ka." Allister had come to respect his *ichiban*'s knowledge of Russian literature, but shook his head at the man's credulity at believing that a Japanese fighter pilot had brought down an American plane with a rice ball.

When the warm weather set in, Allister's paint gang convinced Kando-san that time given to ogling and some cavorting with the girls who worked in the Nippon Company's kitchen, "rovu-timu" (love time), was time well spent. The scam almost came to an end one warm day when Rifleman Ralph St. John pushed things too far and, wanting to continue lying in the sun, told Kando-san, "Me go *benjo*—bye now." Kando-san flew into a rage. Allister, who interposed, caught the brunt of it. "What do you think you're doing, you bastard!" screamed Allister after Kando-san hit him with a scraper.

For several days, Allister kept a discreet distance from the man. Risking a beating, Allister told Kando-san that in Canada "a gentleman—*jenorumano*—didn't strike another gentleman without losing his friendship, so we were no longer friends." His point made, and even more importantly, Kando-san's favour needed, a few days later Allister made up with him. Kando-san was later removed after being caught engaging in some sort of trade for the prisoners outside the camp.

At first Allister was lucky with the next painting master, who, when he found out that Allister was an artist, asked to see samples of his work. The *ichiban* liked them and arranged for Allister to begin painting still lifes. Soon, a surprising number of factory workers were coming to his little studio. Here too Allister practised *sur m shon,* as he made a big show of each brush stroke, sometimes stopping in mid-air as if the spirit was suddenly not moving his art. After a few months, Allister's sponsor wanted a painting of a photo that enraged Allister: the surrender of Singapore. Milking the opportunity for all it was worth, Allister told him that it would take time, for he would have to do sketches of each individual first. The *ichiban* was less and less pleased when he realized that day by day the Japanese grew more ugly and malevolent while the British faces "began to look gentle and beautiful."[9] In retaliation, the *ichiban* sent Allister back to the ship-painting gang.

Some Canadians engaged in sabotage. Since inspecting rivets is relatively easy, work gangs would not shear rivets or would drive them in incorrectly. George MacDonell did risk certain death, had he been caught, by putting iron filings in grease caps that were installed on the ball bearing assemblies of the driveshafts of ships being constructed at *Marutson.* In the mines, sabotage ranged from adding one too many light bulbs to a wire—which, because the lights were powered by direct current, caused an overload (and sometimes small fires)—to leaving brake levers less than fully engaged. The cars would then slip back down the track so fast that when they came to a curve, they jumped the track, closing that part of the mine, sometimes for days.

. . .

As much as the POWs' survival depended on the food in the Red Cross parcels and as much as those parcels represented tangible evidence of a world beyond the war, their arrival also touched off a frenzy of trading reminiscent of a cattle auction. Men who just days earlier were sunk in lethargy soon called out, "Butter fer jam, anybody! . . . M&V [stew] for chocolate! . . . Two decks of Chesterfields for chocolate," while others, thinking the price was too dear, called back "Up yours!"[10]

Some men gorged themselves, often causing stomach cramps and diarrhea. Others paced themselves, stretching out the vital protein in a can of Hereford, the fats in oleomargarine, butter or chocolate, or the nutrients in cheese. At the Argyle Street camp, some of the food was pooled, which allowed cooks to prepare stew and, a few times during the year, even a cake.* Allister, who had husbanded his tins of butter, saw the price rise from three rations of rice and beans to twelve rations of beans (which gave him twelve days of going to work on a full stomach) and then to twelve half-rations of rice and twelve of beans, which allowed him to begin gaining weight.

Soon, however, the parcels were empty and the men were again eating far fewer calories than are needed by men at hard labour. While the parcels surely saved some lives, when they gave out, men sickened again and some became unhinged. Energized by their parcels, Grenadiers Harvey Berry and one of the Caruso brothers discussed their plans for a restaurant. But as their hunger returned, the plans came apart. Unbelievably for starving men, the dispute was over whether Caruso, a trained pastry chef, would also be the chief chef. "They nearly came to blows," recalled Allister. "We watched, following the argument closely. What was so unsettling about this was that not only were *they* going bonkers but *we* considered their antics quite normal."[11]

. . .

The generation the POWs came from did not speak, as we do today, of "coping mechanisms" or "finding mental space." Still, to survive,

---

* The cooks fought a constant battle not only with inadequate supplies but with tasteless rice. At times the cooks used grease that was meant for their shoes and tooth powder to flavour rice.

to protect their sanity, each man had to find a way to come to terms with the horror of his daily existence. Some did this by walling off their emotions and hopes and focusing, almost automaton-like, on daily tasks. Others either fell back on their faith or turned to the padres, all of whom wrote of men who sought to know what Jesus' suffering meant for theirs. Still others, like Corrigan, Allister and another POW Allister calls "Bob," found themselves grappling with age-old philosophical questions.

Spurred by his reading of Pierre Van Paassen's *The Days of Our Years*, in which the Unitarian minister writes of his experiences in Fascist Italy and of being briefly interned in the Dachau concentration camp, on 30 November, Corrigan admitted to his diary that he held the "heretical viewpoint that the R[oman] C[atholic] church as it exists today, and the R.C. doctrine as laid out by the founders of our church are not one and the same thing."* He criticized the Church's role in "oppression, suppression and intrigue," its concentration on sin and hell, the wealth of the Church and its subordination of learning to doctrine. "Surely Christ's religion," he wrote, "ought to be able to withstand the onslaught of learning." The high school dropout ended this several-page entry with the sophisticated argument (echoing the philosopher René Descartes) that even though he believed in Christ, "doubt" and reason should be "openly encouraged."

Even as Verreault continued to be his mate, Allister found himself in deep conversations with Bob, who grew up in Verdun, on the other side of the tracks as it were from Allister's Montreal. Though uneducated, Bob shared Allister's interest in ideas. His description of their discussions shows again how thoughts are free:

---

* One must assume that the Japanese did not know what Paassen's book was about and allowed it into the camp only because it had been a bestseller in 1939/40.

He sucked up the rain of new ideas in books, theories, authors I offered like a dry thirsting plant. Plato, Socrates, Aristotle were tasted, licked, swallowed. . . . We fed each other.

Marching along [to and from their work site] we visited each other's habitats. He joined me in my bohemian days in New York, doing satirical sketches at the Village Vanguard in Greenwich Village or wandering down 42nd Street past the rows of cheap movie houses and porn shows. . . . Carefree days full of hilarity and adventure. Could anything be more opposite to this dreary, anxiety-ridden, hunger-filled existence.[12]

.   .   .

It is a measure of how difficult the lives of the men in Japan had become that Allister equates the discomfort of constant cold that settled on Japan late in the year with that of their unwashed skin. The unexpected arrival of a coal shipment banished both, at least temporarily. Hot water was put into two cement tubs, each large enough to hold fifty men at a time. Following Japanese bathing practice, the five hundred men went through them in sequence, which meant the first group bathed in hot clean water and the last in barely lukewarm, dark, slimy water. "But we were happy for a bath on any terms."[13]

On 9 December, a little over two years since the war began, each man was issued forty sheets of toilet paper. Their previous issue of this standard ten days' supply had been forty-one days earlier. In the interim, they had used their hands and wiped them on the wall when they got through—and during this period they had no soap.

.   .   .

Throughout the year men in the prime of their lives continued to die, six in January and five in February. From April through August the pace of death slowed to about three men per month, and five Canadians died in September, a much higher rate than in German POW camps that held Western soldiers.

One who survived was Henry Lyons. Sick from malnutrition and jaundice, for months his life hung in the balance. Just before they left on the April draft to Japan, officials allowed Riflemen Reggie Haley, Lyons' cousin, and an old friend, Jimmy Irvine, to visit Lyons at the Bowen Road Hospital. He so weak he could barely talk.

Haley placed ¥35 next to Lyons' pillow and told him, "I'm going to leave you this here and you are going to be able to get something to keep you going." Knowing how little he was capable of eating and how little food could be bought, Lyons responded, "It will be no good to me. I can't get nothing here." Tears running down his face, Haley insisted as he felt the weight of Lyons' head as he pushed the notes under the pillow. "You might get something and I'm leaving it."

As they walked out of the hospital, Haley told Irvine through his sobs, "We've looked on Henry for the last time, Jim. Henry's gone." Irvine said the only thing he could: "He'll hang on."

Lyons continued to weaken. Then one day, he heard the orderly direct a man toward his bed. "You're Lyons. You know who I am." Lyons must have hesitated a moment, because the man then said, "I'm Major MacAuley. I'm here to leave you some food," a tangerine. At first Lyons, who had prayed to die, refused it. MacAuley insisted that Lyons eat the tangerine. That night, thinking of his wife, Isabelle, and his young son, Vimy, Lyons beseeched the Lord to send him a sign in his dream to tell him if he was going to return home alive.

"I couldn't walk. I could barely see and I felt gone. But that night I dreamt I come home and what a terrible time I was having getting up the hill, the hill this house is on. My grandmother was still alive. I woke up and I put it all together. The Lord's sent this dream so I would put up a fight." It took him three days to find the strength to get out of bed. "When I did, I didn't even have the strength to crawl on my hands and knees, so I pulled myself on my butt to visit Lawson Moores, who was in bed at the end of the hall."[*]

Lyons wasn't well enough to leave the hospital until toward the end of the year. On 11 November 1943 in Yokohama, Haley died of beriberi, catarrh and pneumonia.

. . .

Haley's death was only one of sixteen in that bitterly cold November. Forsyth's diary for the month taps a terrible tattoo:

Nov. 6th   A Yank died today.

Nov. 9th   Reid of Rifles died today. Makes eleven since we
             arrived here.

Nov. 13th   An American died today.

Nov. 16th   Another Rifle died during the night named Sardy.

Nov. 19th   Another Yank died today.

Nov. 20th   Fischer a Dutchman died early this morning.

Nov. 21st   Rifleman [B.] Haley died today.

Nov. 22nd   Knapp of Rifles died early this morning.
             Cpl.Breen a little later.

Nov. 23rd   Evans died today, and Stan Hunter.

Nov. 29th   Robertson died today.

Nov. 30th   Nick Charuk died today.

December was even more deadly; eighteen Canadians died in four camps across Japan and in Hong Kong. Among these dead

---

[*] Lyons continues, "When I got home, I climbed the hill to my house. It was muddy just like in the dream. Just as I came up, I saw my grandmother." My interview with him took place in that same house.

was Lance-Sergeant Murray Goodenough, in Tsurumi. Over the course of the year, sixty-three Canadians died, all victims of diseases brought on by malnutrition and overwork or accidents in unsafe mines, factories and shipyards. On 28 December, two more Canadians died (bringing the total of POWs to die in the last eighteen weeks since the camp opened to forty-one), prompting Forsyth to write with a power that belies his grade 10 education: "Bitterly cold today, a piercing wind, stumbled back later thru mud and slush in the dark. Wallace has died, one of the Rifles, should never have been in the army at all. Harding, another Rifle died at lights out."

CHAPTER 18

"We Just Breathed Coal Dust and Ash"

Slave Labour in Japan
1944

*And one morning we were . . . coming down the track
and here's a big black cat that had been cut in two
laying right on a rail. And, and Jenkins said, "That's
something for the soup."*
—GRENADIER TOM FORSYTH

As 1943 slipped into 1944, snow fell across southwestern Japan; almost four feet would fall that winter. At 3:30 a.m. (Tokyo time), about the time Tom Forsyth's family in Winnipeg sat down to lunch on the last Friday of 1943, the weight of the snow became too much for a POW hut in Niigata 5B. The hut's support beams creaked and squealed with strain. Then the roof pulled away from the bay in the wall into which Jean-Paul Dallain's bunk had been built.

Before the crash of wood and *wumpf* of falling snow died away, the frigid night air was filled with "awful screams of men crushed and trapped beneath the wreckage," recalled Forsyth, who, though caught in the rubble, was unhurt. To his right he saw the already dead body of Rifleman David Sword; to his left lay Grenadier Joseph Furey, equally lifeless.

Woken by the breaking apart of his hut, Dallain saw the stars—not the roof—above him. Then the screams registered. He never knew if one was the death cry of Royal Rifles Sergeant Lester Sauson, who grew up a mere fifteen miles up the Gaspé coast from Dallain's hometown of New Carlisle. Dallain awoke on an angle, the head of his bed still attached to the wall. "It was a cold night, so I was fully dressed, and once I had the boots on I wanted to rush for the rubble. But by then, the Jap guards had arrived and they ordered us out of what was left of the hut so that they could count and recount us," recalls Dallain.

Lacking heavy equipment, the POWs' rescuers had to clamber over the slippery, jagged pieces of snow-covered wood "without knowing if their additional weight on the roof was crushing us more," recalled Forsyth. "It was a night of horror, the cries of the suffering men unable to move . . . when the first boards were ripped up above me, I felt the wind and the drifting snow on my face. Eight Canadians died that night; seventeen were badly injured and sent to the hospital."

The horror did not end with daybreak. The dead laid out in an unheated room had frozen. To fit them into the crude, short coffins, their naked frozen bodies had to be broken. Survivors with cracked ribs and pelvises were put in body casts. Their lousy bodies soon "endured the tortures of the damned," wrote Forsyth.

. . .

On 28 January 1944, Canada's fusty Prime Minister King rose in the House of Commons and, echoing a speech given hours earlier in the British Parliament by Sir Anthony Eden, told Canadians that there was evidence of "Japanese brutality and organized sadism" against Canadian and other Allied prisoners. His words stood in stark contrast to the formulaic lines—"Treatment here is all right, can't kick"; "The Nipponese show a respectful attitude toward us and nothing we ask of them is too much for them to do"—drunk up by families across the country. A government report concluded that the very ubiquity of these phrases meant that they should be discounted.* Both ministers said that Japanese "guilt [for violating the Geneva Convention] will not be forgotten." As King spoke, two Riflemen were suffering the effects of cruel tortures.

. . .

Blacky Verreault's ordeal at Tsurumi again involved Amana, who slammed the butt of his rifle into Verreault's leg when the Canadian ignored the order to move his feet from his bunk and eat with his feet on the floor. The blow lit a fury that burned through the POW's sense of self-preservation. As he might have during a barroom brawl in Ville-Émard, Quebec, he picked Amana "up by the scruff of the neck and the seat of his pants" and threw him over the nearest table.[1]

Snake Eyes left the hut but soon returned with two guards, bayonets at the ready, who took Verreault out into the snow and beat him black and blue. Then they made him stand coatless and bootless through the night at attention. By morning, one side of Verreault's face was frozen white. The next day, he showed the first signs of pneumonia. For more than a month, Verreault's life hung in the balance.

Three hundred miles away at Niigata, Rifleman James Mortimer endured a similar torture. Dressed only in a shirt and trousers, he

---

* The government did not, however, tell the families this balesome fact. In September, it went further and issued a public report that misled Canadians, saying that at Shamshuipo, "Large vegetable gardens are under cultivation and there are pig and poultry farms. . . . and canteens are open daily for the sale of cigarettes, syrup, soya milk powder and daily necessities" (quoted in Penny, 253f).

was tied to a rope affixed to a stake driven into the snowy ground. To keep from freezing, Mortimer and an American prisoner being punished the same way had to run around the stake all night long. The next morning the Japanese guards clubbed their frostbitten heads. The American died of a broken skull. A few days later, one of Mortimer's legs turned gangrenous. Nothing could be done to stop the putrefaction of his flesh; he would suffer an agonizing death in April.

In March, guards at Omine discovered that the POWs were planning to rise up against their captors as soon as the Allies invaded Japan. Staff Sergeant Harry Lim of the Hong Kong Volunteer Defence Corps had prepared maps and the men had managed to smuggle eight hundred sticks of dynamite out of the mine; these were to be their weapons. In addition to Lim, six Canadians, including Ross, Sergeant Maurice D'Avignon and Rifleman Yank Burns* "were locked in a dungeon and made to stand at attention for 31 hours. Guards prodded anyone who wavered with sharpened bamboo poles; they used them to beat anyone who fell. The torture included being given very small portions of rice and only salted water," reported the *Canada Gazette* in June 1946.

Only the fast intervention of George Grant saved William Allister from being beheaded by a guard named Yamanaka. Yamanaka had objected when Allister wore a new warm cap with the earflaps down, which prevented Allister from hearing Yamanaka's order to remove it. Yamanaka ripped the cap off Allister's head and started slapping

---

* John Burns's nickname came about because he was an American. His family holidayed in northern New York and he crossed the border in mid-1940 and joined the Canadian Army. Burns was one of the 206 men who joined the Rifles as the regiment's train made its way to Vancouver in October 1941. He was one of twenty Americans who joined the Canadian Army. These men were the first to come under fire by the Japanese Army; the attacks on Pearl Harbor and the Philippines were carried out by the Japanese Navy and Air Force. Burns was also adept at smuggling newspapers and medicines into the camp.

him with it. Then he began clubbing the Canadian over the head with his rifle, stunning and enraging Allister.

Grant ran over to interpret. When Allister answered that he had not heard the order to remove the cap, Yamanaka continued to beat him. Blood ran down Allister's face as Yamanaka pulled his sword and, through Grant, began questioning Allister again: "He wants to know how you'd like it if he cut your head off." Two years of bile rose in Allister. "Tell him my boss doesn't want his men working without their heads," he said, before jerking his own head toward the sword-carrying guard in an act of disdain.

"I can't tell him that," Grant hissed. "He'll blow his stack!"
"Tell him anything," [Allister] said, beyond caring, beyond sanity.[2]

Grant's apologetic answer couldn't stop another blow, but together with the blood running down Allister's face, it mollified Yamanaka.

On 22 June Grenadier Nicholas Berzenski and George MacDonell were beaten by Privates Yamanaka, Shibata and Baba. Berzenski had been accused of stealing a can of salmon at the shipyard. MacDonell, his section chief, accompanied Berzenski to the guardroom. After determining that Berzenski was guilty and that MacDonell had lied to protect him, the Japanese hit and kicked the two Canadians. "Then, with our hands tied to an iron grating above our heads, we were beaten with three-foot staves about two inches in diameter," recalled MacDonell, who passed blood for days from what he feared was permanent kidney damage; the beating maimed Berzenski for life.[3]

Kanao Inouye, the Kamloops Kid, had left Hong Kong, but cruelty remained. A moment of kindness to a little girl whose kite had flown into the garden Rifleman Donald Languedoc tended at Shamshuipo almost cost him his life. Languedoc asked permission to climb between the rows of barbed wire and retrieve the girl's kite. When the guard did not refuse, Languedoc retrieved the kite and gave it to the guard to give to the girl. A few hours later, eight other guards dragged Languedoc to the camp commandant, who accused him of engaging in espionage with the Chinese. The guards punched, kicked and beat Languedoc with rifle butts before dumping him unconscious on the campgrounds.

· · ·

In his January speech to the House, King said that the Canadians held in Hong Kong were better treated than the Canadians held in Japan. He was marginally correct. For one thing, by the end of 1943, the heavy labour at Kai Tak was finished. The Japanese occupying Hong Kong continued to make use of illegal labour—manhandling bombs and oil drums—but the need was less and most men did not have to work more than two out of every three days. By contrast, the undernourished men who had left Hong Kong on *Toyama Maru* at the end of December 1943 and arrived in Nagoya, Japan, in early January found themselves working fourteen-hour days in a locomotive factory.

Even as he was forced to contribute to the Japanese war machine, Royal Rifles Sergeant Colin Standish was almost constantly reminded of Canada. Many of the pieces of iron his unprotected hands pushed into sharp steel knives that moved up and down at great speed were stamped "CANADA." The copper ingots he pushed into the machine were imprinted with a maple leaf, which showed they had been mined at Copper Cliff, Ontario, just outside Sudbury.

At Oeyama, John Duguay worked hammering steel for locomotive boilers. While Duguay escaped being beaten, others accused of stealing food did not. Like his comrades at Tsurumi, Omine and Niigata, Duguay slept on a tatami mat and was given a single thin blanket to cover himself. In two and a half years, he received one let-ter; the single letter his family received from him had been rewritten by a Japanese censor.

On a few days, such as 27 August, when the Japanese inexplica-bly delivered a brace of twenty-two pheasants, and 8 September, when liver was served for supper, the officers in Hong Kong ate well. In the days that followed their receipt of Red Cross parcels in August, Chaplain Laite put on fourteen pounds.* Such days, how-ever, were the exception. In Hong Kong, the Canadians' daily calorie count averaged twenty-three hundred, rising above twenty-seven hundred calories only in February. Although the existence in both Hong Kong camps of vegetable and small livestock farms added important variety—and much-needed vitamins and minerals—to the diet, the farms were not large enough to produce adequate food to significantly raise the calorie content or prevent disease. Pellagra and beriberi remained rampant, the latter killing Grenadier George Sokalski on 30 May. In Japan, earlier that month, Lance Ross recorded a meal of soup made from six 12-inch ferns. In June, 145 men suffered from semi-blindness due to avitaminosis. On 16 July, Kenneth Baird noted he had not eaten meat in a year. In August, a man in the dysentery ward was found to have seventy-four worms, some of them eight inches long.

In November, the pigs at Shamshuipo farm neared the slaugh-ter. Divided among nine hundred men, they'd provide a third of a pound of pork per man—*for one day only.* The ton of vegetables harvested in early November worked out to 3½ pounds per man or about *1.8 ounces per man per day for a month.*

The men held in Hong Kong had two additional sources of food: the official canteen and the black market. The canteen, which had

---

* Packed in 1942, by the time the Japanese released these parcels, much of the cheese was filled with weevils and the raisins, prunes and chocolates were somewhat mouldy.

been established in 1942 when the Japanese sold the POWs stocks of food looted from the British and Canadian dumps, had by 1944 withered into irrelevance.

The black market could not have existed without the connivance of the Japanese guards. They provided most of the cash by pay-ing thousands of yen for Red Cross blankets (contained in comfort packages that started arriving in the camps in 1944) and as much as ¥10,000 for gold watches. Prices on the black market were steep: a pound of dry beans cost ¥150.

In Japan—where men often laboured for fifteen days straight—calories were fewer, often less than a thousand a day. Over the course of 1944, at least seventy men died in Japan from diseases linked to malnutrition. In March in Niigata, the Japanese looted the Red Cross parcels of their powdered milk. On 3 April, Forsyth ate a fish head, eyes included, for breakfast. The most common vegetable the POWs ate was a daikon (a large white radish) that was about 95 per-cent water; daikons are, however, high in vitamin C, which explains why the Canadians escaped the torment of scurvy. More than once, hunger drove Forsyth and the others to eat grasshoppers, always being careful to remove the hind legs because they "had barbs that would tear the inside of your mouth." They were also driven to remove undigested beans and corn from their feces and eat them again. On 22 March 1944, thirteen men suffered from beriberi, sev-enteen from electric feet, thirty-four from swelling and four from optic neuritis. Men who had weighed on average 171 pounds when captured and 134 pounds when drafted to Japan were now down to 126 pounds.

At Tsurumi in January, Grenadier Charles Trick recorded "small" rations seven times and "terribly small" rations three times. In February, because of a lack of fuel, his mess ate its rice uncooked. The Japanese appear to have calibrated when to release better food. "One day we eat good, the next day we don't," Trick wrote at the end

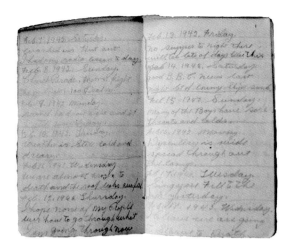

19. Page from Lance Ross's diary.

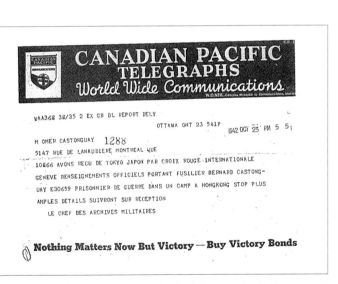

20. Telegram received on 23 October 1942 by Rifleman Claude Castonguay's family, telling them that the Red Cross had received official information that Fusilier Bernard Castonguay was a Prisoner of War in a Hong Kong Camp.

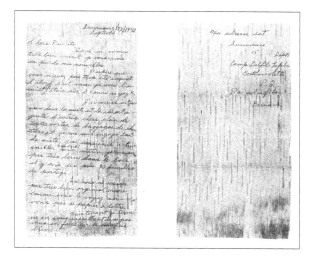

21. Letter from Rifleman Claude Castonguay to his parents, written while he was a POW.

22. Letter from Mrs. MacWhirter to her son Bill while he was a POW.

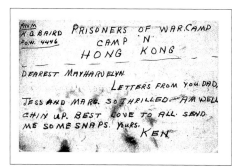

23. Postcard from Major Baird to his wife and daughter.

24. Copy of letter from Harvelyn Baird to her father, Major Kenneth Baird.

DEAR DADDY.

HOW ARE you? I hope you ARE well. WE ARE uP AT NANA'S NOW. I pASSED TO GRADE sEVEN THIS yEAR. SO now I AM FINISHED. GROSVENOR school. I AM gRowiNg SO much you wouldN'T KNow ME, I weigh 103 AND AM NOW NEARly AS TAll AS MUm. DiANE AND I hAD A LovELy TWO WEEKS AT THE LAKE. I AM 5 FEET 3 inches TALL. WE ARE EnclosiNg Two SnAp shots, which wE hopE you LiKE. I LOVE siNgiNg Now AND I MAY TAKE LEssons This yEAR. WELL I HopE I sEE you soon. MUch LOVE AND KiSSES. HARVElyn

25. Sonny Castro playing a woman in a show put on by POWs in Shamshuipo.

26. Sketch of primitive medical equipment available to doctors in Hong Kong after the Japanese looted the Bowen Road Military Hospital.

27. Rifleman Jean-Paul Dallain in 1943, while a POW in Japan.

28. Molly Baird, wife of Major Kenneth Baird.

29. Rifleman Jean-Paul Dallain and Grenadier Tom Forsyth survived the collapse of this hut in Niigata in the early hours of 1 January 1944. Eight other Canadians were crushed to death on that frigid night. Note the snow on the roofs.

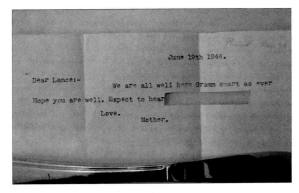

30. Lance Ross's censored mail.

31. POW camp Niigata 5B in August 1945. Note the writing on the roof to alert American pilots of the location of the camp.

32. Sergeant George MacDonell (Royal Rifles), while a POW in Japan.

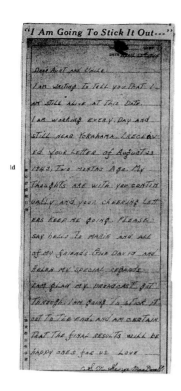

"I Am Going To Stick It Out---"

Dear Aunt and Uncle

I am writing to tell you that I am still alive at this date. I am working every day and still near Yokahama. I received your letter of August 22 1943, two months ago. My thoughts are with you continually and your cheering letters keep me going. Please say hello to Marie and all of my friends. Give David and Helen my special regards. I am glad my broadcast got through. I'm going to stick it out to the end, and am certain that the final results will be happy ones for us. Love

Cpl. M. George MacDonell

33. George MacDonell's letter home, 22 April 1944.

35. Canadian POWs at Tsurumi pushed coal cars like those seen here.

34. Squalid conditions of POW hut in Niigata.

36. Canadian and British POWs at Shamshuipo awaiting the landing party from HMCS Prince Robert.

37. Lieutenant Commander Fred Dey of HMCS *Prince Robert* with newly liberated Canadian POWs in Hong Kong.

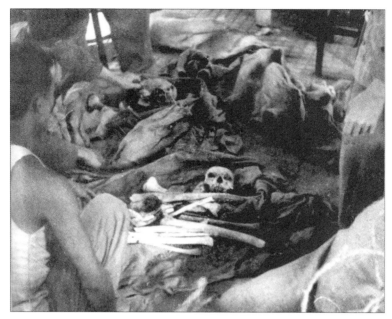

38. Remains of Canadian soldiers that have been gathered together for a proper burial.

39. Hong Kong Veterans Commemorative Association Memorial Wall in Ottawa, dedicated 15 August 2009.

of February when he was down to 121 pounds. On 17 March, the day Trick wrote that "the boys are getting very weak," Captain Saito, commandant of the camp, released 181 twelve-ounce cans of bully beef that was made into a stew.

On 27 March, seventeen men shared a bucket of rice, five more than had shared a bucket two days earlier. On 7 May, the cookhouse threw out the rotten fish the Japanese gave the Canadians for dinner. At the end of the month, to ensure that each of the 460 inmates got his share of the fifty eggs brought into the camp, the cooks made a soup out of them. On 7 July, the Japanese gave them some horse bones for soup. Thanks to an inspection on 28 July, Trick was able to write, "We sure ate good. We had more rice than we have had for weeks. At noon we had a bowl of spaghetti besides a bowl of rice." The first part of August was also good; by the 19th, however, nineteen men were sharing a bucket of rice. On 5 December, there was almost no dinner; the Japanese had given the cooks rotten cow guts to cook.

The black market was less developed in Japan than in Hong Kong. Still, in Tsurumi, both civilian workers and guards traded food for cigarettes. Since there was almost nothing to buy in the canteen, the few times the men were paid, the men used those funds to buy illicit food and smokes.

Trading in the shipyard, coal yard or factory was relatively easy compared with getting the cigarettes back into camp. At one point while working with a trading group, Signalman Gerry Gerrard carried a load of five packs of cigarettes into the camp by secreting them in the crotch of his pants. Another time, while working with another trading group, Gerrard was given a load that was too large to hide on his person. He recruited a sergeant because officers were not usually searched upon returning to camp. But for some reason, the sergeant's lunch was searched and the smokes discovered. The sergeant saved Gerrard from a beating, but not from coming under such close observation that he was unable to retrieve the cigarettes he had hidden away for himself.

Canadian prison camps never descended into the dog-eat-dog world of James Clavell's novel *King Rat* or the South Asian camp where two Americans ran a futures trading market in rice that resulted in other Americans dying of starvation before their eyes. The Canadians were not, however, boy scouts. As he had in 1943, Allister traded for rice rations and in many cases men went hungry when they sold their rations for cigarettes.

. . .

For Ed Shayler and forty-seven other Canadians who travelled to Japan on *Naura Maru*, the hard labour was even worse than it had been at Kai Tak.* In Hong Kong, working in temperatures of 100°F or more, the heat had wrung the sweat from their brows. But at least Shayler could see clearly beneath the broiling sun and breathe the air, even if it was humid. In the pits of Furukawa Mining Company, "We just breathed coal dust and ash," says Shayler, who had the same job Bob Barter did at Omine—bracing the roof of the mine. The pace of work there too was determined by guards' fists, who "if they thought a guy was not producing enough would take him and beat the hell out him," recalls Shayler.

. . .

By the end of 1944, the Canadians had been prisoners of war for 1,102 days. For the most part, morale and order held. As terrible as the strain of being on the Hell Ships was, Canadians experienced nothing like the madness that broke out in the holds of *Oryokk*

---

* The ship also carried 115 Hong Kong Volunteers and 58 British troops.

Maru in December of 1944 when some American POWs turned on others and killed them, while hundreds of other American POWs and their officers looked on.

The removal of the officers to Argyle Street POW Camp and the Japanese decision to exclude officers from the drafts to Japan may have accorded with the Geneva Convention's stipulations about the treatment of officers (that is, excluding them from work and allowing them to keep their batmen). However, as evidenced from the sword whipping meted out to Governor Sir Mark Young, who was imprisoned on Formosa and later in Mukden (China), and the mistreatment of General Maltby, the Japanese overseers were not overly concerned with the Convention's articles that pertained to officers. Rather, the Japanese isolated the men from their officers to remove rallying points and thus render the ordinary ranks compliant.

At Tsurumi, according to MacDonell, "Daily orders and crime sheets for disobedience were in effect. We were an organized military unit, with its formal structure [including messes] and fully operational. No unit was left outside this formal, regimental organization, and each individual was constantly reminded that he was a Canadian soldier who was only temporarily under the control of the Japanese." The command structure was not as formal at Niigata. Even though the NCOs had little power to influence the Japanese, "The sergeant was still the sergeant. We did not lose respect for our officers because we were prisoners," recalls Dallain.

For reasons that are unclear, as the war wore on, the command structure frayed at Shamshuipo, in Hong Kong. Phil Doddridge recalls, "Sergeant so-and-so became simply Bill." More important, however, than a certain hierarchical slovenliness, for which the Canadians were justly famous, was the fact that the Camp Liaison Officer, (British) Major Cecil Boon, became a tool of the captors. Boon took control of the Canadian work parties out of Canadian hands. The coup was triggered by an act of insubordination by Company Sergeant-Major Colin McFayden following the American bombing of Kai Tak in March.

While the bombing heartened the POWs, it also increased the danger of working near the aerodrome. In order to spread the risk fairly, Royal Rifles Captain Everette Denison ordered that officers, who previously had not been assigned to work outside the camp, would take their turns.

One day, Denison learned that Boon had removed McFayden from the work party list and substituted someone else. Denison went to Boon and asked on what authority he had interfered with the detailing of a Canadian work party. Boon denied making any changes but then said that he had posted the list under the authority of the camp's interpreter. When Denison asked, "Who recommended them?" Boon flew into a rage and threw Denison out of his office. Denison's appeal to the Japanese was unsuccessful.

Denison ordered Captains William Leboutillier and Njall Bardal to investigate. Bardal discovered that after seeing his name on the list, McFayden had requested that Boon remove it. Bardal also reported that "two of his officers, Captains [William] Golden and [Edward] Walker had advised CSM McFayden in the matter." Denison never regained control of the Canadian work parties.*

Later in the year at Oeyama, Winnipeg Grenadier Company Sergeant-Major Marcus Tugby and three British NCOs combined to do the Japanese dirty work for them. According to historian

---

* As soon as he could after liberation, Denison reported the matter to "C" Force Commander Lieutenant-Colonel William Home; Bardal and Major George Trist filed other reports. Canadian authorities were, however, aware of Boon's activities before these reports, courtesy of a report sent to Ottawa after Royal Naval New Zealand Reserve Volunteer Lieutenant R.B. Goodwin, who escaped from Hong Kong on 17 July 1944, was debriefed in London in August 1944.

Charles Roland, "The Big Four met in what was described as the Blue Room, where punishment of wrongdoers was sometimes carried out in the presence of the camp commandant and some of his staff. A man who committed a petty crime might be beaten severely by Tugby and the others."[4] Worse, Tugby was seen pilfering food from Red Cross parcels that the Japanese had released to him to give to sick men and used his power to distribute parcels to bribe men into joining work parties when they were ill.[*]

. . .

On 27 February Lance Ross in Omine received his first letter. As Laite and Baird had done with theirs more than a year earlier, Ross copied the letter, which his mother had written in September 1942, into his diary. Although mail delivery in Hong Kong improved, it remained haphazard; a letter written in 1943 arrived before two written in 1942. White received his first mail in March, while Laite received six in the first half of the year.

White's windfall consisted of three letters from his wife, none written after December 1942, and two from his brother in England, the most recent dated 1 January 1943. "It was wonderful," he wrote in his diary, "couldn't keep the tears out of my eyes." Still, by mid-March 1944, the letters were almost a year and a half old. This delay undercut the joy White and others felt at receiving the mail. White wrote: "After reading them over several times comes a let-down feeling. They are so old, anything might have happened since. How is Maxine holding up, is Don still okay??, etc."

Less than a month later, White received a letter that eased his worry. As he wrote in his diary on 7 April: "One letter, Aug. 27/43

---

[*] Tugby's 1946 court martial in Winnipeg ended with a reprimand.

with picture of Maxine, sure great." In August, he received three letters written in January 1943.

One of the two letters Jean-Paul Dallain received made him blush: he read that his sister, Alice, and her baby were doing fine. "How could she have a child out of wedlock?" he thought, forgetting how much time had passed since he'd left New Carlisle, Quebec. Dallain smiled at the fleeting sense of family shame after his friend Phil Gallie asked, "Didn't it ever occur to you that she's married?"

. . .

"News," Henry Lyons recalls, "was life itself." As they had been in 1943, the men in Hong Kong remained better informed about the details of the war than the POWs in Japan. Although he misidentified D-Day (6 June) as "Dunkirk Day," Laite recorded hearing of the invasion of Europe five days after one hundred and fifty thousand men invaded Europe, including fourteen thousand Canadians who stormed onto Juno Beach. In mid-August, after a hiatus of several weeks, the Japanese again allowed the *Hong Kong News* into the camp, and Laite learned of the replacement of Tōjō's government by General Kuniaki Koiso's, the failure of von Stauffenberg's attempt on Hitler's life and Allied advances in Europe.

The Canadians at Tsurumi were the first to learn that their countrymen were fighting in Burma. In June, a Royal Air Force officer brought a patient to the camp's doctor, Captain John Reid. After tending to the patient, Reid discovered that the officer was the Royal Canadian Air Force Flight Officer Len Birchall, shot down in April 1943 while trying to determine the number and type of ships in a convoy heading for Ceylon. Birchall had earned the sobriquet "The Saviour of Ceylon" from Churchill for managing to get off a message warning of the Japanese invasion before his plane crashed into the sea.*

In Omine, Harry Lim translated scraps of newspapers that Japanese civilians used to wrap the lunches and then conveniently left around the factories. On 24 August, the Allies were not fighting "on German territory," as Verreault believed. The Russians had, however, pushed the Germans out of Romania and the 1st Canadian Army was fighting a desperate battle to close the Falaise pocket; mistakes by Field Marshal Montgomery and the same General Crerar that sent "C" Force to Hong Kong allowed some hundred thousand German soldiers to escape. Nor did the Canadians learn that in September their comrades had captured Dieppe and Ostend in Belgium or that in October they were liberating the Netherlands. None of the Canadians knew of the role the Canadians played in defeating Japan's attack on India.

Large formations of American B-29 bombers delivered the most important news right to the POWs' doorsteps. The dreaded *B-nijukus* bombed factories around Tsurumi in June, August, November and in a huge raid on Christmas Eve. On 12 September, Ross heard that Tokyo had been bombed two days earlier. The Americans bombed Hong Kong in October and every second night in December.

The raids on Hong Kong sent Laite and his hutmates scrambling for safety under their steel beds. At Tsurumi, POWs took shelter in "funk holes" covered with some old timbers and piles of dirt. Despite the danger of being caught directly under the bombs, the Canadians welcomed them with both fatalism and grim satisfaction. Baird thought the raid by forty bombers on 8 December a decent payback for the raid that three years earlier had announced the beginning of the Battle for Hong Kong. "We had to hustle back

---

* Birchall commanded 412 Squadron, the first Canadian squadron stationed outside North America or Britain.

to our huts [from the garden], but on the way I saw our planes diving and heard the roar of bombs; quite exciting, the more the merrier."[5]

By late 1944, the POWs had still one more way of telling how the war was going for Japan. Though he did not know that American submarines had all but destroyed the Japanese merchant fleet, Laite realized that the "grow it at home" policy meant that the Empire's ability to import food had been disrupted. The POWs in Japan knew too. Not only had their meagre rations declined again, they could tell that the Japanese civilians in the foundries, shipyards and mines were themselves beginning to go hungry.

Despite Allister's claim that he had adopted a hyperrealistic attitude to survive, he could not help but identify with these poor Japanese civilians. "We had more in common with the workers than with our well-fed countrymen up there [in the planes]. We worked together, suffered the U.S. blockade together, went hungry together, feared the military together, dodged bombs together."[148] Marsh, whose physical sufferings in battle surely would have excused much bitterness, also extended empathy to the Japanese civilians bombed nearby. "I asked one Jap workman how he made out. He smiled and replied 'Wife dead, two children gone!' He reached out, patted me, and then walked away."

. . .

In October, the Japanese military issued the following directive:

> The P.W.s will be concentrated and confined in their present location under heavy guard as the preparation for the final disposition will be made.
> (a) Whether they are destroyed individually or in groups, or however it is done, with mass bombing, poisonous smoke,

poisons, drownings, decapitation, or what, dispose of them as the situation dictates.

(b) In any case, it is the aim not to allow the escape of a single one, to annihilate them all and not leave any traces.

While this directive, which was reiterated in 1945, explains the Japanese massacre of hundreds of thousands of Chinese POWs and their mistreatment of Allied POWs, at least at Tsurumi things were somewhat more complicated. Even as malnourished men were kept at hard labour, a medical orderly told Captain Reid, the Camp Medical Officer, "a new order had come from headquarters—previously when prisoners died it was very good, but now very bad." Perhaps someone up the chain of command had realized that the war was lost and wanted to begin currying favour with the POWs. Perhaps he realized that the death of a POW removed his labour from Japan's fast-eroding war machine. In any case, on 5 November, after Royal Rifles Sergeant-Major Earl Todd was killed when a crane dropped a ton of wood on him, the camp commandant ordered an investigation into the cause of Todd's death.[*]

Since at least the beginning of 1944, the dead at Tsurumi had been treated with more dignity than elsewhere. As already noted, the bodies of those killed in Niigata early New Year's morning had to be further broken before they were cremated. In 1943 in the same camp, when Shorty Pope and Rifleman Bill Knapp each died in his arms, Ken Cambon had been tasked with stuffing each man's mouth and rectum with paper, the Japanese having refused to issue cotton-wool for this last ritual. Neither body had received a blessing before it was carted off to the crematorium.

---

[*] Whatever the reason for or extent of the officials' concern for safety, the Japanese did not take one obvious step: replacing the canvas shoes, many of which lacked complete soles, or the straw boots (an eight-inch-long pad tied with straw to the big toe and around the ankle) with some of the hundreds of boots issued by the Red Cross.

By contrast, at Tsurumi, when twenty-year-old Rifleman Stirling McKinley died in April 1944 from malnutrition, he was, wrote Ross, buried "out on the hill-side among the Pines." In July, after a mining accident killed Riflemen Ralph Campbell and Charles Fitzpatrick, the commandant allowed a major and Sergeant Maurice D'Avignon to preside over a Protestant and Catholic funeral respectively.

Commandant Saito went much further following Todd's death. Eight hundred yen were deposited into the POW account for his family. A Roman Catholic priest from outside the camp was brought in for the funeral, and it ended with the playing of the "Last Post." Todd's body was taken to the crematorium by an honour guard of six Royal Rifles NCOs.

. . .

At no point did the Canadian or other POWs suffer from the Stockholm Syndrome, in which captives begin to identify with their captors. Still, the camps had become their homes. Some, like Verreault, who picked up writing his diary in July after a six-month hiatus, wondered what freedom was like. In the face of the ever-present brutality of the guards and the POWs' poor physical condition, they did what they could to give their lives a semblance of normality.

Again, the experience of the men in Hong Kong differed greatly from those in Japan. Indeed, until April 1944, Mr. Francis O'Neill of the Canadian Auxiliary Service and the British mounted shows on a stage that the POWs built at Shamshuipo. During the eighteen months ending June 1944, a twenty-piece orchestra performed; in the latter part of 1944, the Japanese allowed quartets to perform in different huts each night. In September, the Canadians convinced the camp's commandant that bingo was entertainment (not gambling) and were thereupon allowed to organize games. The small library established in 1942 had grown (thanks mainly to Red Cross shipments) to more than three thousand in 1944; the number of men borrowing books, however, was much smaller due to the discontinuance of electric light and eye damage brought on by malnutrition. In July, basketball became all the rage.

Because he was a padre, Laite could move about the camp more than others, thus making his memoir a valuable source of information at the same time as it depicts atypical freedom. Following the arrival of a Red Cross parcel or when the men scrimped and saved from their meagre rations, better meals for birthdays or even anniversaries were prepared. On 28 August, Laite copied a baking recipe into his diary to memorialize a visit to a Middlesex hut where he was given a cup of milk and a piece of cake.

In 1944, Father Deloughery said 367 masses (in front of a total of six thousand men) and performed 110 evening services. He gave 4,371 Holy Communions and prepared two men for death.

In Japan, labour regimens that kept the Canadians working as many as fifteen days in a row left less time for what the author of the report on Shamshuipo termed "amenities." Still, when not at forced labour, time needed to be filled. On 27 July, his first day off in a fortnight, Verreault washed his laundry, which included several very worn shirts, socks, pants and the sarong worn by Canadians in the warm weather. Four days later, after a dinner during which he discussed his mother's pies, Verreault spent the evening in a silent reverie of chocolate, pie and the sound of the radio in the kitchen of his parents' house. Allister filled much of his time reading. He also clashed with an American officer named Quinn, who decided that each man could borrow only one book a month. When Quinn discovered several books on a shelf above Allister's bed, he did not accept the Canadian's explanation that other men preferred to keep their books on his shelf.

There was no library in Niigata. Cambon took great pleasure in furtively reading *A Pocket Book of Verse,* which he had smuggled from Hong Kong. He and the rest of the camp also enjoyed the small combo organized by a certain George: "The sound of 'Star Dust' bursting out of George's trumpet created a warm civilized aura that masked the cold reality around us."[7]

. . .

As much as the Canadians sought to get along with their captors (at Narumi, Standish gave a guard named Captain Tanaka French lessons), the Dominion's soldiers remained men at war, their only weapon being sabotage. In Tsurumi, they took advantage of lax safety procedures and started fires in heaps of oil-soaked rags. In the steel mill at *Shintetsu,* they burned the steel so that it would break apart when it was forged. Allister did not let his "friendship" with the interpreter Kagurami get in the way of his slow work or of what the Japanese took to be more insulting, farting during *tenko* (roll call).

On 20 January, Canadian Postal Corps Staff Sergeant Charles Clark and Royal Canadian Ordnance Corpsman Private Kenneth Cameron crippled the Nippon Kokan Shipyards. During the afternoon, they hid a lit candle surrounded with celluloid shavings behind some soap boxes. At 8:00 p.m., the fire reached the shavings, which acted as an accelerant. The blueprint office burned, as did the yard's supply of ship's stores, the fitter's shop and other important areas. According to a U.S. Navy report, the fire cut back production of destroyers and other ships totalling eight thousand tons a month by 60 percent. On the strength of the report, which ended "If the part that Sergeant Clark and Private Cameron played in this sabotage had been discovered, undoubtedly they would have been executed or tortured to death," Clark earned a Distinguished Conduct Medal and Cameron a Military Medal.

At the Furukawa Mining Company, sabotaging the train that pulled the cars loaded with a ton of coal each to the surface at around thirty miles per hour was relatively easy. By pulling the clevis pin—which locked the cotter pin into the C-shaped shackle that connected the cars to each other—out a little bit, "when the cars went over the humps or around the sharp turns, the pin would break or work loose and then the cars would jump the track. Once forty cars broke loose and came hurtling down the shaft. The Japs never did figure out what happened. But the shaft was closed until it was dug out," recalls Ed Shayler.

In early December in Niigata, Rifleman Johnny Stroud ensured that his comrades would have a few days off work when he passed around sticks with his feces so that the Japanese believed that the highly infectious disease of amoebic dysentery had broken out.

. . .

The approach of Christmas raised the emotional pitch for the POWs. Allister, though Jewish, spent weeks preparing Christmas decorations. Verreault and others who had formed a choir prepared a concert during which he sang "O Holy Night." The distribution of Red Cross parcels on Christmas Day meant not only full stomachs but tastes of home: chocolate, jam and coffee.

The text for the Protestant Christmas Eve Communion Service sermon at Shamshuipo, "There was no room for Him in the Inn" (Luke 2:7), was especially poignant. It underlined how the quotidian world closed its eyes to the divine within it, even as it asserted a vital thing to remember for men who would be beginning their fourth Christmas as POWs: the stable too lay within the sight of the Lord.

Laite and White spent part of the day visiting the sick together. Their diary entries written at about the times their families were waking on Christmas morning capture the swirl of emotions experienced by the Canadians now spread out among seven POW camps. "All thoughts are with home folk today. The distance from here to our respective homes may be long, and the waiting wearisome, but the distance does not divide our thoughts and affections today. . . . I know that Grayson and Florence will give Mom all cheer possible today," wrote Laite.

White's prose is somewhat earthier: "Another Christmas in this bloody hole! Will there be more? I sincerely hope not." He also remembered to record that he had gone to the hospital to distribute "what few fags I could scrape together."

CHAPTER 19

"They'd Never Let the Fires Go Out— Unless . . ."

Survival
1 January to 17 August 1945

In the heady days after the liberation of Paris on 25 August 1944 and the Russians reaching Germany's eastern border a week later, the optimists in General Dwight D. Eisenhower's command believed that the war in Europe could be over by Christmas. The men of the 2nd Canadian Division, who avenged the humiliation of August 1942 by taking Dieppe on 31 August 1944, believed so too. It was not to be. At the turning of the year, more than eight hundred thousand Allied troops held off half a million Germans in Hitler's last desperate gamble, the Battle of the Bulge.

By contrast, at no point in 1944 did General Douglas MacArthur's or Admiral Chester Nimitz's staffs think that 31 December 1944 would be anything but another day of war in the Pacific. The Marines had landed on Guam on 21 July, and in mid-October at the Battle of Leyte Gulf, the Japanese lost ten thousand men on their four aircraft carriers, three battleships, eight cruisers and twelve destroyers. Yet, despite these setbacks and the loss of fifty-five thousand troops in a bid to invade India earlier in the year, the Japanese were strong enough to commit four hundred thousand men to Operation *Ichi-Go,* which on 6 December 1944 had effectively cut China in two.

About two weeks later, an aged B-24 Liberator bomber, named Earthquake McGoon by her Canadian crew, took off from an aerodrome in India. Eleven and a half hours later, after the plane came under fire, Flight Officer Zeke Hughes called "For God's sake get your bloody head down" to Flight Officer William A. Cosway, who, wanting to enjoy watching the fruits of his navigational labours, had his head up in the plane's dome. Doing his commander one better, Cosway lay down on Pilot Officer Frank Stiegel's back as he looked into the plane's Norden bombsight and guided the plane over their target at Mile 41 on the Burma/Siam railway. During seconds that seemed to stretch out endlessly, Stiegel called up to Hughes, "Left! Left!" or "Right!" An instant after he called out "Bombs away," the fifteen-ton plane lurched upward. A few seconds later, the bridge at Shiutpuit, which the Canadian airmen had dubbed Shitpit, was a tangled wreck.[1]

. . .

To keep even a crudely drawn map showing the slow but steady advance of Allied troops would have invited instant and savage retribution.* The maps that the POWs instead kept safely tucked in their heads were shaped by three forces: rumours, news and the relentless string of bombers overhead.

---

* The previous August, one Rifleman caught a break when a guard discovered his atlas. After some fast talking, the guard agreed not to punish him if the offending book was burned immediately. Within minutes, it went up in flames in a kitchen stove.

On 6 January 1945 in Shamshuipo, Laite heard that the Japanese ambassador had left Berlin, that Montgomery had replaced Eisenhower and that American planes were flying out of France; only this last was true. Two weeks later, the *Hong Kong News* reported heavy fighting in Burma, China and the Philippines. On 29 January, Laite was aware of the Battle for Manila.

At Tsurumi, Verreault recorded (correctly) that the Russians had reached Warsaw on 12 January. The next day, he recorded a windfall of news brought by an American submarine crew captured a mere four months earlier. Whoever told Lance Ross on 27 March that the battleship HMS *King George V* and the carrier HMS *Illustrious* were "taking part in the fight at the Riv Kiv [*sic*] islands," was wrong. The carrier was undergoing refit, but the rumour's very plausibility testified to the Allies' inexorable movement closer to Japan. The rumour that the Americans had landed on Okinawa was true and, Okinawa being part of the prefecture of Tokyo, told the POWs that Japan itself was not beyond the reach of Allied boots.

Verreault knew of Franklin Roosevelt's death on 17 April, five days after he died and three weeks after Verreault recorded the rumour that FDR had said he "will not hear of any talk of peace until he sets foot in Tokyo."* Ross knew of Hitler's death four days after the German dictator died on 30 April.

The most accurate news continued to be gleaned from hundreds of Allied planes pounding Japan and Japanese installations in Hong Kong. By February, the prisoners at Kawasaki noticed that in addition to the B-29s, the air was filled with fighter planes and dive-bombers, which told them that the U.S. Navy was nearby. At Niigata, fighter planes strafed so close to the camp that bullets cut through Jean-Paul Dallain's hut. At Shamshuipo, even though a

---

* This is likely a garbled version of the decision Roosevelt, Churchill and Stalin announced at Yalta to demand Germany's unconditional surrender.

raid in January injured three men, Kenneth Baird cheered when the bombers returned in April. In May, Ross was thankful that at least one bomb was a dud, for it had landed right next to his hut. Hong Kong Volunteer Sub-Lieutenant Lewis Bush likely never forgot those that fell near Yokohama while he was shaving in a hospital on the morning of 29 May. At first there were "great eruptions of black smoke soar[ing] skywards." Then, within five minutes,

> one could not see the sky for smoke and above it all was the roar of those great bombers and the bark of the anti-Aircraft guns. Then came a noise like hailstones on a corrugated and iron roof, the wind started to roar, and soon houses were burning all around us. . . . It was like a dense, black London fog and the wind was howling and flames licked out from the burning houses and tress like the tongues of giant serpents. People bumped into us from out of the blackness which enshrouded everything, and the ghastly hail of incendiary bombs showered all around us, as wave after wave of B29s passed over.[2]

The Canadians at Tsurumi had a ringside seat for the firebombing of Tokyo. Shortly after midnight on 10 March, some three hundred B-29s ignited a firestorm that killed more than a hundred thousand people and destroyed fifteen square miles of Japan's capital, including the homes of one million people.[*]

A few days later, Verreault (with 197 other Canadian POWs) and Allister (and a number of other POWs) were taken through Tokyo on their way to Sendai 4B at Ohashi POW Camp and Tokyo 10B at Sumidagawa POW Camp respectively. The destruction shocked the two Canadian memoirists. According to Allister,

---

[*] More people died in this raid than were killed by the atomic bomb blasts at Hiroshima and Nagasaki combined.

The devastation was complete. Nothing but a few charred sections of low walls had been left standing. We were appalled at the sight before us. Amazing! Rubble as far as the eye could see. Charred rubble. Ashes . . . as after some great sacrifice—which it was. It all seemed pulverized by some gargantuan sledgehammer wielded by a furious god. It *must* be the wrath of God—how could this great Armageddon be the work of man.[3]

Verreault was less drawn to visualizing an angry Jehovah. "Thousands of houses destroyed in the raid from unforgiving flames. As far as the eye can see, all is raised, all is flat and in cinders. Numerous bodies lying in the streets; they [the Canadians] viewed the scene with a strange feeling and no thought of sweet revenge. . . . May God help the poor victims."[4]

．　．　．

The diaries and memoirs tell a less complete story for 1945 than they do for the other years of imprisonment. Ross made no entries between late August 1944 and early March 1945, when he recorded the rumour that Stalin, Roosevelt and Churchill had met at Fairbanks, Alaska; they had, in fact, met at Yalta in February. In the eight months before the end of the war, Ross made a total of sixteen entries. Laite, Tom Marsh and Charles Trick continued writing; however, after more than three years of imprisonment, their entries have a certain perfunctory character. Eight times in January, Trick at Tsurumi wrote simply, "Nothing new." Laite's diary is fairly complete, noting his joy on 28 February when he received a letter from his mother written the previous July. Yet, his entries for 1945 lack the detail and urgency that characterize those of earlier years.

Part of the reason for this difference is, as more than one former POW put it, "One damned day was like another." By early 1945, hunger and deprivation had become the warp and woof of their daily existence. Balancing on rickety scaffolding to drive in rivets or paint ships never became less dangerous—indeed, with bombing raids coming ever more frequently, the danger actually increased. Still, after years of doing it, it had become normal, expected, hardly worth writing about. Likewise for digging in dangerous mines. When Dallain closed his eyes, he heard the steady beat of his sledge-hammer on the die a Japanese worker held atop the glowing piece of steel. Though they dreamed of freedom, the reality of their lives could not help but impress itself on them just as writing and speaking English constantly caused Verreault to lose his French; in March after digging for clams for food, he lamented the fact that he had forgotten the French word for them *(palourdes)*.

Another reason the memoirs and diaries became less urgent is because the mental strain caused by the constant drumbeat of death had abated. In the eight months before their liberation, only eleven POWs died, and several camps saw no deaths at all. And the men also wrote less out of a heightened sense that their ordeal would soon end. Interestingly enough, though the bombings and snatches of news they heard told them the war would soon end, for the most part, they wrote about this hope in guarded language, almost as if they feared that if they stated it too clearly, it would, like a chimera, dissolve.

On 22 June, while in the hospital sick from malaria, malnutrition and worms and near-blind from vitamin deficiency, Laite let his guard down and lost himself in a paragraph-long reverie in which he declared his intention to pick up his seaborne ministry along the coast of British Columbia. He imagined a boat costing $50,000 (almost $700,000 in today's dollars) that, in addition to its crew of about ten, had room for a sick bay that could treat as many as twenty. Laite even considered the details of the crew's uniform.

. . .

Laite would recover from his illness. In Tokyo, Rifleman Beryl Lesieur did not survive what Corporal Arthur Libert of the U.S. Army Medical Corps called in an affidavit an "inefficient operation" for adhesions in the stomach.* Libert and U.S. Major A. Weinstein assisted at the operation conducted by a Captain Tokuda. Instead of dissecting the tissue in Lesieur's stomach, the Japanese doctor tore the adhesions. After it became clear that Lesieur's life was in danger, Tokuda turned the operation over to Weinstein. But even as Weinstein worked to save Lesieur, Tokuda interfered by "probing the open incision with his hands."[5] Lesieur would die three days later.

. . .

By the beginning of 1945, almost all of Japan's merchant shipping fleet lay at the bottom of the ocean. From the point of view of the war effort, the major effect of this loss was the isolation of Japanese garrisons on the South Pacific islands and the reduction in food imports. From the point of view of the POWs, the major effect of the collapse of the Japanese shipping system was a decrease in rations. On 17 January, dinner at Tsurumi consisted of three small oranges. Things were not much better in Hong Kong, where on 2 January, *Hong Kong News* reported that the price of 1 and a third pounds of rice had risen to ¥29, one pound of sugar to ¥50, and ten cigarettes to ¥5. Baird sneered, "Thus the Great East Asian Co-Prosperity Sphere progresses towards its doom."[6] In mid-February, Harry White in Shamshuipo wrote, "Rations low, rice and vegs. only." By March, the price of onions had risen to ¥35 per pound. In

---

* Libert incorrectly identifies Lesieur as Lease and mistakenly indicates the year as 1944.

Hong Kong, the release of Red Cross parcels in late February temporarily improved matters. But the gnawing hunger that returned when he exhausted his parcel prevented Laite from making further plans for his postwar ministry.

In Japan rations also declined, though as far as Verreault could tell from his contact with Japanese civilians in the work camp, their fare was equally bad. Verreault's sarcasm spoke for itself in this entry from 5 January:

> By the way, our Red Cross parcels, which we were due to receive on New Year's Day will only be handed out around the 15th, our hosts, concerned with our good health, don't want to overfeed us. This rich food so soon after the previous parcel. Their thoughtfulness is touching, particularly after starving us for three years.

The parcels were not distributed until the latter part of March.

At Omori, a POW camp situated on a man-made island in Tokyo Bay, whenever the camp's commandant announced that rations were to be increased, the men knew they'd soon be cut. As they struggled to unload 200-pound sacks, the Canadians kept an eye out for those containing sugar, some of which they siphoned off using a bamboo or brass pipe. Guards would look the other way for a couple of cigarettes. The camp's doctor believed he could fight beriberi with a beer-like drink made from yeast and miso paste. The vile mixture contained enough riboflavin, thiamine and other B-vitamins to relieve the pain of electric feet, allowing men to sleep. By March, food had become so scarce that when Grenadier William Bell saw a chocolate bar floating in the water next to the body of a downed American airman, he both violated a taboo and risked severe punishment by snatching the chocolate bar and smuggling it back into camp. In April, the Japanese guards gave the Canadians dog meat; even though the men's stomachs had begun to distend due to malnutrition, their officers feared the meat was unfit for human consumption and refused to allow them to eat it.

For most of the 198 men sent to Ohashi in April, labour consisted of back-breaking work in a lead mine five hundred yards underground. Verreault's knowledge of electrical motors kept him above the surface. Verreault liked the work but soon came down with welder's flash from arc welding without a facemask. MacDonell was so weak that he too worked above ground—in the kitchen that each day had less food to prepare.

According to Verreault, at least at times the camp's commandant meant well. A few days after Germany capitulated, a Japanese guard was arrested for stealing Red Cross parcels. However, by the end of June, the diet of rice and soup had its predictable results. MacDonell lost so much weight that he started losing feeling below his waist. In late July, the Japanese replaced the barley they had been giving the POWs with beans; though more nutritious, the beans played havoc with their digestive systems.

When he arrived in Sumidagawa, a camp near Tsurumi, in March, Allister was stunned to see how well fed the POWs were, especially when he found out that labour there included unloading 100-pound sacks of food or shovelling sixteen tons of coal per man into cars that were then pushed up a trestle to where the coal was dumped. The grub stank. But the opportunities to steal coconut, soybeans and rice were excellent.

The Americans had even set up thirty rice cookers. For the coin of the realm—cigarettes—these cookers provided men with extra food. After George Grant fashioned a hot plate, he and Allister joined the cooking business. Rice was smuggled in hats, shoes, socks and even in the lining of Allister's Red Cross–issued hat. Shortly after arriving at the camp, Allister so overloaded himself with rice that it began leaking from his threadbare sleeves and out of his shoes. To cover his tracks, the men behind him walked in a "long jigging, wriggling procession" during which they kicked up enough dust to obscure the rice.[7] When they got to the camp gate, he still had to endure a pat-down. Luckily, it was perfunctory. So many rice cookers were running that the POWs had to establish a schedule. Despite the hard labour, eating this extra rice allowed them to gain precious pounds.

Then, Allister suspected to protect their market, the Americans started the rumour that a Japanese electrician was going to come investigate the unexplained drain on the electrical system. Everyone but the Americans dismantled their hot plates, and overnight the price of a serving of rice rose from one cigarette to five. When the feared inspection failed to materialize, Allister and Grant began cooking rice again.*

At Niigata, Ken Cambon's stomach turned when he learned that his friend George Francis ate weevils to keep up his protein intake. In early July, they were so hungry that they risked severe punishment in a caper that could have come from *Hogan's Heroes*.

The Camp Commandant, Lieutenant Kato, "Four Eyes," kept a chicken coop in which the same man who beat POWs with the side of his sword lovingly cared for the chickens and collected their eggs. One day, after distracting the guards, Cambon and Francis darted into the coop, grabbed a chicken and ran to the dispensary. As they readied the sterilizer in which they planned to cook it, the chicken, whose neck they thought had been broken, started to squawk. A quick jerk of its neck solved that problem.

Its feathers, however, were another matter. The two men settled

---

* Later, when the officer in charge of the rice platform realized that even a better-fed Allister was not strong enough to carry the heavy sacks of rice, he arranged for Allister to be kept in the camp where he turned out pictures of well endowed hula girls for men who, because they were eating better, experienced a sudden return of their libidos.

on using Cambon's hat to hold them. Francis put the bird into the sterilizer while Cambon snuck outside, where he dug a hole close to the guardhouse and deposited the feathers, carefully leaving a few around to implicate the guards. "Nothing has ever tasted as good as that hen," Cambon later wrote. "We ate the whole bird, sucking the bones dry. It was ecstasy." Francis almost ruined the moment when he asked, "Where's your hat?" and Cambon realized he had left it by the guardhouse. With dawn just moments away, Cambon had to act fast, for the hat had his number stencilled on it. As Francis distracted two guards, Cambon retrieved the hat and made it safely to his hut.

Three days later, Four Eyes noticed that the hen was missing and loosed his fury on the guards. "He jumped up and down, foaming with rage. Then he lined up all the guards and worked them over one by one, slapping them around until they vainly tried to stand at attention."[8]

· · ·

The Canadians never stopped thinking of home and their families. In January 1945, relying on letters written almost three years earlier, Verreault tried to piece together when his brother, who had also joined the army, had moved from Hamilton to Kingston, Ontario. This later date was the key to figuring out if he had been sent overseas to fight in what Verreault, as a veteran of Canada's greatest defeat, imagined to be atrocious fighting across Europe. Laite, Baird and Trick continued to record their joy at the receipt of each letter. Over the course of ten days in February, Trick was especially happy to receive two—albeit two-year-old—letters from his wife.

The passage of time meant that not every letter could bring good news. There is no known case of a "Dear John" letter. However, even as the POWs existed in what Allister later likened to a Rip Van

Winkle–like state, life and death continued unabated. For men who had endured so much suffering and seen so much death, word of death outside the camp came as a heavy blow, as can be seen from Laite's entry on 6 February, which began with a prayer for his own family:

> Mr. Porteous received word today, in a card written in June '44, that his wife died at home in January '44. This news really upset the whole hut, and he has everyone's sympathy. None of us are physically fit to stand a heavy shock, and especially one of this nature would sap one's energy to the breaking point. Porteous has been having a rough time with his health lately, but he is facing this ordeal with commendable courage.

In his entry for 25 July, less than three weeks before the war ended, Baird's stiff upper lip quivered when he wrote of Grenadier Major Harry Hook's death earlier that month. After telling his wife Molly that Hook died when his infected heart gave out, he writes:

> One gets to know a chap pretty well under circumstances such as we have been living during the past three years and a half. He was a damned good officer and soldier, the best in the force that came out here and to think that now it is nearly over, to have to pass on. I hope his heart will find all the things he desires and liked on the other side.[9]

. . .

On 8 May, tens of thousands would take to the streets of Halifax, Ottawa, Montreal, Winnipeg and Vancouver to celebrate VE Day. But amid the festiveness there was little mention of the more than fifteen hundred men of "C" Force then passing their 1,231st day of captivity. The silence is partially explainable by the sheer size of Canada's contribution to the epic struggle against Nazi Germany. A nation of barely eleven million saw more than a million men and women put on its uniform, and tens of thousands more serve in the merchant marine. At a cost of over forty-five thousand dead and even more wounded, Canada had played major roles in the Battle of the Atlantic, the bombing campaign and the liberation of Europe. After making no mention of the men languishing in Japan and Hong Kong on VE Day, on 9 May the *Globe and Mail* ran an editorial that referred to the controversy about the Hong Kong mission (and Dieppe)—but not to the men still imprisoned. The next day, in the middle of an editorial that chided a Canadian senator for making a callous statement about China, the paper said, "As Pearl Harbor and Hong Kong and many another example well showed, they [Japan] are the enemies of all free men, even as Germany."

Placing the attack against the home of America's Pacific Fleet ahead of the attack on the Canadians and the British Empire to which the Dominion of Canada belonged, and for which Canadians bled, is indicative of how the war against Japan came to be viewed as America's war—despite the hundreds of thousands of British and Canadian forces in the China-India-Burma (C-I-B) theatre and despite the men who had fought, bled and died in Hong Kong and the POW camps.*

Bill MacWhirter's, Verreault's and Baird's families well understood the euphoria of VE Day, many having, of course, other sons, brothers and husbands who had fought in Europe. Still, the day was bittersweet for the families of the men of "C" Force. "I was in grade 8, and we were all terribly, terribly excited," recalls Harvelyn McInnis, Baird's daughter. "We heard the boys with the newspapers yelling 'Extra! Extra!' We had reached one goal but we had one more

---

* Some five hundred Canadians died in the C-I-B theatre.

to go, and I thought of my dad. I wondered if he and the others had heard the news. The victory brought forth such excitement and also a fear. I was old enough to realize how vicious the Japanese were and what their retaliatory powers were."

. . .

Despite a dearth of official comment about the ongoing Pacific War, King's government was seized by the issue. Indeed, in the fall of 1944, the Cabinet War Committee had begun planning for Canada's participation in the final push against Japan. However, having narrowly avoided a second conscription crisis that fall, when manpower needs in Europe trumped political promises and forced King to despatch almost thirteen thousand conscripts to bolster the Canadians in Northwest Europe, King opposed simply transferring soldiers from Europe to Asia.

In early April 1945, King decided that Canada would send only volunteers to the Pacific and that before shipping out for Asia, they would undergo training in the United States.* These volunteers would be entitled to thirty days' disembarkation leave as well as any other leave they had built up while in Europe, which would delay putting Canadian boots on Asian ground for many months. The atomic bomb that brought an end to the war would obviate the need for the eighty thousand Canadian troops who volunteered to fight in the Pacific.

---

* This decision applied to the navy as well, and led on 19 April to one of the strangest naval signals ever sent: "Commanding Officers are to explain the situation and give all officers and ratings an opportunity to sign the following undertaking: 'I hereby volunteer for service in the war against Japan and agree to serve in the Pacific Theatre and/or any other theatre for the duration of hostilities should my service be required.'" While many officers and ratings were incensed by the signal, others were not. Eighty percent of the men about the cruiser HMCS *Uganda*, which fought as part of the Pacific Fleet, opted not to sign the undertaking, and soon she sailed for home.

. . .

The Canadian POWs knew nothing about their government's decision to ask soldiers to revolunteer. Nor, indeed, did they know
that King had been re-elected in June on a platform that promised
among other things money to help veterans buy land or start busi-
nesses, public housing and family allowances. The POWs were unaware that hundreds of their countrymen formed squadrons flying
out of India and helping to push back the Japanese, sometimes at
the rate of thirty miles a day. By 14 July, however, those in Ohashi
knew that the U.S. Navy lay just off shore. For, on that day, a wood-
gathering party that had climbed a hill saw a naval bombardment
destroy the smelter at Kamaishi.

The secret 1944 order to not "allow the escape of a single one
[POW], to annihilate them all, and not leave any traces" was not
a secret any longer. At Niigata, Cambon did not have to hear of
Field Marshal (Count) Hisaichi Teruauchi's 1945 order—"At the
moment the enemy lands on Honshu [Japan's largest island, on
which Tokyo is located], all prisoners are to be killed"—to know
his captors' intentions.[10] In the late summer, the POWs were forced
to dig a large pit outside the camp that resembled nothing so much
as an open mass grave. Cambon and his friend George responded
by putting food aside and planning "to break out of [the] camp
and head into the countryside" when they sensed the Japanese were
ready to act on Teruauchi's order.[11]

One guard at Niigata told Cambon that he was a socialist
opposed to the war, and more importantly, smuggled medicines
into the camp, but he remained the exception. Despite the obvious
collapse of the Japanese war effort, no camp commandant reduced
the work required from the POWs, and many guards continued to
mistreat them. In late July, Dallain watched helplessly as a guard
worked Mort, a British POW, to death.

. . .

Word of the bombing of Hiroshima on 6 August reached Prime Minister King in Ottawa and MacDonell at Ohashi at about the same time. King learned of it at that quintessential Canadian event: a federal/provincial conference. A verbal sparring match with the new premier of Ontario, the same George Drew who had pushed for the royal commission that examined "C" Force, was cut short by a note from Minister of Munitions and Supply Clarence D. Howe, who was then telling the press about the dropping of the bomb and hinting at Canada's role in developing it. MacDonell heard about it from a secret radio. "We didn't know what an atomic bomb was," he later wrote, "but we knew one bomb had destroyed the entire city."[12]

Politicians that they were, King and the provincial leaders were as taken with the fact that the development of the atomic bomb had remained a secret as they were with the belief that it would hasten the end of the war. MacDonell had more prosaic concerns: "We closely watched the camp commander and our guards for some reaction. None! They didn't know anything about the destruction of Hiroshima."[13]

. . .

The most famous event of 9 August, the day after the Soviet Union declared war on Japan and invaded Manchuria, was the dropping of a second atomic bomb on Nagasaki. Ross's diary entry for this day, which crows about the "super machine of destruction" that destroyed an entire city, makes two things clear that time (and victor's guilt over the bombing of Hiroshima and Nagasaki) have obscured. First, the bombing of Nagasaki was not the only action that day, and second, even three days after Hiroshima, the Empire of Japan was still using POWs as slave labour. "It's just hell on earth now. Our planes are just smashing everything to pieces. When we go down in the mine now, we can't tell when we may get up again."

A day after Hirohito's government asked the Swiss government to inform the Allies that if the Emperor's position could be guaranteed, Japan would surrender, White in Hong Kong was so hungry he sold his greatcoat for fifty pounds of beans. That day the POWs were given only porridge of rice and beans to eat while the Camp Commandant, Hideo Wada, continued to withhold hundreds of tons of Red Cross supplies.

.   .   .

Over the next few days, as Hirohito's government angled for diplomatic language that would allow the emperor to remain on the throne, the fighting and imprisonment continued. On 10 August, waves of British and American aircraft destroyed or damaged more than seven hundred Japanese aircraft that had been evacuated to the northern part of Honshu Island, and White in Hong Kong heard the rumour that the Russians had attacked the Japanese; they had in fact, two days earlier. The next day, White kept tight rein on his emotions when a work party returned saying that people in the street had said "Peace has been declared." It had not.

On 12 October, after a requisitioned work party returned with the same rumour, White wrote, "Everyone on edge speculating on everything. Trying not to get excited. Hoping for the best." The rumour was again premature; earlier that day a Japanese torpedo bomber attacked and damaged the USS *Pennsylvania* near Okinawa, and a Japanese submarine sank an American destroyer and thousands of B-29s bombed cities across Japan. On 13 August, as more than fifteen hundred B-29s flew over Tokyo dropping leaflets that explained the state of peace negotiations and Tokyo radio said that

Japan would surrender, the commandant of Shamshuipo conducted his second inspection in a week. White picked up the signal that "something is in the wind."* The next day, Emperor Hirohito recorded the famous message in which he informed his subjects that they must "bear the unbearable." During the night, B-29s kept up the pressure by bombing near Tokyo and the Akita-Aradi oil refinery, the last functioning refinery in the country.

. . .

The pictures of the thousands who poured out onto the streets on VJ Day obscure the complex reality of 15 August 1945 (and, indeed, of the weeks that followed). Japan's cities lay in ruins and its navy, air force and industry had all but ceased to exist. However, Hirohito still had armies, albeit depleted ones, numbering in the millions in Burma, China and, of course, in Japan itself. The Americans, who had withstood the Japanese suicide charges at Iwo Jima, Truck and Okinawa, and the British, who had done the same in Burma and Imphal, knew that unless the surrender was accepted by the soldiers at the sharp end and by millions of Japanese civilians who had been trained as suicide fighters, tens (if not hundreds) of thousands of Allied soldiers would die before the fighting was finished. Accordingly, even as Washington waited for word of the surrender, American navy flyers took off for another massive raid against Tokyo. The planes were recalled when President Harry Truman accepted the surrender. As the American planes turned back, the commander of the kamikazes led a group of seven dive-bombers toward the American fleet near Okinawa; navy flyers shot each one down.

---

* In Ottawa, the Minister of Munitions and Supply, C.D. Howe, issued a press release giving details of Canada's role in the development of the atomic bomb.

On 15 August, Harvelyn McInnis was visiting an aunt in Vancouver. "I was in my aunt's garden reading a book and eating cherries from a beautiful big cherry tree. And she came running out saying, 'It's over, it's over.' I knew she meant the war because I already knew of the atom bombs and we were waiting with bated breath to see what the Japanese would do.

"Aunt Katie took me downtown in Vancouver. There were thousands of people and young navy men. I was kissed about twenty times by sailors and so many others. Everyone was screaming and tears streaming down all our cheeks."

. . .

As Harvelyn and the other families of POWs celebrated, it never crossed their minds that the Canadians were not yet free. It appears that the POWs at Kawasaki and Ohashi were the first to learn that the war had ended. Even though the war had ended at noon, Japanese guards kept Ross and the others at Kawasaki working in the mine until the end of their shift. The next day, the guards told them they did not have to go down the mine. At Ohashi, MacDonell feared that the Japanese were readying to act on the order to kill the POWs; at 11:00 a.m., he assembled his men in an unused section of the mine where an explosive charge would have easily brought down the roof. After an agonizing two-hour wait, the sergeant of the guard came and said to MacDonell, "*Hancho*, tell your men we are going back to camp—no more work today." A few minutes later, after telling MacDonell that the emperor had just spoken on the radio, the sergeant winked at the Canadian officer, smiled and said, "*Hancho*, you go Canada now."[14]

Harvelyn's father, Kenneth Baird, did not hear of the surrender until a Chinese newspaper was smuggled into the camp on 16 August. Even then, Wada, the Camp Commandant, refused to confirm anything, though the absence of the guards spoke for itself. The next day, British Lieutenant-Colonel Simon White took matters into his own hands and demanded to know why no one had informed him that the war was over. A short time later, Wada sent White a copy of the Imperial Rescript, signed the day before, ordering the Imperial Japanese Army to surrender. The British officer ordered the Japanese to deliver more food, especially meat, and to get outside the wire.

Jean-Paul Dallain is unsure of the day he and his comrades learned that the war was over, though it was likely 16 August. "We got up in the morning and they told us that there was no work that day. We looked out at Shintesto and for the first time since we came to Niigata, there was no smoke coming from the chimneys. We knew that since it takes five to six days to get the furnaces hot, they'd never let the fires go out—unless. . . . Once we saw that there was no smoke, right away we realized that at long last the war was over, we had survived, and that we were going home to Canada."

CHAPTER 20

"What the Hell Took You So Long to Get Here?"

Liberation
18 August to 25 December 1945

In the days that followed Japan's capitulation, generals and admirals arranged for the liberation of countries and the occupation of Japan. On 18 August, the Japanese in the Philippines surrendered. The next day, the Japanese Army in South China surrendered to Chiang Kai-shek, and the million-man army in Manchuria began surrendering to the Russians. On the 22nd, MacArthur ordered Japan to prepare for the arrival of American troops by, among other things, removing all land and sea obstacles around Tokyo Bay. The first American troops landed in Japan on 28 August while HMCS *Prince Robert,* laden with supplies for the Canadian POWs, steamed for Hong Kong. A few days later, the first Allied POWs (from camps around Yokohama) were liberated, the Canadian government disbanded its Pacific Army and the British fleet reached Hong Kong. On 3 September, the Japanese in Hong Kong surrendered and the

Canadians at Kowloon were liberated.* The next day, the *Globe and Mail* quoted both Royal Rifles Lieutenants Collinson Blaver and Frank Power in an article that sketched out just how badly the Japanese had mistreated their POWs.

On 25 August, American planes began dropping supplies to the camps; to facilitate this, huge signs saying POW or PW were pasted on the top of huts or in open areas. In a few cases, the parachute-equipped crates or forty-gallon steel drums carrying the supplies smashed through the roofs of the huts; one missed Ken Cambon by mere inches. After a few days of nine tons of food arriving *per day,* the officer in command of Ohashi ordered the POW sign changed to "no more!"

Not every plane dropped supplies. To make sure the men still in the camps were not, as Royal Rifles Staff Sergeant John Thomson put it, "pushed around," for three days American fighter planes flew over the camp in Fukushima early in the morning and in the late afternoon firing their machine guns and cannons before putting on a circus. "Flying flat over the tree tops and bank over at a steep angle . . . , the pilots would stand up out of the cock-pit and with that lovely American salute, the hand from forehead [saying,] 'Hiya, boys.'"

Attacks on the former POWs by either civilians angered at the destruction of their country or rogue military units failed to materialize. In most camps, the cruellest guards vanished overnight; some committed hara-kiri. At Omine the men took control of the camp a few days after the capitulation. In others, a few guards remained on duty, saying that their orders were now to protect the emperor's guests until they could be escorted home.

---

* A Canadian representative was present at the famous signing of the surrender on the deck of the USS *Missouri*; he erred by signing one line below Canada's assigned place.

• • •

Starved for so long, many men gorged themselves on canned fruit and chocolate to the point that they became ill. Over two days, Verreault ate thirty chocolate bars. Some men ate so much that by the time Allied armies reached them two weeks later or so, they were no longer emaciated. In addition to the food, medicine (including a new drug, penicillin, that worked miracles before their eyes) and cigarettes, the men could not get enough of the magazines, which reconnected them to the world they had lost. Cambon was only one of many moved to tears by letters dropped with the supplies like this one signed by four crewmembers of USS *Lexington:*

> Some of us here on the ships and on the Islands like to tell ourselves it has been a tough war and we really had it rugged. But we know that you are the ones who have made the sacrifices and we humbly doff our white caps in admiration and respect. Accept our deep gratitude for the deeds you have performed and the suffering you have endured in hastening this day of final and complete victory.[1]

• • •

Even before the British arrived to take possession of the Crown Colony of Hong Kong, the former POWs moved to assert sovereignty. On 17 August, British Colonel Simon White at Shamshuipo placed Major Cecil Boon and four of his followers under protective custody. Reveille the next day saw the raising of the Union Jack on one pole and the naval ensign on another. The plan was for the men to then sing "Abide with Me" and "God Save the King," but Grenadier Harry White wrote in his diary, "there was not much singing, hearts were too full, a choking sensation in the throat, many tears in evidence. I couldn't keep them back. We all realized more than ever before, the meaning of Freedom, the British heritage, what it really meant in our lives." Hastily sewn flags were raised at the camps in Japan. At Sendai 1B, Tom Marsh presented a homemade American flag to a Lieutenant Finn. Not having expected the Stars and Stripes to be raised, the American officer clutched the flag and choked up.

. . .

Even as tens of thousands of soldiers back in Canada were demobilized, the Canadians in Hong Kong and Japan remained soldiers, subject to both military discipline and orders. White is the only Canadian officer to address the fact that the Dominion soldiers arrogated to themselves the power of granting liberty, to borrow a naval term. "I am having my hands full trying to keep them in line, many are going over the fence. I don't really blame them, I'd like to go myself but of course I can't very well. So long as they are in camp for morning roll-call, I am not going to worry them," he wrote in a diary entry. He also noted that the day before a Chinese prostitute had been brought back to camp and that two men had afterward sought treatment from the medical officer. In order to help the men work off their returning energy, on 28 August, White led them on a five-mile hike to the beach where, for the first time in four years, they had a swim. The men enjoyed it but, no doubt, were even happier when they heard that beginning that very day, each day they'd receive both an ounce of brandy and an ounce of gin.

In Niigata, Cambon, George Francis and three American Marines knocked a hole in the fence and walked into the city where, to their amazement, they ran into a freelancing American Navy pilot who had landed at the local airport and started looking for POWs. Later, after the pilot, whom they had brought back to their camp for an impromptu party, was once again airborne, Cambon and some others went back to town to find a bar. Allied soldiers, who only days earlier had been slave labourers, now found themselves wealthy in the only coin that mattered: cigarettes. Cambon drank a few cups of sake and passed out. When he awoke a few hours later, he had a pounding headache and the attention of several kimono-clad women.

At Omine, Bill MacWhirter and his friends weren't overly concerned with military protocol when they left the camp and found a warehouse. With the help of an old man who had learned English during twenty-five years in California, they told the guards to hand over fifty-five cases of beer: "On MacArthur's orders."

No doubt, the most courtly out-of-camp experience was Allister's. Burning for sex, Allister, Smitty and George Grant, the man with whom Allister had run a rice-cooking business, went in search of a brothel. Before they found one, they came upon a group of elderly women and children. The children fascinated the men who had been through so much. The men offered them Hershey bars, but the children—who, Allister realized, were recoiling at what to them looked like giants—were too frightened to accept them. "They had never seen or tasted chocolate, or much of any other joys, for that matter, being as deprived as we were, part of the unseen casualties of war. . . . We showed them how to eat it, watching their expression as they chewed. "*Maika* [good]?" "*Hai,*" they nodded, joining us in the first taste of freedom."[2]

A short time later, Allister found himself in front of a beautiful young woman. As members of the defeated people, the women "knew the role they must play out." An inner voice said, "You have the power—the right. Use it." His nerve wavered. Seeing him hesitate, the girl slipped away, unharmed. As Allister's better angel said, "You knew, it could go no other way," he walked to the table she had been at and saw that she was an art student; the painting she was working on showed that she had not yet mastered light, shadow and form.[3] Before he knew it, Allister found himself sitting on her bench, her brushes in hand, correcting her errors.

. . .

It took more than three months after the end of the war for the last Canadian to return home. The first to be liberated were in Hong Kong. On the very afternoon HMCS *Prince Robert* steamed into view, 30 August, Major Baird visited it, and in his last diary entry, commented warmly about the glasses of rye whisky given to him. Eleven days later, Grenadier Harry White, Baird and the other Canadians boarded HMTS *Empress of Australia* (a ship that before the war had belonged to Canada Pacific Steamship Lines) bound for Manila, where the men underwent medical tests. On 9 October, they arrived in Pearl Harbor.

The Americans liberated the bulk of the Canadians. The most cinematic liberation was of Sumidagawa, which held 246 men, including fifty-five Canadians. Armed Marines arrived in PT boats, recalled Allister. "They came in crouching double, edging cautiously around the corners of the huts, guns pointed, trigger fingers poised," only to find a motley-dressed group of Canadians who quickly told them to point their guns somewhere else. The leathernecks were shocked when they saw the huts the POWs lived in and the bug-infested tatami mats on which they slept. A few hours later, Allister and the others were on a U.S. hospital ship where they showered, were examined, received clean U.S. naval uniforms and were offered unfathomable amounts of food: "What'll it be: fruit? bacon and eggs? sausages? toast? porridge? pancakes? fried spuds?" Old habits died hard. When the Canadians were seen pocketing a few oranges, they were quickly told "the fruit's there all day and you can have all you want, doncha understand?"[4]

On or about 10 September, MacDonell and the other, now well-fed, men at Ohashi were surprised when, instead of Marines or heavily armed troops, a single Canadian Army captain and a corporal arrived at the camp. When the pair had set out by train, the captain knew from American flyers that there was a camp at Ohashi, but no one knew which nationalities were in it. The captain did not bring the news the men wanted most—when they would begin their trip home—though he brought something almost as valuable: word that Colonel Tokunaga and others in Hong Kong were in custody and were to be tried for war crimes, including murder. No doubt, the heartiest cheers went up after he said that among those to be tried was Kanao Inouye, the Kamloops Kid.

On 15 September, a day after a plane dropped a note saying that the men at Ohashi would be delivered from their purgatory the next day, American warships sailed into Kamaishi harbour. After an armed amphibious landing, the colonel leading the Americans asked the captain commanding the former POWs if he had any questions. The strong, healthy Americans smiled when the captain said, "Yes, I have one. What the hell took you so long to get here?" Not long after, on boarding the hospital ship USS *Rescue,* MacDonell and the others were instructed to strip and throw their ragged clothes over the side, and were then sprayed with DDT before being sent to the showers. After lunch, the Canadian sergeant was informed that he was to be transferred to a cruiser, where he would be the admiral's guest. Before dinner with the admiral, the soldier who had led the last charge in the Battle for Hong Kong "was escorted to a gleaming, spotless cabin by two Filipino mess attendants who turned down the white sheets on my bunk and said they would be back for me at 6:45 p.m."

At 6:00 a.m. on 22 September, more than a full month after Emperor Hirohito signed the Imperial Rescript ordering his men to lay down their arms, Bill MacWhirter, Bob Barter, Lance Ross and one hundred and sixty other Canadians climbed aboard a train bound for Nagasaki, where they were to board the British carrier

HMS *Speaker* to take them on to Okinawa. Given everything they had been through—terrible battle, hunger, illnesses stemming from malnutrition, torture, physical deprivation, the sorrow of watching comrades die inhuman deaths, and the pain of being separated from their families for years, much of it without the solace of mail—Ross's diary entry is striking in its simple humanity. "We are now in Nagasaki, and it is a complete ruins, even the hills are all twisted for miles around. That bomb is a deadly thing, what misery there. People are now hungry and when the winter comes on it is going to be terrible."[5]

After spending two days in Okinawa, where they were given medical tests, the men boarded USS *Rainville* for Manila. They stayed in the Philippine capital for just over a week. There they were given more medical tests (and dewormed if necessary) and were debriefed. And most importantly, they were given their back pay and letters from home. Writing of these days years later, Cambon asked, "Who was Frank Sinatra?" How did General Douglas MacArthur, who was known in the camps as "Dug-Out Doug" for his penchant for staying inside the island fortress at Corregidor until he left it some weeks before it fell, become a great hero?

. . .

The picture of HMCS *Prince Robert* arriving in Esquimalt on 21 October 1945, which serves as the image of the troops' return home, misrepresents the reality of their return.[6] Only fifty-five men walked down her gangplank onto Canadian soil. Indeed, *Prince Robert* was the fourth ship to tie up at Esquimalt with Canadian soldiers coming home. Between 3 and 15 October, three American ships, carrying three, seventy-seven and eleven Canadians, arrived at the Vancouver Island naval base.[7] By then, however, more than five hundred men had landed in U.S. ports and come to Canada by rail, beginning with thirteen men who came home on 14 September.

The group commanded by MacDonell that arrived in San Francisco aboard USS *Catron* on 19 October was accorded the highest honour an American warship's captain can give: after reviewing the men on the deck, he allowed a foreign army to march onto the American shore ahead of an American officer. As the welcome band played and the crowd cheered, one soldier could not resist a moment of cheek. Halfway down the gangplank, he stopped, turned around and, as the crowd fell silent, he said, "If you Yanks have any more trouble with the Japanese, you know where to find us."[8]

Almost 350 men, including Jean-Paul Dallain, Chaplain Uriah Laite and Major Maurice Parker, arrived on 5 October. Lance Ross, Chaplain Francis Deloughery and Harvelyn Baird's father Kenneth were part of a group of thirteen who arrived on 18 October. Ross was met in Vancouver by his Aunt Eve, who took him to her house for a home-cooked meal and to rest for the night before he boarded the train east. When he asked how everyone in the family was, he expected to hear that his grandmother, Eve's mother, had died. This aunt, however, told him that his brother, Stuart, had died when his bomber was shot down over Europe. "Dad then screamed in pain," says Mitzi Ross, Lance's daughter.*

Shortly before Harvelyn and Molly Baird left for the station to meet Kenneth, the postman delivered a box. They had seen it before and could still make out the postmark stamped on it on 25 November 1942 when they'd shipped it, filled with sweaters, pants, underwear, socks and toiletries, to Japan. Returned as undeliverable, the box now contained only an old pair of socks and some tooth powder,

---

* In the early 2000s while the elderly Ross was wintering with Mitzi in Ottawa, she showed him a letter Stuart wrote to his mother in which he said that he was joining the army because Lance was a POW and he wanted to do something to try to save him; in the end he joined the air force. "After reading that, Dad just sat very quiet, feeling, I guess, survivor's guilt," she recalls.

neither of which would be needed by the man for whom Harvelyn had dressed up in a plaid skirt and red sweater. Her mother had also agreed that the fifteen-year-old could complete her outfit by, for the first time, wearing lipstick—Revlon Bravo, a very bright red that, she recalls, "must have made me look like Mini Mouse."

Baird—who, they knew, had been in the hospital in the Philippines—looked better than they expected. "He came up and threw his arms around us and said, 'I'm here, and I am never going to leave again.' And we cried." The Baird family shared their first meal together with Baird's oldest friend, a fellow First World War veteran named Clifford Medland. "He stayed until about 2:00 a.m. talking. But I'm sure that Dad wanted to push him out of the door so that he could be alone with my mother," Harvelyn recalls.

There was no grand homecoming for "C" Force followed by a last public parade. There was, however, a train dubbed the "Hong Kong Special" and a series of tearful reunions in train stations across the country and warm welcomes by civic-minded committees along the way. For the bulk of the Grenadiers, the trip home took about another day—long enough for men anxious to see wives, mothers, fathers, sisters and brothers.

MacDonell's trip ended at Union Station in Toronto. Waiting in the crowd were the four members of the Hay family. His aunt Irma and uncle, George Hay, who had been a star player of the Chicago Black Hawks in the 1930s, had adopted him after MacDonell's widowed mother (Irma's sister) died when he was but thirteen years old. They had never thought this day would come. "For such a long time they believed I'd been killed," recalls MacDonell. But shortly after the war ended a telegram had come telling them that he was, indeed, alive.

Some of MacDonell's men who were going on to Montreal and the Gaspé had gotten off the train with him to say their goodbyes. So MacDonell was in the middle of a knot of men when his aunt and uncle first saw him. "My uncle walked up and suddenly there was almost silence as he put his big arms around me. They had given up hope so long ago." Then he saw Aunt Irma's tear-stained face looking at his, still swollen from beriberi. "My family took me home, to our beautiful old three-storey house in Stratford, where, after a wonderful dinner, I went to my room and collapsed into my bed."

For Doddridge, Barter, Duguay, MacWhirter and his half-brother Arley Enright, the trip across Canada did not end in Montreal, as it did for Allister. In the darkest of days, he'd imagined the moment: a conductor calls out "Next Stop, Montreal!" and minutes later with his kit bag on his shoulder, he exits a train in Central Station. But now, as that moment arrived, a few scant steps from the family he so desperately missed, the emotion became too much and he started shaking. As his mother, father, sisters, brothers and other family members cried tears of joy, Allister stood dry-eyed, an effect of the years of having to secure his heart "against all painful emotional onslaughts." (Many of the returning POWs reported that they too did not cry tears of joy.) The touches, perfumes and lively faces seemed the stuff of dreams until his father's "big, rough, straw-textured moustache bestowed a Russian kiss" on his lips, unlocking a flood of warm childhood memories.[9] As his father stepped back, Allister caught a look in his eye that told him that his father alone realized that what others took to be the soldier's full-bodied face was really swelling caused by beriberi.

Verreault, Allister soon learned, was already home. *La Patrie* of 17 October ran a picture of Verreault, tie askew but rakish moustache regrown, surrounded by his family and hugging the two brothers who had served in Europe and about whom he had been so worried. Verreault soon picked up his career as a lineman with Bell Canada.

For Doddridge, Barter, Duguay and hundreds of other men who came from eastern Quebec and the Maritimes, Montreal was a place to stretch their legs and change trains; MacWhirter and Enright fell into the arms of their younger siblings before boarding a train for Gaspé, another day's travel away. After a joyous reunion with his family in the whistle-stop station of Black Cape, MacWhirter's father handed him the keys to a Pontiac. Later that night, MacWhirter added to the diary he had kept with him for so long: "A car to drive on the coast looking at the mountains, the sea, the rivers, my people."

In Montreal, Dallain was introduced to his brother-in-law, the one he did not know about in 1943 when he was embarrassed by reading in a letter that his sister was pregnant. He left the "Hong Kong Special" in Quebec, but not for a real-life version of his dream—going to the Clarendon Hotel and having a hot bath and breakfast in bed. Instead, he was welcomed by his Aunt Yvonne's family, who gave him champagne and surrounded him with animated conversation that the thin veteran who had been through so much found overwhelming. Aunt Yvonne had twelve children, so a Mrs. Corbett, who had gone to school with Dallain's mother, took Dallain to her house for the night. A few days later, he was back on the train bound for Matapédia where his mother and father met him.

. . .

In 1946, no one had ever heard of post-traumatic stress disorder or given much thought to how to reintegrate men who went through what the survivors of "C" Force had endured. For many it was a wrenching experience, dulled all too often by alcohol. Allister recalled how difficult it was to listen to stories about the frustrations of meat, butter and sugar rationing. At times he felt as though he lived in a goldfish bowl or that his family plumbed simple statements like "Pass the sugar" for hidden meaning. He feared that though he survived, he'd be forever cursed as an emotional Flying Dutchman: "I could enjoy everything, yet not really enjoy it." The world he'd remembered now seemed a place of "make-believe." What he recognized as "mad desire to be back in 3-D, where everything really *existed*," vanished only after he left Montreal and visited Bob, another former POW, who was in a veterans' hospital. The two of them reminisced about their time in the camps, an experience that underscored for Allister that that part of his life was now securely in the past.[10]

MacDonell too had a difficult time adjusting. He enrolled at the University of Toronto but found the freedom of university life painful. "No one tells you what to do. There were no parades and no orders," he recalls. In the end he excelled at university, but soon after starting school began having a recurring chilling dream. Asleep in the men's residence, he'd find himself back in Japan in front of an Imperial Japanese Army officer saying "we would never be allowed to be free, never allowed to go home. After we capture Canada, we would never be allowed to go home." Pains in his solar plexus led him to seek the help of Colonel Line, a psychology professor at the university. Line told him, "'The fact that you are alive is not your fault.' He helped me see that I was very upset that so many men in my company had not returned, as I had. Only gradually did I come to realize that I was truly free," MacDonell, who in the 1980s rose to become a deputy minister in Ontario, told me in an emotion-filled tone.*

---

* Some stories of readjustment include humorous moments. Some months after coming home, Baird caused his daughter, Harvelyn, to dissolve into tears when she found that he, following the army's protocol that shoes must be shined, polished her saddle shoes—when being in style meant having them as scuffed as possible. "He caught on pretty quickly, however," she recalls. "When he arrived home he'd never heard of Frank Sinatra, but the next Christmas he bought me a 'Sinatra jacket,' the body of which was tweed while the arms were plain brown. Sinatra had made the jacket style famous by wearing it at a concert."

Forty-five percent of the 1,418 members of "C" Force who came home "suffered from diseases directly attributable to deprivation of food and water."[11] Kenneth Baird, who worked for the Unemployment Insurance agency, died in 1957. Ten percent of his comrades died by 1965; Blacky Verreault died a year later. By 1987, 46 percent or 660 survivors of "C" Force were dead. One hundred percent of the 758 left alive had chronic ailments that stemmed from their mistreatment at the hands of the Japanese: 50 percent had psychiatric problems, 29 percent problems with their feet, 30 percent ophthalmological problems, 29 percent heart ailments and 29 percent impaired respiratory systems. Many men suffered from multiple ailments.

· · ·

The four Dallain boys had survived the war. To celebrate, during Christmas Jean-Paul's father broke out the bottle of champagne that he'd saved from his daughter's wedding. In January, Jean-Paul and Charles were demobilized. Using his back pay, his veteran's grant and a loan from his mother, Jean-Paul bought land on which he built a hardware store that opened in June 1946. In February 1947, trouble with his eyes and a persistent cough led him to seek medical care at the Veterans' Hospital in Quebec City. Dallain was told that he had double pneumonia and was sent to another hospital. Only after he got there did he discover that it was a tuberculosis ward.

Weakened from years of deprivation, the disease took hold and ravaged the twenty-seven-year-old. After three and a half years in a POW camp, including months in hospital at Bowen Road, Dallain was desperate not to remain in the hospital, a sick man, suffering anew. The tuberculosis bacteria were as pitiless as the Kempeitai, and

fate appeared to care not that Dallain had had his quota of suffering.*
Given his advanced condition, the doctors did not think he would
suffer long. But suffer he did, through fits of coughing, fever, nine
bronchoscopes (during which thick, green matter was scooped from
his lungs) and, once again, poor food.

The defeat at Hong Kong sentenced Dallain to three and a half
years of hell. Twice that amount of time passed before he could
begin again what he had joined the army to protect, the life of a free
Canadian, first as a travelling salesman for electrical goods and later
as the postmaster in New Carlisle.

---

* Dallain credits the seriousness of his medical condition with preventing him from going
through a lot of the psychological traumas that many of his fellow veterans of "C" Force
experienced.

CODA

War Crimes Trials

U nlike today, when Canadians strongly support the International Criminal Tribunal for Rwanda and the International Criminal Tribunal for the former Yugoslavia, Prime Minister W.L. Mackenzie King's government was lukewarm on the idea of prosecuting Axis political leaders.* Even after the United States and Great Britain announced that these leaders would be prosecuted, lawyers at External Affairs fretted about *ex post facto* (or victor's) justice. In July 1943, Ottawa instructed Vincent Massey, Canada's High Commissioner in London, to tell the United Nations commission charged with organizing war crimes trials that Canada believed "it would be a mistake . . . to weigh too heavily punishment of war criminals as expression of United Nations policy."†

---

* Between 1996 and1999, Canadian jurist Louise Arbour was the chief prosecutor at both international war crimes trials.

† External Affairs was nothing if not consistent. In August 1945, even as Canada was playing a central role in the formation of the United Nations, King's government abstained on a vote that

At the same time, King established the War Crimes Advisory Committee, an arm's-length committee headed by an honorary adviser, that met infrequently and issued reports arguing against trying Hitler and other senior Nazis, and Tōjō and other senior Japanese officials. The committee held that while civilians suffered, they "were victims of [the] hardships of war." As for crimes against Canadian soldiers, the government assumed that while there would likely be some cases of individual enemy soldiers having committed war crimes, the committee believed such cases were a European problem.

In December 1943 the committee declared, "There is some justification for the view that atrocities committed may have been confined to the brief period of time before proper discipline was restored in the occupied territory." The Department of National Defence strongly dissented from this view. Indeed, it is difficult to understand how Norman Robertson, Under Secretary of State for External Affairs, under whom the advisory committee functioned and who had had in his possession proof of Japanese atrocities for more than two years, could have accepted the committee's report.

King cloaked the War Crimes Advisory Committee under the secrecy of the War Measures Act in order to keep the issue of war crimes trials out of the news. His plan began to unravel within hours of D-Day when SS *Brigadeführer* Kurt Meyer ordered his fanatical Hitlerjugend that made up the 25 S Panzer Grenadier Regiment "in violation of the laws and usages of war" to deny quarter to Allied troops who surrendered. Meyer's men murdered twenty-three Canadians. In total, Meyer was charged with five counts of violating the Geneva Convention and with the murder of fifty-five

---

decided that "crimes against peace" and "crimes against humanity" fell within the jurisdiction of the UN War Crimes Commission. Nor did Canada agree with the American declaration that the Gestapo, the SS and other Nazi organizations were criminal conspiracies.

Canadians. He was tried by a Canadian military court convened by the General Officer Commanding the Canadian Occupation Force, 3rd Canadian Infantry Division, Major-General Christopher Vokes. The court found Meyer guilty and sentenced him to death by hanging; Vokes commuted the sentence to life in prison.*

The opening of the Auschwitz, Buchenwald and other concentration and death camps led to the Nuremberg Trials. Despite the Canadian government's doubts about the trials, Toronto-born Philip Pinkus, who had been seconded from the Canadian Air Force because of his fluent German, presented the original indictment against leading Nazis, including Hermann Göring, Rudolph Hess, Albert Speer, Jules Streicher and Martin Bormann, and which named the Nazi Party, the SA, the SS and the Gestapo as criminal conspiracies.

King's government was not much more enthusiastic about trying Japanese war criminals. Pushed by the Americans, who had wanted three Canadian judges appointed to the Tokyo trials, King agreed to appoint one to serve in Tokyo and other officials to look after Canadian interests at trials held at Yokohama and in Hong Kong. The Tokyo trials heard evidence that implicated Lieutenant Masao Uwamori, the Camp Commandant of Tokyo 3D, in the beatings and deaths of seventy-nine Canadians, including Private Lyle L. Ellis, Rifleman Murray Goodenough, Grenadier George A. Lowe and other Allied POWs. Uwamori received a sentence of three years, thanks in part to a letter from Captain Reid, which said that in comparison to other camp commandants, Uwamori was "fair and considerate."[1] The Tokyo trials convicted seven other guards of mistreating Canadians; the sentences ranged from four to twelve years.

---

* Meyer served five years of his sentence in Dorchester Penitentiary in New Brunswick before being transferred to a British prison in West Germany; he was released in 1954.

In Hong Kong, Major George Puddicombe successfully prosecuted Major-General Ryosaburo Tanaka (229th Regiment), whose men attacked the Salesian Mission medical station on 19 December 1941 and killed Dr. Orloff and several other men. Tanaka denied issuing the order that Captain Martin Banfill and his staff "must die." As well, Tanaka was charged with responsibility for the murders at Eucliffe Castle and at Overbays House on 20 December. The court sentenced Tanaka to twenty years in prison.

Puddicombe also prosecuted Colonel Isao Tokunaga, Captain Shunkichi Saito and Information Officer Honda Tanaka for the deaths of the four Grenadiers who escaped from Shamshuipo: Sergeant John Payne, Lance-Corporal George Berzenski and Privates John Adams and Percy Ellis. Tokunaga admitted that he had ordered their execution not for having escaped per se but for disobeying the Imperial Japanese order not to escape. Saito told the court that the four Canadians died instantly from shots to their hearts. Puddicombe, however, had evidence that a certain Sergeant Yoshida "had boasted about killing the four Canadians with his sword."[2]

Despite evidence from Winnipeg Grenadiers Sergeant Tom Marsh and others, the court acquitted Toshishige Shoji (230th Regiment) of ordering atrocities in the battle for Jardine's Lookout. General Ito was sentenced to twelve years for the murders of seven British soldiers captured near the Repulse Bay Hotel.

Dr. Shunkichi Saito stood trial for denying Dr. J. Crawford the serum he needed to fight the diphtheria epidemic that ravaged the POWs in 1942. The court heard also that Saito ordered Crawford not to record diphtheria as the cause of death on the death certificates and that before the end of the war, Saito destroyed many of the camp's medical records. The court rejected Saito's claim that he had not recognized the seriousness of the diphtheria outbreak because he was at the same time fighting a cholera outbreak among the Japanese, that he had no control over the food supplies, and that the Canadians were malnourished because their occidental metabolisms could not adjust to diets with more carbohydrates than fat. The court sentenced Saito to death. As did the court sitting in Nuremberg, the court in Hong Kong refused to accept Colonel Tokunaga's defence that he was simply "following orders" when he ordered the torture and execution of the four Winnipeg Grenadiers who escaped from North Point in 1942 and five British soldiers who tried to escape later.

.   .   .

Because of his Canadian birth, the prosecution of Kanao Inouye, the Kamloops Kid, raised procedural questions not present in the other cases. Basing itself on the Treason Act of 1351, enacted three years after the Black Death during the reign of Edward III (and which by virtue of the British North American Act was Canadian law), External Affairs recommended that Inouye be returned to Canada to face the charge of treason. King's cabinet disagreed and allowed Inouye to be tried as a Japanese soldier by a British war crimes court. Puddicombe prosecuted this case also, presenting evidence of Inouye's beatings of Captain John Norris and Major Frank Atkinson on 21 December 1942. The court also heard of the water torture of Hong Kong Volunteer Lam Sik (who was accused of communicating with Nationalist Chinese via a hidden wireless set), of a civil servant named Ramphal Ghilote and of Mrs. Mary Power. The fifty-five-year-old woman endured water torture, more than six hours of being hung by her hands (so that her toes barely touched the ground) and burning with a cigarette of her hands and face.

Inouye's lawyers argued that while he did beat the two Canadian officers, he did so under orders—and that had he not carried out those orders, he would have been guilty of mutiny and thus have faced a Japanese death sentence. The fact that he apologized for the beatings afterward was offered as proof that he was not culpable for them. As well, his lawyers argued that Inouye was present at Sik's, Ghilote's and Power's interrogations only as an interpreter. Given what the Canadians had told Puddicombe about Inouye's statements about his hatred of Canada and his mistreatment as a child in British Columbia, the Canadian prosecutor was surprised to hear Inouye's lawyers tell the court that Inouye enjoyed his childhood in Canada and that he "was struck by the extreme chauvinism of Japanese life" after he had moved to Japan in 1936.[3] His lawyers offered as proof that the man was anything but a fanatical member of the Kempeitai the fact that in February 1945—while the nation was girding for invasion and millions of civilians were readying to be kamikazes—he wrangled a discharge so he could go work in a civilian company.

The court would have none of it. Its president, Lieutenant-Colonel J.C. Stewart, stated:

> "Some of these acts involved such wanton and barbarous cruelty that it was a mere accident of fate whether the victims survived or not. Your culpability is greatly aggravated by the fact that you were the guest of the Dominion of Canada in your youth and there you received kindness and free education which should have impressed on your mind the decent ways of civilized people and made it impossible for you to be concerned, directly or indirectly, in such an outrage against humanity."[4]

Unlike verdicts in civil and criminal trials, verdicts in military trials must be confirmed by the commander responsible for the military district. On 19 November 1946, the confirming authority ruled that Inouye should not have been tried in a military court because he was a British subject—Canadians were British subjects until 1948 when the Canadian Parliament passed the Citizenship Act. After some toing and froing as to whether Inouye had in fact been born in Tokyo or had renounced his British citizenship, Canadian authorities agreed that Inouye was, indeed, a British subject and should be tried as a civilian under the medieval Treason Act. The Statement of Offence presented to his second trial read:

> High treason by adhering to the King's Enemies elsewhere than in the King's Realm, to wit, in the Colony of Hong Kong and its Dependencies—contrary to the Treason Act, 1351 (25 Edw.3.St.5, c.2).

The evidence at this second trial was substantially the same as it was at his first trial. What differed was Inouye's attitude toward Canada and the Japanese emperor. Now, he claimed to be "embittered against the Canadian people" because of his treatment as a child in British Columbia, which included, as he had told William Allister, not being allowed to attend a birthday party when he was ten years old because he was a "yellow bastard."* "My body is the Japanese emperor's body—my mind and my body belong to the Japanese emperor!" he declared extemporaneously.

Whatever Inouye's real beliefs, his performance was designed to support his lawyers' claim that this trial too was invalid, though for the opposite reason his first trial was. Inouye's first trial was overturned because his lawyers convinced the confirming authority that Inouye was a British subject and thus could not be tried in a military court. Now, they argued that Inouye could not be tried for

---

* In Allister's memoir, while he damns Inouye and records his heinous crimes, he also writes that he, the Jewish outsider in Montreal, understood what it was like to grow up "isolated, insulted and jeered at" (Allister, 80).

treason against a sovereign to whom he did not owe fealty. Inouye's bond was to Emperor Hirohito and not the King of Canada.

Neither the presiding judge nor the jury accepted this argument. It took the jury only ten minutes to convict Inouye. An appeal that recapitulated the citizenship argument failed because there was no evidence showing that Inouye had officially renounced his status as a British subject.

Inouye was executed on 25 August 1947. The man the POWs called Slap Happy went to his death shouting "*Banzai!*"

ACKNOWLEDGEMENTS

M ore than I can say here, I am indebted to the men who agreed to give me their time and relive the pain and horror of their battle in Hong Kong and the POW camps some three score and ten years ago. In telling this story, I sat on the shoulders of ordinary men who stood tall against everything fate—no, not fate, the Imperial Japanese Army—could throw at them. The years have bent their backs and weakened their eyes, but the years have not condemned them or the witness they bear against the cruelty of their captors, the torture inflicted upon them or the murders of their comrades.

To William Allister, Bob Barter, Flash Clayton, Phil Doddridge, John Duguay, Henry Lyons, George MacDonell, Bill MacWhirter, Eric Maloney, Ed Shayler and Johnny Stroud, all of whom spent long hours being interviewed and keeping me from error, I say thank you.

À Jean-Paul Dallain, *qui j'ai interviewé aussi, je vous remercie.*

Without the help of Vince Lopata, who is writing a regimental history of the Winnipeg Grenadiers, this book would have been much more difficult and much less precise; Vince's maps serve as the basis for the maps in this book, and for this, and for his attentive reading of the manuscript, I also thank him. Mitzi Ross, the daughter of Lance-Sergeant Lance Ross (a title and name that is surely the curse of copy editors), graciously gave me access to her father's diary and wartime memorabilia.

Tony Banham, who has spent decades studying the battle and whose *Not the Slightest Chance: The Defence of Hong Kong, 1941,* is a model history, has also given unstintingly of his time, expertise and personal records. Tony's keen eye caught errors, both big and small, in the manuscript.

Both Dr. Alec Douglas and Dr. Bill Rawling, two of Canada's exemplary military historians, will recognize where their comments improved this text. Thank you both for your support of my work.

My chairs at Algonquin College during the three years I've been writing his book, Pam Wilson and Peter Larock, have also facilitated my work, sometimes by authorizing time for research and sometimes by understanding that when it looks like I'm a million miles away it's because in my mind's eye, I'm still writing. Likewise, I would like to thank my dean, Russell Mills, for his interest in my writing. Jennifer Vandenberg, the inter-library loans librarian at the college, can find the proverbial needle in the haystack. Miki Ko, a student at the college, translated parts of the Japanese official history.

My agent, David Johnston, makes sure the i's are dotted and the t's are crossed and thus allows me to worry about getting the history right and telling the story.

A writer could not wish for a more skilful and attentive editor than I have in Jim Gifford.

I thank also a Japanese diplomat who, at his request, cannot be named. He helped me understand how the Imperial Japanese Army functioned and identified for me what parts of the Japanese official history had to be translated. His help on this project and his generosity of spirit is a testament to the healing of the terrible wounds opened at Hong Kong.

Finally, I want to thank my children, Pascale and Nicolas, who will be enjoying the rigours of university when this book comes out.

All errors in the foregoing are, of course, mine.

APPENDIX I

The Order of Battle

Japanese Invasion Force (ranks given as of December 1941):
23rd Army (Lieutenant-General Takashi Sakai)
Southern Expeditionary Army Group (Lieutenant-General
    Osamu Tsukada)
38th Division (Lieutenant-General Sano Tadayoshi)
228th Regiment (Colonel Teihichi Doi)
229th Regiment (Colonel Ryosaburo Tanaka)
230th Regiment (Colonel Toshishige Shoji)

Canadian Force:
Royal Rifles of Canada
Winnipeg Grenadiers
Royal Canadian Corps of Signals

British Forces (including Indian and Volunteers):
Infantry:
2nd Battalion/Royal Scots
1st Battalion/Middlesex Regiment
5th Battalion/7th Rajput Regiment
2nd Battalion/14th Punjabi Regiment
Hong Kong Chinese Regiment

Hong Kong Volunteer Defence Corps (HKVDC):
Artillery:
8th Coast Regiment, Royal Artillery
12th Coast Regiment, Royal Artillery
956th Defence Battery, Royal Artillery
Hong Kong and Singapore Volunteer Artillery

Brigadier Cedric Wallis's War Diary, Appendix H

This typescript of Appendix H of Brigadier Cedric Wallis's East Brigade War Diary is reproduced here (exactly as written) because there is no copy of it in the archives of either the Government of Canada or the Department of National Defence. As the foregoing pages make clear, my research shows that as a record of the Royal Rifles' service in the Battle for Hong Kong, this diary is almost useless; Wallis's attitude toward the Canadians who served under him is, quite simply, shocking. I reproduce this Appendix not because of its value as a military document but, rather, to put on record the quality of the military mind under which the Royal Rifles of Canada served during the Battle for Hong Kong.*

---

* The report is reproduced verbatim save for regularizing the spellings and punctuation somewhat and not following the military practice of capitalizing proper nouns.

THE ROYAL RIFLES OF CANADA

I fear that the contents of my War Diary Narrative are far from complimentary to this unit. It is therefore fitting that a record should now be made while events are clearly in my memory. Moreover it would be unfair if their war record was not balanced by any good points which are known.

It must be realized that my only acquaintance with the battalion was from 14 Dec. 1941 throughout the Island Battle until the surrender of Stanley Force on 26 Dec. 41. After that in the POW camps at Stanley and North Point until about 15 Jan. 1942, when I was temporarily admitted to the Bowen Road hospital.

I found the R.R.C. [Royal Rifles of Canada] in occupation of their defences in East Brigade Sector on 7 Dec. (approximately). Before that date there had been one skeleton [force?] manning by officers and NCOs and one full manning trial of some 3 days duration. The unit had a fair knowledge of its sub-sector, of the location and cooperative functions of the other units and arms in their sector. The battalion was very well found as regards arms and equipment. Their vehicular transport had not, however, arrived from Canada. Portable W/T [radio] sets had not arrived and the training of personnel was commenced before hostilities commenced. Their most serious shortcoming was obviously in training. Brigadier Lawson, whom I met towards the end of 1941, told me that the R.R.C. had unfortunately nothing like the training he would have liked. When commanding the Hong Kong Infantry Brigade, I had been asked about the 20th Nov. To supply a liberal complement of good NCO instructors to the Canadians to teach weapon training—Vickers machine gun, anti-tank, rifle, mortars and Thompson sub-machine gun. So it was evident that their proficiency in these weapons is in doubt.

On the 14th Dec., I took over at Tytam [i.e., Tai Tam] Headquarters from Lieutenant Colonel W.J. Home, M.C., Commanding the

R.R.C. on the formation of the new East Infantry Brigade. As well as Home, I met Major Price (2nd in Command), Captain Atkinson (Adjutant), Major MacAuley (3rd in Command) and the other officers. I inspected as many company and platoon positions as possible during the next few days. The Commanding Officer, Major MacAuley, the Adjutant and some others had seen service in the Great War. I thought they looked of strong character and reliable. All ranks appeared very cheerful and verbally, at any rate, showed a sort of "toughness." The only qualms I had were due to their lack of training, the short time they had to master their role in the Defence Scheme and the impression they gave of being used to good living. I doubted whether they were physically "tough" or hardened, particularly after their long sea voyage. I had gained the impression they did not do all they might to quickly get "fit" and hard. For, they seemed too ready to demand and ride in motor transport rather than march. But, I hoped they would prove satisfactory, and I was comforted in knowing their role was that of "Defence" in carefully prepared pre-selected positions linked by a good telephone system.

During the next few days, I was constantly in their Headquarters and took my meals with them. I grew to like them. Lieutenant Colonel Home struck me as steady though slow in decision and in action—decidedly ponderous.

The first shock I received was on the night of 18/19 Dec. 41 when after landing, the enemy detachment gradually worked south from Pakshwan-Aldrich Bay and drove "C" Company under Major Bishop to a position on the lower east slope of Mount Parker just north of the 6 battery. This company had not reacted well to the enemy shelling and mortar fire and the air attacks on Lyemun Gap and the Saiwan 6 position. They were inclined to leave their positions and take cover in the various concrete shelters and were loath to return and occupy their weapon pits. Their failure to counter-attack at Saiwan is recorded [elsewhere]. In spite of repeated contradictions at the time by the Commanding Officer, I was gradually forced to conclude this company did not fully pull its weight and had left much of the fighting to Captain Bompas, Royal Artillery and his gunners. They should have held their positions at all costs as ordered. But they withdrew and once more set an example which had ruined the defence of C Battalion Sector on the Mainland of retrograde movement.* As far as I can judge from the accounts of Captain Bompas, R.A. (dec.) and Officer Commanding Armoured Cars who went to reinforce them, Major Bishop did his best, but the men would not hang on.

The next phase involved the rapid collection of any available reinforcing platoons and the occupation of Mount Parker and the reinforcing of Sanatorium Gap. Three platoons in all were send but none reached their objective. The platoon for Sanatorium Gap lost its way. Keeping the great massif of Mount Parker on his right, any platoon commander of average intelligence should have been able to make his way [to] Boa Vista without difficulty even at night. The men were not fit enough to climb hills quickly and were badly hampered by their thick woollen battle dress which was far too heavy for such operations. It quickly became apparent that the unit had no conception of field communication. They were unable to lay and man a field cable to keep their battalion headquarters in touch with the progress of these platoons. The operation proved too much for the Canadians and the enemy quickly grasped Mount Parker and occupied Sanatorium Gap.

Next came the withdrawal to Stone Hill and Stanley. A description will be found [elsewhere]. On these and subsequent pages will be found accounts of their disorganization, failures in intercommunication and tactical handling. By the night of 20 Dec. 1941 after little success in the Repulse Bay area against Violet Hill

---

* Wallis appears here to be conflating the Royal Rifles with the Royal Scots, whom he blamed for the collapse of the mainland defences.

and Middle Spur, all the former bombast and over confidence departed the R.R.C.* I had hoped that in an "advance" operation they might show greater determination than on 18/19 Dec., but was not so. The hills, their lack of training and unfitness were once more too much for them and their discipline was very lax. Much jettisoning of equipment occurred. In the defence positions held on Stone Hill–Stanley Mound, food and water were a grave problem. Sub-units would not wait for food to be carried forward. They kept on withdrawing to the road to feed, leaving far too [few of ?] this detachment to hold the high ground. Once down on Island Road, men did not hurry to return to their positions, in some cases slipping off to the battalion cooking area near Stanley Police Station.

On 21 Dec. 41, the advance guard was led by Major MacAuley, R.R.C. aided by Major Templer, Royal Artillery, and the battalion fought with determination; the men on Bridge Hill put up a good fight and had a hand to hand grenade struggle. But their slowness up the hills, lack of any communications and inability to feed in forward positions rendered the result indecisive.

It was clear from the fighting on 20 and 21 Dec. 1941 that provided they had good leaders the men were brave enough and would follow. But the use of regular officers as section commanders was terribly costly and no more were available.

Two examples of bad leadership are noticeable. Firstly, on 20 Dec. 41 D Company under Major Parker were sent to occupy a position

---

* I hasten to remind the reader that Wallis began this report with the words: "I fear that the contents of my War Diary Narrative are far from complimentary to this unit. It is therefore fitting that a record should now be made while events are clearly in my memory. Moreover it would be unfair if their war record was not balanced by any good points which are known." In neither this Appendix nor in the hourly part of this report does he speak of any incidence of "bombast." Rather, above he wrote, "All ranks appeared very cheerful and verbally, at any rate, showed a sort of 'toughness,'" which, one would think, a commander would consider virtues.

on the north east of Violet Hill. They failed to do so and threw away their 3 mortars. Instead of occupying the best positions they could, the company simply withdrew having failed to send back any information. Secondly: This same company when given clear orders as to the counterattack it was to carry out on 25 December 41 near Stanley Prison [the Christmas Day attack], failed through not obeying orders and [instead] attacking by the most exposed route and out of control. (See [elsewhere].) Again, instead of holding the positions reached, the whole company withdrew more than a mile to the fort.

Discipline was bad. The unit threw away its 3 mortars as the men so no point in carrying such heavy loads. They lost almost all field telephones. They men would wander off and pick up anything they fancied. Far too many slunk off to the rear to Stanley Village and fort and were out of battle positions for long periods.

On the night of 23 December 41 one company withdrawing to new positions near St. Josephs College, poured into the Prison Club. In this building there was a large room with tables and chairs where Lieutenant-Colonel Wilcox, Prison Superintendant used to feed his warders. The Canadians simply came in and took the place over, rather than going to their new positions. It was only with delay and difficulty that they were eventually got out by the Brigade Major.

My Brigade Major reports that then he had to issue order to an officer of the R.R.C.*, the order and its suitability or otherwise (as they saw it) would be discussed in a sort of "soviet" by any present at the time. If the Canadians thought the action ordered was a good thing it would be obeyed. If those present did not care for it, in all probability it would not be carried out.

---

* Wallis places the following note here: "This was not confined to the men only. About 27 Dec 41 the Commanding Officer [Home] was found to be wearing a good pair of boots belonging to Major Forrester, Royal Artillery which he found in the 965 Battery offices he had been given to live in." This charge left more than a few veterans speechless. George MacDonell, who knew Home well, says of the commander of the Royal Rifles, "quite simply, he was an officer and a gentleman."

The R.R.C. were like untrained against trained boxers. Inadequately trained, heavily clad and not well enough conditioned, they could not fight the well trained and well led, fit Japanese troops they were opposed to.

After 19 Dec. 1941, I was finding more and more how very reluctant and slow they were to execute orders. The Commanding Officer was showing a slowly increasing hostility towards Brigade Headquarters. I felt I was being regarded as a hard taskmaster who insisted in trying to make Canadians fight. The Commanding Officer and his officers showed they felt that the hurry and urgency were not necessary. As time passed, I saw more and more clearly that Home had not the drive and determination to fight a losing battle. He was too quickly oppressed by failure—far to slow in issuing his orders—far too prone to say his unit couldn't do it or was short of men—always too far back under cover in an advance.

I am convinced that Home's shortcomings went far to detract from the value of the R.R.C. A good battalion commander can make or mar any unit. (I feel I have the right to say this—I commanded a training battalion for a time, a territorial battalion for year and the 5/7 Rajputs for 3½ years and feel in a position to judge.)

From the evening of 21 December 1941 onwards commended a never ending struggle to keep Lt. Col. Home and the R.C.C. going. Home first showed openly that night he had no more heart left for fighting. I was utterly shocked and astonished by his attitude. It seemed amazing that he should talk of "Canadian lives" as being wasted—as if they were of higher value than those of other members of His Majesty's Forces. I wondered at time whether it was not all a bad dream. Could a Canadian officer and one who looked a gentleman, have made what seemed to me to be a dishonourable request.

Details of the R.R.C. final demand to surrender prematurely will be found in the account on Stanley fighting [elsewhere].

We lost Hong Kong. Nothing the R.R.C. might have done could have averted that end. It would be highly unjust to put the blame on the Canadians.

Their lack of training and their other shortcomings I can understand and forgive. That their failures should have led to a loss of confidence and lower their morale, I can appreciate. That they should know fear (and I knew it myself) I can sympathize with. But, I cannot forget or forgive their failures to overcome their fears—their complete loss of morale and attempt to force Stanley Force to surrender on 24 Dec. 1941.

I consider that much of the blame rests with Lt. Col. Home, M.C., whom I judge to be a bad commander.* But his 2nd in Command (Major Price) and several of his senior officers were little better and have some share of responsibility. All officers were of the same mind as their commanding officer.

I feel convinced that the men of the R.R.C. better led and commanded would, in spite of their lack of training have rendered a better account of themselves.†

Signed
C. Wallis
Brigadier, Commanding East Infantry Brigade
1st October, 1942

---

* The Canadian government passed judgment on Home after he returned to Canada in 1945 when he was promoted to Brigadier-General.

† It is notable that Wallis does not mention here the successful attacks on Red, Bridge and Notting hills.

Honours and Awards

Victoria Cross
Sergeant-Major John Robert Osborn, Winnipeg Grenadiers
  (posthumous)

Distinguished Service Order
Major Wells Bishop, E.D., Royal Rifles of Canada
Major Ernest Hodkinson, Winnipeg Grenadiers

Military Cross
Captain Frederick Atkinson, Royal Rifles of Canada
Lieutenant Alexander Blackwood, Winnipeg Grenadiers
Lieutenant Collinson Blaver, Royal Rifles of Canada
Honorary Captain Uriah Laite, Winnipeg Grenadiers
Lieutenant William Nugent, Winnipeg Grenadiers
Captain Robert Philip, Winnipeg Grenadiers
Lieutenant Francis Power, Royal Rifles of Canada

Distinguished Conduct Medal
Staff Sergeant Charles Clark, Canadian Postal Corps
Corporal Derrek Rix, Winnipeg Grenadiers
Company Quartermaster Sergeant Colin Standish, Royal Rifles
  of Canada

Military Medal

Lance-Corporal Ronald Atkinson, Winnipeg Grenadiers

Rifleman Ernest Bennett, Royal Rifles of Canada

Sergeant Emile Bernard, Royal Rifles of Canada

Private Kenneth Cameron, Royal Canadian Ordnance Corps

Lance-Sergeant Murray Goodenough, Royal Rifles of Canada
(posthumous)

Private William Morris, Winnipeg Grenadiers

Lance-Corporal Meirion Price, Winnipeg Grenadiers

Corporal Lionel Speller, Royal Canadian Corps of Signals

Sergeant Grant Stoddard, Royal Rifles of Canada

Lance-Corporal John Varley, Royal Rifles of Canada

Lance-Sergeant Cecil Whalen, Winnipeg Grenadiers

Company Quartermaster-Sergeant Stanley Wright, Royal Rifles
of Canada

Mentioned in Despatches
Royal Rifles:
Lieutenant William Bradley

Private Bernard Castonguay

Private Morgan Davies

Sergeant Maurice D'Avignon

Corporal Joseph Fitzpatrick (K.I.A.)

Rifleman Nelson Gailbraith

Corporal Edwin Harrison (K.I.A.)

Corporal Lorne Latimer (K.I.A.)

Major Thomas MacAuley, D.C.M., E.D.

Sergeant George MacDonell

Corporal George McRae

Sergeant Kenneth Porter

Private Lloyd Roblee

Lieutenant James Ross (K.I.A.)

Lieutenant Arthur Scott
Sergeant Leslie Stickles
Private James Wallace

Winnipeg Grenadiers:
Private Frank Brown
Major Henry Hook
Lieutenant John Dunderdale
Private Aurbrey Flegg
Corporal Lorne Latimer (K.I.A.)
Corporal Ernest Macfarland (K.I.A.)
Private Norman Matthews
Private Sydney Sheffer
Private Edwin Smith
Private James Thom
Sergeant Charles Watson

Royal Canadian Corps of Signals:
Private Robert Damant
Sergeant Charles Sharp (K.I.A.)

In Memoriam

Their name liveth for evermore
—Ecclesiasticus*

---

* This saying from the Bible is inscribed on the Altar of Remembrance at Sai Wan Military Cemetery in Hong Kong, where 1,505 British Empire soldiers died either in the Battle of Hong Kong or in the POW camps. Four hundred and forty-four graves hold the remains of unidentified soldiers. The Sai Wan Memorial lists some two thousand names, including more than two hundred Canadians.

CANADIANS KILLED IN THE BATTLE FOR HONG KONG

Regiment	Last Name	Rank	First Name	Hometown	Cemetery Name
Brigade	Hennessy	LIEUTENANT COLONEL	Patrick	Ottawa, ON	Sai Wan Cemetery
Brigade	Lawson	BRIGADIER	John K.	Ottawa, ON	Sai Wan Cemetery
Brigade	Lyndon	MAJOR	Charles A.	Edmonton, AB	Sai Wan Memorial
Corps of Military Staff Clerks	Black	SERGEANT	Marvin F.	Rolling Dam, NB	Sai Wan Cemetery
Corps of Military Staff Clerks	Jewitt	SERGEANT	Charles L.	London, ON	Sai Wan Memorial
Corps of Military Staff Clerks	Phillips	SERGEANT	William E.	Victoria, BC	Sai Wan Memorial
Royal Canadian Army Pay Corps	Davies	CAPTAIN	Roslyn M.	Winnipeg, MB	Sai Wan Cemetery
Royal Canadian Army Service Corps	Berger	PRIVATE	Max	Sarnia, ON	Sai Wan Memorial
Royal Canadian Army Service Corps	Hickey	CAPTAIN	Overton S.	New York, NY	Sai Wan Memorial
Royal Canadian Army Service Corps	Jackson	PRIVATE	Albert	Montreal, QC	Sai Wan Memorial
Royal Canadian Army Service Corps	Melville	PRIVATE	David S.	Toronto, ON	Stanley Military Cemetery
Royal Canadian Army Service Corps	Newsome	PRIVATE	Ambrose	Montreal, QC	Sai Wan Memorial
Royal Canadian Corps of Signals	Damant	SIGNALMAN	Robert	Montreal, QC	Stanley Military Cemetery
Royal Canadian Corps of Signals	Fairley	SIGNALMAN	John L.	Port Alberni, BC	Stanley Military Cemetery
Royal Canadian Corps of Signals	Greenberg	SIGNALMAN	Hymie	Winnipeg, MB	Stanley Military Cemetery
Royal Canadian Corps of Signals	Horvath	SIGNALMAN	James E.	Pine Falls, BC	Sai Wan Memorial
Royal Canadian Corps of Signals	Sharp	SIGNALMAN	Charles G.	Victoria, ON	Stanley Military Cemetery
Royal Canadian Corps of Signals	Thomas	SIGNALMAN	Ernest R.	Lynnmour, BC	Sai Wan Memorial

Regiment	Last Name	Rank	First Name	Hometown	Cemetery Name
Royal Canadian Ordnance Corps	Deroches	CORPORAL	Gerard G.	Ottawa, ON	Sai Wan Memorial
Royal Canadian Ordnance Corps	Jackman	STAFF SERGEANT	George	Ottawa, ON	Sai Wan Memorial
Royal Canadian Ordnance Corps	McGuire	PRIVATE	Frank C.	Kingston, ON	Sai Wan Memorial
Royal Rifles of Canada	Acorn	RIFLEMAN	John	Deer Lake, ON	Sai Wan Memorial
Royal Rifles of Canada	Acorn	RIFLEMAN	Joseph	Peters Road, PEI	Sai Wan Memorial
Royal Rifles of Canada	Adams	RIFLEMAN	Bryce	Mill Stream, QC	Sai Wan Cemetery
Royal Rifles of Canada	Allen	RIFLEMAN	Louis	St. Zacharie, QC	Sai Wan Memorial
Royal Rifles of Canada	Andrews	RIFLEMAN	Albert	Lac Megantic, QC	Sai Wan Memorial
Royal Rifles of Canada	Arseneau	RIFLEMAN	Jules	Adams Gulch, NB	Sai Wan Memorial
Royal Rifles of Canada	Atwood	RIFLEMAN	Percy	Barrington, NS	Sai Wan Memorial
Royal Rifles of Canada	Baker	RIFLEMAN	John	Campbellton, NB	Stanley Military Cemetery
Royal Rifles of Canada	Barnett	RIFLEMAN	Clifford	Toronto, ON	Sai Wan Memorial
Royal Rifles of Canada	Bate	RIFLEMAN	Ernest	Maxelsfield, British Isles	Sai Wan Memorial
Royal Rifles of Canada	Beacroft	RIFLEMAN	Ronald		Sai Wan Memorial
Royal Rifles of Canada	Beattie	SERGEANT	Leonard	Iberville, QC	Sai Wan Memorial
Royal Rifles of Canada	Bertin	RIFLEMAN	Edmund	New Mills, NB	Sai Wan Memorial
Royal Rifles of Canada	Best	RIFLEMAN	William	Grand Cascapedia, QC	Sai Wan Memorial
Royal Rifles of Canada	Boudreau	RIFLEMAN	Vance	Glen Levit, NB	Sai Wan Memorial
Royal Rifles of Canada	Bouley	RIFLEMAN	Narcisse	Campbellton, NB	Sai Wan Memorial
Royal Rifles of Canada	Briand	RIFLEMAN	Rannie	Douglastown, QC	Sai Wan Memorial
Royal Rifles of Canada	Bujold	RIFLEMAN	Hubert	Cross Point, QC	Sai Wan Memorial
Royal Rifles of Canada	Burgess	RIFLEMAN	Walter	Cornwall, ON	Sai Wan Memorial
Royal Rifles of Canada	Calder	RIFLEMAN	George	Broadlands, QC	Sai Wan Memorial
Royal Rifles of Canada	Chalmers	RIFLEMAN	Ralph	Thornhill, ON	Sai Wan Memorial

Regiment	Last Name	Rank	First Name	Hometown	Cemetery Name
Royal Rifles of Canada	Chatterton	RIFLEMAN	Orrin	Carlisle, QC	Sai Wan Cemetery
Royal Rifles of Canada	Coleman	CORPORAL	John	Scotstown, QC	Stanley Military Cemetery
Royal Rifles of Canada	Collins	CORPORAL	Alger	Albert, NB	Sai Wan Memorial
Royal Rifles of Canada	Cormier	RIFLEMAN	Frank	Amherst, NS	Stanley Military Cemetery
Royal Rifles of Canada	Crosman	RIFLEMAN	Philip	Little Pabos, QC	Sai Wan Memorial
Royal Rifles of Canada	Cuzner	SERGEANT	John	Montreal, QC	Sai Wan Memorial
Royal Rifles of Canada	Cyr	RIFLEMAN	Euclide	New Richmond, QC	Sai Wan Cemetery
Royal Rifles of Canada	Delaney	RIFLEMAN	Joseph	House Harbour, QC	Sai Wan Memorial
Royal Rifles of Canada	Delaney	RIFLEMAN	Morris	New Carlisle, QC	Sai Wan Memorial
Royal Rifles of Canada	Dixon	RIFLEMAN	Alfred	Toronto, ON	Sai Wan Memorial
Royal Rifles of Canada	Doran	RIFLEMAN	Alexander	Newcastle, NB	Sai Wan Memorial
Royal Rifles of Canada	Doucet	RIFLEMAN	Edgar	West Bathurst, NB	Sai Wan Memorial
Royal Rifles of Canada	Doyle	RIFLEMAN	Joseph	Montreal, QC	Sai Wan Memorial
Royal Rifles of Canada	Dupont	RIFLEMAN	Elroy	Pembroke, ON	Sai Wan Cemetery
Royal Rifles of Canada	Evans	RIFLEMAN	Joseph	Asbestos, QC	Sai Wan Cemetery
Royal Rifles of Canada	Fallow	LANCE-CORPORAL	William	New Richmond, QC	Sai Wan Memorial
Royal Rifles of Canada	Firlotte	RIFLEMAN	John	Bathurst, NB	Sai Wan Memorial
Royal Rifles of Canada	Fitzpatrick	CORPORAL	John	Quebec, QC	Sai Wan Memorial
Royal Rifles of Canada	Forsyth	RIFLEMAN	Delmar	Chicoutimi, QC	Stanley Military Cemetery
Royal Rifles of Canada	Fry	LIEUTENANT	William	Westmount, QC	Sai Wan Memorial
Royal Rifles of Canada	Gallant	RIFLEMAN	Benjamin	Glencoe, QC	Sai Wan Memorial
Royal Rifles of Canada	Gallant	RIFLEMAN	Clement	Cross Point, QC	Sai Wan Memorial
Royal Rifles of Canada	Gammack	RIFLEMAN	Maurice	Stirlingshire, Scotland	Sai Wan Memorial
Royal Rifles of Canada	Gander	HONORARY SERGEANT	(attached)	Gander, NF	Memorial Wall, Ottawa, ON
Royal Rifles of Canada	Geraghty	RIFLEMAN	Oliver	Oak Bay Mills, QC	Sai Wan Memorial

Regiment	Last Name	Rank	First Name	Hometown	Cemetery Name
Royal Rifles of Canada	Grieves	RIFLEMAN	Willis	Campbellford, ON	Sai Wan Memorial
Royal Rifles of Canada	Halley	RIFLEMAN	George	Bury, QC	Sai Wan Memorial
Royal Rifles of Canada	Harrison	LANCE-CORPORAL	Argyle	Bury, QC	Sai Wan Memorial
Royal Rifles of Canada	Harrison	LANCE-CORPORAL	Edwin	Grand Cascapedia, QC	Sai Wan Memorial
Royal Rifles of Canada	Henderson	RIFLEMAN	Elzie	Haliburton, ON	Sai Wan Memorial
Royal Rifles of Canada	Hickey	RIFLEMAN	Charles	Nash Creek, NB	Sai Wan Cemetery
Royal Rifles of Canada	Hopgood	RIFLEMAN	Leslie	Weston, ON	Sai Wan Cemetery
Royal Rifles of Canada	Hughes	SERGEANT	Harold	Hamilton, ON	Sai Wan Memorial
Royal Rifles of Canada	Hunchuck	RIFLEMAN	Harold	Weston, ON	Stanley Military Cemetery
Royal Rifles of Canada	Irvine	RIFLEMAN	Bertram	Flatlands, NB	Sai Wan Memorial
Royal Rifles of Canada	Irvine	RIFLEMAN	Crandel	Mann Settlement, QC	Sai Wan Memorial
Royal Rifles of Canada	Irvine	RIFLEMAN	Gordon	Mann Settlement, QC	Sai Wan Memorial
Royal Rifles of Canada	Jackson	RIFLEMAN	Ray	Chesley, ON	Sai Wan Cemetery
Royal Rifles of Canada	Jacques	RIFLEMAN	Daniel	Fontenelle, QC	Sai Wan Memorial
Royal Rifles of Canada	Keating	RIFLEMAN	Edward	Toronto, ON	Sai Wan Memorial
Royal Rifles of Canada	Kinnie	RIFLEMAN	Ronald	Beaverbrook, NB	Stanley Military Cemetery
Royal Rifles of Canada	Lafferty	RIFLEMAN	Harvey	Thorold, ON	Sai Wan Cemetery
Royal Rifles of Canada	Lapointe	RIFLEMAN	Joseph	Montreal, QC	Sai Wan Memorial
Royal Rifles of Canada	Latimer	CORPORAL	Lorne	Detroit, MI	Sai Wan Cemetery
Royal Rifles of Canada	Lebel	RIFLEMAN	Valmont	Campbellton, NB	Sai Wan Memorial
Royal Rifles of Canada	Linn	RIFLEMAN	James	Marmora, ON	Sai Wan Memorial
Royal Rifles of Canada	Little	LANCE-CORPORAL	Orval	Athens, GA	Sai Wan Cemetery
Royal Rifles of Canada	Long	RIFLEMAN	John	Tide Head, NB	Sai Wan Memorial
Royal Rifles of Canada	Lyons	CORPORAL	Jack	Mann Settlement, QC	Sai Wan Memorial
Royal Rifles of Canada	Lyster	LIEUTENANT	Franklin	South Durham, QC	Sai Wan Memorial

Regiment	Last Name	Rank	First Name	Hometown	Cemetery Name
Royal Rifles of Canada	MacLean	RIFLEMAN	Charles	Cape Breton, NS	Sai Wan Memorial
Royal Rifles of Canada	Mahoney	RIFLEMAN	Murray	Sussex, NB	Sai Wan Memorial
Royal Rifles of Canada	Main	RIFLEMAN	James	Dawsonville, NB	Sai Wan Memorial
Royal Rifles of Canada	Major	RIFLEMAN	Kenneth	Williamstown, ON	Sai Wan Memorial
Royal Rifles of Canada	Major	RIFLEMAN	Wilson	Hopetown, QC	Sai Wan Memorial
Royal Rifles of Canada	Mann	RIFLEMAN	James	Oak Bay Mills, QC	Sai Wan Memorial
Royal Rifles of Canada	Martel	CORPORAL	George	Quebec, QC	Sai Wan Memorial
Royal Rifles of Canada	Martin	RIFLEMAN	Paul	Restigouche, NB	Sai Wan Memorial
Royal Rifles of Canada	McClellan	CORPORAL	Wendell	New Westminster, BC	Sai Wan Memorial
Royal Rifles of Canada	McGrath	RIFLEMAN	William	McGrath Cove, NB	Sai Wan Memorial
Royal Rifles of Canada	McGuire	RIFLEMAN	Ralph	Port Daniel West, QC	Sai Wan Cemetery
Royal Rifles of Canada	McIsaac	RIFLEMAN	Joseph	Inverness, NS	Sai Wan Memorial
Royal Rifles of Canada	McKay	RIFLEMAN	John	Nash Creek, NB	Sai Wan Memorial
Royal Rifles of Canada	McNab	SERGEANT	Lorne	Kenogami, QC	Sai Wan Memorial
Royal Rifles of Canada	McRae	CORPORAL	George	Chandler, QC	Sai Wan Memorial
Royal Rifles of Canada	McWhirter	LANCE-CORPORAL	John	New Richmond, QC	Sai Wan Memorial
Royal Rifles of Canada	Meredith	LANCE-CORPORAL	Eddie	Montreal, QC	Sai Wan Memorial
Royal Rifles of Canada	Mohan	RIFLEMAN	James	Midland, ON	Sai Wan Memorial
Royal Rifles of Canada	Moir	RIFLEMAN	Andrew	Lindsay, ON	Stanley Military Cemetery
Royal Rifles of Canada	Moore	RIFLEMAN	Claude	New Richmond, QC	Sai Wan Memorial
Royal Rifles of Canada	Moore	RIFLEMAN	Walter	Kentville, NS	Sai Wan Memorial
Royal Rifles of Canada	Murphy	RIFLEMAN	Claud	Halifax, NS	Sai Wan Memorial
Royal Rifles of Canada	Murphy	RIFLEMAN	Reynald	New Richmond, QC	Sai Wan Memorial
Royal Rifles of Canada	Nellis	RIFLEMAN	Leo	Flatlands, NB	Sai Wan Memorial
Royal Rifles of Canada	Newell	RIFLEMAN	Lorne	Lisgar, QC	Sai Wan Memorial

Regiment	Last Name	Rank	First Name	Hometown	Cemetery Name
Royal Rifles of Canada	Noel	RIFLEMAN	William	Durham Centre, NB	Sai Wan Memorial
Royal Rifles of Canada	Noseworthy	RIFLEMAN	Percy	St. John's, NF	Sai Wan Memorial
Royal Rifles of Canada	Oakley	RIFLEMAN	Raymond	Midland, ON	Sai Wan Memorial
Royal Rifles of Canada	Poag	RIFLEMAN	Russell	Caledonia, ON	Stanley Military Cemetery
Royal Rifles of Canada	Pollock	RIFLEMAN	Duncan	Glen Levit, NB	Sai Wan Memorial
Royal Rifles of Canada	Pollock	RIFLEMAN	Frederick	Norton, NB	Sai Wan Memorial
Royal Rifles of Canada	Potts	RIFLEMAN	William	Port Hope, ON	Sai Wan Memorial
Royal Rifles of Canada	Pratt	RIFLEMAN	Porter	Matapédia, QC	Sai Wan Memorial
Royal Rifles of Canada	Rattie	RIFLEMAN	Alexander	Cross Point, QC	Sai Wan Cemetery
Royal Rifles of Canada	Reid	RIFLEMAN	Colin	Quebec, QC	Sai Wan Memorial
Royal Rifles of Canada	Robertson	RIFLEMAN	Oscar	New Richmond, QC	Sai Wan Memorial
Royal Rifles of Canada	Rooney	RIFLEMAN	Leonard	Douglastown, QC	Sai Wan Memorial
Royal Rifles of Canada	Ross	LIEUTENANT	James	Spencerwood, QC	Sai Wan Memorial
Royal Rifles of Canada	Sannes	LANCE-CORPORAL	Aksel	Campbellton, NB	Sai Wan Cemetery
Royal Rifles of Canada	Scobie	RIFLEMAN	Garnet	Haley's Station, ON	Sai Wan Memorial
Royal Rifles of Canada	Scott	LIEUTENANT	Arthur	Preston Park, QC	Sai Wan Memorial
Royal Rifles of Canada	Sheldon	RIFLEMAN	Bertram	Toronto, ON	Stanley Military Cemetery
Royal Rifles of Canada	Smith	RIFLEMAN	William	Chatham, NB	Sai Wan Memorial
Royal Rifles of Canada	Sommerville	LANCE-CORPORAL	Reginald	Bergerville, QC	Sai Wan Memorial
Royal Rifles of Canada	Sullivan	RIFLEMAN	Fergus	Shigawake East, QC	Sai Wan Memorial
Royal Rifles of Canada	Surette	RIFLEMAN	Henry	Port Bickerton, NS	Sai Wan Cemetery
Royal Rifles of Canada	Swanson	RIFLEMAN	Kurt		Stanley Military Cemetery
Royal Rifles of Canada	Tapp	RIFLEMAN	Harry	Barachois, QC	Sai Wan Memorial
Royal Rifles of Canada	Thompson	RIFLEMAN	Morton	Glen Levit, NB	Sai Wan Cemetery
Royal Rifles of Canada	Thorn	LIEUTENANT	Raymond	Quebec, QC	Sai Wan Memorial

Regiment	Last Name	Rank	First Name	Hometown	Cemetery Name
Royal Rifles of Canada	Travers	LANCE-CORPORAL	Charles	Sault Ste. Marie, ON	Sai Wan Memorial
Royal Rifles of Canada	Trites	RIFLEMAN	Leverette	Moncton, NB	Sai Wan Memorial
Royal Rifles of Canada	Vigneault	RIFLEMAN	Laureat	Boisville, QC	Sai Wan Memorial
Royal Rifles of Canada	Vincent	RIFLEMAN	Robert	River Charlo, NB	Sai Wan Memorial
Royal Rifles of Canada	Watts	RIFLEMAN	Eric		Sai Wan Memorial
Royal Rifles of Canada	Williams	LIEUTENANT	Gerard	Quebec, QC	Sai Wan Cemetery
Royal Rifles of Canada	Wills	RIFLEMAN	John	Mount Dennis, ON	Sai Wan Cemetery
Royal Rifles of Canada	Wonnacott	SERGEANT	Alfred	Echo Bay, ON	Sai Wan Cemetery
Royal Rifles of Canada	Woodside	LIEUTENANT	Arnold	Quebec, QC	Sai Wan Memorial
The Winnipeg Grenadiers	Abgrall	PRIVATE	Harvey	St. Boniface, MB	Sai Wan Memorial
The Winnipeg Grenadiers	Agerbak	PRIVATE	Tage J.	Pilot Bank, MB	Sai Wan Memorial
The Winnipeg Grenadiers	Aitken	PRIVATE	John A.	St. James, MB	Sai Wan Memorial
The Winnipeg Grenadiers	Atkinson	PRIVATE	William L.	Black Hawk, ON	Sai Wan Memorial
The Winnipeg Grenadiers	Baptiste	PRIVATE	Edgar H.	Red Pheasant, SK	Sai Wan Memorial
The Winnipeg Grenadiers	Barrett	PRIVATE	Wilfred P.	Miniota, MB	Sai Wan Memorial
The Winnipeg Grenadiers	Barron	PRIVATE	Oliver A.	Winnipeg, MB	Sai Wan Memorial
The Winnipeg Grenadiers	Beltz	CORPORAL	Charles M.	Winnipeg, MB	Sai Wan Memorial
The Winnipeg Grenadiers	Birkett	LIEUTENANT	George A.	St. Vital, MB	Sai Wan Memorial
The Winnipeg Grenadiers	Blanchard	PRIVATE	Robert	Winnipeg, MB	Sai Wan Cemetery
The Winnipeg Grenadiers	Bowman	CAPTAIN	Allan S.	Waskada, MB	Sai Wan Memorial
The Winnipeg Grenadiers	Boyd	LANCE-CORPORAL	David V.	Winnipeg, MB	Sai Wan Memorial
The Winnipeg Grenadiers	Brady	PRIVATE	James J.	North Kildonan, MB	Sai Wan Memorial
The Winnipeg Grenadiers	Carberry	PRIVATE	Samuel R.	Winnipeg, MB	Sai Wan Cemetery
The Winnipeg Grenadiers	Carcary	PRIVATE	William T.	Carman, MB	Sai Wan Memorial

Regiment	Last Name	Rank	First Name	Hometown	Cemetery Name
The Winnipeg Grenadiers	Caswill	PRIVATE	Gabriel J.	Winnipeg, MB	Sai Wan Memorial
The Winnipeg Grenadiers	Chaboyer	PRIVATE	Marcel	St. Laurent, MB	Sai Wan Memorial
The Winnipeg Grenadiers	Cooper	PRIVATE	Kenneth S.	Mather, MB	Sai Wan Memorial
The Winnipeg Grenadiers	Crawford	PRIVATE	William	Winnipeg, MB	Sai Wan Memorial
The Winnipeg Grenadiers	David	SECOND LIEUTENANT	James A.	Winnipeg, MB	Sai Wan Memorial
The Winnipeg Grenadiers	Davis	PRIVATE	Albert H.	St. Vital, MB	Sai Wan Memorial
The Winnipeg Grenadiers	Deslaurier	PRIVATE	Leon	Winnipeg, MB	Sai Wan Memorial
The Winnipeg Grenadiers	Donovan	PRIVATE	Valentine A.	Winnipeg, MB	Sai Wan Memorial
The Winnipeg Grenadiers	Dowswell	PRIVATE	Melvin S.	Dryden, ON	Sai Wan Memorial
The Winnipeg Grenadiers	Dunsford	SERGEANT	Edward C.	Winnipeg, MB	Sai Wan Memorial
The Winnipeg Grenadiers	Eccles	PRIVATE	Norman C.	Flin Flon, MB	Sai Wan Memorial
The Winnipeg Grenadiers	Edgley	PRIVATE	Charles R.	Winnipeg, MB	Sai Wan Memorial
The Winnipeg Grenadiers	Ferguson	LANCE-SERGEANT	Charles E.	St. Vital, MB	Sai Wan Memorial
The Winnipeg Grenadiers	Folster	PRIVATE	Donald H.	Winnipeg, MB	Sai Wan Memorial
The Winnipeg Grenadiers	Folster	PRIVATE	Herbert T.	Winnipeg, MB	Sai Wan Memorial
The Winnipeg Grenadiers	Foord	PRIVATE	Frank M.	Manson, MB	Sai Wan Memorial
The Winnipeg Grenadiers	Foster	SERGEANT	Russell M.	St. Charles, MB	Sai Wan Memorial
The Winnipeg Grenadiers	French	LIEUTENANT	Charles D.	Norwood, MB	Sai Wan Memorial
The Winnipeg Grenadiers	Frobisher	PRIVATE	Donald	St. Rose du Lac, MB	Sai Wan Memorial
The Winnipeg Grenadiers	Fryatt	WARRANT OFFICER	Walter B.	St. Vital, MB	Sai Wan Memorial
The Winnipeg Grenadiers	Gagne	PRIVATE	Louis	St. Marie Beauce, QC	Sai Wan Cemetery
The Winnipeg Grenadiers	Geekie	PRIVATE	Victor E.	Winnipeg, MB	Sai Wan Memorial
The Winnipeg Grenadiers	Girard	PRIVATE	David	Therien, AB	Sai Wan Cemetery
The Winnipeg Grenadiers	Goodman	PRIVATE	Oscar	Selkirk, MB	Sai Wan Memorial
The Winnipeg Grenadiers	Grace	PRIVATE	Robert W.	Winnipeg, MB	Sai Wan Memorial

Regiment	Last Name	Rank	First Name	Hometown	Cemetery Name
The Winnipeg Grenadiers	Granger	PRIVATE	Albert A.	Estevan, SK	Sai Wan Memorial
The Winnipeg Grenadiers	Grantham	PRIVATE	William O.	Sidney, MB	Sai Wan Memorial
The Winnipeg Grenadiers	Gray	PRIVATE	John A.	Langruth, MB	Sai Wan Memorial
The Winnipeg Grenadiers	Green	PRIVATE	Albert R.	Winnipeg, MB	Sai Wan Cemetery
The Winnipeg Grenadiers	Gresham	MAJOR	Albert B.	Winnipeg, MB	Sai Wan Memorial
The Winnipeg Grenadiers	Grierson	PRIVATE	Hugh L.	Woodlands, MB	Sai Wan Memorial
The Winnipeg Grenadiers	Gunn	PRIVATE	John J.	Winnipeg, MB	Sai Wan Cemetery
The Winnipeg Grenadiers	Hallett	PRIVATE	Lloyd McD.	Fisherton, MB	Sai Wan Memorial
The Winnipeg Grenadiers	Hardisty	PRIVATE	William L.	Woodlands, MB	Sai Wan Memorial
The Winnipeg Grenadiers	Hargraves	PRIVATE	John	Ladywood, MB	Sai Wan Memorial
The Winnipeg Grenadiers	Hooper	LIEUTENANT	Ronald J.	Winnipeg, MB	Sai Wan Cemetery
The Winnipeg Grenadiers	Johnson	SERGEANT	Harvey H.	Winnipeg, MB	Sai Wan Memorial
The Winnipeg Grenadiers	Johnson	PRIVATE	Cecil H.	St. James, MB	Sai Wan Memorial
The Winnipeg Grenadiers	Johnson	PRIVATE	Lorne W.	Bulyea, SK	Sai Wan Memorial
The Winnipeg Grenadiers	Jonsson	PRIVATE	Theodore	Baldur, MB	Sai Wan Memorial
The Winnipeg Grenadiers	Kasijan	PRIVATE	Michael	Portage la Prairie, MB	Sai Wan Memorial
The Winnipeg Grenadiers	Kellas	PRIVATE	William A.	North Kildonan, MB	Sai Wan Memorial
The Winnipeg Grenadiers	Kelly	PRIVATE	Laurence B.	St. Vital, MB	Stanley Military Cemetery
The Winnipeg Grenadiers	Kelso	CORPORAL	Henry	Winnipeg, MB	Sai Wan Memorial
The Winnipeg Grenadiers	Kelso	CORPORAL	John R.	Winnipeg, MB	Sai Wan Memorial
The Winnipeg Grenadiers	KilFoyle	PRIVATE	Wesley N.	MacGregor, MB	Sai Wan Memorial
The Winnipeg Grenadiers	Land	PRIVATE	Gordon S.	Carman, MB	Sai Wan Memorial
The Winnipeg Grenadiers	Land	PRIVATE	Royal C.	Carman, MB	Sai Wan Memorial
The Winnipeg Grenadiers	Larsen	PRIVATE	Robert E.	Winnipeg, MB	Sai Wan Memorial
The Winnipeg Grenadiers	Law	PRIVATE	George	Winnipeg, MB	Sai Wan Memorial

Regiment	Last Name	Rank	First Name	Hometown	Cemetery Name
The Winnipeg Grenadiers	Lawrie	PRIVATE	Keith R.	Morris, MB	Sai Wan Memorial
The Winnipeg Grenadiers	Little	PRIVATE	Francis	Winnipeg, MB	Sai Wan Memorial
The Winnipeg Grenadiers	Long	SERGEANT	John	Winnipeg, MB	Sai Wan Memorial
The Winnipeg Grenadiers	Lousier	PRIVATE	Ernie J.	Bowsman, MB	Sai Wan Memorial
The Winnipeg Grenadiers	Lowe	PRIVATE	James A.	Montreal, QC	Sai Wan Memorial
The Winnipeg Grenadiers	MacFarlane	PRIVATE	George W.	Winnipeg, MB	Stanley Military Cemetery
The Winnipeg Grenadiers	Maltese	PRIVATE	James	Winnipeg, MB	Stanley Military Cemetery
The Winnipeg Grenadiers	Matte	PRIVATE	Thomas	Winnipeg, MB	Sai Wan Memorial
The Winnipeg Grenadiers	Matthews	PRIVATE	Denis	Winnipeg, MB	Sai Wan Cemetery
The Winnipeg Grenadiers	Maxwell	PRIVATE	Ralph C.	Transcona, MB	Sai Wan Memorial
The Winnipeg Grenadiers	McBride	PRIVATE	William	Winnipeg, MB	Sai Wan Memorial
The Winnipeg Grenadiers	McCorrister	PRIVATE	Mervin S.	Winnipeg, MB	Sai Wan Memorial
The Winnipeg Grenadiers	McGowan	PRIVATE	Robert C.	Gladstone, MB	Sai Wan Memorial
The Winnipeg Grenadiers	McKillop	LIEUTENANT	Orville W.	Portage la Prairie, MB	Sai Wan Cemetery
The Winnipeg Grenadiers	Meades	PRIVATE	Raymond A.	La Rivière, MB	Sai Wan Memorial
The Winnipeg Grenadiers	Mitchell	LIEUTENANT	Eric L.	Winnipeg, MB	Sai Wan Cemetery
The Winnipeg Grenadiers	Mitchell	LIEUTENANT	William V.	Winnipeg, MB	Sai Wan Memorial
The Winnipeg Grenadiers	Morgan	LANCE-CORPORAL	Albert W.	Winnipeg, MB	Sai Wan Memorial
The Winnipeg Grenadiers	Morris	PRIVATE	John I.	Winnipeg, MB	Sai Wan Memorial
The Winnipeg Grenadiers	O'Neill	LANCE-CORPORAL	Dori J.	Winnipeg, MB	Sai Wan Memorial
The Winnipeg Grenadiers	Orvis	PRIVATE	Harry	Grand Marais, MB	Sai Wan Memorial
The Winnipeg Grenadiers	Osadchuk	PRIVATE	Nicholas A.	Winnipeg, MB	Sai Wan Memorial
The Winnipeg Grenadiers	Osborn	WARRANT OFFICER	John R.	St. Vital, MB	Sai Wan Memorial
The Winnipeg Grenadiers	Ouellette	PRIVATE	Alfred J.	Winnipeg, MB	Stanley Military Cemetery
The Winnipeg Grenadiers	Owen	PRIVATE	Richard	Winnipeg, MB	Sai Wan Memorial

Regiment	Last Name	Rank	First Name	Hometown	Cemetery Name
The Winnipeg Grenadiers	Pare	PRIVATE	Gabriel J.	Winnipeg, MB	Sai Wan Memorial
The Winnipeg Grenadiers	Parenteau	PRIVATE	Walter J.	Reynaud, SK	Sai Wan Memorial
The Winnipeg Grenadiers	Paterson	SERGEANT	George H.	Stonewall, MB	Sai Wan Memorial
The Winnipeg Grenadiers	Peppin	PRIVATE	Louis	St. Lazare, MB	Sai Wan Memorial
The Winnipeg Grenadiers	Piasta	PRIVATE	Henry	Rossburn, MB	Sai Wan Cemetery
The Winnipeg Grenadiers	Pontius	PRIVATE	Ira W.	Faulkner, MB	Sai Wan Memorial
The Winnipeg Grenadiers	Poulsen	PRIVATE	Aage	Winnipeg, MB	Sai Wan Memorial
The Winnipeg Grenadiers	Prieston	PRIVATE	William A.	Benito, MB	Sai Wan Memorial
The Winnipeg Grenadiers	Procinsky	PRIVATE	Peter	Northbank, AB	Sai Wan Memorial
The Winnipeg Grenadiers	Rodgers	SERGEANT	Edward H.	Winnipeg, MB	Sai Wan Cemetery
The Winnipeg Grenadiers	Ross	PRIVATE	Victor	Meadow Lake, SK	Sai Wan Memorial
The Winnipeg Grenadiers	Rutherford	PRIVATE	George A.	Wood Bay, MB	Sai Wan Cemetery
The Winnipeg Grenadiers	Shatford	PRIVATE	Howard E.	Winnipeg, MB	Sai Wan Memorial
The Winnipeg Grenadiers	Shkolny	PRIVATE	Max	Winnipeg, MB	Sai Wan Memorial
The Winnipeg Grenadiers	Shore	PRIVATE	William C.	Winnipeg, MB	Sai Wan Cemetery
The Winnipeg Grenadiers	Silkey	PRIVATE	Samuel	Selkirk, MB	Sai Wan Memorial
The Winnipeg Grenadiers	Simpson	PRIVATE	Kenneth	Winnipeg, MB	Sai Wan Memorial
The Winnipeg Grenadiers	Smelts	PRIVATE	Edgar C.	Elgin, MB	Sai Wan Memorial
The Winnipeg Grenadiers	Smith	PRIVATE	Cecil E.	Winnipeg, MB	Sai Wan Memorial
The Winnipeg Grenadiers	Smith	PRIVATE	Charles	Regina, SK	Sai Wan Memorial
The Winnipeg Grenadiers	Smith	PRIVATE	Robert C.	Climax, SK	Sai Wan Memorial
The Winnipeg Grenadiers	Specht	PRIVATE	William J.	Beaconia, MB	Sai Wan Memorial
The Winnipeg Grenadiers	Starrett	PRIVATE	Ewart G.	Winnipeg, MB	Sai Wan Memorial
The Winnipeg Grenadiers	Starrett	PRIVATE	William J.	Winnipeg, MB	Sai Wan Memorial
The Winnipeg Grenadiers	Stodgell	PRIVATE	Stanley F.	Fisher Branch, MB	Sai Wan Memorial

Regiment	Last Name	Rank	First Name	Hometown	Cemetery Name
The Winnipeg Grenadiers	Swanson	PRIVATE	Edwin	Vassar, MB	Sai Wan Memorial
The Winnipeg Grenadiers	Tarbuth	CAPTAIN	Lyle T.	Winnipeg, MB	Sai Wan Memorial
The Winnipeg Grenadiers	Teasdale	PRIVATE	Gowan	Winnipeg, MB	Sai Wan Memorial
The Winnipeg Grenadiers	Tompkins	PRIVATE	John E.	Winnipeg, MB	Sai Wan Memorial
The Winnipeg Grenadiers	Vickers	CORPORAL	Jack F.	Winnipeg, MB	Sai Wan Memorial
The Winnipeg Grenadiers	Walker	PRIVATE	Norman C.	Minota, MB	Sai Wan Memorial
The Winnipeg Grenadiers	Warr	PRIVATE	Leslie M.	Saskatoon, MB	Sai Wan Memorial
The Winnipeg Grenadiers	Whalen	PRIVATE	Bernard B.	Winnipeg, MB	Sai Wan Memorial
The Winnipeg Grenadiers	White	PRIVATE	Thomas C.	Badger, MB	Sai Wan Memorial
The Winnipeg Grenadiers	Whiteside	PRIVATE	Edwin E.	Kenora, MB	Sai Wan Memorial
The Winnipeg Grenadiers	Wiebe	PRIVATE	Henry	Carman, MB	Sai Wan Memorial
The Winnipeg Grenadiers	Williams	PRIVATE	Jack G.	Stonewall, MB	Sai Wan Memorial
The Winnipeg Grenadiers	Willis	PRIVATE	Charles	Winnipeg, MB	Sai Wan Memorial
The Winnipeg Grenadiers	Wilson	PRIVATE	William J.	Winnipeg, MB	Sai Wan Memorial
The Winnipeg Grenadiers	Wojnarsky	PRIVATE	John	Elphinstone, MB	Sai Wan Memorial
The Winnipeg Grenadiers	Woods	LANCE-SERGEANT	Albert T.	Winnipeg, MB	Sai Wan Memorial
The Winnipeg Grenadiers	Woytowich	PRIVATE	Frank	Howden, MB	Sai Wan Cemetery
The Winnipeg Grenadiers	Wright	PRIVATE	Roland F.	Winnipeg, MB	Sai Wan Memorial
The Winnipeg Grenadiers	Young	LIEUTENANT	Hugh J.	Winnipeg, MB	Sai Wan Cemetery

CANADIANS WHO DIED IN JAPANESE POW CAMPS

Regiment	Last Name	Rank	First Name	Hometown	Cemetery Name
Canadian Dental Corps	Paul	CORPORAL	Glen	East Angus, QC	Sai Wan Cemetery
Canadian Provost Corps	Lavoie	PRIVATE	Joseph	St. Jean, QC	Sai Wan Cemetery
Canadian Provost Corps	Emo	SERGEANT	James	Montreal, QC	Yokohama War Cemetery
Canadian Provost Corps	Hope	SERGEANT	Alexander	Montreal, QC	Yokohama War Cemetery
Royal Canadian Army Pay Corps	Ellis	SERGEANT	Lyle	San Jose, CA	Yokohama War Cemetery
Royal Canadian Army Pay Corps	Lumb	SERGEANT	David	London, ON	Sai Wan Cemetery
Royal Canadian Army Pay Corps	Terry	CAPTAIN	Edward	Ottawa, ON	Sai Wan Cemetery
Royal Canadian Army Service Corps	Carter	SERGEANT	Albert	Toronto, ON	Sai Wan Cemetery
Royal Canadian Army Service Corps	Pearce	PRIVATE	William	Toronto, ON	Sai Wan Cemetery
Royal Canadian Army Service Corps	Sword	STAFF SERGEANT	David	Toronto, ON	Yokohama War Cemetery
Royal Canadian Corps of Signals	Little	SIGNALMAN	John	Terrace, BC	Sai Wan Cemetery
Royal Canadian Corps of Signals	Redhead	SIGNALMAN	Thomas	Victoria, BC	Sai Wan Cemetery
Royal Canadian Corps of Signals	White	LANCE-CORPORAL	Wesley	Abbotsford, BC	Sai Wan Cemetery
Royal Canadian Ordnance Corps	Cusson	PRIVATE	Paul	Nanaimo, BC	Sai Wan Cemetery
Royal Rifles of Canada	Aitkens	RIFLEMAN	Deighton	Quebec, QC	Sai Wan Cemetery
Royal Rifles of Canada	Aitkens	RIFLEMAN	Edward C.	Magdalen Island, QC	Yokohama War Cemetery

Regiment	Last Name	Rank	First Name	Hometown	Cemetery Name
Royal Rifles of Canada	Allen	CORPORAL	William H.	East Angus, QC	Yokohama War Cemetery
Royal Rifles of Canada	Antilla	RIFLEMAN	Leo S.	Kenogami, QC	Sai Wan Cemetery
Royal Rifles of Canada	Bacon	RIFLEMAN	Laureat	Quebec, QC	Sai Wan Cemetery
Royal Rifles of Canada	Barclay	RIFLEMAN	Robert M.	Durham Centre, NB	Sai Wan Cemetery
Royal Rifles of Canada	Barclay	RIFLEMAN	William J.	Tide Head, NB	Sai Wan Cemetery
Royal Rifles of Canada	Barnes	RIFLEMAN	Kenneth	Escuminac, QC	Yokohama War Cemetery
Royal Rifles of Canada	Bent	RIFLEMAN	Howard N.	Halifax, NS	Yokohama War Cemetery
Royal Rifles of Canada	Benwell	RIFLEMAN	Marvin M.	Marcil, QC	Yokohama War Cemetery
Royal Rifles of Canada	Bisson	RIFLEMAN	George S.	Paspebiac, QC	Yokohama War Cemetery
Royal Rifles of Canada	Blandk	RIFLEMAN	Elmer W.	Seven Sisters, MB	Yokohama War Cemetery
Royal Rifles of Canada	Bottie (Pottie)	RIFLEMAN	Leo J.	West Lardoise, NS	Yokohama War Cemetery
Royal Rifles of Canada	Boudreau	RIFLEMAN	Sylvestre	St. Jules de Maria, QC	Sai Wan Cemetery
Royal Rifles of Canada	Boutin	RIFLEMAN	Marius	Breakeyville, QC	Sai Wan Cemetery
Royal Rifles of Canada	Breen	CORPORAL	Frederick	Kirkland Lake, ON	Yokohama War Cemetery
Royal Rifles of Canada	Campbell	RIFLEMAN	Ralph W.	Campbellton, NB	Yokohama War Cemetery
Royal Rifles of Canada	Chenell	RIFLEMAN	Albert B.	Magdalen Island, QC	Yokohama War Cemetery
Royal Rifles of Canada	Chenell	LANCE-CORPORAL	James M.	Magdalen Island, QC	Sai Wan Cemetery
Royal Rifles of Canada	Chenell	RIFLEMAN	William R.	Magdalen Island, QC	Yokohama War Cemetery
Royal Rifles of Canada	Chicoine	RIFLEMAN	Gaston	Barachois, QC	Sai Wan Cemetery
Royal Rifles of Canada	Clapperton	RIFLEMAN	Albert G.	Grand Cascapedia, QC	Sai Wan Cemetery
Royal Rifles of Canada	Coates	RIFLEMAN	Russell	Bury, QC	Sai Wan Cemetery
Royal Rifles of Canada	Coffin	RIFLEMAN	Ninian A.	Gaspé Harbour, QC	Sai Wan Cemetery
Royal Rifles of Canada	Cole	STAFF SERGEANT	Elmer W.	Sussex, NB	Yokohama War Cemetery
Royal Rifles of Canada	Cormier	RIFLEMAN	Leo A.	Gaspé Harbour, QC	Sai Wan Cemetery
Royal Rifles of Canada	Coughlin	RIFLEMAN	Peter G.	Point-a-la-Garde, QC	Sai Wan Cemetery

Regiment	Last Name	Rank	First Name	Hometown	Cemetery Name
Royal Rifles of Canada	Culleton	RIFLEMAN	Wellington	Matapédia, QC	Yokohama War Cemetery
Royal Rifles of Canada	Cyr	RIFLEMAN	Clement	New Richmond, QC	Yokohama War Cemetery
Royal Rifles of Canada	Danyluck	RIFLEMAN	Nicholas	Black Donald, ON	Sai Wan Cemetery
Royal Rifles of Canada	Doucett	RIFLEMAN	Peter	Jardinville, QC	Yokohama War Cemetery
Royal Rifles of Canada	Dubois	RIFLEMAN	Leo P.	Sawyerville, QC	Sai Wan Cemetery
Royal Rifles of Canada	Englehart	RIFLEMAN	Rupert	Wyer's Brook, NB	Yokohama War Cemetery
Royal Rifles of Canada	Firlotte	RIFLEMAN	James B.	Durham Centre, NB	Yokohama War Cemetery
Royal Rifles of Canada	Firth	RIFLEMAN	Malcolm	Dawsonville, NB	Sai Wan Cemetery
Royal Rifles of Canada	Fitzpatrick	RIFLEMAN	Charles J.	Quebec, QC	Yokohama War Cemetery
Royal Rifles of Canada	Forsyth	RIFLEMAN	Robert	Pittsburgh, PA	Sai Wan Cemetery
Royal Rifles of Canada	Gee	CORPORAL	John M.	Quebec, QC	Yokohama War Cemetery
Royal Rifles of Canada	Gibbons	RIFLEMAN	Harold E.	Southampton, ON	Yokohama War Cemetery
Royal Rifles of Canada	Gibbs	CORPORAL	Douglas A.	Melbourne, QC	Sai Wan Cemetery
Royal Rifles of Canada	Goodenough	LANCE-SERGEANT	Murray T.	Sherbrooke, QC	Yokohama War Cemetery
Royal Rifles of Canada	Gover	RIFLEMAN	Ronald A.	South River, ON	Sai Wan Cemetery
Royal Rifles of Canada	Guitard	RIFLEMAN	Gabriel	Nash Creek, NB	Yokohama War Cemetery
Royal Rifles of Canada	Gunter	RIFLEMAN	Merlin	South Durham, QC	Sai Wan Cemetery
Royal Rifles of Canada	Haley	RIFLEMAN	Reginald	Matapédia, QC	Yokohama War Cemetery
Royal Rifles of Canada	Hamilton	RIFLEMAN	Sterling	Campbellton, NB	Yokohama War Cemetery
Royal Rifles of Canada	Harding	RIFLEMAN	Robert W.	Andover, MA	Yokohama War Cemetery
Royal Rifles of Canada	Harrison	RIFLEMAN	Edmond C.	Bury, QC	Yokohama War Cemetery
Royal Rifles of Canada	Hicks	RIFLEMAN	Frank	Kingsville, ON	Yokohama War Cemetery
Royal Rifles of Canada	Huntington	RIFLEMAN	Ralph	New Carlisle, QC	Sai Wan Cemetery
Royal Rifles of Canada	Ingalls	RIFLEMAN	Keith C.	Cowansville, QC	Yokohama War Cemetery
Royal Rifles of Canada	Irvine	RIFLEMAN	Glenford	Flatlands, NB	Sai Wan Cemetery

Regiment	Last Name	Rank	First Name	Hometown	Cemetery Name
Royal Rifles of Canada	Irvine	RIFLEMAN	Ronald		Sai Wan Cemetery
Royal Rifles of Canada	Irving	RIFLEMAN	Morton A.	Matapédia, QC	Yokohama War Cemetery
Royal Rifles of Canada	Jacquard	RIFLEMAN	Angus J.	Little River Harbour, NS	Yokohama War Cemetery
Royal Rifles of Canada	Kellaway	RIFLEMAN	Gordon G.	Lansing, ON	Sai Wan Cemetery
Royal Rifles of Canada	Kendall	RIFLEMAN	Donald	Windsor Mills, ON	Sai Wan Cemetery
Royal Rifles of Canada	Knapp	RIFLEMAN	William A.	Quebec, QC	Yokohama War Cemetery
Royal Rifles of Canada	Lamb	RIFLEMAN	Patrick		Yokohama War Cemetery
Royal Rifles of Canada	Lapointe	RIFLEMAN	Valmore	Rivière-du-Loup, QC	Sai Wan Cemetery
Royal Rifles of Canada	Lawrence	RIFLEMAN	Bert		Sai Wan Memorial
Royal Rifles of Canada	Legacy	RIFLEMAN	John F.		Sai Wan Cemetery
Royal Rifles of Canada	Lesieur	RIFLEMAN	Beryl	La Tuque, QC	Sai Wan Cemetery
Royal Rifles of Canada	MacAllister	RIFLEMAN	Arthur	Nash Creek, NB	Sai Wan Cemetery
Royal Rifles of Canada	MacArthur	RIFLEMAN	John E.	Scotstown, QC	Sai Wan Cemetery
Royal Rifles of Canada	MacDonald	STAFF SERGEANT	Lorne M.	Scotstown, QC	Yokohama War Cemetery
Royal Rifles of Canada	MacLaughlin	RIFLEMAN	Thomas	Bass River, NS	Sai Wan Cemetery
Royal Rifles of Canada	MacNaughton	RIFLEMAN	Alden L.	Matapédia, QC	Yokohama War Cemetery
Royal Rifles of Canada	MacRae	CORPORAL	Allan H.	Scotstown, QC	Yokohama War Cemetery
Royal Rifles of Canada	Maloney	RIFLEMAN	Eddie J.	Barachois, QC	Yokohama War Cemetery
Royal Rifles of Canada	Mann	LANCE-CORPORAL	Lindsay R.	Runnymede, QC	Sai Wan Cemetery
Royal Rifles of Canada	Mann	RIFLEMAN	Maxwell A.	Upsaiquitch, NB	Sai Wan Cemetery
Royal Rifles of Canada	Martin	SERGEANT	James	Quebec, QC	Yokohama War Cemetery
Royal Rifles of Canada	Matheson	RIFLEMAN	Harold	Compton, QC	Yokohama War Cemetery
Royal Rifles of Canada	Mazerolle	RIFLEMAN	Emile	Peters Mill, NB	Yokohama War Cemetery
Royal Rifles of Canada	McAra	RIFLEMAN	William R.		Sai Wan Cemetery
Royal Rifles of Canada	McKinley	RIFLEMAN	Sterling W.	Broadlands, QC	Yokohama War Cemetery

Regiment	Last Name	Rank	First Name	Hometown	Cemetery Name
Royal Rifles of Canada	McLeod	RIFLEMAN	Roderick	Powell River, ON	Yokohama War Cemetery
Royal Rifles of Canada	Medhurst	RIFLEMAN	George	Cobourg, ON	Sai Wan Cemetery
Royal Rifles of Canada	Mortimer	RIFLEMAN	James L.	Dundalk, ON	Yokohama War Cemetery
Royal Rifles of Canada	Mullim	RIFLEMAN	Elmer O.	Brassett, QC	Sai Wan Cemetery
Royal Rifles of Canada	Murray	RIFLEMAN	George W.	Walled Lake, MI	Yokohama War Cemetery
Royal Rifles of Canada	Nicholson	RIFLEMAN	William	Toronto, ON	Sai Wan Cemetery
Royal Rifles of Canada	Noble	RIFLEMAN	Russell G.	Melbourne, QC	Sai Wan Cemetery
Royal Rifles of Canada	Patterson	RIFLEMAN	James R.	Sussex, NB	Sai Wan Cemetery
Royal Rifles of Canada	Pelletier	RIFLEMAN	Gerard J.	Rouyn, QC	Sai Wan Cemetery
Royal Rifles of Canada	Perreault	LANCE-CORPORAL	Arthur	Fontenelle, QC	Yokohama War Cemetery
Royal Rifles of Canada	Phillips	CORPORAL	Edward	Sawyerville, QC	Yokohama War Cemetery
Royal Rifles of Canada	Pidgeon	RIFLEMAN	Joseph A.	Percé, QC	Yokohama War Cemetery
Royal Rifles of Canada	Pomeroy	RIFLEMAN	George R.	Castleton, ON	Sai Wan Cemetery
Royal Rifles of Canada	Pope	SERGEANT	Colin C.	Cookshire, QC	Yokohama War Cemetery
Royal Rifles of Canada	Pope	SERGEANT	William R.	Cookshire, QC	Sai Wan Cemetery
Royal Rifles of Canada	Post	RIFLEMAN	John R.	Aroostock, NB	Sai Wan Cemetery
Royal Rifles of Canada	Ray	RIFLEMAN	Irvin K.	St. Mary's River, NS	Yokohama War Cemetery
Royal Rifles of Canada	Reid	RIFLEMAN	Lloyd G.	Almonte, ON	Yokohama War Cemetery
Royal Rifles of Canada	Richards	SERGEANT	Thomas M.	St. John, NB	Yokohama War Cemetery
Royal Rifles of Canada	Roblee	RIFLEMAN	Lloyd L.	Springhill, NS	Yokohama War Cemetery
Royal Rifles of Canada	Ross	RIFLEMAN	Cyril M.	Hopetown, QC	Sai Wan Cemetery
Royal Rifles of Canada	Rowland	RIFLEMAN	Roney	Durham, NS	Yokohama War Cemetery
Royal Rifles of Canada	Russell	SERGEANT	Robert L.	Quebec, QC	Yokohama War Cemetery
Royal Rifles of Canada	Sarty	RIFLEMAN	Perry	Mersey Point, NS	Yokohama War Cemetery
Royal Rifles of Canada	Sauson	CORPORAL	Edward L.	Skigawake, QC	Sai Wan Cemetery

Regiment	Last Name	Rank	First Name	Hometown	Cemetery Name
Royal Rifles of Canada	Sauson	SERGEANT	Lester L.	Skigawake, QC	Yokohama War Cemetery
Royal Rifles of Canada	Savoy	RIFLEMAN	Edward J.	St. John, NB	Yokohama War Cemetery
Royal Rifles of Canada	Smith	RIFLEMAN	Lawrence	Trenholmville, QC	Sai Wan Cemetery
Royal Rifles of Canada	Smith	RIFLEMAN	Norman A.	Clayton, ON	Yokohama War Cemetery
Royal Rifles of Canada	Snear	RIFLEMAN	Thomas W.		Yokohama War Cemetery
Royal Rifles of Canada	Snedden	RIFLEMAN	Jack G.	Toronto, ON	Yokohama War Cemetery
Royal Rifles of Canada	Splude	RIFLEMAN	George R.	Moncton, NB	Sai Wan Cemetery
Royal Rifles of Canada	Stevens	RIFLEMAN	Clarence G.	Danville, ON	Sai Wan Cemetery
Royal Rifles of Canada	Suits	RIFLEMAN	William R.	Dowanaic, MI, USA	Sai Wan Cemetery
Royal Rifles of Canada	Sweetman	RIFLEMAN	Herbert F.	Bonaventure, QC	Sai Wan Cemetery
Royal Rifles of Canada	Syvret	RIFLEMAN	David	Belle Anse, QC	Yokohama War Cemetery
Royal Rifles of Canada	Taylor	RIFLEMAN	Reginald S.	East Kildonan, MB	Yokohama War Cemetery
Royal Rifles of Canada	Thompson	RIFLEMAN	John A.	Dawsonville, NB	Sai Wan Cemetery
Royal Rifles of Canada	Todd	WARRANT OFFICER	Earl E.	Bergerville, QC	Yokohama War Cemetery
Royal Rifles of Canada	Vermette	CORPORAL	Patrick	Campbellton, NB	Sai Wan Cemetery
Royal Rifles of Canada	Wallace	RIFLEMAN	Herbert A.	Kingsbury, ON	Yokohama War Cemetery
Royal Rifles of Canada	Walsh	CORPORAL	James S.	Entry Island, QC	Sai Wan Cemetery
Royal Rifles of Canada	Waterhouse	RIFLEMAN	William E.	Melbourne, QC	Yokohama War Cemetery
Royal Rifles of Canada	Welsh	RIFLEMAN	Allen	Magdalen Islands, QC	Sai Wan Cemetery
Royal Rifles of Canada	Welsh	RIFLEMAN	Delbert W.	Magdalen Islands, QC	Sai Wan Cemetery
Royal Rifles of Canada	Welsh	RIFLEMAN	Melvin	Magdalen Islands, QC	Yokohama War Cemetery
Royal Rifles of Canada	Whalen	RIFLEMAN	Joseph M.	Kirkfield, ON	Sai Wan Cemetery
Royal Rifles of Canada	Wilbur	RIFLEMAN	Clarence J.	South Bathurst, NB	Sai Wan Cemetery
Royal Rifles of Canada	Willett	RIFLEMAN	Frederick	Cross Point, QC	Yokohama War Cemetery
Royal Rifles of Canada	Willey	RIFLEMAN	Ivan E.	Danville, QC	Sai Wan Cemetery

Regiment	Last Name	Rank	First Name	Hometown	Cemetery Name
Royal Rifles of Canada	Wood	RIFLEMAN	Donald G.	Frontenac County, QC	Yokohama War Cemetery
Royal Rifles of Canada	Wrywas	RIFLEMAN	Frederick A.	Inverness, NS	Yokohama War Cemetery
The Winnipeg Grenadiers	Abel	SERGEANT	Frederick J.	Langruth, MB	Sai Wan Cemetery
The Winnipeg Grenadiers	Adams	PRIVATE	John H.	Winnipeg, MB	Sai Wan Cemetery
The Winnipeg Grenadiers	Armstrong	PRIVATE	George	Winnipeg, MB	Sai Wan Cemetery
The Winnipeg Grenadiers	Atkinson	PRIVATE	Ronald E.	Winnipeg, MB	Sai Wan Cemetery
The Winnipeg Grenadiers	Badger	PRIVATE	George C.	Kamsack, SK	Sai Wan Cemetery
The Winnipeg Grenadiers	Bazinet	PRIVATE	Henry J.	Deer Horn, MB	Yokohama War Cemetery
The Winnipeg Grenadiers	Bell	PRIVATE	Gordon	Winnipeg, MB	Yokohama War Cemetery
The Winnipeg Grenadiers	Berezenski	LANCE-CORPORAL	George	Binscarth, MB	Sai Wan Cemetery
The Winnipeg Grenadiers	Blanchard	PRIVATE	Arthur J.	Hudson Bay Junction, SK	Yokohama War Cemetery
The Winnipeg Grenadiers	Blueman	LANCE-CORPORAL	Henry K.	Sudbury, ON	Yokohama War Cemetery
The Winnipeg Grenadiers	Boswell	PRIVATE	Ernest A.	Roblin, MB	Sai Wan Cemetery
The Winnipeg Grenadiers	Boulding	PRIVATE	Albert E.	Radisson, SK	Yokohama War Cemetery
The Winnipeg Grenadiers	Bowes	PRIVATE	David W.	Dryden, ON	Yokohama War Cemetery
The Winnipeg Grenadiers	Bross	PRIVATE	Carl J.	St. Boniface, MB	Yokohama War Cemetery
The Winnipeg Grenadiers	Brown	PRIVATE	Alexander	Renwer, MB	Sai Wan Cemetery
The Winnipeg Grenadiers	Caruso	PRIVATE	Frank T.	Winnipeg, MB	Yokohama War Cemetery
The Winnipeg Grenadiers	Chaboyer	PRIVATE	David J.	St. Laurent, MB	Yokohama War Cemetery
The Winnipeg Grenadiers	Chapman	PRIVATE	James E.	Sturgeon Creek, MB	Sai Wan Cemetery
The Winnipeg Grenadiers	Charuk	PRIVATE	Nickolas J.	Oak Bluff, MB	Yokohama War Cemetery
The Winnipeg Grenadiers	Chewter	PRIVATE	George W.	St. Boniface, MB	Sai Wan Cemetery
The Winnipeg Grenadiers	Coady	PRIVATE	John A.	Luseland, SK	Sai Wan Cemetery
The Winnipeg Grenadiers	Colvin	PRIVATE	Frederick J.	Carman, MB	Yokohama War Cemetery

Regiment	Last Name	Rank	First Name	Hometown	Cemetery Name
The Winnipeg Grenadiers	Danyluik	PRIVATE	William	Ward, SK	Yokohama War Cemetery
The Winnipeg Grenadiers	Davis	PRIVATE	John J.	Winnipeg, MB	Sai Wan Cemetery
The Winnipeg Grenadiers	Delorme	PRIVATE	George D.	Carman, MB	Yokohama War Cemetery
The Winnipeg Grenadiers	Dumaine	PRIVATE	Joseph A.	St. Norbert, MB	Yokohama War Cemetery
The Winnipeg Grenadiers	Eastholm	PRIVATE	Eric E.	Winnipeg, MB	Sai Wan Cemetery
The Winnipeg Grenadiers	Ellis	PRIVATE	Percy J.	Wawanesa, MB	Sai Wan Cemetery
The Winnipeg Grenadiers	Evans	PRIVATE	Robert D.	Winnipeg, MB	Yokohama War Cemetery
The Winnipeg Grenadiers	Fifer	PRIVATE	Royal V.	Winnipeg, MB	Sai Wan Cemetery
The Winnipeg Grenadiers	Forbes	PRIVATE	James P.	Winnipeg, MB	Sai Wan Cemetery
The Winnipeg Grenadiers	Foster	PRIVATE	Stanley	Winnipeg, MB	Sai Wan Cemetery
The Winnipeg Grenadiers	Fox	PRIVATE	Erwin A.	Semans, SK	Yokohama War Cemetery
The Winnipeg Grenadiers	Foxall	PRIVATE	Reginald	Winnipeg, MB	Sai Wan Cemetery
The Winnipeg Grenadiers	Freeman	PRIVATE	Edward J.	Norwood, MB	Sai Wan Cemetery
The Winnipeg Grenadiers	Friesen	PRIVATE	John U.	Plum Coulee, MB	Yokohama War Cemetery
The Winnipeg Grenadiers	Furey	PRIVATE	Joseph	Firdale, MB	Yokohama War Cemetery
The Winnipeg Grenadiers	Gard	PRIVATE	James P.	Fisherton, MB	Yokohama War Cemetery
The Winnipeg Grenadiers	Gemmell	PRIVATE	David	Winnipeg, MB	Sai Wan Cemetery
The Winnipeg Grenadiers	Grainger	LANCE-CORPORAL	William A.	Beulah, MB	Yokohama War Cemetery
The Winnipeg Grenadiers	Hallett	PRIVATE	Lawrence G.	Fisherton, MB	Yokohama War Cemetery
The Winnipeg Grenadiers	Hamelin	PRIVATE	Francois F.	Fisher Branch, MB	Sai Wan Cemetery
The Winnipeg Grenadiers	Harkness	PRIVATE	William	Winnipeg, MB	Sai Wan Cemetery
The Winnipeg Grenadiers	Harper	LIEUTENANT	George B.	Regina Beach, MB	Sai Wan Cemetery
The Winnipeg Grenadiers	Hawes	LANCE-CORPORAL	Malcolm J.	Selkirk, MB	Yokohama War Cemetery
The Winnipeg Grenadiers	Hawkes	PRIVATE	Douglas	St. Andrews, MB	Sai Wan Cemetery
The Winnipeg Grenadiers	Hendry	PRIVATE	David	West Kildonan, MB	Yokohama War Cemetery

Regiment	Last Name	Rank	First Name	Hometown	Cemetery Name
The Winnipeg Grenadiers	Heuft	PRIVATE	Ernest	Winnipeg, MB	Yokohama War Cemetery
The Winnipeg Grenadiers	Holmstrom	PRIVATE	Stuart	Onanole, MB	Sai Wan Cemetery
The Winnipeg Grenadiers	Hook	MAJOR	Henry W.	Winnipeg, MB	Sai Wan Cemetery
The Winnipeg Grenadiers	Howard	PRIVATE	Harry S.	Swan River, MB	Sai Wan Cemetery
The Winnipeg Grenadiers	Hull	PRIVATE	Herbert J.	Fort Garry, MB	Yokohama War Cemetery
The Winnipeg Grenadiers	Hunter	CORPORAL	Stanley H.	Meadows, MB	Yokohama War Cemetery
The Winnipeg Grenadiers	Iles	PRIVATE	Percy J.	Arrow River, MB	Sai Wan Cemetery
The Winnipeg Grenadiers	Irwin	PRIVATE	Roy R.	Melita, MB	Yokohama War Cemetery
The Winnipeg Grenadiers	Iverach	CORPORAL	John A.	Isabella, MB	Sai Wan Cemetery
The Winnipeg Grenadiers	Johnson	PRIVATE	Edward T.	Otterburn, MB	Yokohama War Cemetery
The Winnipeg Grenadiers	Johnston	PRIVATE	David	Letellier, MB	Sai Wan Cemetery
The Winnipeg Grenadiers	Jones	PRIVATE	Harold B.	Winnipeg, MB	Yokohama War Cemetery
The Winnipeg Grenadiers	Kirk	PRIVATE	Roy L.	Riding Mountain, MB	Yokohama War Cemetery
The Winnipeg Grenadiers	Kitteringham	PRIVATE	John H.	Gladstone, MB	Yokohama War Cemetery
The Winnipeg Grenadiers	Laplante	PRIVATE	Gabriel D.	Shortdale, MB	Sai Wan Cemetery
The Winnipeg Grenadiers	Laplante	PRIVATE	Roman J.	Marchand, MB	Sai Wan Cemetery
The Winnipeg Grenadiers	Lariviere	PRIVATE	Ernest	St. Vital, MB	Sai Wan Cemetery
The Winnipeg Grenadiers	Lavallee	PRIVATE	Ernest	St. Laurent, MB	Yokohama War Cemetery
The Winnipeg Grenadiers	Lavarie	PRIVATE	Cecil F.	Winnipeg, MB	Yokohama War Cemetery
The Winnipeg Grenadiers	Lewis	PRIVATE	Joseph M.	Winnipeg, MB	Sai Wan Cemetery
The Winnipeg Grenadiers	Lovell	CORPORAL	Roy T.	La Rivière, MB	Yokohama War Cemetery
The Winnipeg Grenadiers	Lowe	CORPORAL	George A.	Winnipeg, MB	Yokohama War Cemetery
The Winnipeg Grenadiers	Lucas	PRIVATE	Harold F.	Barford, SK	Sai Wan Cemetery
The Winnipeg Grenadiers	Mabb	PRIVATE	Herbert H.	Fisher Branch, MB	Sai Wan Cemetery
The Winnipeg Grenadiers	Mannell	PRIVATE	John W.	Winnipeg, MB	Sai Wan Cemetery

Regiment	Last Name	Rank	First Name	Hometown	Cemetery Name
The Winnipeg Grenadiers	Marsh	PRIVATE	Clifford J.	Fort Francis, ON	Yokohama War Cemetery
The Winnipeg Grenadiers	Matthews	PRIVATE	Norman C.	Winnipeg, MB	Yokohama War Cemetery
The Winnipeg Grenadiers	McGinnis	PRIVATE	William J.	Nokomis, SK	Yokohama War Cemetery
The Winnipeg Grenadiers	McLaughlin	PRIVATE	George R.	Hamiota, MB	Yokohama War Cemetery
The Winnipeg Grenadiers	McLellan	PRIVATE	Earl J.	East Kildonan, MB	Yokohama War Cemetery
The Winnipeg Grenadiers	McLeod	PRIVATE	Robert	Winnipeg, MB	Yokohama War Cemetery
The Winnipeg Grenadiers	McTaggart	LANCE-CORPORAL	Hugh P.	Portage la Prairie, MB	Yokohama War Cemetery
The Winnipeg Grenadiers	Moffatt	PRIVATE	John A.	Norwood, MB	Sai Wan Cemetery
The Winnipeg Grenadiers	Moore	PRIVATE	Bertrand C.	Winnipeg, MB	Yokohama War Cemetery
The Winnipeg Grenadiers	Moore	PRIVATE	Douglas H.	Elgin, MB	Sai Wan Cemetery
The Winnipeg Grenadiers	Moore	PRIVATE	Wilfred S.	Winnipeg, MB	Sai Wan Cemetery
The Winnipeg Grenadiers	Neufeld	PRIVATE	Benjamin	Morris, MB	Yokohama War Cemetery
The Winnipeg Grenadiers	Nichol	LANCE-CORPORAL	David S.	Darlingford, MB	Sai Wan Cemetery
The Winnipeg Grenadiers	Oige	PRIVATE	Joseph H.	Selkirk, MB	Sai Wan Cemetery
The Winnipeg Grenadiers	Olafson	PRIVATE	Budvar P.	Portage la Prairie, MB	Yokohama War Cemetery
The Winnipeg Grenadiers	Panco	PRIVATE	Michael	Winnipeg, MB	Yokohama War Cemetery
The Winnipeg Grenadiers	Pastuck	PRIVATE	Nicholas	Sleeman, ON	Sai Wan Cemetery
The Winnipeg Grenadiers	Paul	PRIVATE	Ernest J.	Carman, MB	Yokohama War Cemetery
The Winnipeg Grenadiers	Payne	SERGEANT	John O.	St. Vital, MB	Sai Wan Cemetery
The Winnipeg Grenadiers	Pearson	PRIVATE	Douglas E.	Austin, MB	Sai Wan Cemetery
The Winnipeg Grenadiers	Pott	PRIVATE	Norman A.	Birch River, MB	Yokohama War Cemetery
The Winnipeg Grenadiers	Proulx	PRIVATE	Ernest	Ste. Anne	Yokohama War Cemetery
The Winnipeg Grenadiers	Raites	PRIVATE	Edward	Winnipeg, MB	Sai Wan Cemetery
The Winnipeg Grenadiers	Rees	PRIVATE	Ralph C.	McAuley, MB	Yokohama War Cemetery
The Winnipeg Grenadiers	Robertson	PRIVATE	Gilbert A.	Winnipeg, MB	Yokohama War Cemetery

Regiment	Last Name	Rank	First Name	Hometown	Cemetery Name
The Winnipeg Grenadiers	Robidoux	PRIVATE	Marcel E.	Headingly, MB	Sai Wan Cemetery
The Winnipeg Grenadiers	Robinson	PRIVATE	Henry	Vancouver, BC	Sai Wan Cemetery
The Winnipeg Grenadiers	Rodd	PRIVATE	Orville W.	Winnipeg, MB	Sai Wan Cemetery
The Winnipeg Grenadiers	Rousell	PRIVATE	Leo	Brachois, QC	Yokohama War Cemetery
The Winnipeg Grenadiers	Rutherford	LANCE-SERGEANT	Archibald R.	Winnipeg, MB	Yokohama War Cemetery
The Winnipeg Grenadiers	Samson	PRIVATE	Albert J.	Piney, MB	Sai Wan Cemetery
The Winnipeg Grenadiers	Sayers	PRIVATE	George W.	Battleford, SK	Sai Wan Cemetery
The Winnipeg Grenadiers	Shayler	PRIVATE	Harry A.	St. Vital, MB	Yokohama War Cemetery
The Winnipeg Grenadiers	Singleton	LANCE-CORPORAL	Benjamin W.	Eden, MB	Sai Wan Cemetery
The Winnipeg Grenadiers	Sioux	PRIVATE	Anthony J.	St. Laurent, MB	Sai Wan Cemetery
The Winnipeg Grenadiers	Skene	PRIVATE	William J.	Grand Marais, MB	Yokohama War Cemetery
The Winnipeg Grenadiers	Smith	PRIVATE	John S.	Elmwood, MB	Sai Wan Cemetery
The Winnipeg Grenadiers	Smith	PRIVATE	William A.	Swan River, MB	Sai Wan Cemetery
The Winnipeg Grenadiers	Smith	PRIVATE	Victor G.	Inwood, MB	Yokohama War Cemetery
The Winnipeg Grenadiers	Sokalski	PRIVATE	George	Winnipeg, MB	Sai Wan Cemetery
The Winnipeg Grenadiers	Stodgell	PRIVATE	Garnett J.	Fisher Branch, MB	Sai Wan Cemetery
The Winnipeg Grenadiers	Sumner	PRIVATE	William J.	Winnipeg, MB	Sai Wan Cemetery
The Winnipeg Grenadiers	Sutcliffe	LIEUTENANT COLONEL	John L.	Fort Garry, MB	Sai Wan Cemetery
The Winnipeg Grenadiers	Thomas	PRIVATE	Clifford	Traverse Bay, MB	Sai Wan Cemetery
The Winnipeg Grenadiers	Thomasson	PRIVATE	Thomas	Baldur, MB	Sai Wan Cemetery
The Winnipeg Grenadiers	Till	PRIVATE	Earl B.	Minitonas, MB	Sai Wan Cemetery
The Winnipeg Grenadiers	Townsend	CORPORAL	George H.	Mapletown, MB	Yokohama War Cemetery
The Winnipeg Grenadiers	Watson	PRIVATE	Richard H.	Vantage, SK	Yokohama War Cemetery
The Winnipeg Grenadiers	Webster	CORPORAL	Robert W.	Winnipeg, MB	Yokohama War Cemetery
The Winnipeg Grenadiers	Whillier	PRIVATE	Walter C.	Brandon, MB	Sai Wan Cemetery

Regiment	Last Name	Rank	First Name	Hometown	Cemetery Name
The Winnipeg Grenadiers	Whitbread	PRIVATE	Sydney G.	Tisdale, SK	Sai Wan Cemetery
The Winnipeg Grenadiers	Woodward	PRIVATE	Cyril S.	St. Vital, MB	Yokohama War Cemetery
The Winnipeg Grenadiers	Young	PRIVATE	Lewis E.	Winnipeg, MB	Yokohama War Cemetery
The Winnipeg Grenadiers	Zedan	PRIVATE	Michael	Alonsa, MB	Yokohama War Cemetery

I thank Vince Lopata for graciously providing me with these lists of Canadian heroes.

Notes

Preface

1   I have not dealt with the decision of the Canadian government to intern Japanese Canadians. The mental anguish, family dislocation and loss of property suffered by these Canadians (and by Americans of Japanese origin) are to be regretted. In September 1988, Prime Minister Brian Mulroney officially apologized for the internment and announced a compensation package.

Introduction

1   Bix, 199.
2   Quoted in Donaghy and Roy, 84.
    "Japan may have been warlike, but at present we do not see any reason why she should not be one of the great factors in preserving the peace of the world. She must have room for expansion."
3   Quoted in Donaghy and Roy, 87.
4   Quoted in Vincent, 9.
5   Churchill, quoted in Vincent, 11.
6   Quoted in Vincent, 20.
7   Quoted in Dickson, 102.
8   Quoted in Vincent, 26.
9   Quoted in Vincent, 29.
10 Scott, F.R., "W.L.M.K.," accessed from www.library.utoronto.ca/canpoetry/scott_fr/poem5.htm.
11 Quoted in Vincent, 44.
12 Quoted in Vincent, 46.
13 Verreault, 1 November 1941.
14 Quoted in Vincent, 121.
15 Quoted in Bix, 433.
16 Quoted in Ferguson, 32.

Chapter 1

1   Lindsay, *Battle for Hong Kong*, 62f.

Chapter 2

1   Quoted in Ferguson, 54.
2   Quoted in Ferguson, 53.
3   Proulx, 23.
4   Quoted in Muir, 92.
5   Quoted in Lindsay, *Battle*, 75.
6   Muir, 102.

Chapter 3

1   Quoted in Lindsay *Lasting Honour*, 50. 26
2   Allister, 19.
3   Proulx, 24.
4   Quoted in Banham, *Slightest Chance*, 344, note 67. The inquest found that the disin-
       tegration of the Scots' line led to the collapse of "the whole defence of the mainland."
5   Second Lieutenant J.A. Ford quoted in Lindsay, *Battle*, 78.
6   Quoted in Lindsay, *Honour*, 50.

Chapter 4

1   Dew, 51f.
2   Quoted in Lindsay, *Honour*, 64.
3   Dew, 53.
4   Second Lieutenant J.A. Ford quoted in Lindsay, *Battle*, 95.
5   Wenzell Brown quoted in Banham, *Slightest Chance*, 101.
6   Proulx, 29-31.

Chapter 5

1   Colonel Noonan quoted in Ferguson, 140
2   Quoted in Lindsay, *Honour*, 86
3   Maltby, *Draft*, 5.
4   E-mail to author.
5   Quoted in Dower, 26.
6   Quoted in Warren, 50.

Chapter 6

1   Allister, 9, 25.

2   Allister, 27.

3   Ishikawa.

4   Hynes, 22.

5   Wallis's vituperative language about Bishop's withdrawal is hard to square with the fact that he nominated Bishop for a Distinguished Service Order for directing the withdrawal and Company Quartermaster-Sergeant Colin Standish for a Distinguished Service Medal for his role in it. The citation that accompanied Bishop's award praises "His skilful retreat when heavily outnumbered had saved the situation from turning into a complete disaster. He personally covered the retirement and his courage, skill and devotion to duty so inspired his men that they were able to cope with enormously superior forces until the reinforcements came."

6   Quoted in Tim Carew, 130f.

7   Allister, 27f.

8   Ferguson, 130.

Chapter 7

1   Report No. 163, entitled "Canadian Participation in the Defence of Hong Kong: December 1941," prepared in the late 1940s by the Historical Section of the Department of National Defence, states (paragraph 159): "Reports of the subsequent action are somewhat confused. It appears that part of 'A' Coy pushed right through to Mount Butler, and captured the top of the hill soon after first light, which was 0700. The position was held for two or three hours, when a heavy enemy counterattack forced a retirement towards Jardine's Lookout and Wong Nei Chong."

Oliver Lindsay endorses this view. Based on his reading of the Winnipeg Grenadier's War Diary written by Major George Trist and the testimony of Corporal Keith Geddes, Sergeant William Pugsley and Private Harry Atkinson, Vince Lopata, who is writing a regimental history of the Grenadiers, agrees.

Tony Banham disagrees. In several emails to me, he has made the following arguments. First, there is no archaeological evidence for the Canadians having been on Mount Butler. Second, in order to reach the mountain, Gresham's men would have had to pass through Lieutenant Charles French's No. 5 Platoon, which was then in the cul between Mount Butler and Jardine's Lookout. (French's platoon was destroyed sometime after 7:00 a.m. French was wounded covering the retreat and, after avoiding capture for several hours, was killed by a Japanese patrol near 9:00 a.m.)

Third, Banham cites Atkinson, who on a tour of the battlefield identified a place on Jardine's Lookout as being where he fought. Fourth, the topography described in Pugsley's report fits better with Jardine's Lookout than it does Mount Butler.

To make matters even more complicated, Atkinson's memoir says that he was on Mount Butler. Japanese records offer little help.

Determining exactly where Gresham's men fought their desperate battle is impossible. If they did fight on Jardine's Lookout, they had to be far enough away from Birkett's men that they did not clash. If they reached Mount Butler, then we must assume that they missed seeing French's platoon.

For the reader's sake, I have refrained from placing "scare quotes" around the references to Mount Butler here. But keep in mind that the actions described here may have occurred a thousand or so yards to the west. While the exact location of where Gresham's men fought is in doubt, we know much about what happened to these Canadians 1,400 feet above the South China Sea.

2   Ferguson, 145f.

3   Quoted in Lindsay, *Honour*, 87.

4   Ishikawa.

5   Allister, 28.

6   Ferguson, 161.

7   There is some debate about exactly when Bowman attacked and when he died. Chaplain Laite's and Major Trist's (post war) reports give different times.

8   Quoted in Greenhous, 86.

9   Stacey, 481.

10   Carew, 136.

11   Ferguson, 164.

Chapter 8

1   Garneau, 267f.

2   On 29 December 1941, the *Hong Kong News* estimated that the Japanese suffered almost 8,000 casualties, 2,000 of whom were men killed in action. Other estimates run from 675 to 7,000 killed in action, while the number of wounded is put at 7,000 to 20,000. Historian Tony Banham, who lives in Hong Kong, suggests that the number of Japanese casualties was approximately 13,000, or 60 percent of the 20,000 committed to battle. The Japanese cremated their dead. The regiments that attacked Hong Kong were destroyed at Guadalcanal in 1942/43 (quoted in Banham, *Slightest Chance*, 318).

3   Quoted in Muir, 117.

4   Basing his argument on the fact that there is no archaeological evidence for this action, Tony Banham contends that Hodkinson could not have surprised the Japanese here. As with the debate about whether Gresham's men were on Jardine's Lookout or Mount Butler, in effect this is a distinction without a difference. Mistaking one hill for another in Hong Kong may cause historians to fret, but what is important is that this Grenadier detachment destroyed a Japanese force.

5   Allister, 29f.

6   Allister, 37f.

Chapter 9

1   Quoted in Vincent, 225. Carew's characterization of the Canadians is based on Malt-
     by's "Operations in Hong Kong from 8th to 25th December, 1941" report published
     the *London Gazette* (and thus in the semi-official history of the battle), which itself
     echoes many of Wallis's egregious statements. Maltby wrote: "These two [Canadian]
     battalions proved to be inadequately trained for modern war. Though possessing
     first class material, this lack of training rendered them incapable of fire and move-
     ment and consequently when launched in many local counter-attacks (and it was on
     these counter-attacks that the defence of the island depended) they suffered heavily
     and accomplished little." This report, it is worth noting, was toned down in the ma-
     jor general's final report after an intervention by Field Marshal Bernard Montgom-
     ery made at the behest of the Canadian government.
2   Quoted in Ferguson, 178.
3   Proulx, 45–51.
4   Quoted in Garneau, 267.
5   Proulx, 56.
6   Proulx, 60.

Chapter 10

1   Major Young's recce patrol left the Repulse Bay Hotel near 7:30 a.m. on orders of
     General Maltby. All that is certain is that the order was prompted by a call from
     British Major C.M. Manners. There are two versions of what Manners said and what
     Maltby thought. In the first draft of his report, after saying that the major had called,
     Maltby wrote, "He said the Canadians are doing nothing, the defences appeared to
     be quite inadequate, and the Officer Commanding Coy [Young] was the worse for
     drink. With the women and children in the Hotel helpless, he viewed the situation
     with extreme pessimism." Canadian officials, including Hume Wrong, the Acting
     Under Secretary for External Affairs, objected to this (and other) statements. With
     the help of Field Marshal Bernard Montgomery, who had his own rocky relationship
     with Canadians under his command, this (and other offending) sections were either
     excised or significantly altered.
        Thus, in the version published in the *London Gazette* in 1948, Maltby wrote, "He
     [Manners] said the defences appeared to be quite inadequate, and with women and
     children in the Hotel helpless, he viewed the situation with extreme pessimism." As for
     Maltby's own thoughts about Major Young, who earned a Distinguished Service Order
     in the First World War, in his original report he wrote, "At 0725 hours Major Young at
     Repulse Bay Hotel was ordered to organize two strong patrols, recce Westwards from
     the Hotel and clear up the situation at the junction of Island Road [position] 593942
     with the road to [Little] Hong Kong where some troops were coming down from The

Ridge Advanced Ordinance Depot had been ambushed over-night. Major Young *appeared to understand the orders*" (emphasis added). The published version leaves out the position number and the charge of drunkenness against Major Young.

2　Proulx, 67f.

3　Cambon, 21.

4　Cambon, 22.

5　Two other veterans dispute this, saying Murphy was shot. I have included Mac-Whirter's version in order to give an indication of the type of enemy these young Canadians faced.

6　Banham suggests this occurred on 22 December.

Chapter 11

1　Cambon, 24f. Cambon records the machine gunner's statement as, "What the hell have you stupid s.o.b.s been?" but then adds that this is a cleaned-up version of the soldier's language that was filled with expletives, which, warrants, I believe, my interpolation. I have rendered the Middlesex machine gunner's words as they likely were.

2　Marsman, 67.

3　Quoted in Garneau, 81.

4　Cambon, 29.

5　Proulx, 87–90.

6　Marsman, 72.

7　Quoted in Lindsay, *Honour*, 120.

Chapter 12

1　Verreault, 43

2　Marsman, 80f.

Chapter 13

1　Garneau, 162

2　Quoted in Banham, *Slightest Chance*, 236.

3　Proulx, 115

4　Marsman, 96, 98.

5　Quoted in Banham, *Slightest Chance*, 242.

Chapter 14

1　MacDonell, 82.

2　MacDonell, 82.

3　MacDonell, 82.

4 Quoted in Luff, *Hidden Years,* 125.

5 Quoted in Lindsay, *Honour,* 151.

Chapter 15

1 The *Regina Leader Post*'s headline read "HONG KONG OVERCOME: Glorious Canadian Chapter: 101 Saskatchewan Men."

  The loss of the Winnipeg Grenadiers was, of course, of major concern to the *Winnipeg Free Press* and *Winnipeg Tribune,* both of which ran a number of articles through the second week of January.

2 Quoted in Craddock, 88.

3 Allister, 49.

4 Allister, 50.

5 Quoted in Garneau, 99f.

  Cholera, which can kill in just a few hours, however, was another matter. It terrified the Japanese, who protected their soldiers with shots every six months and boosters every three. In late February, the POWs were inoculated against the disease.

6 Allister, 76f.

7 Allister, 60.

8 Verreault, 65.

9 MacArthur, 177.

10 Daws, 139.

11 Allister, 53.

12 Quoted in Banham, *Suffer,* 31.

Chapter 16

1 Quoted in Banham, *Suffer,* 45.

2 Allister, 152.

3 Garneau, 103.

4 Allister, 73. Choosing whom to send was, Captain John Reid told a post war interview, a horrific exercise in playing God. "We graded the men, a, b, c, d, and e, and it was just a matter of starting at the top and getting enough for the work party and a lot of sick men had to go to work."

5 Quoted in MacDonell, 99f.

6 Quoted in Garneau, 105.

7 Quoted in Roland, 122.

8 Daws, 88.

9 Allister, 76.

10 Daws, 88.

11 Verreault, 89.

12 Allister, 86.

13   *The Canadian Medical Association Journal*, 1947, 594.

14   For an interesting discussion of the difference between how POWs (stoically) viewed bombings and how the bombings enraged camp guards, see Grossman, 56–60.

15   Quoted in Garneau, 115.

16   Quoted in McIntosh, 52.

17   Allister, 75.

18   Baird, 141, 143.

19   Allister, 86.

Chapter 17

1   On 25 September 1942, 1,816 British POWs boarded the *Lisbon Maru* bound for Japan. Early on the morning of 1 October, the U.S. submarine *Grouper* torpedoed what its captain thought was a Japanese freighter being used as a troop ship. As the ship's crew struggled to keep the ship afloat, the Japanese tied over the hatches that led to the holds holding the POWs. Later in the day, a destroyer and another freighter evacuated some 750 Japanese soldiers. Sick with dysentery and diarrhea, the POWs manned pumps. At one point, the Japanese lowered a bucket of liquid to the exhausted POWs; it was filled with urine.

    Near dawn on 2 October, when it became clear that the *Lisbon Maru* was going to sink, some POWs broke out of the hold. The Japanese on deck opened fire, killing one man. Shortly after the POWs retreated to the hold, the sinking ship hit a sandbar. Another group of POWs then broke out. As the water rushed into the hold via an open porthole and some of their comrades drowned, discipline held and the Royal Scots climbed on deck in an orderly fashion.

    They jumped into the water. Some swam toward a nearby island, others toward four small Japanese ships. As they reached the rope ladders dangling from these ships, Japanese sailors kicked at the British and stepped on their fingers, preventing them from climbing aboard the ships. Several nearby junks picked up the men they could. About 200 POWs made it to the nearby islands, where they were sheltered by Chinese villagers until the Japanese came to pick them up. More than 840 POWs drowned or were shot to death.

2   Allister, 93.

3   Cambon, 56.

4   Quoted in MacDonell, 112.

5   Allister 99, 102.

6   Verreault, 115.

7   Quoted in McIntosh, 152.

8   Quoted in Baird, 175.

9   Allister, 123.

10   Allister, 137f.

The behaviour Allister describes is consistent with "starvation neurosis" (Jackson, 110), which can occur when an individual loses 25 percent of his or her body weight due to lack of food.

11   Allister, 139.
12   Allister, 124.
13   Allister, 143.

Chapter 18

1   Verreault, 126.
2   Allister, 154.
3   MacDonell, 110.
4   Roland, 229.
5   Baird, 220.
6   Allister, 168.
7   Cambon, 78f.

Chapter 19

1   Cosway, 62.
2   Quoted in Banham, *Suffer*, 200.
3   Allister, 177.
4   Verreault, 221.
5   Quoted in McIntosh, 158.
6   Baird, 226.
7   Allister, 197.
8   Cambon, 89f.
9   Baird, 256.
10   Cambon. This order accords with one from Borneo that divided internees into groups and indicated how each was to be liquidated (www.mansell.com/pow_resources/ Formosa/date_set.html):
     "1. Women, children, nuns—to be given poisoned rice. 2. Internee men and Catholic fathers to be shot and burnt. 3. 500 British-American-Dutch and Australian POWs to be marched to the mountains to be shot and burnt. 4. The sick and weak left at Lintang Main Camp to be bayoneted and the entire camp destroyed by fire."
11   Cambon, 83.
12   MacDonell, 133.
13   MacDonell, 133.
14   MacDonell, 135.

Chapter 20

1   Cambon, 96f.
2   Allister, 224.
3   Allister, 225.
4   Allister, 230.
5   Ross's recognition of and sympathy for the plight of the Nagasakians should not be taken to mean that he or his comrades opposed the use of the atomic bombs. Though Ross died before I could interview him, from reading his diary, speaking to his daughter, Mitzi, and his comrades, I feel safe in saying that, as did most of his comrades, had Ross been given a choice, he would have voted to use the atomic bomb.

Was, as many revisionist historians claim, impressing the Russians part of the reason U.S. President Harry Truman chose to drop the bomb? Possibly. Would he have dropped it on Germany, another white, Christian country? Nothing I have seen suggests not, though it is plausible that doing so might have been more difficult given that wartime propaganda had not dehumanized the Germans to the extent it had the Japanese. (One must immediately add that American wartime propaganda was matched racial insult and racial stereotype by Japanese war time propaganda.)

Ross and his comrades were in a different position than the American president. There is no doubt that an invasion of the Home Islands would have resulted in their executions. There is no doubt that the dropping of the bombs obviated the need for such an invasion. To a man, the veterans of "C" Force I interviewed have, often with sorrow in the voices, said that the atomic bombings saved their lives.

6   The dates in what follows may not match several memories. The official records of who arrived when and on which ship are incomplete and scattered between different Canadian and American archives. What follows is largely based on Vince Lopata's spade work. I apologize in advance for any controversy that may ensue and trust that veterans and their families will find that while the actual dates may be in question, their stories and their loved ones' stories are correct.

7   USS *General W.C. Langfitt* reached Esquimalt on 3 October; USS *Admiral C.F. Hughes* did so on 9 October and USS *General R.L. Howse* on 15 October.

8   MacDonell, 156.
9   Allister, 236.
10   Allister, 238.
11   Colonel James E. Hunter, Assistant Director of Canadian Army Medical Services, quoted in McIntosh, 250.

Coda

1   Quoted in McIntosh, 177.

2   Quoted in McIntosh, 41.
3   Brode, 173.
4   Brode in quoted, 173.

Bibliography

Allister, William. *A Handful of Rice*. London: Secker and Warburg, 1961.

———. *Where Life and Death Hold Hands*. Toronto: Stoddart, 1989.

Baird, Major Kenneth G. *Letters to Harvelyn from Japanese POW Camps: A Father's Letters to His Young Daughter during World War II*. Toronto: HarperCollins, 2002.

Banham, Tony. *Not the Slightest Chance: The Defence of Hong Kong, 1941*. Vancouver: UBC Press, 2003.

———. *We Shall Suffer There: Hong Kong's Defenders Imprisoned, 1942–45*. Hong Kong: Hong Kong University Press, 2009.

Bayly, Christopher, and Tim Harper. *Forgotten Armies: Britain's Asian Empire and the War with Japan*. New York: Penguin, 2004.

Beauregard, Claude. *Guerre et censure au Canada, 1939–1945*. Silberry, Quebec: Septentrion, 1998.

Bell, Christopher M. "'Our Most Exposed Outpost': Hong Kong and British Far Eastern Strategy, 1921–1941." *The Journal of Military History*, Vol. 60 (Jan. 1996), 61–88.

Bercuson, David J. *Maple Leaf against the Axis: Canada's Second World War*. Toronto: Stoddart, 1995.

Bergerud, Eric. *Touched with Fire: The Land War in the South Pacific*. New York: Penguin, 1996.

Bess, Michael. *Choices under Fire: Moral Dimensions of World War II*. New York: Vintage, 2006.

Birch, Alan, and Martin Cole. *Captive Christmas: The Battle of Hong Kong—December 1942*. Hong Kong: Heinemann Asia, 1979.

Bix, Herbert P. *Hirohito and the Making of Modern Japan*. New York: HarperCollins, 2000.

Bosanquet, David. *Escape through China.* London: Robert Hale, 1983.

Bourke, Johanna. *An Intimate History of Killing.* London, Granta, 1999.

Bourrie, Mark. *The Fog of War: Canada's Media Censorship in World War II.* Toronto: Key Porter, 2010.

Brode, Patrick. *Casual Slaughter and Accidental Judgements: Canadian War Crimes Prosecutions, 1944–1948.* Toronto: Osgoode Hall, 1997.

Burke, Penny D. *Beyond the Call: Royal Canadian Corps of Signals Brigade Headquarters, "C" Force Hong Kong and Japan 1941–1945.* Ottawa: The Hong Kong Veterans Commemorative Association, 2009. (www.hkvca.ca)

Burton, John. *Fortnight of Infamy: The Collapse of Allied Airpower West of Pearl Harbor.* Annapolis, Maryland: The Naval Institute Press, 2006.

Bush, Lewis. *Clutch of Circumstance.* Tokyo: Okuyama, 1956.

Cambon, Kenneth. *Guest of Hirohito.* Vancouver: PW Press, 1990.

"Canadian Participation in the Defence of Hong Kong: December 1941." Historical Section, Canadian Military Headquarters, Report No. 163.

Carew, Tim. *The Fall of Hong Kong.* London: White Lion Publishers, 1960.

Castonguay, Bernard. *Prisonnier de guerre au Japon (1941–1945).* n.p. 2005.

Chang, Iris. *The Rape of Nanking.* New York: Penguin, 1997.

Chater, Les. *Behind the Fence: Life as a POW in Japan 1942–1045.* St. Catharines, Ontario: Vanwell, 2001.

Clarkson, Adrienne. *Heart Matters: A Memoir.* Toronto: Viking, 2006.

Clavell, James. *King Rat.* New York: Random House, 1962.

Cook, Haruko Taya, and Theodore F. Cook. *Japan at War: An Oral History.* New York: The New Press, 1992.

Copp, Terry. "The Defence of Hong Kong December 1941." *Canadian Military History,* Vol. 10, No. 4 (Autumn 2001), 5–20.

Corrigan, Family, and Lieutenant L.B. *A Hong Kong Diary Revisited.* Cobourg, Ontario: Frei Press, 2008.

Costello, John. *The Pacific War 1941–1945.* New York, Quill, 1981.

Cosway, W.A. (Navigator, RCAF). *Earthquake McGoon: A Memoir of the "Forgotten War" in South East Asia.* Victoria, B.C.: Trafford, 2006.

Craddock, John. *First Shot: The Untold Story of the Minisubs that Attacked Pearl Harbor.* New York: McGraw-Hill, 2006.

Crawford, J.N. "A Medical Officer in Hong Kong." *The Manitoba Medical Review,* Vol. 26, No. 2, (February 1946), 63–68.

———. "Men and Books: Barbed Wire Humour." *The Canadian Medical Association Journal,* Vol. 57 (1947), 593–596.

Dancocks, Daniel. *In Enemy Hands: Canadian Prisoners of War 1939–45.* Toronto: McClelland and Stewart, 1990.

Daws, Gavan. *Prisoners of the Japanese: POWs of World War II in the Pacific.* New York: William Morrow, 1994.

Dew, Gwen. *Prisoner of the Japs.* Toronto: Ryerson, 1943.

Dickson, Paul. "Crerar and the Decision to Garrison Hong Kong." *Canadian Military History,* Vol. 3, No. 1. (1994), 97–109.

Donaghy, Greg, and Patricia Roy, eds. *Contradictory Impulses: Canada and Japan in the Twentieth Century.* Vancouver: UBC Press, 2008.

Douglas, W.A.B., and Brereton Greenhous, eds. *Out of the Shadows: Canada in the Second World War.* 2nd Revised Edition. Toronto: Dundurn, 1995.

Dower, John W. *War Without Mercy: Race and Power in the Pacific War.* New York: Pantheon, 1986.

Ednacott, G.B. *Hong Kong Eclipse.* Oxford: Oxford University Press, 1978.

Farquharson, Robert H. *For Your Tomorrow: Canadians and the Burma Campaign 1941–1945.* Toronto: n.p., 2004.

Fedorowich, Kent. "'Cocked Hats and Swords and Small, Little Garrisons': Britain, Canada and the Fall of Hong Kong, 1941." *Modern Asian Studies,* Vol. 37, No. 1 (2003), 111–157.

Ferguson, Ted. *Desperate Siege: The Battle for Hong Kong.* Toronto: Doubleday Canada, 1980.

Fletcher-Cooke, John. *The Emperor's Guest 1942–45.* London: Leo Cooper, 1971.

Frank, Richard B. *Downfall: The End of the Imperial Japanese Empire.* New York: Penguin, 1999.

Garneau, Grant S. *The Royal Rifles of Canada in Hong Kong 1941–1945.* Ottawa: The Hong Kong Veterans Commemorative Association, 2001.

Gibney, Frank, ed. *Sens: The Japanese Remember the Pacific War*. Expanded Edition. London: M.E. Sharpe, 2007.

Gilbert, Adrian. *POW: Allied Prisoners in Europe 1939–1945*. London: John Murray, 2006.

Glusman, John A. *Conduct under Fire 1941–1945: Four American Doctors and Their Fight for Life as Prisoners of the Japanese*. New York: Penguin, 2005.

Goldstein, Donald M., and Katherine V. Dillon. *The Pacific War Papers: Japanese Documents of World War II*. Washington, D.C.: Potomac Books, 2006.

Granatstein, J. L. *Canada's Army: Waging War and Keeping the Peace*. Toronto: University of Toronto Press, 2002.

Granatstein, J. L., and Desmond Morton. *Canada and the Two World Wars*. Toronto: Key Porter, 2003.

Greenfield, Nathan M. *Baptism of Fire: The Second Battle of Ypres and the Forging of Canada, April 1915*. Toronto: HarperCollins, 2007.

Greenhous, Brereton. *"C" Force to Hong Kong: A Canadian Catastrophe 1941–1945*. Toronto: Dundurn, 1997.

Grossman, Lt. Col. Dave. *On Killing: The Psychological Cost of Learning to Kill in War and Society*. Revised Ed. Boston: Little, Brown and Co., 2009.

Guest, Captain Freddie. *Escape from the Bloodied Sun*. London: Jarrold, 1956.

Hastings, Max. *Nemesis: The Battle for Japan, 1944–45*. New York: HarperCollins, 2007.

Holmes, Richard. *Acts of War: The Behavior of Men in Battle*. New York: The Free Press, 1985.

Hoyt, Edwin P. *Japan's War: The Great Pacific Conflict*. New York: Cooper Square Press, 2001.

Hynes, Samuel. *The Soldier's Tale: Bearing Witness to Modern War*. London: Penguin, 1997.

Jackson, Joe: *A Furnace Afloat: The Wreck of the Hornet and the 4,300-Mile Voyage of Its Survivors*. London: Phoenix, 2004.

Jenson, Kurt F. *Cautious Beginnings: Canadian Foreign Intelligence 1939–1951*. Vancouver: UBC Press, 2008.

Kakehashi, Kumiko. *So Sad to Fall in Battle: An Account of War Based on General Tadamichi Kuribayashi's Letters from Iwo Jima*. New York: Ballantine Books, 2007.

Keegen, John. *The Face of Battle.* New York: Viking, 1976.

Kuribayashi, Tadamichi (ed. Tsuyuko Yoshida). *Picture Letters from the Commander in Chief.* San Francisco: VIZ Media, 2007.

Lindsay, Oliver. *The Battle for Hong Kong 1941–1945 : Hostage to Fortune.* Montreal: McGill-Queen's University Press, 2005.

———. *The Lasting Honour: The Fall of Hong Kong 1941.* London: Sphere Books, 1980.

Lopata, Vince. *History of the Winnipeg Grenadiers, "Y" and "C" Force, World War II.* Forthcoming; a copy is in possession of the author.

Luff, John. *The Hidden Years.* Hong Kong: South China Morning Post, 1967.

———. *Hong Kong Cavalcade.* Hong Kong: South China Morning Post, 1968.

MacArthur, Brian. *Surviving the Sword: Prisoners of the Japanese 1942–45.* London: Abacus, 2005.

MacDonell, George S. *One Soldier's Story 1939–1945: From the Fall of Hong Kong to the Defeat of Japan.* Toronto: Dundurn, 2002.

Maltby, General Cedric. "Operations in Hong Kong from 8th to 25th December, 1941." Supplement to the *London Gazette,* 20 January 1948.

———. Draft for "Operations in Hong Kong from 8th to 25th December, 1941," D-Hist, 93/75.

Marsman, Jan Henrik. *I Escaped from Hong Kong.* New York: Reynal & Hitchcock, 1942.

Marston, Daniel, ed. *The Pacific War Companion: From Pearl Harbor to Hiroshima.* New York: Osprey, 2005.

McGuire, C.R. "The Postal History of Canada's World War II Hong Kong Field Force." *Stampex Canada.* The Royal Philatelic Society of Canada, July 2, 1982, n.p.

McIntosh, Dave. *Hell on Earth: Aging Faster, Dying Sooner: Canadian Prisoners of War of the Japanese during World War II.* Toronto: McGraw-Hill Ryerson, 1997.

Melnyk, T.W. *Canadian Flying Operations in South East Asia 1941–1945.* Ottawa: Ministry of Supply and Services Canada, 1976.

Michno, Gregory F. *Death on the Hellships: Prisoners at Sea in the Pacific War.* Annapolis, Maryland: Naval Institute Press, 2001.

Miller, Robert W. "War Crimes Trials at Yokohama." *Brooklyn Law Review,* Vol. XV, No. 2 (April 1949), 191–209.

Muir, Augustus. *The First of Foot: The History of the Royal Scots (The Royal Regiment).* Edinburgh: The Royal Scots History Committee, 1961.

Nitobe, Inazo. *Bushido: The Soul of Japan: A Classic Essay on Samurai Ethics* (1905). Rpt. New York: Kodansha International, 2002.

Philips, Richard. *Prison Doctor: An Account of a Royal Air Force Medical Officer during the Japanese Occupation of Indonesia, 1942–1945.* Sussex, England: The Book Guild, 1996.

Proulx, Benjamin A. *Underground from Hong Kong.* New York: E.P. Dutton and Co, 1943.

Roland, Charles G. *Long Night's Journey into Day: Prisoners of War in Hong Kong and Japan, 1941–1945.* Waterloo, Ontario: Wilfrid Laurier University Press, 2001.

Rottman, Gordon L. *Japanese Army in World War II: Conquest of the Pacific, 1941–42.* New York: Osprey, 2005.

———. *Japanese Army in World War II: The South Pacific and New Guinea, 1942–43.* New York: Osprey, 2005.

———. *Japanese Infantryman 1937–45.* New York: Osprey, 2005.

Roy, Patricia E., et al. *Mutual Hostages: Canadians and Japanese during the Second World War.* Toronto: University of Toronto Press, 1990.

Russell, Lord. *The Knights of Bushido: A Short History of Japanese War Crimes.* London: Cassell, 1958.

Schom, Alan. *The Eagle and the Rising Sun: The Japanese–American War 1941–1943.* New York: W.W. Norton & Co., 2004.

Skvorzov, Lieutenant A.V. *Hong Kong Prisoners of War Camp Life: 25 December, 1941–30 August, 1945.* SCMP Books, n.d.

Snow, Philip. *The Fall of Hong Kong: Britain, China and the Japanese Occupation.* New Haven: Yale University Press, 2003.

Soper, Roland. *Sword of Wood.* Toronto: Balsam House, 1993.

Stacey, Colonel C.P. *Six Years of War: The Army in Canada, Britain and the Pacific.* Ottawa: Queen's Printer, 1966.

Stacey, General C.P. *Arms, Men and Governments: The War Policies of Canada 1935–1945.* Ottawa, Queen's Printer, 1970.

Stanton, John. "Reluctant Vengeance: Canada and the Tokyo War Crimes Tribunal." *Journal of American and Canadian Studies,* 17 (1999), accessed through www.info. sophia.ac.jp/amecana/Journal/17–4.htm

Stewart, Major Evan. *A Record of the Actions of the Hong Kong Volunteer Defence Corps.* Hong Kong: Ye Olde Printerie, 1953.

Tamayam, Kazuo, and John Nunneley. *Tales by Japanese Soldiers.* London: Cassell, 1992.

Toland, John. *The Rising Sun: The Decline and Fall of the Japanese Empire, 1936–1945.* New York: Random House, 1970.

Toman, Cynthia. *An Officer and a Lady: Canadian Military Nursing and the Second World War.* Vancouver: UBC Press, 2008.

Vance, Jonathan F. *Objects of Concern: Canadian Prisoners of War through the Twentieth Century.* Vancouver: UBC Press, 1994.

Verreault, Georges "Blacky." *Diary of a Prisoner of War in Japan 1941–1945.* Rimouski, Quebec: Vero, 1995.

Veterans Affairs Canada. *Canadians in Hong Kong.* Ottawa: Veterans Affairs Canada, 2005.

Vincent, Carl. *No Reason Why: The Canadian Hong Kong Tragedy—An Examination.* Stittsville, Ontario: Canada's Wings, 1981.

Wai-Chung, Lawrence Lai. "The Battle of Hong Kong: A Note on the Literature and the Effectiveness of the Defence." *The Journal of the Hong Kong Branch of the Royal Asiatic Society,* Vol. 39 (1999), 115–136.

War History Office. Strategy on Hong Kong/Chang Sha (1941) Vol. 47, *Senshi Sosho* (*War History Series*). Tokyo: Asagumo News Bureau, 1971.

Warner, Philip. *Japanese Army of World War II.* New York: Osprey, 1973.

Warren, Alan. *Britain's Greatest Defeat: Singapore, 1942.* London: Hambledon Continuum, 2002.

Webster, Donovan. *The Burma Road: The Epic Story of the China–Burma–India Theater in World War II.* New York: HarperCollins, 2003.

Canadian Online Memoirs

The following memoirs can be found at the website of the Hong Kong Veterans Commemorative Association (www.hkvca.ca):

Atkinson, Henry

Babin, Alfred

Bell, William

Cadoret, Bruce

Christensen, Frank

Chistie, Kay

Deloughery, Father Francis

Doddridge, Phil

Fotsythe, Tom

James, John

Laite, Padre Uriah

Marsh, Tom

Parker, Maurice

Peterson, George

Shayler, Ed

Trick, Charles

Wilson, Dick

Unpublished Memoirs/Diaries/Interviews in Possession of the Author

Allister, William :	Interview with the author
Barter, Bob:	Interview with the author
Clayton, Flash:	Interview with the author
Dallain, Jean-Paul:	Memoir/Interview with the author
Doddridge, Phil:	Interview with the author
Duguay, John:	Interview with the author
Hallada, George:	Interview with the author
Lyons, Henry:	Interview with the author
MacDonell, George:	Interview with the author

MacWhiter, Bill:	Diary/Interview with the author
Maloney, Eric:	Interview with the author
Ross, Lance:	Diary
Shayler, Ed:	Interview with the author
Stroud, Johnny:	Interview with the author

Canadian War Diaries and Postwar Reports in Archival Collections

Department of National Defence, History Secretariat

Barnett, Honorary Captain James (Anglican Chaplain)

Bush, Captain Howard

Canivet, Private Leslie

Corrigan, Lieutenant William

Deloughery, Honorary Captain Francis (Roman Catholic Chaplain)

Galbraith, Private Nelson

Lawson, Brigadier-General Lawson, diary

Myatt, Sergeant Victor

Poy, William (Adrienne Clarkson's father)

Proulx, Lieutenant Benjamin

Reid, Captain John, M.D.

Russell, Stretcher-Bearer John

Skelton, Private Sydney

Winnipeg Grenadiers, War Diary

Library and Archives Canada

Bush, Captain Howard

Callahan, Mrs. Jean (correspondence)

Clark, Colonel

Doucet, Mrs. M. (correspondence with Norman Robertson)

Kanao Inouye (Kamloops Kid), War Crimes Trial Documents

Home, Colonel William, War Diary

History of the Japanese 38th Division

Langueduc, Private Donald

Pugsley, William

Royal Rifles, War Diary

Thomas, Mrs. E. R. (correspondence)

Thomson, Lieutenant J.

Wilson, Mrs. Charles

Young, Major Charles

War Museum Archives

Martyn, Corporal Francis

White, Lieutenant Harry (Winnipeg Grenadiers)

JAPANESE MEMOIRS

Ishikawa, Sakae. "Memoir of an Infantry Gunner." Jugun no Omoide. Jugun Kaikoroku
   Kankokai, Gifu, 1974, n.p.

Kubo, Yoshiaki. "Memoir of a Bomber Pilot." 97 Shiki Jubakugekitai Kusenki. Tokyo:
   Kojinsha, 1997.

Nakamura, Susumu. "Memoirs of an Infantryman, 230th Infantry Regiment." Jugun
   no Omoide. Jugun Kaikoroku Kankokai, Gifu, 1974, n.p.

Shimoda, Iwao. "Memoir of an Artilleryman." Gairo wo hanemawatta kyodan.
   Ichiokunin no Showashi—Nihon no Senshi 7—Taiheiyo Senso 1, *Mainichi
   Newspapers,* 1978, n.p.

Taki, Soichi (Munekazu/Muneichi). "Memoirs of an Infantryman, 230th Infantry
   Regiment." Jugun no Omoide. Jugun Kaikoroku Kankokai, Gifu, 1974, n.p.

Photo Credits

1. Courtesy of Bill MacWhirter
2. Courtesy of Jean-Paul Dallain
3. Courtesy of Library and Archives Canada/PA37483
4. Courtesy of Library and Archives Canada/PA116459
5. Courtesy of Library and Archives Canada/PA116457
6. Courtesy of Library and Archives Canada/PA116456
7. *Hong Kong Prisoner of War Camp Life, 25 December, 1941 – 30 August, 1945,* drawings by Lieut. A.V. Skvorzov. Hong Kong: SCMP Book Publishing Limited, 2005.
8. Courtesy of Library and Archives Canada/PA37419
9. Courtesy of Library and Archives Canada/PA114878
10. Courtesy of Library and Archives Canada/PMR-79-166/e010789741
11. Courtesy of Library and Archives Canada/PA114818
12. Courtesy of Library and Archives Canada/PA166425
13. Courtesy of Library and Archives Canada/PA155526
14. Courtesy of Library and Archives Canada PMR-77-531/e010789744
15. Courtesy of Library and Archives Canada/PA116804
16. Courtesy of Library and Archives Canada/PA145352
17. *Letters to Harvelyn.* Courtesy of Harvelyn McInnis
18. *Letters to Harvelyn.* Courtesy of Harvelyn McInnis
19. Courtesy of Mitzi Ross
20. Bernard Castonguay, *Prisonnier de guerre au Japon (1941–1945)*, Bibliotheque nationale du Quebec, 2005
21. Bernard Castonguay, *Prisonnier de guerre au Japon (1941–1945)*, Bibliotheque nationale du Quebec, 2005

22. Courtesy of Bill MacWhirter

23. *Letters to Harvelyn.* Courtesy of Harvelyn McInnis

24. *Letters to Harvelyn.* Courtesy of Harvelyn McInnis

25. Courtesy of Library and Archives Canada/PA114875

26. *Hong Kong Prisoner of War Camp Life, 25 December, 1941 – 30 August, 1945,* drawings by Lieut. A.V. Skvorzov. Hong Kong: SCMP Book Publishing Limited, 2005.

27. Courtesy of Jean-Paul Dallain

28. *Letters to Harvelyn.* Courtesy of Harvelyn McInnis

29. Courtesy of Library and Archives Canada/PA187673

30. Courtesy of Mitzi Ross

31. Courtesy of Mrs. Ken Cambon

32. Courtesy of George MacDonell

33. Courtesy of George MacDonell

34. Courtesy of Library and Archives Canada/PA187672

35. Courtesy of Library and Archives Canada/PA187675

36. Courtesy of Library and Archives Canada/PA114811

37. Courtesy of Library and Archives Canada/PA151738

38. Courtesy of Library and Archives Canada/PMR-79-812

39. Courtesy of Hong Kong Veterans Commemorative Association

Index